SpringBoard®

English Language Arts
California Edition

Grade 6

CollegeBoard

ABOUT THE COLLEGE BOARD

The College Board is a mission-driven not-for-profit organization that connects students to college success and opportunity. Founded in 1900, the College Board was created to expand access to higher education. Today, the membership association is made up of over 6,000 of the world's leading educational institutions and is dedicated to promoting excellence and equity in education. Each year, the College Board helps more than seven million students prepare for a successful transition to college through programs and services in college readiness and college success — including the SAT® and the Advanced Placement Program®. The organization also serves the education community through research and advocacy on behalf of students, educators, and schools. For further information, visit www.collegeboard.org.

ISBN: 1-4573-0462-7
ISBN: 978-1-4573-0462-0

1 2 3 4 5 6 7 8   19 20 21 22
Printed in the United States of America

ACKNOWLEDGMENTS

The College Board gratefully acknowledges the outstanding work of the classroom teachers and writers who have been integral to the development of this revised program. The end product is testimony to their expertise, understanding of student learning needs, and dedication to rigorous and accessible English Language Arts instruction.

Pat Bishop
Writing Coach (Retired)
Hillsborough Schools
Tampa, Florida

Amanda Breuer
English Teacher
Tetzlaff Accelerated Learning
Academy
Cerritos, California

Susie Challancin
English Teacher
Bellevue School District 405
Bellevue, Washington

Bryant Crisp
English Teacher
Charlotte Mecklenburg
Schools Charlotte, North
Carolina

Paul DeMaret
English Teacher
Poudre School District
Fort Collins, Colorado

Kathy Galford
English Teacher
Chesapeake Public Schools
Chesapeake, Virginia

Michelle Lewis
Curriculum Coordinator
Spokane Public Schools
Spokane, Washington

Julie Manley
English Teacher
Bellevue School District 405
Bellevue, Washington

Le'Andra Myers
English Teacher
Pasco School District
Pasco, Washington

Stephanie Sharpe
English Teacher
Hillsborough Schools
Tampa, Florida

Susan Van Doren
English Teacher
Douglas County School
District Minden, Nevada

SPRINGBOARD ENGLISH LANGUAGE ARTS DEVELOPMENT

Lori O'Dea
Executive Director
Content Development

Doug Waugh
Executive Director
Product Management

Joely Negedly
Senior Director
Grades 6–12 English and
Social Studies Curriculum and
Instruction

JoEllen Victoreen
English Language Arts
Instructional Manager

Sarah Balistreri
English Language Arts Editor

Jennifer Duva
English Language Arts Editor

Rebecca Grudzina
English Language Arts Editor

Spencer Gonçalves
Assistant ELA Editor

Jessica Pippin
Assistant ELA Editor

RESEARCH AND PLANNING ADVISORS

We also wish to thank the members of our SpringBoard Advisory Council and the many educators who gave generously of their time and their ideas as we conducted research for both the print and online programs. Your suggestions and reactions to ideas helped immeasurably as we planned the revisions. We gratefully acknowledge the teachers and administrators in the following districts.

ABC Unified School District
Cerritos, California

Bellevue School District 405
Bellevue, Washington

Charleston County School District
Charleston, South Carolina

Clark County School District
Las Vegas, Nevada

Denver Public Schools
Denver, Colorado

Hillsborough County Public Schools
Tampa, Florida

Kenton County School District
Fort Wright, Kentucky

Los Angeles Unified School District
Los Angeles, California

Milwaukee Public Schools
Milwaukee, Wisconsin

Newton County Schools
Covington, Georgia

Noblesville Schools
Noblesville, Indiana

Oakland Unified School District
Oakland, California

Orange County Public Schools
Orlando, Florida

Peninsula School District
Gig Harbor, Washington

Quakertown Community School
    District
Quakertown, Pennsylvania

St. Vrain School District
Longmont, Colorado

Scottsdale Public Schools
Phoenix, Arizona

Seminole County Public Schools
Sanford, Florida

Spokane Public Schools
Spokane, Washington

Contents

Unit 1   Stories of Change

Activities

Unit 2 The Power to Change

Activities

Unit 3 Changing Perspectives

Activities

Unit 4 The Final Act

Activities

To the Student

WELCOME TO SPRINGBOARD!

Dear Student,

Welcome to the SpringBoard program! This program has been created with you in mind: it contains the English Language Arts content you need to learn, the tools to help you learn, and tasks to strengthen the critical thinking skills that prepare you for high school and beyond.

In SpringBoard, you will explore compelling themes through reading, writing, discussions, performances, and research. You will closely read short stories, novels, poems, historical texts, and articles. You'll also view and interpret films, plays, and audio texts while comparing them to their related print versions. With frequent opportunities to write creatively and analytically throughout the program, you will develop fluency, research skills, and an understanding of how to craft your writing based on audience and purpose. Through collaborative discussions, presentations, performances, and debates with your peers, you will deepen your understanding of the texts you've read and viewed and learn how to convey your ideas with clarity and voice.

Tools to help you learn are built into every lesson. At the beginning of each activity, you will see suggested learning strategies, each of which is explained in full in the Resources section of your book. These strategies will help you deeply analyze text, collect evidence for your writing, and critically think about and discuss issues and ideas. Within the activities, you'll also notice explanations about essential vocabulary and grammar concepts that will enrich your ability to read and write effectively.

With high school right around the corner, now is the time to challenge yourself to develop skills and habits you need to be successful throughout your academic career. The SpringBoard program provides you with meaningful and engaging activities built on the rigorous standards that lead to high school, college, and career success. Your participation in SpringBoard will help you advance your reading, writing, language, and speaking and listening skills, all while helping you build confidence in your ability to succeed academically.

We hope you enjoy learning with the SpringBoard program. It will give you many opportunities to explore ideas and issues collaboratively and independently and to cultivate new skills as you prepare for your future.

Sincerely,

SpringBoard

AP CONNECTIONS

When you reach high school, you may have an opportunity to take Advanced Placement (AP) classes or other rigorous courses. When the time comes to make that decision, we want you to be equipped with the kind of higher-order thinking skills, knowledge, and behaviors necessary to be successful in AP classes and beyond. You will see connections to AP in the texts that you read, the strategies you use, and the writing tasks you encounter throughout the course.

Connections to AP Language and Literature will help you

- Read closely and analyze both literary and nonfiction texts

- Analyze relationships among author's purpose, literary/stylistic devices, rhetorical appeals, and desired effects for intended audiences

- Write with attention to selecting textual evidence and organizational patterns according to purpose and audience

- Write to interpret and evaluate multiple perspectives in literature

- Develop the control of language and command of conventions required for academic writing

THE SPRINGBOARD DIFFERENCE

SpringBoard is different because it provides instruction with hands-on participation that involves you and your classmates in daily discussions and analysis of what you're reading and learning. You will have an opportunity to

- Discuss and collaborate with your peers to explore and express your ideas

- Explore multiple perspectives by reading a variety of texts—both fiction and nonfiction—that introduce you to different ways of thinking, writing, and communicating

- Examine writing from the perspective of a reader and writer and learn techniques that good writers use to communicate their message effectively

- Gain a deep understanding of topics, enabling you to apply your learning to new and varied situations

- Take ownership of your learning by practicing and selecting strategies that work for you

- Reflect on your growth and showcase your best work as a reader, writer, speaker, and listener in a working Portfolio

MIDDLE SCHOOL AT A GLANCE
Grade 6

SpringBoard grade 6 is developed around the thematic concept of **change**. During the year, you will learn how writers use that theme to tell stories in poetry, short stories, and nonfiction texts. Among the many authors whose work you will read is Langston Hughes, a famous writer who was part of the Harlem Renaissance. Sharon Creech explores change resulting from the loss of a parent in her novel *Walk Two Moons*. Gary Soto and Sandra Cisneros tell vivid stories about the awkward changes that can be part of growing up. John Steinbeck takes you on a trip around the country with his dog, Charley. Scenes from one of William Shakespeare's plays take you into the world of drama. As you read these texts and make connections to experiences in your own life, you will begin to see how writers use the details of everyday life to create stories that we all enjoy.

Reading and writing go hand in hand, and SpringBoard grade 6 gives you opportunities to write your own stories (narrative writing), explain information (expository writing), and create an argument to persuade an audience (argumentative writing). Specific strategies for writing and revising support your writing efforts from planning to drafting, revising, and editing. You will be writing a personal narrative and a short story, essays in which you share your ideas about a fictional story and a real-life story, and an argumentative letter to persuade others to support your position on an issue.

You will also be asked to deepen your understanding by analyzing how film presents a topic and by conducting research on topics of interest. In this grade you will view a video biography of Temple Grandin while also reading about her life and how she has coped with autism.

Grade 7

In SpringBoard grade 7, you will investigate the thematic concept of **choice**. All of us make choices every day. Some of those choices have a short-term impact (like what to have for lunch), while others have a greater impact (like whether to study in school or to goof off!). By reading from his autobiography, you will learn about Nelson Mandela's choice to fight segregation in South Africa—even though it meant going to jail. A famous poem by Robert Frost, the novel *Tangerine*, Sojourner Truth's historic speech on slavery, and a drama by Shakespeare all show you the choices that real and imaginary characters make and how those choices affect their lives. Close reading strategies will help you to determine what each text says explicitly and to make logical inferences from what it does not say explicitly. Writing and speaking will focus on text-based evidence. For example, you and your peers will write a literary analysis of a novel and include findings from research to produce a multimedia biographical presentation. Much like in 6th grade, you will be asked to write in narrative, expository, and argumentative modes.

You will also look at print texts and then examine how those same texts are portrayed in film. Dramas are like a film performed on stage, and you will get to star in a performance of a scene from another of Shakespeare's plays.

Grade 8

In SpringBoard grade 8, units of study focus on the theme of **challenge**. Among the many texts that you will read are an essay about Civil War heroes, narratives about the Holocaust, a novel and short story by Ray Bradbury, Elie Wiesel's Nobel Prize acceptance speech, poetry by Walt Whitman, and a play by Shakespeare.

These texts take you into the world of heroes—both everyday heroes and extraordinary ones—who face challenges and take actions to overcome them. You will learn about the archetype of "hero," which is a model that writers follow in creating stories about heroes. Writing and speaking opportunities are varied and engaging. For example, you will write a hero's journey narrative about a hero of your choice, along with essays and an argument that presents your position on an issue in a compelling way. Using research on an issue of national or global significance, you will create an informative multimedia presentation. Viewing film is also a part of researching and analyzing what authors are communicating. As part of studying comedy and Shakespeare, you will analyze scenes from the play *A Midsummer Night's Dream* and then view those scenes in film to determine how and why a film director may have changed the scenes.

CLASSROOM TOOLS

As you move through each SpringBoard unit, your teacher will guide you to use tools that will help you develop strong study habits, keep your work organized, and track your learning progress.

Reader/Writer Notebook

Your **Reader/Writer Notebook** is a place to record and keep track of vocabulary words, grammar practice, notes and reflections on readings, some writing assignments, brainstorms, and other items as determined by your teacher. You will use your Reader/Writer Notebook often, so think of it as an extension of the main SpringBoard book.

Word Wall

Your teacher will regularly add new vocabulary words to the class **Word Wall**. The Word Wall gives you and your classmates a visual reminder of the words you are learning throughout the unit of study. Also, you can use the Word Wall to easily check the spelling of new words.

Performance Portfolio

Your **Performance Portfolio** is a place to keep your assignments organized so that you can see your growth and learning across the school year. Keeping a portfolio will make it easier to share your work with others, reflect on what you are learning, revise certain pieces of work, and set goals for future learning.

Your teacher will guide you to include items in your portfolio that illustrate a wide range of work, such as first drafts, final drafts, quickwrites, notes, reading logs, graphic organizers, audio and video examples, and graphics that represent a variety of genres, forms, and media created for a multitude of purposes. As you progress through the course, you will have opportunities to revisit prior work, revise it based on new learning, and reflect on the learning strategies and activities that help you be successful.

Independent Reading

Based on your personal interests and preferences, you will be encouraged to select books, articles, and other texts to read independently. Reading independently not only reinforces the learning you're doing in class, but it also gives you a chance to expand your knowledge about topics that fascinate you.

You can find **Independent Reading Lists** in the Resources section at the back of your book. The lists provide ideas for texts that complement the reading you're doing in each SpringBoard unit. These are suggestions to get you started, but you may also choose other readings with input from your teacher, family, and peers.

While you work your way through each SpringBoard unit, your teacher will give you time to read independently. You can record general thoughts or reactions to your independent reading in the **Independent Reading Log** in the Resources section of your book. You may also use the Independent Reading Log to respond to the occasional **Independent Reading Links** that you'll encounter in each SpringBoard unit. These links prompt you to think about your independent reading by responding to questions, doing research, making connections between texts and themes, discussing ideas in book groups, and recommending titles to your classmates.

We hope you enjoy exploring the texts, topics, and themes in SpringBoard and that you feel inspired to deepen your reading, writing, speaking, and analytic skills through the program.

California Common Core State Standards

Reading Standards for Literature

Key Ideas and Details	RL.6.1	Cite textual evidence to support analysis of what the text says explicitly as well as inferences drawn from the text.
	RL.6.2	Determine a theme or central idea of a text and how it is conveyed through particular details; provide a summary of the text distinct from personal opinions or judgments.
	RL.6.3	Describe how a particular story's or drama's plot unfolds in a series of episodes as well as how the characters respond or change as the plot moves toward a resolution.
Craft and Structure	RL.6.4	Determine the meaning of words and phrases as they are used in a text, including figurative and connotative meanings; analyze the impact of a specific word choice on meaning and tone. **(See grade 6 Language standards 4–6 for additional expectations.) CA**
	RL.6.5	Analyze how a particular sentence, chapter, scene, or stanza fits into the overall structure of a text and contributes to the development of the theme, setting, or plot.
	RL.6.6	Explain how an author develops the point of view of the narrator or speaker in a text.
Integration of Knowledge and Ideas	RL.6.7	Compare and contrast the experience of reading a story, drama, or poem to listening to or viewing an audio, video, or live version of the text, including contrasting what they "see" and "hear" when reading the text to what they perceive when they listen or watch.
	RL.6.8	(Not applicable to literature)
	RL.6.9	Compare and contrast texts in different forms or genres (e.g., stories and poems; historical novels and fantasy stories) in terms of their approaches to similar themes and topics.
Range of Reading and Text Complexity	RL.6.10	By the end of the year, read and comprehend literature, including stories, dramas, and poems, in the grades 6–8 text complexity band proficiently, with scaffolding as needed at the high end of the range.

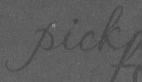

Reading Standards for Informational Text

Key Ideas and Details	RI.6.1	Cite textual evidence to support analysis of what the text says explicitly as well as inferences drawn from the text.
	RI.6.2	Determine a central idea of a text and how it is conveyed through particular details; provide a summary of the text distinct from personal opinions or judgments.
	RI.6.3	Analyze in detail how a key individual, event, or idea is introduced, illustrated, and elaborated in a text (e.g., through examples or anecdotes)
Craft and Structure	RI.6.4	Determine the meaning of words and phrases as they are used in a text, including figurative, connotative, and technical meanings. **(See grade 6 Language standards 4–6 for additional expectations.) CA**
	RI.6.5	Analyze how a particular sentence, paragraph, chapter, or section fits into the overall structure of a text and contributes to the development of the ideas.
	RI.6.5a	**Analyze the use of text features (e.g., graphics, headers, captions) in popular media. CA**
	RI.6.6	Determine an author's point of view or purpose in a text and explain how it is conveyed in the text.
Integration of Knowledge and Ideas	RI.6.7	Integrate information presented in different media or formats (e.g., visually, quantitatively) as well as in words to develop a coherent understanding of a topic or issue.
	RI.6.8	Trace and evaluate the argument and specific claims in a text, distinguishing claims that are supported by reasons and evidence from claims that are not.
	RI.6.9	Compare and contrast one author's presentation of events with that of another (e.g., a memoir written by and a biography on the same person).
Range of Reading and Text Complexity	RI.6.10	By the end of the year, read and comprehend literary nonfiction in the grades 6–8 text complexity band proficiently, with scaffolding as needed at the high end of the range.

Writing Standards

Text Types and Purposes	W.6.1	Write arguments to support claims with clear reasons and relevant evidence.
	W.6.1a	Introduce claim(s) and organize the reasons and evidence clearly.
	W.6.1b	Support claim(s) with clear reasons and relevant evidence, using credible sources and demonstrating an understanding of the topic or text.
	W.6.1c	Use words, phrases, and clauses to clarify the relationships among claim(s) and reasons.
	W.6.1d	Establish and maintain a formal style.
	W.6.1e	Provide a concluding statement or section that follows from the argument presented.
	W.6.2	Write informative/explanatory texts to examine a topic and convey ideas, concepts, and information through the selection, organization, and analysis of relevant content.
	W.6.2a	Introduce a topic **or thesis statement**; organize ideas, concepts, and information, using strategies such as definition, classification, comparison/contrast, and cause/effect; include formatting (e.g., headings), graphics (e.g., charts, tables), and multimedia when useful to aiding comprehension. **CA**
	W.6.2b	Develop the topic with relevant facts, definitions, concrete details, quotations, or other information and examples.
	W.6.2c	Use appropriate transitions to clarify the relationships among ideas and concepts.
	W.6.2d	Use precise language and domain-specific vocabulary to inform about or explain the topic.
	W.6.2e	Establish and maintain a formal style.
	W.6.2f	Provide a concluding statement or section that follows from the information or explanation presented.
	W.6.3	Write narratives to develop real or imagined experiences or events using effective technique, relevant descriptive details, and well-structured event sequences.
	W.6.3a	Engage and orient the reader by establishing a context and introducing a narrator and/or characters; organize an event sequence that unfolds naturally and logically.
	W.6.3b	Use narrative techniques, such as dialogue, pacing, and description, to develop experiences, events, and/or characters.
	W.6.3c	Use a variety of transition words, phrases, and clauses to convey sequence and signal shifts from one time frame or setting to another.

Writing Standards

Text Types and Purposes	W.6.3d	Use precise words and phrases, relevant descriptive details, and sensory language to convey experiences and events.
	W.6.3e	Provide a conclusion that follows from the narrated experiences or events.
Production and Distribution of Writing	W.6.4	Produce clear and coherent writing in which the development, organization, and style are appropriate to task, purpose, and audience. (Grade-specific expectations for writing types are defined in standards 1–3 above.)
	W.6.5	With some guidance and support from peers and adults, develop and strengthen writing as needed by planning, revising, editing, rewriting, or trying a new approach. (Editing for conventions should demonstrate command of Language standards 1–3 up to and including grade 6.)
	W.6.6	Use technology, including the Internet, to produce and publish writing as well as to inter act and collaborate with others; demonstrate sufficient command of keyboarding skills to type a minimum of three pages in a single sitting.
Research to Build and Present Knowledge	W.6.7	Conduct short research projects to answer a question, drawing on several sources and refocusing the inquiry when appropriate.
	W.6.8	Gather relevant information from multiple print and digital sources; assess the credibility of each source; and quote or paraphrase the data and conclusions of others while avoiding plagiarism and providing basic bibliographic information for sources.
	W.6.9	Draw evidence from literary or informational texts to support analysis, reflection, and research.
	W.6.9a	Apply *grade 6 Reading standards* to literature (e.g., "Compare and contrast texts in different forms or genres [e.g., stories and poems; historical novels and fantasy stories] in terms of their approaches to similar themes and topics").
	W.6.9b	Apply *grade 6 Reading standards* to literary nonfiction (e.g., "Trace and evaluate the argument and specific claims in a text, distinguishing claims that are supported by reasons and evidence from claims that are not").
Range of Writing	W.6.10	Write routinely over extended time frames (time for research, reflection, and revision) and shorter time frames (a single sitting or a day or two) for a range of discipline-specific tasks, purposes, and audiences.

Speaking and Listening Standards

Comprehension and Collaboration	SL.6.1	Engage effectively in a range of collaborative discussions (one-on-one, in groups, and teacher-led) with diverse partners on *grade 6 topics, texts, and issues*, building on others' ideas and expressing their own clearly.
	SL.6.1a	Come to discussions prepared, having read or studied required material; explicitly draw on that preparation by referring to evidence on the topic, text, or issue to probe and reflect on ideas under discussion.
	SL.6.1b	Follow rules for collegial discussions, set specific goals and deadlines, and define individual roles as needed.
	SL.6.1c	Pose and respond to specific questions with elaboration and detail by making comments that contribute to the topic, text, or issue under discussion.
	SL.6.1d	Review the key ideas expressed and demonstrate understanding of multiple perspectives through reflection and paraphrasing.
	SL.6.2	Interpret information presented in diverse media and formats (e.g., visually, quantitatively, orally) and explain how it contributes to a topic, text, or issue under study.
	SL.6.3	Delineate a speaker's argument and specific claims, distinguishing claims that are supported by reasons and evidence from claims that are not.
Presentation of Knowledge and Ideas	SL.6.4	Present claims and findings **(e.g., argument, narrative, informative, response to literature presentations),** sequencing ideas logically and using pertinent descriptions, facts, and details **and nonverbal elements** to accentuate main ideas or themes; use appropriate eye contact, adequate volume, and clear pronunciation. **CA**
	SL.6.4a	**Plan and deliver an informative/explanatory presentation that develops a topic with relevant facts, definitions, and concrete details; uses appropriate transitions to clarify relationships; uses precise language and domain specific vocabulary; and provides a strong conclusion. CA**
	SL.6.5	Include multimedia components (e.g., graphics, images, music, sound) and visual displays in presentations to clarify information.
	SL.6.6	Adapt speech to a variety of contexts and tasks, demonstrating command of formal English when indicated or appropriate. (See grade 6 Language standards 1 and 3 for specific expectations.)

Language Standards

Conventions of Standard English	L.6.1	Demonstrate command of the conventions of standard English grammar and usage when writing or speaking.
	L.6.1a	Ensure that pronouns are in the proper case (subjective, objective, possessive).
	L.6.1b	Use **all pronouns, including** intensive pronouns (e.g., *myself, ourselves*) **correctly. CA**
	L.6.1c	Recognize and correct inappropriate shifts in pronoun number and person.
	L.6.1d	Recognize and correct vague pronouns (i.e., ones with unclear or ambiguous antecedents).
	L.6.1e	Recognize variations from standard English in their own and others' writing and speaking, and identify and use strategies to improve expression in conventional language.
	L.6.2	Demonstrate command of the conventions of standard English capitalization, punctuation, and spelling when writing.
	L.6.2a	Use punctuation (commas, parentheses, dashes) to set off nonrestrictive/parenthetical elements.
	L.6.2b	Spell correctly.
Knowledge of Language	L.6.3	Use knowledge of language and its conventions when writing, speaking, reading, or listening.
	L.6.3a	Vary sentence patterns for meaning, reader/ listener interest, and style.
	L.6.3b	Maintain consistency in style and tone.
Vocabulary Acquisition and Use	L.6.4	Determine or clarify the meaning of unknown and multiple-meaning words and phrases based on *grade 6 reading and content*, choosing flexibly from a range of strategies.
	L.6.4a	Use context (e.g., the overall meaning of a sentence or paragraph; a word's position or function in a sentence) as a clue to the meaning of a word or phrase.
	L.6.4b	Use common, grade-appropriate Greek or Latin affixes and roots as clues to the meaning of a word (e.g., *audience, auditory, audible*).
	L.6.4c	Consult reference materials (e.g., dictionaries, glossaries, thesauruses), both print and digital, to find the pronunciation of a word or determine or clarify its precise meaning or its part of speech.
	L.6.4d	Verify the preliminary determination of the meaning of a word or phrase (e.g., by checking the inferred meaning in context or in a dictionary).

Language Standards

Vocabulary Acquisition and Use	L.6.5	Demonstrate understanding of figurative language, word relationships, and nuances in word meanings.
	L.6.5a	Interpret figures of speech (e.g., personification) in context.
	L.6.5b	Use the relationship between particular words (e.g., cause/effect, part/whole, item/category) to better understand each of the words.
	L.6.5c	Distinguish among the connotations (associations) of words with similar denotations (definitions) (e.g., *stingy, scrimping, economical, unwasteful, thrifty*).
	L.6.6	Acquire and use accurately grade-appropriate general academic and domain-specific words and phrases; gather vocabulary knowledge when considering a word or phrase important to comprehension or expression.

California English Language Development Standards

Part I: Interacting in Meaningful Ways

Communicative Modes	Standard Code	Emerging	Expanding	Bridging
Collaborative	PI.6.1	**Exchanging information/ideas** Engage in conversational exchanges and express ideas on familiar topics by asking and answering *yes–no* and *wh-* questions and responding using simple phrases.	**Exchanging information/ideas** Contribute to class, group, and partner discussions by following turn-taking rules, asking relevant questions, affirming others, adding relevant information, and paraphrasing key ideas.	**Exchanging information/ideas** Contribute to class, group, and partner discussions by following turn-taking rules, asking relevant questions, affirming others, adding relevant information and evidence, paraphrasing key ideas, building on responses, and providing useful feedback.
	PI.6.2	**Interacting via written English** Engage in short written exchanges with peers and collaborate on simple written texts on familiar topics, using technology when appropriate.	**Interacting via written English** Engage in longer written exchanges with peers and collaborate on more detailed written texts on a variety of topics, using technology when appropriate.	**Interacting via written English** Engage in extended written exchanges with peers and collaborate on complex written texts on a variety of topics, using technology when appropriate.
	PI.6.3	**Supporting opinions and persuading others** Negotiate with or persuade others in conversations (e.g., to gain and hold the floor or ask for clarification) using basic learned phrases (e.g., *I think ...* , *Would you please repeat that?*), as well as open responses.	**Supporting opinions and persuading others** Negotiate with or persuade others in conversations (e.g., to provide counter-arguments) using an expanded set of learned phrases (*I agree with X, but ...*), as well as open responses.	**Supporting opinions and persuading others** Negotiate with or persuade others in conversations using appropriate register (e.g., to reflect on multiple perspectives) using a variety of learned phrases, indirect reported speech (e.g., *I heard you say X, and Gabriel just pointed out Y*), as well as open responses.
	PI.6.4	**Adapting language choices** Adjust language choices according to social setting (e.g., classroom, break time) and audience (e.g., peers, teacher).	**Adapting language choices** Adjust language choices according to purpose (e.g., explaining, persuading, entertaining), task, and audience.	**Adapting language choices** Adjust language choices according to task (e.g., facilitating a science experiment, providing peer feedback on a writing assignment), purpose, task, and audience.

Communicative Modes	Standard Code	Emerging	Expanding	Bridging
Interpretive	PI.6.5	**Listening actively** Demonstrate active listening in oral presentation activities by asking and answering basic questions with prompting and substantial support.	**Listening actively** Demonstrate active listening in oral presentation activities by asking and answering detailed questions with occasional prompting and moderate support.	**Listening actively** Demonstrate active listening in oral presentation activities by asking and answering detailed questions with minimal prompting and support.
	PI.6.6a	**Reading/viewing closely** Explain ideas, phenomena, processes, and text relationships (e.g., compare/contrast, cause/effect, problem/solution) based on close reading of a variety of grade-level texts and viewing of multimedia with substantial support.	**Reading/viewing closely** Explain ideas, phenomena, processes, and text relationships (e.g., compare/contrast, cause/effect, problem/solution) based on close reading of a variety of grade-level texts and viewing of multimedia with moderate support.	**Reading/viewing closely** Explain ideas, phenomena, processes, and text relationships (e.g., compare/contrast, cause/effect, problem/solution) based on close reading of a variety of grade-level texts and viewing of multimedia with light support.
	PI.6.6b	**Reading/viewing closely** Express inferences and conclusions drawn based on close reading of grade-level texts and viewing of multimedia using some frequently used verbs (e.g., *shows that, based on*).	**Reading/viewing closely** Express inferences and conclusions drawn based on close reading of grade-level texts and viewing of multimedia using a variety of verbs (e.g., *suggests that, leads to*).	**Reading/viewing closely** Express inferences and conclusions drawn based on close reading of grade-level texts and viewing of multimedia using a variety of precise academic verbs (e.g., *indicates that, influences*).
	PI.6.6c	**Reading/viewing closely** Use knowledge of morphology (e.g., affixes, roots, and base words), context, reference materials, and visual cues to determine the meaning of unknown and multiple-meaning words on familiar topics.	**Reading/viewing closely** Use knowledge of morphology (e.g., affixes, roots, and base words), context, reference materials, and visual cues to determine the meaning of unknown and multiple-meaning words on familiar and new topics.	**Reading/viewing closely** Use knowledge of morphology (e.g., affixes, roots, and base words), context, reference materials, and visual cues to determine the meaning, including figurative and connotative meanings, of unknown and multiple-meaning words on a variety of new topics.

Communicative Modes	Standard Code	Emerging	Expanding	Bridging
Interpretive	PI.6.7	**Evaluating language choices** Explain how well writers and speakers use language to support ideas and arguments with detailed evidence (e.g., identifying the precise vocabulary used to present evidence, or the phrasing used to signal a shift in meaning) with substantial support.	**Evaluating language choices** Explain how well writers and speakers use specific language to present ideas or support arguments and provide detailed evidence (e.g., showing the clarity of the phrasing used to present an argument) with moderate support.	**Evaluating language choices** Explain how well writers and speakers use specific language resources to present ideas or support arguments and provide detailed evidence (e.g., identifying the specific language used to present ideas and claims that are well supported and distinguishing them from those that are not) with light support.
	PI.6.8	**Analyzing language choices** Explain how phrasing or different common words with similar meaning (e.g., choosing to use the word *cheap* versus the phrase *a good saver*) produce different effects on the audience.	**Analyzing language choices** Explain how phrasing, different words with similar meaning (e.g., describing a character as *stingy* versus *economical*), or figurative language (e.g., *The room was depressed and gloomy.*) produce shades of meaning and different effects on the audience.	**Analyzing language choices** Explain how phrasing, different words with similar meaning (e.g., *stingy-economical-unwasteful-thrifty*), or figurative language (e.g., *The room was depressed and gloomy.*) produce shades of meaning, nuances, and different effects on the audience.
Productive	PI.6.9	**Presenting** Plan and deliver brief oral presentations on a variety of topics and content areas.	**Presenting** Plan and deliver longer oral presentations on a variety of topics and content areas, using details and evidence to support ideas.	**Presenting** Plan and deliver longer oral presentations on a variety of topics and content areas, using reasoning and evidence to support ideas, as well as growing understanding of register.
	PI.6.10a	**Writing** Write short literary and informational texts (e.g., an argument for protecting the rainforests) collaboratively (e.g., with peers) and independently.	**Writing** Write longer literary and informational texts (e.g., an argument for protecting the rainforests) collaboratively (e.g., with peers) and independently using appropriate text organization.	**Writing** Write longer and more detailed literary and informational texts (e.g., an argument for protecting the rainforests) collaboratively (e.g., with peers) and independently using appropriate text organization and growing understanding of register.

Communicative Modes	Standard Code	Emerging	Expanding	Bridging
Productive	PI.6.11a	**Justifying/arguing** Justify opinions by providing some textual evidence (e.g., quoting from the text) or relevant background knowledge with substantial support.	**Justifying/arguing** Justify opinions or persuade others by providing relevant textual evidence (e.g., quoting from the text or referring to what the text says) or relevant background knowledge with moderate support.	**Justifying/arguing** Justify opinions or persuade others by providing detailed and relevant textual evidence (e.g., quoting from the text directly or referring to specific textual evidence) or relevant background knowledge with light support.
	PI.6.11b	**Justifying/arguing** Express attitude and opinions or temper statements with some basic modal expressions (e.g., *can, has to*).	**Justifying/arguing** Express attitude and opinions or temper statements with a variety of familiar modal expressions (e.g., *maybe/ probably, can/could, must*).	**Justifying/arguing** Express attitude and opinions or temper statements with nuanced modal expressions (e.g., *probably/certainly/ definitely, should/would, might*) and phrasing (e.g., *In my opinion …*).
	PI.6.12a	**Selecting language resources** Use a select number of general academic words (e.g., *author, chart*) and domain-specific words (e.g., *scene, cell, fraction*) to create some precision while speaking and writing.	**Selecting language resources** Use a growing set of academic words (e.g., *author, chart, global, affect*), domain-specific words (e.g., *scene, setting, plot, point of view, fraction, cell membrane, democracy*), synonyms, and antonyms to create precision and shades of meaning while speaking and writing.	**Selecting language resources** Use an expanded set of general academic words (e.g., *affect, evidence, demonstrate, reluctantly*), domain-specific words (e.g., *scene, setting, plot, point of view, fraction, cell membrane, democracy*), synonyms, antonyms, and figurative language to create precision and shades of meaning while speaking and writing.
	PI.6.12b	**Selecting language resources** Use knowledge of morphology to appropriately select affixes in basic ways (e.g., *She likes* X.).	**Selecting language resources** Use knowledge of morphology to appropriately select affixes in a growing number of ways to manipulate language (e.g., *She likes X. That's impossible.*).	**Selecting language resources** Use knowledge of morphology to appropriately select affixes in a variety of ways to manipulate language (e.g., changing *observe ⤳ observation, reluctant ⤳ reluctantly, produce ⤳ production*, etc.).

Part II: Learning About How English Works

Language Processes	Standard Code	Emerging	Expanding	Bridging
Structuring Cohesive Texts	PII.6.1	**Understanding text structure** Apply basic understanding of how different text types are organized to express ideas (e.g., how a narrative is organized sequentially with predictable stages versus how arguments are organized around ideas) to comprehending texts and writing basic texts.	**Understanding text structure** Apply growing understanding of how different text types are organized to express ideas (e.g., how a narrative is organized sequentially with predictable stages versus how arguments are structured logically around reasons and evidence) to comprehending texts and writing texts with increasing cohesion.	**Understanding text structure** Apply increasing understanding of how different text types are organized to express ideas (e.g., how a historical account is organized chronologically versus how arguments are structured logically around reasons and evidence) to comprehending texts and writing cohesive texts.
	PII.6.2a	**Understanding cohesion** Apply basic understanding of language resources for referring the reader back or forward in text (e.g., how pronouns refer back to nouns in text) to comprehending texts and writing basic texts.	**Understanding cohesion** Apply growing understanding of language resources for referring the reader back or forward in text (e.g., how pronouns or synonyms refer back to nouns in text) to comprehending texts and writing texts with increasing cohesion.	**Understanding cohesion** Apply increasing understanding of language resources for referring the reader back or forward in text (e.g., how pronouns, synonyms, or nominalizations refer back to nouns in text) to comprehending texts and writing cohesive texts.
	PII.6.2b	**Understanding cohesion** Apply basic understanding of how ideas, events, or reasons are linked throughout a text using a select set of everyday connecting words or phrases (e.g., *first/next, at the beginning*) to comprehending texts and writing basic texts.	**Understanding cohesion** Apply growing understanding of how ideas, events, or reasons are linked throughout a text using a variety of connecting words or phrases (e.g., *for example, in the first place, as a result, on the other hand*) to comprehending texts and writing texts with increasing cohesion.	**Understanding cohesion** Apply increasing understanding of how ideas, events, or reasons are linked throughout a text using an increasing variety of academic connecting and transitional words or phrases (e.g., *consequently, specifically, however, moreover*) to comprehending texts and writing cohesive texts.

Language Processes	Standard Code	Emerging	Expanding	Bridging
Expanding and Enriching Ideas	PII.6.3	**Using verbs and verb phrases** Use a variety of verb types (e.g., doing, saying, being/having, thinking/feeling), tenses (e.g., present, past, future), and aspects (e.g., simple, progressive) appropriate for the text type and discipline (e.g., simple past and past progressive for recounting an experience) on familiar topics.	**Using verbs and verb phrases** Use various verb types (e.g., doing, saying, being/having, thinking/feeling, reporting), tenses (e.g., present, past, future), and aspects (e.g., simple, progressive, perfect) appropriate for the task, text type, and discipline (e.g., simple present for literary analysis) on an increasing variety of topics.	**Using verbs and verb phrases** Use various verb types (e.g., doing, saying, being/having, thinking/feeling, reporting), tenses (e.g., present, past, future), and aspects (e.g., simple, progressive, perfect) appropriate for the task, text type, and discipline (e.g., the present perfect to describe previously made claims or conclusions) on a variety of topics.
	PII.6.4	**Using nouns and noun phrases** Expand noun phrases in simple ways (e.g., adding a sensory adjective to a noun) in order to enrich the meaning of sentences and add details about ideas, people, things, etc.	**Using nouns and noun phrases** Expand noun phrases in a variety of ways (e.g., adding comparative/superlative adjectives to noun phrases or simple clause embedding) in order to enrich the meaning of sentences and add details about ideas, people, things, etc.	**Using nouns and noun phrases** Expand noun phrases in an increasing variety of ways (e.g., adding comparative/superlative and general academic adjectives to noun phrases or more complex clause embedding) in order to enrich the meaning of sentences and add details about ideas, people, things, etc.
	PII.6.5	**Modifying to add details** Expand sentences with simple adverbials (e.g., adverbs, adverb phrases, prepositional phrases) to provide details (e.g., time, manner, place, cause) about a familiar activity or process.	**Modifying to add details** Expand sentences with an increasing variety of adverbials (e.g., adverbs, adverb phrases, prepositional phrases) to provide details (e.g., time, manner, place, cause) about a familiar or new activity or process.	**Modifying to add details** Expand sentences with a variety of adverbials (e.g., adverbs, adverb phrases and clauses, prepositional phrases) to provide details (e.g., time, manner, place, cause) about a variety of familiar and new activities and processes.

Language Processes	Standard Code	Emerging	Expanding	Bridging
Connecting and Condensing Ideas	PII.6.6	**Connecting ideas** Combine clauses in a few basic ways to make connections between and join ideas (e.g., creating compound sentences using *and, but, so*).	**Connecting ideas** Combine clauses in an increasing variety of ways (e.g., creating compound and complex sentences) to make connections between and join ideas, for example, to express a reason (e.g., *He stayed at home on Sunday to study for Monday's exam*) or to make a concession (e.g., *She studied all night even though she wasn't feeling well*).	**Connecting ideas** Combine clauses in a wide variety of ways (e.g., creating compound and complex sentences) to make connections between and join ideas, for example, to express a reason (e.g., *He stayed at home on Sunday to study for Monday's exam*), to make a concession (e.g., *She studied all night even though she wasn't feeling well*), or to link two ideas that happen at the same time (e.g., *The students worked in groups while their teacher walked around the room*).
	PII.6.7	**Condensing ideas** Condense ideas in simple ways (e.g., by compounding verbs, adding prepositional phrases, or through simple embedded clauses or other ways of condensing as in, This is a story about a girl. The girl changed the world. ⟶ This is a story about a girl *who changed the world*.) to create precise and detailed sentences.	**Condensing ideas** Condense ideas in an increasing variety of ways (e.g., through various types of embedded clauses and other ways of condensing, as in, Organic vegetables are food. They're made without chemical fertilizers. They're made without chemical insecticides. ⟶ Organic vegetables are foods *that are made without chemical fertilizers or insecticides*.) to create precise and detailed sentences.	**Condensing ideas** Condense ideas in a variety of ways (e.g., through various types of embedded clauses, ways of condensing, and nominalization as in, They *destroyed* the rainforest. Lots of animals *died*. ⟶ The *destruction* of the rainforest led to the *death* of many animals.) to create precise and detailed sentences.
Foundational Literacy Skills: **Literacy in an Alphabetic Writing System** • Print concepts Phonological awareness • Phonics & word recognition • Fluency	PIII.6	**See Appendix A for information on teaching reading foundational skills to English learners of various profiles based on age, native language, native language writing system, schooling experience, and literacy experience and proficiency. Some considerations are:** • Native language and literacy (e.g., phoneme awareness or print concept skills in native language) should be assessed for potential transference to English language and literacy. • Similarities between native language and English should be highlighted (e.g., phonemes or letters that are the same in both languages). • Differences between native language and English should be highlighted (e.g., some phonemes in English may not exist in the student's native language; native language syntax may be different from English syntax).		

Stories of Change

Visual Prompt: A butterfly goes through several changes in its life. It starts as an egg, becomes a caterpillar and then a chrysalis, and finally emerges as a beautiful butterfly. In what ways do people change as they move through the stages of their lives?

Unit Overview

Unit 1 introduces the idea of "change" as the conceptual focus for the year. By reading, analyzing, and creating texts, you will examine changes that happen in your life as well as in the world around you. Through your responses to texts, you will better understand that change is threaded through all of our lives and is something we can tell stories about.

Stories of Change

Contents

Activities

*Texts not included in these materials.

Language and Writer's Craft
- Pronouns (1.5)
- Vivid Verbs (1.6)
- Transitions (1.8)
- Revising for Transitions (1.9)
- Varied Sentence Patterns (1.13)

MY INDEPENDENT READING LIST

_____

_____

_____

_____

_____

_____

_____

_____

_____

_____

_____

_____

_____

_____

_____

_____

_____

_____

_____

_____

_____

_____

_____

Previewing the Unit

ACADEMIC VOCABULARY

When you **analyze**, you separate something into parts and study how the parts are related. This **analytical** approach allows you to understand how the parts work together so you can better understand them. For example, an **analysis** of a patient's symptoms will help a doctor understand a patient's illness.

My Notes

Learning Targets

- Preview the big ideas, academic vocabulary, and literacy terms for the unit.
- Identify and analyze the skills and knowledge needed to complete Embedded Assessment 1 successfully.

Making Connections

When you think about change, what thoughts come to your mind? Have you perhaps changed schools? Have you made new friends? Has an old friend moved away? Change is a part of life. In this unit, you will **analyze** stories about change, as well as write your own ideas and stories about change.

Essential Questions

Based on your current knowledge, how would you answer these questions?

1. How can change be significant?
2. What makes a good story?

Introducing the Strategy: QHT

QHT is a strategy for thinking about your own understanding of vocabulary words. The letters stand for **Questions, Heard,** and **Teach:**

Q: words you may have seen but you are not sure about their meaning
H: words you have heard before but may not know them well
T: words you know so well you could teach them to someone else

To use **QHT**, think about how well you know each term, and label each term with a letter.

Developing Vocabulary

Look at the Academic Vocabulary and Literary Terms on the Contents page. Apply the QHT strategy to see which words you may already know and which you will need to learn more about.

Unpacking Embedded Assessment 1

Read the assignment for Embedded Assessment 1: Writing a Personal Narrative.

Your assignment is to write a personal narrative that includes a well-told incident, a response to the incident, and a reflection about the significance of the incident.

In your own words, paraphrase the assignment and then summarize what you will need to know to complete this assessment successfully. With your class, create a graphic organizer to represent the skills and knowledge you will need to complete the tasks identified in the embedded assessment.

What Makes a Narrative?

Learning Targets

- Define the concept of change through the reading of a narrative.
- Apply understanding of narrative elements to reading and writing.
- Write a narrative using sequence of events.

Narratives

The following passage is an example of a **narrative**. Narratives can be made up or based on real events. Generally, a narrative includes elements such as **characters, dialogue,** a **setting,** and the events or actions that lead to and follow a **conflict**. Authors often use the narrative form to write about changes in their lives, the lives of those around them, and in the world. In "The Circuit," author Francisco Jiménez uses events from his own childhood to write about how change affects a Mexican boy and his immigrant family.

Preview

In this activity, you will read a narrative and identify the elements of characters, setting, dialogue, and conflict.

Setting a Purpose for Reading

- As you read the narrative the first time, underline words and phrases that indicate when the action of the story is taking place and think about the events in chronological order.
- Put a star next to the changes that the narrator and his family experience.
- Circle unknown words and phrases. Try to determine their meaning using context clues, word parts, or a dictionary.

Introducing the Strategy: Close Reading and Marking the Text

This strategy involves reading a text word by word, sentence by sentence, and line by line to develop a complete understanding of it. Close reading is characterized by marking the text as a way of reading actively. Marking the text means to make notes or write questions that help you to understand the text.

> **LEARNING STRATEGIES:**
> Graphic Organizer, Note-taking, Close Reading, Marking the Text

> **Literary Terms**
> A **narrative** tells a story or describes a sequence of events. The act of creating characters is **characterization**. The **setting** is the time and place where the story takes place, while **conflict** is a struggle between characters or opposing forces. **Dialogue** is conversation between people. In a story, it is the words that characters say.

WORD CONNECTIONS

Roots and Affixes

The Greek word *chron-* in *chronological* means "time." *Chronological* means "ordered by time." Other English words having to do with time also contain this root. Based on this new knowledge, determine the meaning of the words *chronicle, chronic, chronology,* and *synchronize.*

My Notes

_____

_____

_____

_____

_____

_____

What Makes a Narrative?

WORD CONNECTIONS

Content Connections

A *bracero* is a Spanish word that means "one who works with his arm." The word was used to describe Mexicans who were invited to come to the United States to work as laborers during World War II. With so many Americans overseas at war, workers were needed in industries such as agriculture and rail transportation. Braceros often worked under extreme conditions for low pay. The U.S. government Bracero program ended in 1964.

sharecropper: a farmer who farms another person's property in exchange for a share of the crops or the sale of them

My Notes

ABOUT THE AUTHOR

Francisco Jiménez (1943–) was born in Tlaquepaque, Mexico, and grew up in a family of migrant workers in California. He spent much of his childhood moving around California with no permanent home or regular schooling, yet despite incredible odds he went on to have a distinguished academic career. A graduate of Santa Clara University, he also attended Harvard University and received both a master's degree and a PhD from Columbia University. A longtime writer of academic works for adults, Jiménez's entry into writing for young people came through an award-winning short story, "The Circuit," based on his childhood.

Short Story

The Circuit

by Francisco Jiménez

1   It was that time of year again. Ito, the strawberry **sharecropper,** did not smile. It was natural. The peak of the strawberry season was over and the last few days the workers, most of them *braceros,* were not picking as many boxes as they had during the months of June and July.

2   As the last days of August disappeared, so did the number of *braceros.* Sunday, only one—the best picker—came to work. I liked him. Sometimes we talked during our half-hour lunch break. That is how I found out he was from Jalisco, the same state in Mexico my family was from. That Sunday was the last time I saw him.

3   When the sun had tired and sunk behind the mountains, Ito signaled us that it was time to go home. "*Ya esora,*" he yelled in his broken Spanish. Those were the words I waited for twelve hours a day, every day, seven days a week, week after week. And the thought of not hearing them again saddened me.

4   As we drove home Papá did not say a word. With both hands on the wheel, he stared at the dirt road. My older brother, Roberto, was also silent. He leaned his head back and closed his eyes. Once in a while he cleared from his throat the dust that blew in from outside.

5   Yes, it was that time of year. When I opened the front door to the shack, I stopped. Everything we owned was neatly packed in cardboard boxes. Suddenly I felt even more the weight of hours, days, weeks, and months of work. I sat down on a box. The thought of having to move to Fresno and knowing what was in store for me there brought tears to my eyes.

6   That night I could not sleep. I lay in bed thinking about how much I hated this move.

7   A little before five o'clock in the morning, Papá woke everyone up. A few minutes later, the yelling and screaming of my little brothers and sisters, for whom the move was a great adventure, broke the silence of dawn. Shortly, the barking of the dogs accompanied them.

8   While we packed the breakfast dishes, Papá went outside to start the "*Carcanchita*." That was the name Papá gave his old '38 black Plymouth. He bought it in a used-car lot in Santa Rosa in the winter of 1949. Papá was very proud of his little **jalopy**. He had a right to be proud of it. He spent a lot of time looking at other cars before buying this one. When he finally chose the *Carcanchita*, he checked it thoroughly before driving it out of the car lot. He examined every inch of the car. He listened to the motor, tilting his head from side to side like a parrot, trying to detect any noises that spelled car trouble. After being satisfied with the looks and sounds of the car, Papá then insisted on knowing who the original owner was. He never did find out from the car salesman, but he bought the car anyway. Papá figured the original owner must have been an important man because behind the rear seat of the car he found a blue necktie.

9   Papá parked the car out in front and left the motor running. "*Listo,*" he yelled. Without saying a word, Roberto and I began to carry the boxes out to the car. Roberto carried the two big boxes and I carried the two smaller ones. Papá then threw the mattress on top of the car roof and tied it with ropes to the front and rear bumpers.

10   Everything was packed except Mamá's pot. It was an old large galvanized pot she had picked up at an army surplus store in Santa María the year I was born. The pot had many dents and nicks, and the more dents and nicks it acquired the more Mamá liked it. "*Mi olla,*" she used to say proudly.

11   I held the front door open as Mamá carefully carried out her pot by both handles, making sure not to spill the cooked beans. When she got to the car, Papá reached out to help her with it. Roberto opened the rear car door and Papá gently placed it on the floor behind the front seat. All of us then climbed in. Papá sighed, wiped the sweat off his forehead with his sleeve, and said wearily: "*Es todo.*"

12   As we drove away, I felt a lump in my throat. I turned around and looked at our little shack for the last time.

13   At sunset we drove into a **labor** camp near Fresno. Since Papá did not speak English, Mamá asked the camp foreman if he needed any more workers. "We don't need no more," said the foreman, scratching his head. "Check with Sullivan down the road. Can't miss him. He lives in a big white house with a fence around it."

14   When we got there, Mamá walked up to the house. She went through a white gate, past a row of rose bushes, up the stairs to the front door. She rang the doorbell. The porch light went on and a tall husky man came out. They exchanged a few words. After the man went in, Mamá clasped her hands and hurried back to the car. "We have work! Mr. Sullivan said we can stay there the whole season," she said, **gasping** and pointing to an old garage near the stables.

WORD CONNECTIONS

Cognates
The Spanish cognate for *adventure* is *aventura*.

jalopy: an old car worn down by use

My Notes

_____

_____

_____

_____

_____

_____

_____

_____

_____

_____

_____

_____

_____

_____

labor: work that a person is paid for. Mexican migratory laborers (braceros) were sometimes housed in **labor** camps near their field work.

gasp: speak with deep, difficult breaths

What Makes a Narrative?

strain: pulled or stretched by force

My Notes

15   The garage was worn out by the years. It had no windows. The walls, eaten by termites, **strained** to support the roof full of holes. The dirt floor, populated by earth worms, looked like a gray road map.

16   That night, by the light of a kerosene lamp, we unpacked and cleaned our new home. Roberto swept away the loose dirt, leaving the hard ground. Papá plugged the holes in the walls with old newspapers and tin can tops. Mamá fed my little brothers and sisters. Papá and Roberto then brought in the mattress and placed it on the far corner of the garage. "Mamá, you and the little ones sleep on the mattress. Roberto, Panchito, and I will sleep outside under the trees," Papá said.

17   Early next morning Mr. Sullivan showed us where his crop was, and after breakfast, Papá, Roberto, and I headed for the vineyard to pick.

18   Around nine o'clock the temperature had risen to almost one hundred degrees. I was completely soaked in sweat and my mouth felt as if I had been chewing on a handkerchief. I walked over to the end of the row, picked up the jug of water we had brought, and began drinking. "Don't drink too much; you'll get sick," Roberto shouted. No sooner had he said that than I felt sick to my stomach. I dropped to my knees and let the jug roll off my hands. I remained motionless with my eyes glued on the hot sandy ground. All I could hear was the drone of insects. Slowly I began to recover. I poured water over my face and neck and watched the dirty water run down my arms to the ground.

19   I still felt a little dizzy when we took a break to eat lunch. It was past two o'clock and we sat underneath a large walnut tree that was on the side of the road. While we ate, Papá jotted down the number of boxes we had picked. Roberto drew designs on the ground with a stick. Suddenly I noticed Papá's face turn pale as he looked down the road. "Here comes the school bus," he whispered loudly in alarm. Instinctively, Roberto and I ran and hid in the vineyards. We did not want to get in trouble for not going to school. The neatly dressed boys about my age got off. They carried books under their arms. After they crossed the street, the bus drove away. Roberto and I came out from hiding and joined Papá. "*Tienen que tener cuidado,*" he warned us.

20   After lunch we went back to work. The sun kept beating down. The buzzing insects, the wet sweat, and the hot dry dust made the afternoon seem to last forever. Finally the mountains around the valley reached out and swallowed the sun. Within an hour it was too dark to continue picking. The vines blanketed the grapes, making it difficult to see the bunches. "*Vámonos,*" said Papá, signaling to us that it was time to quit work. Papá then took out a pencil and began to figure out how much we had earned our first day. He wrote down numbers, crossed some out, wrote down some more. "*Quince,*" he **murmured**.

murmur: speak softly or quietly

21   When we arrived home, we took a cold shower underneath a water-hose. We then sat down to eat dinner around some wooden crates that served as a table. Mamá had cooked a special meal for us. We had rice and tortillas with *carne con chile,* my favorite dish.

22   The next morning I could hardly move. My body ached all over. I felt little control over my arms and legs. This feeling went on every morning for days until my muscles finally got used to the work.

23 It was Monday, the first week of November. The grape season was over and I could now go to school. I woke up early that morning and lay in bed, looking at the stars and **savoring** the thought of not going to work and of starting sixth grade for the first time that year. Since I could not sleep, I decided to get up and join Papá and Roberto at breakfast. I sat at the table across from Roberto, but I kept my head down. I did not want to look up and face him. I knew he was sad. He was not going to school today. He was not going tomorrow, or next week, or next month. He would not go until the cotton season was over, and that was sometime in February. I rubbed my hands together and watched the dry, acid stained skin fall to the floor in little rolls.

24 When Papá and Roberto left for work, I felt relief. I walked to the top of a small grade next to the shack and watched the "Carcanchita" disappear in the distance in a cloud of dust.

25 Two hours later, around eight o'clock, I stood by the side of the road waiting for school bus number twenty. When it arrived I climbed in. Everyone was busy either talking or yelling. I sat in an empty seat in the back.

26 When the bus stopped in front of the school, I felt very nervous. I looked out the bus window and saw boys and girls carrying books under their arms. I put my hands in my pant pockets and walked to the principal's office. When I entered I heard a woman's voice say: "May I help you?" I was startled. I had not heard English for months. For a few seconds I remained speechless. I looked at the lady who waited for an answer. My first instinct was to answer her in Spanish, but I held back. Finally, after struggling for English words, I managed to tell her that I wanted to enroll in the sixth grade. After answering many questions, I was led to the classroom.

27 Mr. Lema, the sixth grade teacher, greeted me and assigned me a desk. He then introduced me to the class. I was so nervous and scared at that moment when everyone's eyes were on me that I wished I were with Papá and Roberto picking cotton. After taking roll, Mr. Lema gave the class the assignment for the first hour. "The first thing we have to do this morning is finish reading the story we began yesterday," he said enthusiastically. He walked up to me, handed me an English book, and asked me to read. "We are on page 125," he said politely. When I heard this, I felt my blood rush to my head; I felt dizzy. "Would you like to read?" he asked hesitantly. I opened the book to page 125. My mouth was dry. My eyes began to water. I could not begin. "You can read later," Mr. Lema said understandingly.

28 For the rest of the reading **period** I kept getting angrier and angrier with myself. I should have read, I thought to myself.

29 During recess I went into the restroom and opened my English book to page 125. I began to read in a low voice, pretending I was in class. There were many words I did not know. I closed the book and headed back to the classroom.

30 Mr. Lema was sitting at his desk correcting papers. When I entered he looked up at me and smiled. I felt better. I walked up to him and asked if he could help me with the new words. "Gladly," he said.

31 The rest of the month I spent my lunch hours working on English with Mr. Lema, my best friend at school.

savor: to enjoy something and make it last

My Notes

period: a specific length of time

What Makes a Narrative?

My Notes

32 One Friday during lunch hour Mr. Lema asked me to take a walk with him to the music room. "Do you like music?" he asked me as we entered the building.

33 "Yes, I like *corridos*," I answered. He then picked up a trumpet, blew on it, and handed it to me. The sound gave me goose bumps. I knew that sound. I had heard it in many *corridos*. "How would you like to learn how to play it?" he asked. He must have read my face because before I could answer, he added: "I'll teach you how to play it during our lunch hours."

34 That day I could hardly wait to get home to tell Papá and Mamá the great news. As I got off the bus, my little brothers and sisters ran up to meet me. They were yelling and screaming. I thought they were happy to see me, but when I opened the door to our shack, I saw that everything we owned was neatly packed in cardboard boxes.

Second Read

- Reread the narrative to answer these text-dependent questions.
- Write any additional questions you have about the text in your Reader/Writer Notebook.

1. **Key Ideas and Details:** Reread the opening paragraphs. What kind of work do the narrator and his family do? Cite details from the story that support your answers.

2. **Key Ideas and Details:** On page 6 and 7, Jiménez describes the family's departure. What do the details of the family's departure help you understand? Cite evidence from the text to support your answer.

3. **Craft and Structure:** What does the figurative phrase "lump in my throat" in paragraph 12 tell you about the impact of events on the narrator so far in the story? Cite other evidence in the story to support your answer.

4. **Key Ideas and Details:** Revisit pages 6 and 7. What do you learn about the narrator? Cite textual evidence to support your answer.

My Notes

5. **Key Ideas and Details:** On page 8, the narrator refers to the garage as home. What actions do the family take to make it a home? What does this tell us about how the family faces change?

6. **Key Ideas and Details:** Starting with paragraph 22, the narrator gets ready for school. What kinds of feelings does he have about leaving the family's work and going to school? Highlight text that helps you answer the question.

7. **Craft and Structure:** Reread page 9. What is the most important episode for the narrator at school? Why is it important?

8. **Key Ideas and Details:** How does the ending to this story reinforce your understanding of the life of migrant workers? Cite evidence from the text to support your answer.

What Makes a Narrative?

ACADEMIC VOCABULARY
To **sequence** something is to put things in an order, so a **sequence** of events is a set of events that follows one after another in a **sequential** or orderly presentation of steps or events.

9. **Craft and Structure:** Think about the words and phrases that you underlined in your first read. How does the author use words that indicate time to create a sequence of events?

Working from the Text

10. Scan the beginning of the story (paragraphs 1–12), thinking about the events that occur. Which events give the reader insight into the narrator's attitude toward change?

11. To help you recognize narrative elements, use the following table to organize details from the text.

Descriptions of Setting (give specific details)	Characterization (use adjectives or nouns to describe how the characters are feeling)	Important Dialogue (quote words and phrases from the text)	External and Internal Conflict (give specific details)

Check Your Understanding

What conclusions can you draw about the narrator's attitude toward change? Provide evidence from the story that supports your conclusion.

Literary Terms
In an **external conflict**, the character struggles with an outside force. In an **internal conflict**, the character struggles with his or her own needs or emotions.

WRITING to SOURCES / **Narrative Writing Prompt**

Imagine a different ending for "The Circuit." Review the end of the story and write a narrative that describes the narrator's experience learning to play the trumpet. How would this change his life? Be sure to

• Use the narrative elements that you learned about in this activity.

• Use the narrative technique of sequencing events to organize the action in your new ending.

• Include details of your character's feelings and dialogue.

Keep this writing piece in your portfolio.

Planning for Independent Reading

Learning Targets
- Examine ways to choose a literary text for independent reading.
- Set goals in an independent reading plan.

Planning Independent Reading

The focus of this unit is on narratives. In previewing Embedded Assessment 1, you have seen that you will be writing your own narrative about a change in your life. Reading other types of narratives—a fictional novel, a memoir, a graphic novel, a biography, or a collection of short stories—will help you see how writers create narratives. Think about these questions to help you choose books to read outside of class.

1. What have you enjoyed reading in the past? What is your favorite book or favorite type of book? Who is your favorite author?

2. Preview the book you have selected: What do the front and back covers show you? What type of visual is shown? What types of fonts and colors are used? Are there awards or brags that tell you about the book?

3. Read the first few pages. Are they interesting? How does the author try to hook you to keep reading? What can you tell about the characters and setting (location and time) so far? Does this seem too hard, too easy, or just right?

Reading Discussion Groups

Your teacher will guide you in a book pass. Practice previewing each book, looking at the covers and reading the first few pages.

4. In your Reader/Writer Notebook, record each book's title and author, something from your previewing that stands out to you, and your rating of the book.

5. After previewing each book and thinking about the goals of this unit, do you want to continue reading the book you brought to the group or choose something else?

6. Create an Independent Reading Plan to help you set personal reading goals. Keep this plan in your Reader/Writer Notebook.

I have chosen to read _____

by (author) _____

because (reason from previewing) _____

_____

I will set aside time to read at (time, place) _____

I should finish this text by (date) _____

7. Record your daily reading pace in your Independent Reading Log. Write a brief daily report in your log responding to what you have read.

LEARNING STRATEGIES:
Collaborative Discussion

INDEPENDENT READING LINK

Read and Respond

As you read, think like a writer by noticing the way writers create characters, construct plots, use details to create a setting, include transitions to move the story forward and indicate a change in time or place, and use dialogue to enhance the readers' understanding of what is happening. Use your Reader/Writer Notebook to create your reading plan and respond to any questions, comments, or reactions you might have to your reading. Your teacher may ask questions about your text, and making notes in your Reader/Writer Notebook will help you answer them.

My Notes

_____

_____

_____

_____

_____

_____

_____

_____

_____

_____

_____

_____

Personal Narrative: Incident-Response-Reflection

LEARNING STRATEGIES:
Predicting, Close Reading, Marking the Text, Graphic Organizer, Visualizing

My Notes

_____

_____

_____

_____

Literary Terms

A **personal narrative** is a story based on one's own life and told in the first person.
Point of view is the perspective from which a story or poem is told. In **first-person point of view**, the narrator is a character in the story using first-person pronouns such as *I* and *we* to tell what he or she sees and knows. In **third-person point of view**, the narrator is someone outside the story using third-person pronouns such as *he*, *she*, and *they* to tell the story.

_____

_____

_____

_____

_____

_____

Learning Target

- Analyze how the response in a personal narrative contributes to the development of the story.
- Identify and use an organizational structure to develop ideas and events in a personal narrative.

Personal Narratives

A **personal narrative** can be defined as a first-person **point of view** autobiographical story. Personal narratives usually include a significant incident, the writer's response to the incident, and a reflection on the meaning of the incident.

A personal narrative may follow this structure:

- **Incident:** the central piece of action that is the focus of the narrative. It may include the setting and dialogue
- **Response:** the immediate emotions and actions associated with the incident
- **Reflection:** a description that explores the significance of the incident

Preview

In this activity, you will read a personal narrative to identify its organizational structure and apply it to your own writing.

Setting a Purpose for Reading

- As you read the following personal narrative, use close reading and mark the text for the setting, the major incident of the story, the narrator's response to the incident, and the reflection about the incident.
- Circle unknown words and phrases. Try to determine the meaning of the words by using context clues, word parts, or a dictionary.

ABOUT THE AUTHOR
Dan Greenburg is a novelist, journalist, screenwriter, playwright, and humorist who has also done stand-up comedy. He has written for both adults and children. His successful series *The Zack Files* was inspired by his own son Zack. Greenburg wanted to write books that his son would like to read.

Personal Narrative

My Superpowers

by Dan Greenburg

1 Do you ever wish you had superpowers?

2 When I was a kid, growing up on the North Side of Chicago and being picked on by bullies, I prayed for superpowers. Like Superman, I wanted to be able to fly faster than speeding bullets, to be more powerful than locomotives, to leap tall buildings at a single bound. Mainly, I wanted to punch bullies in the stomach so hard that my fist came out of their backs.

3 Winters in Chicago are so cold that frost forms leafy patterns on your bedroom window and stays there for months. The wind howls off Lake Michigan, and a thick shell of pitted black ice covers the streets and sidewalks from December to April. To keep warm in winter, I wore a heavy wool coat, a wool muffler, wool mittens, furry earmuffs and—one of my most treasured possessions—a Chicago Cubs baseball cap autographed by a player named Big Bill Nicholson.

4 On the coldest days of winter, three bullies waited for me after school, just for the fun of terrorizing me. The biggest one was a fat ugly kid named Vernon Manteuffel. Vernon and his two buddies would pull off my Cubs cap and tease me with it. They'd pretend to give it back, then toss it around in a game of keep-away.

5 One day in February when the temperature was so low I felt my eyeballs cracking, Vernon and his friends caught up with me on my way home. As usual, they tore off my Cubs cap and started playing catch with it. What made it worse than usual was that on this particular day I happened to be walking home with a pretty girl named Ann Cohn, who lived across the street from me. Ann Cohn had green eyes and shiny black hair and I had a goofy crush on her. As if it wasn't bad enough that these guys humiliated me when I was alone, now they were doing it in front of Ann Cohn.

6 I was so embarrassed, I began to cry. Crying in front of Ann Cohn made me even more embarrassed. I was speechless with shame and anger. Driven by rage, I did what only an insane person would do: I attacked Vernon Manteuffel. I punched him in the chest and grabbed back my Cubs cap.

7 Vernon saw that I had become a madman. People don't know what to do with madmen. Vernon looked shocked and even a little afraid. He backed away from me. I attacked the second boy, who also backed away from me. Encouraged by their backing away, I ran after them, screaming, punching, flailing at them with both fists. I chased them for two blocks before they finally pulled ahead and disappeared. Breathing hard, tears streaming down my face, I felt I had regained my honor, at least temporarily.

8 That weekend, perhaps made braver by my triumph over the three bullies, I kissed Ann Cohn on her sofa. I can't tell you exactly why I did that. Maybe because it was a cold, cloudy Saturday and there was nothing else to do. Maybe because we both wondered what it would feel like. In any case, I could now brag that, at age eight, I had personally kissed an actual girl who wasn't related to me.

9 I never did get those superpowers. Not as a kid, at least.

locomotive: a rail vehicle with the engine that powers a train

possession: something that is owned

terrorize: frighten someone intentionally, such as with threats or violence

GRAMMAR & USAGE
Commas

When listing three or more things in a series, separate them with commas: "...I ran after them, screaming, punching, flailing at them with both fists."

You can also create longer sentences by linking descriptive phrases with commas: "Breathing hard, tears streaming down my face, I felt I had regained my honor..."

Personal Narrative: Incident-Response-Reflection

voodoo: religion practiced in Haiti involving spells and spirits of the dead

My Notes

radioactive: containing powerful, dangerous radiation energy

10 When I grew up, I became a writer. I discovered a particular pleasure in going on risky adventures. I wrote about my real-life adventures for national magazines: I spent four months riding with New York firefighters and running into burning buildings with them. I spent six months riding with New York homicide cops as they chased and captured drug dealers and murderers. I flew upside-down over the Pacific Ocean with a stunt pilot in an open-cockpit airplane. I took part in dangerous **voodoo** ceremonies in Haiti. I spent time on a tiger ranch in Texas and learned to tame two-hundred-pound tigers by yelling "*No!*" and smacking them hard on the nose. I found that tigers were not much different from the bullies of my childhood in Chicago.

11 I also wrote fiction. I created entire worlds and filled them with people I wanted to put in there. I made these people do and say whatever it pleased me to have them do and say. In the worlds I made up, I was all-powerful. I *had superpowers.*

12 I began writing a series of children's books called *The Zack Files*, about a boy named Zack who keeps stumbling into the supernatural. In many of these books I gave Zack temporary powers—to read minds, to travel outside his body, to travel back into the past, to triumph over ghosts and monsters. I created another series called *Maximum Boy*, about a boy named Max who accidentally touches **radioactive** rocks that just came back from outer space and who suddenly develops superpowers. Maximum Boy is me as a kid in Chicago, but with superpowers.

13 Oh yeah, I almost forgot. In *The Zack Files*, I created a fat, stupid kid who sweats a lot and thinks he's cool, but who everyone laughs at behind his back. You know what I named this fool? Vernon Manteuffel. I do hope the real Vernon knows.

Second Read

- Reread the narrative to answer these text-dependent comprehension questions.
- Write any additional questions you have about the text in your Reader/Writer Notebook.

1. **Key Ideas and Details:** What details from the story tell you how the incident of bullying the narrator describes is different from the usual bullying he experiences?

2. **Craft and Structure:** Why did Greenburg name his series *Maximum Boy*? Make an inference about what the word *maximum* means? Use context clues to check your inference. What does it tell you about the series?

3. **Key Ideas and Details:** Where does Greenburg's reflection on the importance of this incident begin? Summarize what he says is the impact of that incident in his later life.

Working from the Text

4. Identify five events in "My Superpowers." Sequence them in chronological order:

First:

Then:

Next:

Afterwards:

Finally:

5. Often, **cause** and **effect** play an important part in a narrative. Give examples of a cause and an effect from "My Superpowers." There may be more than one.

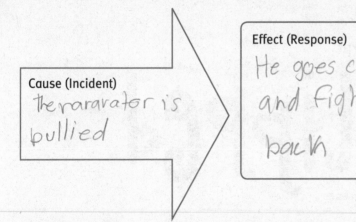

Cause (Incident)
the rararator is bullied

Effect (Response)
He goes crazy and fights back

6. **Quickwrite:** Summarize Greenburg's response and what he learned the day bullies tried for the last time to scare him.

Check Your Understanding

Narrative Writing Prompt

Review the key incident-response-reflection events in "My Superpowers." Then return to the alternative ending you wrote for "The Circuit." Revise it to follow an incident-response-reflection organization. Be sure to

- Use pronouns correctly as you write first-person point of view
- Establish the incident(setting, conflict, character), describe the narrator's response to the incident, and write his reflection to the incident.

ACADEMIC VOCABULARY
Cause and effect describes a relationship in which an action or event will produce or **cause** a certain response or **effect** in the form of another event. It is important to show that a specific effect is directly related to a cause. For example, the effect of a flat tire is caused by driving over a sharp object.

My Notes

INDEPENDENT READING LINK

Read and Discuss

How is the concept of change present in the book you are reading on your own? What is happening to the characters that is causing them to change, or what can you predict will happen? With a small group of your peers, compare how the theme of change is playing out in each of your independent reading books. Add your notes to an Independent Reading section of your Reader/Writer Notebook.

He Said, She Said: Characterization

LEARNING STRATEGIES:
Collaborative Discussion,
Predicting, Close Reading,
Marking the Text, Graphic
Organizer

My Notes

Learning Targets

- Make inferences about a character and provide textual evidence in a short, written response.
- Explain how an author develops the point of view of characters.
- Practice the use and conventions of pronouns and dialogue.

Preview

In this activity, you will read an excerpt from a novel and analyze its characters.

Setting a Purpose for Reading

- Authors develop their characters in various ways. When looking for evidence of characterization, look for words and phrases that describe the character's appearance, what the character says (dialogue), what others say about the character, and the character's actions. As you read the excerpt from *Flipped*, underline evidence that shows how author Wendelin Van Draanen develops her characters.

ABOUT THE AUTHOR

Wendelin Van Draanen started writing for adults but discovered that she much preferred writing for children. She has had much success with her Sammy Keyes mystery series, several of which have won the Edgar Allan Poe Award for best children's mystery. She lives with her family in California.

Novel Excerpt

from

Flipped

by Wendelin Van Draanen

From the chapter "Diving Under"

1 All I've ever wanted is for Juli Baker to leave me alone. For her to back off—you know, just give me some *space.*

2 It all started the summer before second grade when our moving van pulled into her neighborhood. And since we're now about done with the *eighth* grade, that, my friend, makes more than half a decade of strategic avoidance and social discomfort.

3 She didn't just barge into my life. She barged and shoved and wedged her way into my life. Did we invite her to get into our moving van and start climbing all over boxes? No! But that's exactly what she did, taking over and showing off like only Juli Baker can.

catapult: to quickly move up or ahead in position

4 My dad tried to stop her. "Hey!" he says as she's catapulting herself on board. "What are you doing? You're getting mud everywhere!" So true, too. Her shoes were, like, caked with the stuff.

5 She didn't hop out, though. Instead, she planted her rear end on the floor and started pushing a big box with her feet. "Don't you want some help?" She glanced my way. "It sure looks like you *need* it."

6 I didn't like the implication. And even though my dad had been tossing me the same sort of look all week, I could tell—he didn't like this girl either. "Hey! Don't do that," he warned her. "There are some really valuable things in that box."

7 "Oh. Well, how about this one?" She scoots over to a box labeled LENOX and looks my way again. "We should push it together!"

8 "No, no, no!" my dad says, then pulls her up by the arm. "Why don't you run along home? Your mother's probably wondering where you are."

9 This was the beginning of my soon-to-become-acute awareness that the girl cannot take a hint. Of any kind. Does she zip on home like a kid should when they've been invited to leave? No. She says, "Oh, my mom knows where I am. She said it was fine." Then she points across the street and says, "We just live right over there."

10 My father looks to where she's pointing and mutters, "Oh boy." Then he looks at me and winks as he says, "Bryce, isn't it time for you to go inside and help your mother?"

11 I knew right off that this was a ditch play. And I didn't think about it until later, but ditch wasn't a play I'd run with my dad before. Face it, pulling a ditch is not something discussed with dads. It's like, against parental law to tell your kid it's okay to ditch someone, no matter how annoying or *muddy* they might be.

12 But there he was, putting the play in motion, and man, he didn't have to wink twice. I smiled and said, "Sure thing!" then jumped off the liftgate and headed for my new front door.

13 I heard her coming after me but I couldn't believe it. Maybe it just sounded like she was chasing me; maybe she was really going the other way. But before I got up the nerve to look, she blasted right past me, grabbing my arm yanking me along.

14 This was too much. I planted myself and was about to tell her to get lost when the weirdest thing happened. I was making this big windmill motion to break away from her, but somehow on the downswing my hand wound up tangling into hers. I couldn't believe it. There I was, holding the mud monkey's hand!

15 I tried to shake her off, but she just clamped on tight and yanked me along, saying, "C'mon!"

16 My mom came out of the house and immediately got the world's sappiest look on her face. "Well, hello," she says to Juli.

17 "Hi!"

18 I'm still trying to pull free, but the girl's got me in a death grip. My mom's grinning, looking at our hands and my fiery red face. "And what's your name, honey?"

19 "Julianna Baker. I live right over there," she says, pointing with her unoccupied hand.

20 "Well, I see you've met my son," she says, still grinning away.

---

implication: an idea suggested, not directly stated; something implied

GRAMMAR & USAGE
Reflexive and Intensive Pronouns

Words like *myself, yourself, itself, ourselves, yourselves,* and *themselves* can be used as reflexive or intensive pronouns, depending on how they are used in a sentence.

A **reflexive pronoun** is used as an object and refers back to the subject of the sentence.

Example: ". . . as she's catapulting *herself* on board."

An **intensive pronoun** adds emphasis to a noun in the sentence. It can be removed without changing the meaning of the sentence.

Example: "I sent my complaint to the president of the company himself."

immediately: right away; without delay

My Notes

He Said, She Said: Characterization

pick fo

GRAMMAR & USAGE
Punctuating Dialogue

Look at how the writer uses dialogue in paragraphs 16–21. What do you notice about the use of quotation marks? How does the writer indicate who is speaking?

When writing dialogue, remember these points:

- Place a person's spoken words inside quotation marks (beginning and ending).

- Place the period, comma, exclamation mark, or question mark inside the ending quotation mark.

- Capitalize the first word of dialogue.

- Start a new paragraph when a different character speaks.

21 "Uh-huh!"

response

22 Finally I break free and do the only manly thing available when you're seven years old—I dive behind my mother.

23 Mom puts her arm around me and says, "Bryce, honey, why don't you show Julianna around the house?"

24 I flash her help and warning signals with every part of my body, but she's not receiving. Then *she* shakes *me* off and says, "Go on."

25 Juli would've tramped right in if my mother hadn't noticed her shoes and told her to take them off. And after those were off, my mom told her that her dirty socks had to go, too. Juli wasn't embarrassed. Not a bit. She just peeled them off and left them in a crusty heap on our porch.

response

26 I didn't exactly give her a tour. I locked myself in the bathroom instead. And after about ten minutes of yelling back at her that no, I wasn't coming out anytime soon, things got quiet out in the hall. Another ten minutes went by before I got the nerve to peek out the door.

27 No Juli.

28 I snuck out and looked around, and yes! She was gone.

29 Not a very sophisticated ditch, but hey, I was only seven.

reflection

30 My troubles were far from over, though. Every day she came back, over and over again. "Can Bryce play?" I could hear her asking from my hiding place behind the couch. "Is he ready yet?" One time she even cut across the yard and looked through my window. I spotted her in the nick of time and dove under my bed, but man, that right there tells you something about Juli Baker. She's got no concept of personal space. No respect for privacy. The world is her playground, and watch out below—Juli's on the slide!

From the chapter "Flipped"

1 The first day I met Bryce Loski, I flipped. Honestly, one look at him and I became a lunatic. It's his eyes. Something in his eyes. They're blue, and framed in the blackness of his lashes, they're dazzling. **Absolutely** breathtaking.

2 It's been over six years now, and I learned long ago to hide my feelings, but oh, those first days. Those first years! I thought I would die for wanting to be with him.

3 Two days before the second grade is when it started, although the anticipation began weeks before—ever since my mother had told me that there was a family with a boy my age moving into the new house right across the street.

4 Soccer camp had ended, and I'd been so bored because there was nobody, absolutely nobody, in the neighborhood to play with. Oh, there were kids, but every one of them was older. That was dandy for my brothers, but what it left *me* was home alone.

5 My mother was there, but she had better things to do than kick a soccer ball around. So she said, anyway. At the time I didn't think there was anything better than kicking a soccer ball around, especially not the likes of laundry or dishes or vacuuming, but my mother didn't agree. And the danger of being home alone with her was that she'd recruit me to help her wash or dust or vacuum, and she wouldn't tolerate the dribbling of a soccer ball around the house as I moved from chore to chore.

absolutely: with certainty; without question

My Notes

_____

_____

_____

_____

_____

_____

_____

_____

6 To play it safe, I waited outside for weeks, just in case the new neighbors moved in early. **Literally**, it was *weeks*. I entertained myself by playing soccer with our dog, Champ. Mostly he'd just block because a dog can't exactly kick and score, but once in a while he'd dribble with his nose. The scent of a ball must overwhelm a dog, though, because Champ would eventually try to chomp it, then lose the ball to me.

7 When the Loskis' moving van finally arrived, everyone in my family was happy. "Little Julianna" was finally going to have a playmate.

8 My mother, being the truly sensible adult that she is, made me wait more than an *hour* before going over to meet him. "Give them a chance to stretch their legs, Julianna," she said. "They'll want some time to adjust." She wouldn't even let me watch from the yard. "I know you, sweetheart. Somehow that ball will wind up in their yard and you'll just *have* to go retrieve it."

9 So I watched from the window, and every few minutes I'd ask, "Now?" and she'd say, "Give them a little while longer, would you?"

10 Then the phone rang. And the minute I was sure she was good and preoccupied, I tugged on her sleeve and asked, "Now?"

11 She nodded and whispered, "Okay, but take it easy! I'll be over there in a minute."

12 I was too excited not to charge across the street, but I did try very hard to be **civilized** once I got to the moving van. I stood outside looking in for a record-breaking length of time, which was hard because there he was! About halfway back! My new sure-to-be best friend, Bryce Loski.

13 Bryce wasn't really doing much of anything. He was more hanging back, watching his father move boxes onto the liftgate. I remember feeling sorry for Mr. Loski because he looked worn out, moving boxes all by himself. I also remember that he and Bryce were wearing matching turquoise polo shirts, which I thought was really cute. Really *nice*.

14 When I couldn't stand it any longer, I called, "Hi!" into the van, which made Bryce jump, and then quick as a cricket, he started pushing a box like he'd been working all along.

15 I could tell from the way Bryce was acting so guilty that he was supposed to be moving boxes, but he was sick of it. He'd probably been moving things for days! It was easy to see that he needed a rest. He needed some juice! Something.

16 It was also easy to see that Mr. Loski wasn't about to let him quit. He was going to keep on moving boxes around until he collapsed, and by then Bryce might be dead. Dead before he'd had the chance to move in!

17 The tragedy of it catapulted me into the moving van. I had to help! I had to save him!

18 When I got to his side to help him shove a box forward, the poor boy was so exhausted that he just moved aside and let me take over. Mr. Loski didn't want me to help, but at least I saved Bryce. I'd been in the moving van all of three minutes when his dad sent him off to help his mother unpack things inside the house.

19 I chased Bryce up the walkway, and that's when everything changed. You see, I caught up to him and grabbed his arm, trying to stop him so maybe we could play a little before he got trapped inside, and the next thing I know he's holding my hand, looking right into my eyes.

literally: true, without exaggeration

GRAMMAR & USAGE
Sentences and Fragments

Authors often use simple sentences or fragments in dialogue. **Simple sentences** contain an independent clause with a single subject and a verb.

Example: "I live right over there."

Fragments are not complete sentences, as they do not have both a subject and a verb.

Example: "Sure thing!"

Authors may use fragments intentionally in dialogue and for stylistic reasons, but fragments used by mistake take away from the author's credibility.

civilized: normal, respectful behavior

My Notes

_____
_____
_____
_____
_____
_____
_____
_____
_____
_____
_____

He Said, She Said: Characterization

My Notes

20 My heart stopped. It just stopped beating. And for the first time in my life, I had that feeling. You know, like the world is moving all around you, all beneath you, all *inside* you, and you're floating. Floating in midair. And the only thing keeping you from drifting away is the other person's eyes. They're connected to yours by some invisible physical force, and they hold you fast while the rest of the world swirls and twirls and falls completely away.

21 I almost got my first kiss that day. I'm sure of it. But then his mother came out the front door and he was so embarrassed that his cheeks turned completely red, and the next thing you know he's hiding in the bathroom.

22 I was waiting for him to come out when his sister, Lynetta, saw me in the hallway. She seemed big and mature to me, and since she wanted to know what was going on, I told her a little bit about it. I shouldn't have, though, because she wiggled the bathroom doorknob and started teasing Bryce something fierce. "Hey, baby brother!" she called through the door. "There's a hot chick out here waiting for you! Whatsa matter? Afraid she's got cooties?"

23 It was so embarrassing! I yanked on her arm and told her to stop it, but she wouldn't, so finally I just left.

24 I found my mother outside talking to Mrs. Loski. Mom had given her the beautiful lemon Bundt cake that was supposed to be our dessert that night. The powdered sugar looked soft and white, and the cake was still warm, sending sweet lemon smells into the air.

25 My mouth was watering just looking at it! But it was in Mrs. Loski's hands, and I knew there was no getting it back. All I could do was try to eat up the smells while I listened to the two of them discuss grocery stores and the weather forecast.

26 After that Mom and I went home. It was very strange. I hadn't gotten to play with Bryce at all. All I knew was that his eyes were a dizzying blue, that he had a sister who was not to be trusted, and that he'd almost kissed me.

Second Read

- Reread the novel excerpt to answer these text-dependent comprehension questions.
- Write any additional questions you have about the text in your Reader/Writer Notebook.

1. **Key Ideas and Details:** Analyze the first meeting between Juli and Bryce, from Bryce's point of view. Use details from the story to describe what Bryce says and does.

2. **Craft and Structure:** After reading Bryce's first-person telling of this incident, find the part of Juli's story that recounts the exact same part of the incident. Mark the text by highlighting words and phrases in Juli's retelling of the incident that show her attitude toward and her feelings about what is happening.

3. **Craft and Structure:** How does the author pace the narrative? What words or phrases does the author use as transitions?

4. **Craft and Structure:** How does the author's use of different chapters to represent each character contribute to the development of the plot and the different perspectives of the characters?

My Notes

He Said, She Said: Characterization

Literary Terms

Connotation refers to the suggested or implied meaning or emotion associated with a word. In contrast, **denotation** refers to the literal meaning of a word.

My Notes

Working from the Text

5. A writer's diction, or word choices, often uses **connotation** to create an effect or meaning. For example, what do the verbs "barged," "shoved," and "wedged" say about how a character is moving? What image of the character do you get based on these words? In paragraph 17, notice that Juli uses the verbs "charge" and "catapult" to describe how she moves. These verbs mean more than simply "to walk or run"; they have strong connotations. How does the connotative effect of these words describe Juli's attitude toward her friendship with Bryce?

As you continue to work on the characterization of Juli and Bryce in the following questions, use additional examples of connotation to support your responses.

6. Record the textual evidence of the author's characterization in the following graphic organizer.

What Bryce/Juli says:	What Bryce/Juli does:

What others say about Bryce/Juli:	How Bryce/Juli appears:

7. Make an inference about the characters' attitudes in *Flipped*. To support your thinking, include textual evidence about what the characters say and do.

I know Bryce thinks Juli is _____ because he says,

I know Juli thinks Bryce is _____ because she says

My Notes

_____

_____

_____

_____

_____

_____

_____

_____

8. Use evidence from the text to show the differences in Bryce's and Juli's perspective about an incident and how each character responded to it.

	Bryce's Point of View	Juli's Point of View
Incident		
Response		

He Said, She Said: Characterization *picky*

Language and Writer's Craft: Pronouns

Pronouns can be used as both subjects and objects. Look at the graphic organizer below and write in the pronouns of each type.

	Subjective (Subject)		Objective (Object)	
	Singular	Plural	Singular	Plural
First person	I	we	me	us
Second person	you	you	you	you
Third person	he, she, it	they	him, her, it	them

- When would you use a subjective pronoun and an objective pronoun?

Subjective when the pronoun is the subject of the sentence ("I did this", "he did that", "I dive" & and "she says") objective if the pronoun is the object of the verb ("Yanked me", "got me") or object of the preposition ("with her")

- Think about how writers use pronouns. Reread paragraphs 13–14 of the chapter "Flipped." Read the paragraphs using only pronouns and not the names of the characters? Why might this be confusing for readers?

Too many pronouns can be confusing because the reader does not know which character is speaking or being described.

- Reread paragraphs 13–14 aloud to a partner, using only proper names and no pronouns. How does this usage affect the flow of writing?

the writing sounds stilted; a mixture of proper names and pronouns leads to more effective writing.

Possessive Pronouns

The possessive pronouns show ownership. Complete the chart below by writing the possessive pronouns that correspond to the pronouns in the left column. Find examples of how these pronouns are used in *Flipped* and discuss with a partner.

I	my, mine	our, ours
you	your	yours
he/she/they	his, her, their	his, hers, theirs

9. **Collaborative Discussion:** Discuss the following prompt: Describe a time when you and another person (a friend, an adult, a teacher, a sibling) saw the same incident differently. Explain both how you saw the incident and how the other person viewed it.

10. Use the graphic organizer to prewrite about the incident you shared during the collaborative discussion.

I Say . . .	_____ Says . . .
Reflection: What did you learn, how did you grow?	Reflection: What would _____ say you learned or how you grew?

WRITING to SOURCES   **Narrative Writing Prompt**

Write about the incident that you completed the prewrite for in a way that shows the differing attitudes about what happened. Be sure to

- Establish the incident (setting, conflict, character) and describe the response to the incident.
- Create dialogue that incorporates the characters' feelings and punctuate it correctly.
- Use descriptive language: connotative diction and vivid verbs.
- Use proper names and pronouns (including subjective, objective, intensive, and possessive) appropriately; punctuate your narrative correctly.

Return to the text of *Flipped* as a model of how to incorporate these elements in your writing.

INDEPENDENT READING LINK

Read and Recommend
Investigate and record in your Reader/Writer Notebook how the author of the book you are reading independently is developing character. Based on your author's character development, write why you would or would not recommend his or her writing to your peers.

Analyzing Narratives

pick

LEARNING STRATEGIES:
Paraphrasing, Close Reading,
Marking the Text, Graphic
Organizer, Note-taking

Literary Terms
Figurative language
is language used in an
imaginative way to express
ideas that are not literally
true. The most common
examples of figurative
language are **metaphor**
and **simile**. A simile
compares two unlike things
using words such as *like* or
as. *His music is like a fast
trip on a roller coaster*. A
metaphor compares two
unlike things without using
the words *like* or *as*. Often
a form of *to be* is used. *Her
music is a trip to the streets
of Memphis*.

Learning Targets
- Analyze the author's use of descriptive language in a personal narrative and its
  effect on the reader.

Descriptive Language
Writers use descriptive language, such as **figurative language**, vivid verbs, and
sensory language, to add interest, detail, and voice to their writing. Review the
definitions and examples of figurative language in the Literary Terms box.

Preview
In this activity, you will read a personal narrative and analyze the author's use of
descriptive language.

Setting a Purpose for Reading
- Read the personal narrative and underline any examples of figurative language
  such as **simile** and **metaphor**.
- Circle unknown words or phrases. Try to determine the meaning of the words by
  using context clues, word parts, or a dictionary.

ABOUT THE AUTHOR
Gary Soto grew up in Fresno, California, and now lives in Berkeley, California.
In high school, he discovered a love of reading and knew he wanted to be
a writer. Soto started writing while in college. He has written poems, short
stories, and novels, which capture the vivid details of everyday life and which
have won numerous awards and prizes. Of Mexican-American heritage, Soto
speaks Spanish as well as English.

My Notes

_____

_____

_____

_____

_____

_____

_____

_____

_____

_____

_____

_____

Personal Narrative

The Jacket

by Gary Soto

1 My clothes have failed me. I remember the green coat that I wore in fifth and sixth
grades when you either danced like a champ or pressed yourself against a greasy wall,
bitter as a penny toward the happy couples.

2 When I needed a new jacket and my mother asked what kind I wanted, I described
something like bikers wear: black leather and silver studs, with enough belts to hold
down a small town. We were in the kitchen, steam on the windows from her cooking.
She listened so long while stirring dinner that I thought she understood for sure the
kind I wanted. The next day when I got home from school, I discovered draped on
my bedpost a jacket the color of day-old guacamole. I threw my books on the bed
and approached the jacket slowly, as if it were a stranger whose hand I had to shake.
I touched the vinyl sleeve, the collar, and peeked at the mustard-colored lining.

vinyl: a plastic material

incident

3 From the kitchen mother yelled that my jacket was in the closet. I closed the door to her voice and pulled at the rack of clothes in the closet, hoping the jacket on the bedpost wasn't for me but my mean brother. No luck. I gave up. From my bed, I stared at the jacket. I wanted to cry because it was so ugly and so big that I knew I'd have to wear it a long time. I was a small kid, thin as a young tree, and it would be years before I'd have a new one. I stared at the jacket, like an enemy, thinking bad things before I took off my old jacket, whose sleeves climbed halfway to my elbow.

4 I put the big jacket on. I zipped it up and down several times, and rolled the cuffs up so they didn't cover my hands. I put my hands in the pockets and flapped the jacket like a bird's wings. I stood in front of the mirror, full face, then profile, and then looked over my shoulder as if someone had called me. I sat on the bed, stood against the bed, and combed my hair to see what I would look like doing something natural. I looked ugly. I threw it on my brother's bed and looked at it for a long time before I slipped it on and went out to the backyard, smiling a "thank you" to my mom as I passed her in the kitchen. With my hands in my pockets I kicked a ball against the fence, and then climbed it to sit looking into the alley. I hurled orange peels at the mouth of an open garbage can, and when the peels were gone I watched the white puffs of my breath thin to nothing.

similie

5 I jumped down, hands in my pockets, and in the backyard, on my knees, I teased my dog, Brownie, by swooping my arms while making birdcalls. He jumped at me and missed. He jumped again and again, until a tooth sunk deep, ripping an L-shaped tear on my left sleeve. I pushed Brownie away to study the tear as I would a cut on my arm. There was no blood, only a few loose pieces of fuzz. Damn dog, I thought, and pushed him away hard when he tried to bite again. I got up from my knees and went to my bedroom to sit with my jacket on my lap, with the lights out.

6 That was the first afternoon with my new jacket. The next day I wore it to sixth grade and got a D on a math quiz. During the morning recess Frankie T., the playground terrorist, pushed me to the ground and told me to stay there until recess was over. My best friend, Steve Negrete, ate an apple while looking at me, and the girls turned away to whisper on the monkey bars. The teachers were no help: they looked my way and talked about how foolish I looked in my new jacket. I saw their heads bob with laughter, their hands half covering their mouths.

similies

7 Even though it was cold, I took off the jacket during lunch and played kickball in a thin shirt, my arms feeling like braille from goose bumps. But when I returned to class I slipped the jacket on and shivered until I was warm. I sat on my hands, heating them up, while my teeth chattered like a cup of crooked dice. Finally warm, I slid out of the jacket but put it back on a few minutes later when the fire bell rang. We paraded out into the yard where we, the sixth graders, walked past all the other grades to stand against the back fence. Everybody saw me. Although they didn't say out loud, "Man, that's ugly," I heard the buzz-buzz of gossip and even laughter that I knew was meant for me.

response

8 And so I went, in my guacamole-colored jacket. So embarrassed, so hurt, I couldn't even do my homework. I received C's on quizzes and forgot the state capitals and the rivers of South America, our friendly neighbor. Even the girls who had been friendly blew away like loose flowers to follow the boys in neat jackets.

similie

My Notes

braille: a system of writing for blind people that uses raised dots on a page to represent letters

pick

9 I wore that thing for three years until the sleeves grew short and my forearms stuck out like the necks of turtles. All during that time no love came to me—no little dark girl in a Sunday dress she wore on Monday. At lunchtime I stayed with the ugly boys who leaned against the chainlink fence and looked around with propellers of grass spinning in our mouths. We saw girls walk by alone, saw couples, hand in hand, their heads like bookends pressing air together. We saw them and spun our (propellers) so fast our faces were blurs.

propeller: an object with quickly turning blades

10 I blame that jacket for those bad years. I blame my mother for her bad taste and her cheap ways. It was a sad time for the heart. With a friend I spent my sixth-grade year in a tree in the alley, waiting for something good to happen to me in that jacket, which had become the ugly brother who tagged along wherever I went. And it was about that time that I began to grow. My chest puffed up with muscle and, strangely, a few more ribs. Even my hands, those fleshy hammers, showed bravely through the cuffs, the fingers already hardening for the coming fights. But that L-shaped rip on the left sleeve got bigger; bits of stuffing coughed out from its wound after a hard day of play. I finally Scotch-taped it closed, but in rain or cold weather the tape peeled off like a scab and more stuffing fell out until that sleeve shriveled into a **palsied** arm. That winter the elbows began to crack and whole chunks of green began to fall off. I showed the cracks to my mother, who always seemed to be at the stove with steamed-up glasses, and she said that there were children in Mexico who would love that jacket. I told her that this was America and yelled that Debbie, my sister, didn't have a jacket like mine. I ran outside, ready to cry, and climbed the tree by the alley to think bad thoughts and watch my breath puff white and disappear.

reflection

palsy: a condition featuring uncontrolled shaking of a body part

11 But whole pieces still casually flew off my jacket when I played hard, read quietly, or took (vicious) spelling tests at school. When it became so spotted that my brother began to call me "camouflage," I flung it over the fence into the alley. Later, however, I swiped the jacket off the ground and went inside to drape it across my lap and **mope**.

vicious: cruel and dangerous

mope: aimless, unhappy state

12 I was called to dinner: steam silvered my mother's glasses as she said grace; my brother and sister with their heads bowed made ugly faces at their glasses of powdered milk. I gagged too, but eagerly ate big rips of buttered tortilla that held scooped-up beans. Finished, I went outside with my jacket across my arm. It was a cold sky. The faces of clouds were piled up, hurting. I climbed the fence, jumping down with a grunt. I started up the alley and soon slipped into my jacket, that green ugly brother who breathed over my shoulder that day and ever since.

reflection

metaphor

My Notes

_____

_____

_____

_____

_____

_____

_____

_____

_____

_____

_____

_____

Second Read

- Reread the personal narrative to answer these text-dependent comprehension questions.
- Write any additional questions you have about the text in your Reader/Writer Notebook.

1. **Craft and Structure:** Look at the opening sentence. How does the author engage and orient the reader?

   the writer hooks the reader with a strong opening sentence.

2. **Craft and Structure:** What is the point of view of this text? From whose perspective is it written? Cite evidence from the text in your answer.

   its written from first person point of view He uses pronouns like i, my, mine.

3. **Key Ideas and Details:** To show his hatred of his jacket, Soto exaggerates the effect of the jacket on his life. List some effects of the jacket by copying phrases directly from the story.

   9

4. **Craft and Structure:** Paragraphs 7, 8, and 9 have especially vivid examples of similes that describe how the narrator is feeling. Underline examples. Choose one that you consider especially vivid, rewrite it, and explain its effect.

   girls blew away like lose Flowers that means they walked away like flowers blowing away in the wind

5. **Craft and Structure:** In the final paragraph of the narrative, Soto uses the following metaphor to describe his jacket "...my jacket, that green ugly brother who breathed over my shoulder that day and every day since." Based on this line, what can you conclude about the significance of the jacket in Soto's life?

   that jacket made his life worse since he thought it was ugly which blew people away from him.

Analyzing Narratives

GRAMMAR & USAGE
Vivid Verbs

A verb is the part of speech that expresses existence, action, or occurrence. Vivid verbs provide every specific description of an action. For example.

Not vivid: The dog *barked* and *ran* after the cat.

Vivid: The dog *growled* and *sprang* after the cat.

Literary Terms

Sensory language refers to words that appeal to the five senses. Writers use sensory language to help readers create mental images of the characters and story details.

Working from the Text

Language & Writer's Craft: Vivid Verbs

A verb is the part of speech that expresses existence, action, or occurrence.

Example: They *walked* to school.

Vivid verbs describe an action in ways that help the reader create a mental image of the action. How does the action from the sentence above change in your mind when you replace the verb *walked* with one of these verbs?

scrambled, skipped, marched, strode, sauntered

6. Reread paragraphs 4 and 5, and underline the vivid verbs. Choose two and explain how the vivid verbs you chose create mental images of the action. If you change the verbs, how do the images change?

7. In addition to figurative language and vivid verbs, writers use sensory details to enhance their writing. Review the Literary Terms box for **sensory language,** and then read the paragraph below.

   June and her friends were playing baseball in her yard. Billy was up at the plate. When June pitched the ball, Billy hit the ball high into the air. June watched the ball fly into her attic window. The glass shattered. June and Billy looked at each other and ran out of the yard.

   In your Reader/Writer Notebook, revise the story to include sensory details that appeal to any of the five senses.

8. Skim through "The Jacket," looking for examples of descriptive language. Write four examples in the table. Then analyze each example to understand the effect the author is trying to create. Finally, evaluate the example for its effectiveness.

Type of Descriptive Language	Example of Descriptive Language	Analyze the Effect	Evaluate How Effective It Is

9. Summarize the writer's use of descriptive language, including similes, metaphors, vivid verbs, and sensory language. How does his use of descriptive language help express the narrator's response to the incident? Provide textual evidence to support your ideas.

Check Your Understanding

With your group, choose one of the narratives you have read and make a poster that demonstrates your analysis of the story by creatively incorporating the following:

- Title and author of text
- An ending to this sentence: *This narrative is effective because . . .*
- Examples of textual evidence that support the sentence
- Pictures/symbols/color that illustrate the elements of a narrative

As you complete your poster, think about the answer to the Essential Question: What makes a good story?

My Notes

Creating a Narrative

LEARNING STRATEGIES:
Prewriting, Rereading, Drafting, Graphic Organizer

My Notes

Learning Targets

- Brainstorm a personal incident about change to develop a narrative.
- Establish a sequence of events and use organization to plan the details for a narrative.
- Write dialogue and commentary to help establish the context of an incident.

The Writing Process

In creating your personal narrative, you will use the following writing process:

Planning and Prewriting: brainstorm ideas and plan your writing using the incident-response-reflection structure

Drafting: write your narrative with an effective beginning, middle, and end, including interesting details, descriptive language, and transitions

Revising: add words, phrases, sentences, and ideas to enhance your writing

Editing: check for correct grammar and spelling

1. **Prewriting:** Write about changes that have happened in your life and changes that could occur in the future.

In what ways has your life changed since **first grade**?	In what ways has your life changed since **last year**?
• Went to ymca • learned to read • BFF moved	• Im emo now • more classes • shorter classes
How might your life change during the current school year?	**What types of changes might occur when you become a teenager?**
• get new clothes • better grades • new friends	• go to high school • make new friends irl • get a small Job

2. What words, phrases, and images show the kinds of changes you and your classmates have faced? Interview your classmates, and make a list for each of the five areas shown below.

Hobbies	Beliefs	Appearance	School	Responsibilities
• TikTok account • drawing • playing games		• expander fell off • shaved my eyebrows • new style	• more home work • harder classes • more teachers	• take care of pet • wash clothes • take out trash

3. Think about the narratives you have read and how the writers created a story around an incident. List some of the incidents that resulted in some kind of change to your life. An example might be events that happened when changing from elementary school to middle school.

I dressed the way I wanted and expressed myself. I got bullied

4. Choose one memorable incident that you would be willing to share as a visual memory map. Think back to that incident and determine what happened at the beginning, in the middle, and at the end. Try to come up with at least eight to ten events for the entire incident, at least three to four for each part. Use the graphic organizer to list the events of the incident.

My Notes

My Incident:

Events at the Beginning	Events in the Middle	Events at the End

Creating a Narrative

5. Next, brainstorm details of the events. Record descriptive language (connotative diction, sensory details, vivid verbs) and dialogue. Use the questions in the boxes to guide your thoughts.

Structure of a Personal Narrative

Beginning Details	Middle Details	Ending Details
• What was the time and place? (setting) • Who was there? (characters) • What were you (the narrator) doing, thinking, and feeling?	• Describe events in chronological order. Include dialogue. • What happened? (conflict) • What were you and others doing? • What were you thinking and feeling?	• How did it end? • What did you learn, discover, or realize? How did you grow?

Incident	Response	Reflection
_____	_____	_____
_____	_____	_____
_____	_____	_____
_____	_____	_____
_____	_____	_____
_____	_____	_____

My Notes
_____
_____
_____
_____
_____
_____
_____
_____
_____
_____
_____
_____

Creating a Memory Map

For each event you have listed, you will create one panel or page and include the following:

• Write a sentence that gives specific details about the event. Then, write commentary using a different-colored pen. Your **commentary** should explain the importance of the event or explain your feelings and emotions at the time.

• Using a third color, provide one sentence of dialogue for the scene.

• Create a drawing or graphic representation for each event.

• Give your Memory Map a title that will intrigue the reader and represent the narrative.

• Be prepared to present your Memory Map, telling your story to either a small group or the whole class.

You will use your Memory Map in the next activities as you write a narrative.

Creating a Narrative: Prewriting and Drafting

Learning Targets

- Apply an understanding of narrative elements, including characterization and an effective sequence of events, by drafting a narrative.
- Apply the writing process while drafting a personal narrative.
- Use a variety of transition words, phrases, and clauses to create coherence in a narrative.

1. **Prewriting:** Using the topic from your Memory Map or another topic of your choice, think about whether there are additional questions you might ask. Use the reporter's questions (*who, what, when, where, why,* and *how*) to fill in details of the narrative plan.

_____

_____

_____

_____

_____

_____

2. **Planning:** Organize the answers to your questions in a graphic organizer such as the one below (see the Resources for a full-page version).

LEARNING STRATEGIES:
Prewriting, Rereading, Drafting, Graphic Organizer

My Notes

_____

_____

_____

_____

_____

_____

_____

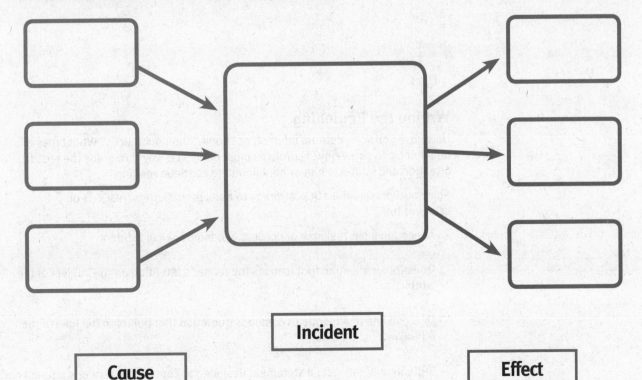

Incident

Cause

Effect

Creating a Narrative: Prewriting and Drafting

3. **Characterization:** Plan the characters by deciding what they say and do.

What the Character Says:	What Others Say:
What the Character Does:	Descriptions of the Character's Appearance:
What the Character Thinks:	Language Techniques:

Writing the Beginning

How have you seen authors interest, or "hook," their audiences? What types of beginnings do you enjoy? Narratives must begin in a way that grabs the reader's attention and interests him or her enough to continue reading.

Some authors use the AQQS strategy to hook their readers. AQQS is an acronym for:

Anecdote: a short sketch or account of a biographical incident

Question: a question that focuses the reader's attention on the subject of the writing

Quote: a line of dialogue or a famous quotation that points to the idea of the narrative

Statement of intrigue: a statement designed to capture the reader's interest and compel him or her to read more

4. Reread the openings of the narratives in Activities 1.2, 1.4, 1.5, and 1.6.
   In the last column of the graphic organizer, describe the type of hook each
   author uses.

	Text	What choice did the author make to hook the reader? Does the author use one of the AQQS strategies?
"The Circuit"	"It was that time of year again. Ito, the sharecropper, did not smile. It was natural. The peak of strawberry season was over and the last few days the workers, most of them *braceros*, were not picking as many boxes as they had during the months of June and July."	
"My Superpowers"	"Do you ever wish you had superpowers?"	
Flipped From the chapter "Diving Under"	"All I've ever wanted is for Juli Baker to leave me alone. For her to back off—you know, just give me some space."	
"The Jacket"	"My clothes have failed me. I remember the green coat that I wore in fifth and sixth grades when you either danced like a champ or pressed yourself against a greasy wall, bitter as a penny toward the happy couples."	

Creating a Narrative: Prewriting and Drafting

5. Which narrative opening do you believe is most effective? Why?

_____

_____

_____

_____

Writing an Ending

6. Reread the endings in the narratives in Activities 1.2, 1.4, 1.5, and 1.6. Then complete the graphic organizer.

Title of Text	Describe how the narrator ends the story.	Summarize how the narrator changes because of the incident. Consider what the narrator learns and how he/she has grown as a person.
"The Circuit"	Jiménez explains	The ending shows that
"My Superpowers"	Greenburg explains	The ending shows that
Flipped From the chapter "Diving Under"	Van Draanen explains	The ending shows that
"The Jacket"	Soto explains	The ending shows that

7. Which narrative ending do you believe is most effective? Why?

_____

_____

_____

_____

ACADEMIC VOCABULARY
When you use **transitions** to connect ideas, you are helping to create **coherence**. Coherence is the clear and orderly presentation of ideas in your writing and speaking. This ability to make your thinking **cohere**, or stick together, is an important skill in writing and thinking about any subject.

Language and Writer's Craft: Transitions

The use of transitions makes an essay or other writing easy for the reader to follow. **Transitions** are words and phrases that link ideas, sentences, and paragraphs. Transitions help you create **coherence** in your writing.

Transitional words help you move from one sentence or thought to another.

- **Transitions that show examples:** *that is, such as, for example, in other words, for instance*
- **Transitions that show time:** *first, next, after, finally, then, at the same time*
- **Transitions that show importance:** *second, more importantly, most important, most of all, least, last but not least*

8. Fill in the blanks in the paragraph below with the most appropriate transitional words and phrases from the list above.

_____, I went to my mom's secret recipe drawer in her bedroom. _____, I grabbed everything I needed from the kitchen. I wasn't going to cook in our kitchen, however. I wanted to keep everyone in the dark about what I was up to, _____ my nosy sister Caitlin. _____, I was going to win this bake-off challenge all by myself.

Check Your Understanding

Narrative Writing Prompt:

Write a draft of your narrative about a change that is significant to you. Remember to refer to your Memory Map, questions and answers about details, and your characterization graphic organizer to help guide you as you write. Be sure to

- Establish the incident (setting, conflict, character), describe the response (events), and include a reflection.
- Write from the first-person point of view and include details of the characters' feelings; use dialogue to develop the characters and the incident.
- Use descriptive language, such as connotative diction, sensory details, and vivid verbs.
- Use transitions, apply correct punctuation, and use different types of pronouns correctly.

My Notes

Creating a Narrative: Revising

LEARNING STRATEGIES:
Revising, Adding, Drafting,
Sharing and Responding

My Notes

Learning Targets

- Examine and use revision strategies to enhance narrative writing.
- Add dialogue and incorporate transitions and sensory details into a final draft.

No one ever creates a perfect piece of writing with just one try. Revision gives you the chance to look at your writing critically and decide how to improve it.

Introducing the Strategy: Adding

The adding strategy is a revision strategy. With this strategy, you make conscious choices to enhance a piece of your writing by adding words, phrases, sentences, or ideas. For example, characters and incidents should be fully developed in narrative writing. Adding details as you revise can make a character come alive for the reader or make the story more appealing.

Adding Dialogue

Adding dialogue is one way to enhance narrative writing. When adding dialogue, it is important to vary your use of dialogue tags. *Dialogue tags* are phrases used to explain who is speaking. For example, look at this line from *Flipped*:

   "No, no, no!" my dad says, then pulls her up by the arm.

The dialogue tag is the phrase "my dad says."

1. Brainstorm words other than "says" that you could use in dialogue tags, categorizing them by beginning letter. These verbs should be vivid and more descriptive than "said."

starts with A-D	starts with E-K	starts with L-P	starts with Q-Z

2. Your teacher will share with you a sample of a comic strip, or you might bring in one of your favorite comic strips. Mark the text with different colors for each character in the comic strip. Then transform the conversation in the comic strip into written dialogue in paragraph form. Remember to punctuate the dialogue correctly and use a variety of dialogue tags.

3. Share your dialogue with a partner and compare how you each wrote the words of the characters in the comic strip. How were your paragraphs alike? How were they different?

_____

_____

_____

_____

_____

_____

_____

Check Your Understanding

Create a Writer's Checklist for using dialogue. Then use the checklist to revise your narrative to include dialogue.

My Notes

Creating a Narrative: Revising

Language and Writer's Craft: Revising for Transitions

Another way of revising your writing is to add transitions. Transitions help the reader follow a narrative by showing how ideas are related. The following words and phrases are examples of common transitions.

again	also	in addition	too	but
still	however	because	then	so
first	second	next	before	afterward
yet	finally	at last	to begin	later
as soon as	not long after	instead	at the last moment	in the end

INDEPENDENT READING LINK

Read and Respond

Outline the sequence of events from your independent reading book. What has happened so far? In your Reader/Writer Notebook, include major events, examples of important dialogue, and transitional words and phrases.

My Notes

4. The following student narrative does not include any transitional words or phrases. It also lacks details to help the reader imagine the scene. Highlight each place where a transition might fit. Underline sentences that would benefit from sensory details and vivid verbs. Circle or draw a box around the pronouns.

When the author Gary Soto was in sixth grade, he needed a new jacket. His mother bought him a green jacket that he did not like at all. It was ugly. It was bad luck for him at school. He did poorly on tests and his friends didn't pay any attention to him. He thought his teachers and classmates all made fun of him and his jacket. The author's luck didn't change over time. No girls came his way. He tried to show his mother how bad his jacket looked. Her glasses were always steamed up. The author blames those bad times on his green jacket.

5. Rewrite the paragraph above, adding transitions, sensory details, and vivid verbs.

Revising Your Opening

6. Reread the opening of your narrative. Does it have a hook that grabs the reader's attention? Review the AQQS strategy:

Anecdote: a short sketch or account of a biographical incident

Question: a question that focuses the reader's attention on the subject of the writing

Quote: a line of dialogue or a famous quotation that points to the idea of the narrative

Statement of intrigue: a statement designed to capture the reader's interest and compel him or her to read more

If needed, revise your narrative opening to use one of these techniques.

Revising the Ending

7. Reread your ending. Does it have a reflection on the incident, following the incident-response-reflection pattern? How can you make your ending stronger? Do you need to add sensory language or transitions? Revise the ending to your narrative.

_____

_____

_____

_____

Creating a Finished Document

8. Among the steps to finishing your narrative is writing a title. To find ideas for the title:

- Skim the narrative for a word or phrase that captures the big idea or theme of the narrative. Use interesting, descriptive words for your title.
- State the change the narrator experienced, in a clever way.
- Make your title unique; an effective title is not just a labeling of the genre or type of text (e.g., Personal Narrative).

9. The last step to creating a final draft is to check that it is correct and as good as you can make it. To prepare your document for publication, do the following:

- Proofread it to ensure that you have caught and fixed any spelling errors. If you are using word-processing software, use its spell-check feature.
- Check that you have used correct grammar and punctuation.
- Use available resources, such as a dictionary and thesaurus, as you edit your narrative and prepare it for publication.

 Independent Reading Checkpoint

Write about how the theme of change is presented in your independent reading book. In a few paragraphs, describe changes that a character experiences and explain the significance of these changes.

My Notes

Writing a Personal Narrative

Assignment

Your assignment is to write a personal narrative that includes a well-told incident, a response to the incident, and a reflection about the significance of the incident.

Planning and Prewriting: Take time to make a plan for your personal narrative.

- What activities have you completed or ideas have you brainstormed that will help you as you think of an appropriate incident to write about?
- How will you make sure you understand all that needs to be part of your personal narrative?
- What prewriting strategies can you use to help you create ideas? Will you work from your Memory Map?

Drafting: Determine the structure of your personal narrative.

- What will you include in the beginning, the middle, and the end of your narrative?
- How will you introduce your incident?
- How will you be sure to write about the significance of the incident in a way that conveys importance?

Evaluating and Revising the Draft: Create opportunities to review and revise in order to make your work the best it can be.

- During the process of writing, have you paused at points to share and respond with others how well you are following the structure of a narrative?
- Are you considering revising your draft to add transitions and additional details to the incident? Once you get suggestions, are you creating a plan to include revision ideas in your draft?
- Have you used the Scoring Guide to help you evaluate how well your draft included the requirements of the assignment?

Checking and Editing for Publication: Confirm that your final draft is ready for publication.

- How will you check for grammatical and technical accuracy?
- How will you make sure that everything is spelled correctly?

Reflection

After completing this Embedded Assessment, think about how you went about accomplishing this assignment, and answer the questions below:

- How did the activities leading up to this Embedded Assessment help you to be successful?
- What activities were especially helpful, and why?

Technology TIP:

As you prepare for publication, don't forget to use spelling and grammar tools provided by your word-processing program to ensure that your final version is as clean as possible.

Writing a Personal Narrative

SCORING GUIDE

Scoring Criteria	Exemplary	Proficient	Emerging	Incomplete
Ideas	The narrative • presents a clearly focused and significant incident • develops experiences, events, and/or characters through thorough and effective use of dialogue, pacing, and descriptive details.	The narrative • presents a focused and significant incident • develops experiences, events, and/or characters through techniques such as dialogue, pacing, and descriptive details.	The narrative • Presents an inconsistently focused incident • Begins to develop experiences, events, and/or characters through some use of dialogue, pacing, and/or descriptive details.	The narrative • presents an unfocused or unclear incident • fails to develop experiences, events, and/or characters; minimal use of elaborative techniques.
Structure	The narrative • engages and orients the reader in an introduction • sequences events in the incident and response logically and naturally • uses a variety of transitional strategies effectively • provides an insightful reflective conclusion.	The narrative • orients the reader with an adequate introduction • sequences events in the incident and response logically • uses transitional words, phrases, and clauses to link events and signal shifts • provides a reflective conclusion.	The narrative • provides a weak or unrelated introduction • sequences events unevenly • uses inconsistent, repetitive, or basic transitional words, phrases, and clauses • provides a weak or disconnected conclusion.	The narrative • lacks an introduction • sequences events illogically • uses few or no transitional strategies • lacks a conclusion.
Use of Language	The narrative • uses precise words and sensory language effectively to convey the experience • demonstrates command of the conventions of standard English capitalization, punctuation, spelling, grammar, and usage (including pronoun use, sentence variety, dialogue tags, and punctuation).	The narrative • uses generally precise words and sensory language to convey the experience • demonstrates adequate command of the conventions of standard English capitalization, punctuation, spelling, grammar, and usage (including pronoun use, sentence variety, dialogue tags, and punctuation).	The narrative • uses few precise words and little sensory language • demonstrates partial or inconsistent command of the conventions of standard English capitalization, punctuation, spelling, grammar, and usage (including pronoun use, sentence variety, dialogue tags, and punctuation).	The narrative • uses limited, vague, and unclear words and language • lacks command of the conventions of standard English capitalization, punctuation, spelling, grammar, and usage; frequent errors obscure meaning.

Previewing Embedded Assessment 2 and Preparing to Write a Short Story

LEARNING STRATEGIES:
QHT, Close Reading, Paraphrasing, Graphic Organizer

My Notes

Learning Targets
- Reflect on prior learning and identify the skills and knowledge necessary to complete Embedded Assessment 2 successfully.
- Reassess knowledge of academic vocabulary and literary terms in the unit.
- Compare and contrast writing a personal narrative and writing a short story.

Making Connections
In the first part of this unit, you thought about changes in your life and learned how to write a personal narrative. In the second part of the unit, you will expand on your writing skills by learning to write a short story that will appeal to an audience.

Essential Questions
1. Reflect on your understanding of the first Essential Question: How can change be significant?
2. Have your ideas about what makes a good story changed?

Developing Vocabulary
Create a graphic organizer with three columns, one each for Q, H, and T. Re-sort the following words from the first half of the unit using the QHT strategy. Compare this sort with your original sort. Where has it changed most? Where has it changed least?

Literary Terms		Academic Vocabulary
narrative	connotation	analyze
characterization	denotation	sequence
setting	simile	cause-effect
conflict (internal/external)	metaphor	transitions
dialogue	sensory language	coherence
	personal narrative	

Unpacking Embedded Assessment 2
Closely read the assignment for Embedded Assessment 2: Writing a Short Story.

> Write a story using dialogue, vivid verbs, and figurative language that captures a real or imagined experience and includes characters, conflict, and a plot with exposition, climax, and resolution.

Also read the Scoring Guide for Embedded Assessment 2 on page 88. With your class, create a graphic organizer to use as a visual reminder of the required knowledge (what you need to know) and skills (what you need to do). Copy the graphic organizer for future reference. After each activity, use this graphic to guide reflection about what you have learned and what you still need to learn in order to be successful on the Embedded Assessment.

3. Based on your current understanding, how do you think writing a personal narrative and a short story are similar? How are they different? Fill in the chart below with your ideas for each genre.

	Personal Narrative	Short Story
Topics		
Setting		
Plot		
Characters		
Dialogue		

4. With a group, discuss your ideas about how personal narratives and short stories may be similar or different. Write down the conclusions you can draw, based on your discussion.

_____

_____

_____

_____

_____

5. What do these similarities and differences mean for you as a writer? Do you think writing a short story will be more or less challenging than writing a personal narrative?

_____

_____

_____

_____

INDEPENDENT READING LINK

Read and Research

To support your learning in the second half of the unit, you might think about reading a collection of short stories by different authors or a collection of short stories by a single author. Research a short story writer to read based on themes, settings, characters, or a style that you might find appealing.

My Notes

_____

_____

_____

_____

_____

_____

_____

_____

_____

_____

_____

_____

_____

_____

_____

_____

_____

_____

_____

What's in a Short Story?

LEARNING STRATEGIES:
Collaborative Discussion,
Note-taking, Drafting

Literary Terms
A **short story** is a fictional narrative that presents a sequence of events, or plot, that include a conflict.

My Notes

Learning Targets
- Identify the theme of a short story by analyzing narrative elements.
- Use narrative writing to develop a character and transform a story from third-person into first-person point of view.

Preview
In this activity, you will read a **short story** and identify its theme by examining the incident that takes place and how the characters respond.

Setting a Purpose for Reading
- Read the short story "Thank You, M'am" by Langston Hughes and underline the main incident of the narrative.
- Place a star next to the characters' responses to the incident.
- Circle unknown words and phrases. Try to determine the meaning of the words by using context clues, word parts, or a dictionary.

ABOUT THE AUTHOR
Langston Hughes (1902–1967) began his writing career early. By 8th grade, he was named the class poet. He regularly wrote verse for his high school magazine. Hughes entered Columbia University in 1921 and discovered the arts scene in Harlem. He became a prominent figure in the Harlem Renaissance. His poetry, plays, and stories frequently focus on the African American experience, particularly on the struggles and feelings of people in a segregated society. His poetry was especially informed by the jazz and blues rhythms of African American music.

Short Story

Thank You, M'am

by Langston Hughes

1   She was a large woman with a large purse that had everything in it but hammer and nails. It had a long strap, and she carried it slung across her shoulder. It was about eleven o'clock at night, and she was walking alone, when a boy ran up behind her and tried to snatch her purse. The strap broke with the single tug the boy gave it from behind. But the boy's weight and the weight of the purse combined caused him to lose his balance so, instead of taking off full blast as he had hoped, the boy fell on his back on the sidewalk, and his legs flew up. The large woman simply turned around and kicked him right square in his blue-jeaned sitter. Then she reached down, picked the boy up by his shirt front, and shook him until his teeth rattled.

2   After that the woman said, "Pick up my pocketbook, boy, and give it here."

3   She still held him. But she bent down enough to permit him to **stoop** and pick up her purse. Then she said, "Now ain't you **ashamed** of yourself?"

4   Firmly gripped by his shirt front, the boy said, "Yes'm."

5   The woman said, "What did you want to do it for?"

6   The boy said, "I didn't aim to."

7   She said, "You a lie!"

8   By that time two or three people passed, stopped, turned to look, and some stood watching.

9   "If I turn you loose, will you run?" asked the woman.

10   "Yes'm," said the boy.

11   "Then I won't turn you loose," said the woman. She did not release him.

12   "I'm very sorry, lady, I'm sorry," whispered the boy.

13   "Um-hum! And your face is dirty. I got a great mind to wash your face for you. Ain't you got nobody home to tell you to wash your face?"

14   "No'm," said the boy.

15   "Then it will get washed this evening," said the large woman starting up the street, dragging the frightened boy behind her.

16   He looked as if he were fourteen or fifteen, frail and **willow**-wild, in tennis shoes and blue jeans.

17   The woman said, "You ought to be my son. I would teach you right from wrong. Least I can do right now is to wash your face. Are you hungry?"

18   "No'm," said the being-dragged boy. "I just want you to turn me loose."

19   "Was I bothering *you* when I turned that corner?" asked the woman.

20   "No'm."

21   "But you put yourself in contact with me," said the woman. "If you think that that contact is not going to last awhile, you got another thought coming. When I get through with you, sir, you are going to remember Mrs. Luella Bates Washington Jones."

22   Sweat popped out on the boy's face and he began to struggle. Mrs. Jones stopped, jerked him around in front of her, put a half-nelson about his neck, and continued to drag him up the street. When she got to her door, she dragged the boy inside, down a hall, and into a large kitchenette-furnished room at the rear of the house. She switched on the light and left the door open. The boy could hear other roomers laughing and talking in the large house. Some of their doors were open, too, so he knew he and the woman were not alone. The woman still had him by the neck in the middle of her room.

23   She said, "What is your name?"

24   "Roger," answered the boy.

25   "Then, Roger, you go to that sink and wash your face," said the woman, whereupon she turned him loose–at last. Roger looked at the door—looked at the woman—looked at the door—*and went to the sink.*

stoop: bend forward and down
ashamed: feeling shame or guilt

My Notes

willow: long and thin, like a willow tree branch

My Notes

26 Let the water run until it gets warm," she said. "Here's a clean towel."

27 "You gonna take me to jail?" asked the boy, bending over the sink.

28 "Not with that face, I would not take you nowhere," said the woman. "Here I am trying to get home to cook me a bite to eat and you snatch my pocketbook! Maybe, you ain't been to your supper either, late as it be. Have you?"

29 "There's nobody home at my house," said the boy.

30 "Then we'll eat," said the woman, "I believe you're hungry—or been hungry—to try to snatch my pocketbook."

31 "I wanted a pair of blue suede shoes," said the boy.

32 "Well, you didn't have to snatch my pocketbook to get some suede shoes," said Mrs. Luella Bates Washington Jones. "You could of asked me."

33 "M'am?"

34 The water dripping from his face, the boy looked at her. There was a long pause. A very long pause. After he had dried his face and not knowing what else to do, dried it again, the boy turned around, wondering what next. The door was open. He could make a dash for it down the hall. He could run, run, run, run, *run!*

35 The woman was sitting on the day-bed. After a while she said, "I were young once and I wanted things I could not get."

36 There was another long pause. The boy's mouth opened. Then he frowned, but not knowing he frowned.

37 The woman said, "Um-hum! You thought I was going to say *but*, didn't you? You thought I was going to say, *but I didn't snatch people's pocketbooks*. Well, I wasn't going to say that." Pause. Silence. "I have done things, too, which I would not tell you, son—neither tell God, if he didn't already know. So you set down while I fix us something to eat. You might run that comb through your hair so you will look presentable."

icebox: refrigerator

38 In another corner of the room behind a screen was a gas plate and an **icebox.** Mrs. Jones got up and went behind the screen. The woman did not watch the boy to see if he was going to run now, nor did she watch her purse which she left behind her on the day-bed. But the boy took care to sit on the far side of the room where he thought she could easily see him out of the corner of her eye, if she wanted to. He did not trust the woman not to trust him. And he did not want to be mistrusted now.

39 "Do you need somebody to go to the store," asked the boy, "maybe to get some milk or something?"

40 "Don't believe I do," said the woman, "unless you just want sweet milk yourself. I was going to make cocoa out of this canned milk I got here."

41 "That will be fine," said the boy.

42 She heated some lima beans and ham she had in the icebox, made the cocoa, and set the table. The woman did not ask the boy anything about where he lived, or his folks, or anything else that would embarrass him. Instead, as they ate, she told him about her job in a hotel beauty-shop that stayed open late, what the work was like, and how all kinds of women came in and out, blondes, red-heads, and Spanish. Then she cut him a half of her ten-cent cake.

43 "Eat some more, son," she said.

44 When they were finished eating she got up and said, "Now, here, take this ten dollars and buy yourself some blue suede shoes. And next time, do not make the mistake of latching onto *my* pocketbook *nor nobody else's*—because shoes come by devilish like that will burn your feet. I got to get my rest now. But I wish you would behave yourself, son, from here on in."

45 She led him down the hall to the front door and opened it. "Goodnight! Behave yourself, boy!" she said, looking out into the street.

46 The boy wanted to say something else other than "Thank you, m'am," to Mrs. Luella Bates Washington Jones, but he couldn't do so as he turned at the barren stoop and looked back at the large woman in the door. He barely managed to say "Thank you" before she shut the door. And he never saw her again.

Second Read

- Reread the short story to answer these text-dependent comprehension questions.
- Write any additional questions you have about the text in your Reader/Writer Notebook.

1. **Key Ideas and Details:** On page 50, how do the details of setting and character set up the conflict of this story?

2. **Key Ideas and Details:** How does Mrs. Luella Bates Washington Jones's comment in paragraph 13, "I got a great mind to wash your face for you" define how she treats Roger? Find other textual evidence based on things Mrs. Jones says to support your answer.

3. **Craft and Structure:** In paragraph 25, Mrs. Jones finally turns Roger loose: "Roger looked at the door—looked at the woman—looked at the door—*and went to the sink*." Why did the author choose to italicize this part of the text?

4. **Craft and Structure:** In paragraph 44, Mrs. Jones states, "Shoes come by devilish like that will burn your feet." State in your own words what Mrs. Jones meant.

My Notes

What's in a Short Story?

My Notes

5. **Key Ideas and Details:** Even though Roger never sees Mrs. Jones again at the end of the story, what evidence supports Mrs. Jones's promise in paragraph 21, "When I get through with you, sir, you are going to remember Mrs. Luella Bates Washington Jones."

Check Your Understanding

What is the story's **theme**? Write a sentence describing what the reader learns about life through the interaction between Roger and Mrs. Luella Bates Washington Jones.

Literary Terms

Theme is the central idea, message, or purpose of a literary work.

WRITING to SOURCES **Writing Prompt**

This story is told from the third-person point of view. Choose a scene or event in the incident and imagine Roger's thoughts and feelings about what is happening. Draft a first-person narrative of his thinking at that point in the story. Be sure to

- Use first-person point of view.
- Maintain the character of Roger as the author presents him.
- Show how Roger's thoughts and feelings fit the theme of the story.
- Use a variety of first-person pronouns (subjective, objective, intensive, and possessive) and ensure that they are in the correct case.

Save this writing response so that you can revisit it when generating ideas for the original short story you will create for Embedded Assessment 2.

Plot Elements

Learning Targets
- Explain how a character responds to change.
- Describe how a well-structured story plot develops.

Elements of Storytelling
Storytellers use the following elements of **plot** to develop and organize ideas.

Exposition: the events that give the reader background information needed to understand the story. The introduction to the story usually reveals the setting, the major characters, and the conflict.

Rising Action: the major events that develop the plot and lead to the climax

Climax: the event that is the turning point in the story, at which the conflict could be resolved in different ways

Falling Action: the events that begin to conclude the story and lead to the ending

Resolution: the events that conclude the story and reveal the theme

Types of Conflict
You learned in the first part of the unit that conflict is an important part of a story. Writers reveal conflict through the dialogue and events of a story. Conflict is used to move the action forward, reveal information about characters, and create a decision or change.

The two main types of conflict are internal conflict and external conflict.
- *Internal conflict* occurs when a character struggles with his or her own needs, desires, or emotions.
- *External conflict* occurs when a character struggles with an outside force, such as another character or something in nature.

Reviewing and Analyzing a Story
Fairy Tales

Fairy tales apply familiar story ideas—such as a quest towards a goal or a rags-to-riches character arc—to the plot elements of storytelling. A rags-to-riches fairy tale involves a poor, struggling person who finds fortune or success. *Cinderella* is a classic example. A quest fairy tale is about a hero on a journey of adventure who achieves something important. *The Lord of the Rings* is a kind of quest fairy tale.

1. After your teacher reads a fairy tale aloud, summarize the story.

_____

_____

_____

_____

LEARNING STRATEGIES:
Note-taking, Graphic Organizer

Literary Terms
Plot is the sequence of related events that make up a story.

WORD CONNECTIONS

Multiple Meaning Words

A single word sometimes has several meanings. For example, the word *exposition* refers to the plot of a short story. It also describes a type of writing. It may also describe a fair or public exhibit.

WORD CONNECTIONS

Roots and Affixes

Resolution is the noun form of *resolve*. The root *-sol-* or *-solve-* means "to set loose or free." This root occurs in *solution, absolution*, and *resolute*.
The Latin prefix *re-* means "back" or "again."

My Notes

Plot Elements

My Notes

2. Write the events you have listed from the fairy tale in the appropriate places on the plot diagram.

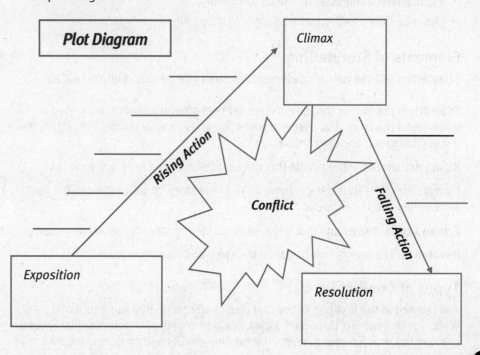

3. After analyzing plot, character, conflict, and setting, what would you conclude is the theme of this story?

Check Your Understanding

Narrative Writing Prompt

Create a plot for a story of your own that follows a rags-to-riches or hero quest plot line. The setting for your story can be any time or place and does not need to use typical fairy tale fantasy characters or magic. Make up and write at least seven events on the provided plot diagram. You might choose one of the following plot outlines and imagine how the story might develop.

- An unhappy young boy with three terrible older brothers is told he can become the eldest if he can outsmart them.

- A poor country girl saves a wealthy woman's life and then their lives turn in the opposite direction.

- A sixth grader faces difficult choices when a story he writes about his hometown is made into a successful Hollywood movie.

- A musical group who can't come up with a good song roam the city searching for inspiration.

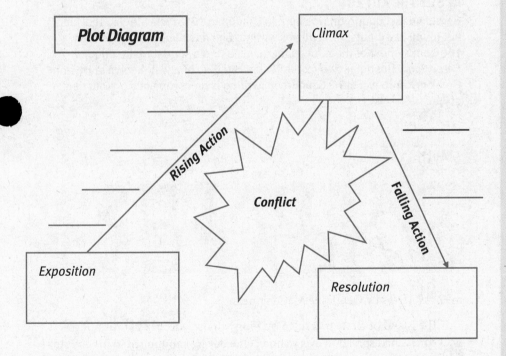

Plot Diagram

Climax

Rising Action

Conflict

Falling Action

Exposition

Resolution

In the Beginning

LEARNING STRATEGIES:
Graphic Organizer, Marking the
Text, Rereading, Brainstorming,
Skimming/Scanning

WORD CONNECTIONS

Roots and Affixes

The suffix *-logy* is from Greek and means "the study of." This much-used word part appears in many words in English, such as *mythology, biology, bacteriology, criminology, ecology*.

My Notes

reputation: how a person is thought of

soaring: rising to a great height

Learning Target

- Identify the elements of the exposition of a story by accurately recording textual evidence that supports interpretation.
- Identify and utilize varied sentence patterns in writing.

Preview

In this activity, you will read a myth and identify the elements of the exposition.

Setting a Purpose for Reading

- As you read the following story, look for and mark the different events in the plot.
- Circle unknown words and phrases. Try to determine the meaning of the words by using context clues, word parts, or a dictionary.

ABOUT THE AUTHOR

Geraldine McCaughrean was born in London in 1951. She studied teaching but found her greatest talent was writing. She has published more than 160 books, most of them for children, including a sequel to the original *Peter Pan*. "Daedalus and Icarus" is her retelling of a well-known story from Greek mythology. For McCaughrean, writing is an escape and a great deal of fun.

Myth

DAEDALUS and ICARUS

from *Greek Myths* by Geraldine McCaughrean

1 The island of Crete was ruled by King Minos, whose **reputation** for wickedness had spread to every shore. One day he summoned to his country a famous inventor named Daedalus. "Come, Daedalus, and bring your son, Icarus, too. I have a job for you, and I pay well."

2 King Minos wanted Daedalus to build him a palace, with **soaring** towers and a high, curving roof. In the cellars there was to be a maze of many corridors—so twisting and dark that any man who once ventured in there would never find his way out again.

3 "What is it for?" asked Daedalus. "Is it a treasure vault? Is it a prison to hold criminals?"

4 But Minos only replied, "Build my labyrinth as I told you. I pay you to build, not to ask questions."

5 So Daedalus held his tongue and set to work. When the palace was finished, he looked at it with pride, for there was nowhere in the world so fine. But when he found out the purpose of the maze in the cellar, he **shuddered** with horror.

6 For at the heart of that maze, King Minos put a creature that was half man, half beast—a thing almost too horrible to describe. He called it the Minotaur, and he fed it on men and women!

7 Then Daedalus wanted to leave Crete at once, and forget both maze and Minotaur. So he went to King Minos to ask for his money.

8 "I regret," said King Minos, "I cannot let you leave Crete, Daedalus. You are the only man who knows the secret of the maze and how to escape from it. The secret must never leave this island. So I'm afraid I must keep you and Icarus here a while longer."

9 "How much longer?" gasped Daedalus.

10 "Oh—just until you die," replied Minos cheerfully. "But never mind. I have plenty of work for a man as clever as you."

11 Daedalus and Icarus lived in great comfort in King Minos's palace. But they lived the life of prisoners. Their rooms were in the tallest palace tower, with beautiful views across the island. They ate **delectable** food and wore expensive clothes. But at night the door of their fine apartment was locked, and a guard stood outside. It was a comfortable prison, but it was a prison, even so. Daedalus was deeply unhappy.

12 Every day he put seed out on the windowsill, for the birds. He liked to study their brilliant colors, the clever overlapping of their feathers, the way they soared on the sea wind. It comforted him to think that they at least were free to come and go. The birds had only to spread their wings and they could leave Crete behind them, whereas Daedalus and Icarus must stay forever in their luxurious cage.

13 Young Icarus could not understand his father's unhappiness. "But I like it here," he said. "The king gives us gold and this tall tower to live in."

14 Daedalus groaned. "But to work for such a wicked man, Icarus! And to be prisoners all our days! . . . We shan't stay. We shan't!"

15 "But we can't get away, can we?" said Icarus. "How can anybody escape from an island? Fly?" He snorted with laughter.

16 Daedalus did not answer. He scratched his head and stared out of the window at the birds pecking seed on the sill.

17 From that day onward, he got up early each morning and stood at the open window. When a bird came for the seed, Daedalus begged it to **spare** him one feather. Then each night, when everyone else had gone to bed, Daedalus worked by candlelight on his greatest invention of all.

18 Early mornings. Late nights. A whole year went by. Then one morning Icarus was awakened by his father shaking his shoulder. "Get up, Icarus, and don't make a sound. We are leaving Crete."

19 "But how? It's impossible!"

20 Daedalus pulled out a bundle from under his bed. "I've been making something, Icarus." Inside were four great folded fans of feathers. He stretched them out on the bed. They were wings! "I sewed the feathers together with strands of wool from my blanket. Now hold still."

shudder: to tremble or shake

My Notes

delectable: very pleasant to taste or smell

spare: to give up something not needed

In the Beginning

My Notes

plunge: to suddenly move downward

flutter: to move with a flapping or waving motion

21 Daedalus melted down a candle and daubed his son's shoulders with sticky wax. "Yes, I know it's hot, but it will soon cool." While the wax was still soft, he stuck two of the wings to Icarus's shoulder blades.

22 "Now you must help me put on my wings, Son. When the wax sets hard, you and I will fly away from here, as free as birds!"

23 "I'm scared!" whispered Icarus as he stood on the narrow window ledge, his knees knocking and his huge wings drooping down behind. The lawns and courtyards of the palace lay far below. The royal guards looked as small as ants. "This won't work!"

24 "Courage, Son!" said Daedalus. "Keep your arms out wide and fly close to me. Above all—are you listening, Icarus?"

25 "Y-y-yes, Father."

26 "Above all, don't fly too high! Don't fly too close to the sun!"

27 "Don't fly too close to the sun," Icarus repeated, with his eyes tight shut. Then he gave a cry as his father nudged him off the windowsill. He **plunged** downward. With a crack, the feathers behind him filled with wind, and Icarus found himself flying. Flying!

28 "I'm flying!" he crowed.

29 The guards looked up in astonishment, and wagged their swords, and pointed and shouted, "Tell the king! Daedalus and Icarus are . . . are . . . flying away!"

30 By dipping first one wing, then the other, Icarus found that he could turn to the left and the right. The wind tugged at his hair. His legs trailed out behind him. He saw the fields and streams as he had never seen them before!

31 Then they were out over the sea. The sea gulls pecked at him angrily, so Icarus flew higher, where they could not reach him.

32 He copied their shrill cry and taunted them: "You can't catch me!"

33 "Now remember, don't fly too high!" called Daedalus, but his words were drowned by the screaming of the gulls.

34 I'm the first boy ever to fly! I'm making history! I shall be famous! thought Icarus, as he flew up and up, higher and higher.

35 At last Icarus was looking the sun itself in the face. "Think you're the highest thing in the sky, do you?" he jeered. "I can fly just as high as you! Higher, even!" He did not notice the drops of sweat on his forehead: He was so determined to outfly the sun.

36 Soon its vast heat beat on his face and on his back and on the great wings stuck on with wax. The wax softened. The wax trickled. The wax dripped. One feather came unstuck. Then a plume of feathers **fluttered** slowly down.

37 Icarus stopped flapping his wings. His father's words came back to him clearly now: "*Don't fly too close to the sun!*"

38 With a great sucking noise, the wax on his shoulders came unstuck. Icarus tried to catch hold of the wings, but they just folded up in his hands. He plunged down, his two fists full of feathers — down and down and down.

39 The clouds did not stop his fall.

40 The sea gulls did not catch him in their beaks.

41 His own father could only watch as Icarus hurtled head first into the glittering sea and sank deep down among the sharks and eels and squid. And all that was left of proud Icarus was a litter of waxy feathers floating on the sea.

Second Read

- Reread the myth to answer these text-dependent comprehension questions.
- Write any additional questions you have about the text in your Reader/Writer Notebook.

1. **Key Ideas and Details:** What event creates a conflict in the story? What is Daedalus's response to the conflict?

2. **Craft and Structure:** What words give you insight into what kind of person King Minos is?

3. **Key Ideas and Details:** What elements in the story are characteristics of a myth?

4. **Key Ideas and Details:** What inference can you make based on paragraphs 34 and 35?

5. **Key Ideas and Details:** What event is a turning point, or climax, in the story? What event is part of the falling action?

My Notes

In the Beginning

Literary Terms

Foreshadowing refers to clues or hints signaling events that will occur later in the plot of a story.

Working from the Text

6. Use the graphic organizer to analyze the beginning of the story—its exposition. The exposition of a story introduces the setting, characters, and conflict. In addition, skim the story to find examples of foreshadowing. Authors use **foreshadowing** to add suspense and expectation about what will happen in a story.

Exposition	Details from the Text	Graphic Representation	What is foreshadowed?
Setting			
Character(s)			
Conflict			

7. What techniques does the author use to create the exposition?

8. Myths often try to explain natural phenomenon (such as earthquakes and volcanos) or teach a lesson (such as "respect your elders"). This myth has a lesson for the reader. What is its lesson or theme?

Language and Writer's Craft: Varied Sentence Patterns

Why is it important to vary your sentence patterns? Adding sentence variety gives life and rhythm to writing. Too many sentences with the same structure and length can become boring for readers. Varying sentence style and structure can also reduce repetition and add emphasis. Long sentences work well for incorporating a lot of information, and short sentences can often emphasize crucial points.

- Dialogue most often consists of short sentences in a simple pattern, usually questions, comments, exclamations, or commands.
- The use of *and* as a coordinating conjunction creates longer sentences.

9. Return to the myth of "Daedalus and Icarus" Choose a section of text to reread and examine the sentences. Mark a variety of sentence patterns, and analyze the beginnings of sentences. Take notes in the My Notes margin.

- Highlight a short sentence. What was the effect of the sentence length or pattern?
- Underline a long sentence, and note when the coordinating conjunction "and" is used. What is the effect of the sentence length or pattern?
- Identify a sentence that stands out to you. Is it long or short, and what is its effect?

Writing Prompt: Think of another natural phenomenon or lesson people should learn. Write the beginning or exposition to your own unique myth. Be sure to

- Establish the story's context by introducing the setting, characters, and conflict of the story.
- Use figurative language.
- Use a variety of sentence lengths and patterns.

My Notes

A Day of Change: Developing the Story

LEARNING STRATEGIES:
Group Discussion, Graphic Organizer

My Notes

Learning Targets
- Analyze how conflicts in a story advance the plot's rising action and climax.

Preview
In this activity, you will read a short story and analyze how conflict advances the plot.

Setting a Purpose for Reading
- As you read this short story, mark the elements of exposition (setting, character, and initial conflict) and the major events in the story.
- Circle unknown words and phrases. Try to determine the meaning of the words by using context clues, word parts, or a dictionary.

ABOUT THE AUTHOR

Sandra Cisneros grew up in Chicago and now lives in San Antonio, Texas. One of her best-known novels, *The House on Mango Street*, reveals the life of a young girl growing up in the Latino section of Chicago. In talking about her writing, Cisneros says she creates stories from things that have touched her deeply; " . . . in real life a story doesn't have shape, and it's the writer that gives it a beginning, a middle, and an end."

Short Story

Eleven

from *Woman Hollering Creek and Other Stories,* by Sandra Cisneros

1 What they don't understand about birthdays and what they never tell you is that when you're eleven, you're also ten, and nine, and eight, and seven, and six, and five, and four, and three, and two, and one. And when you wake up on your eleventh birthday you expect to feel eleven, but you don't. You open your eyes and everything's just like yesterday, only it's today. And you don't feel eleven at all. You feel like you're still ten. And you are—underneath the year that makes you eleven.

2 Like some days you might say something stupid, and that's the part of you that's still ten. Or maybe some days you might need to sit on your mama's lap because you're scared, and that's the part of you that's five. And maybe one day when you're all grown up maybe you will need to cry like if you're three, and that's okay. That's what I tell Mama when she's sad and needs to cry. Maybe she's feeling three.

3 Because the way you grow old is kind of like an onion or like the rings inside a tree trunk or like my little wooden dolls that fit one inside the other, each year inside the next one. That's how being eleven years old is.

4 You don't feel eleven. Not right away. It takes a few days, weeks even, sometimes even months before you say Eleven when they ask you. And you don't feel smart eleven, not until you're almost twelve. That's the way it is.

GRAMMAR & USAGE
Pronouns

Indefinite pronouns refer to nonspecific persons or things. In this excerpt, Rachel mentions *everybody, somebody, nobody*. These indefinite pronouns refer to people who are not specific named.

5 Only today I wish I didn't have only eleven years rattling inside me like pennies in a tin Band-Aid box. Today I wish I was one hundred and two instead of eleven because if I was one hundred and two I'd have known what to say when Mrs. Price put the red sweater on my desk. I would've known how to tell her it wasn't mine instead of just sitting there with that look on my face and nothing coming out of my mouth.

6 "Whose is this?" Mrs. Price says, and she holds the red sweater up in the air for all the class to see. "Whose? It's been sitting in the coatroom for a month."

7 "Not mine," says everybody. "Not me."

8 "It has to belong to somebody," Mrs. Price keeps saying, but nobody can remember. It's an ugly sweater with red plastic buttons and a collar and sleeves all stretched out like you could use it for a jump rope. It's maybe a thousand years old and even if it belonged to me I wouldn't say so.

9 Maybe because I'm skinny, maybe because she doesn't like me, that stupid Sylvia Saldívar says, "I think it belongs to Rachel." An ugly sweater like that, all **raggedy** and old, but Mrs. Price believes her. Mrs. Price takes the sweater and puts it right on my desk, but when I open my mouth nothing comes out.

10 "That's not, I don't, you're not . . . Not mine," I finally say in a little voice that was maybe me when I was four.

11 "Of course it's yours," Mrs. Price says. "I remember you wearing it once." Because she's older and the teacher, she's right and I'm not.

12 Not mine, not mine, not mine, but Mrs. Price is already turning to page thirty-two, and math problem number four. I don't know why but all of a sudden I'm feeling sick inside, like the part of me that's three wants to come out of my eyes, only I squeeze them shut tight and bite down on my teeth real hard and try to remember today I am eleven, eleven. Mama is making a cake for me for tonight, and when Papa comes home everybody will sing Happy birthday, happy birthday to you.

13 But when the sick feeling goes away and I open my eyes, the red sweater's still sitting there like a big red mountain. I move the red sweater to the corner of my desk with my ruler. I move my pencil and books and eraser as far from it as possible. I even move my chair a little to the right. Not mine, not mine, not mine.

14 In my head I'm thinking how long till lunchtime, how long till I can take the red sweater and throw it over the schoolyard fence, or leave it hanging on a **parking meter**, or bunch it up into a little ball and toss it in the alley. Except when math period ends, Mrs. Price says loud and in front of everybody, "Now, Rachel, that's enough," because she sees I've shoved the red sweater to the tippy-tip corner of my desk and it's hanging all over the edge like a waterfall, but I don't care.

15 "Rachel," Mrs. Price says. She says it like she's getting mad. "You put that sweater on right now and no more nonsense."

16 "But it's not—"

17 "Now!" Mrs. Price says.

18 This is when I wish I wasn't eleven, because all the years inside of me—ten, nine, eight, seven, six, five, four, three, two, and one—are pushing at the back of my eyes when I put one arm through one sleeve of the sweater that smells like cottage cheese, and then the other arm through the other and stand there with my arms apart like if the sweater hurts me and it does, all itchy and full of germs that aren't even mine.

My Notes

raggedy: in poor condition; worn, tattered

parking meter: machine next to a street into which people pay for a parking space

A Day of Change: Developing the Story

My Notes

hiccup: a sound in the throat that comes from uncontrolled muscle movements in the chest

19 That's when everything I've been holding in since this morning, since when Mrs. Price put the sweater on my desk, finally lets go, and all of a sudden I'm crying in front of everybody. I wish I was invisible but I'm not. I'm eleven and it's my birthday today and I'm crying like I'm three in front of everybody. I put my head down on the desk and bury my face in my stupid clown-sweater arms. My face all hot and spit coming out of my mouth because I can't stop the little animal noises from coming out of me, until there aren't any more tears left in my eyes, and it's just my body shaking like when you have the **hiccups**, and my whole head hurts like when you drink milk too fast.

20 But the worst part is right before the bell rings for lunch. That stupid Phyllis Lopez, who is even dumber than Sylvia Saldívar, says she remembers the red sweater is hers! I take it off right away and give it to her, only Mrs. Price pretends like everything's okay.

21 Today I'm eleven. There's a cake Mama's making for tonight, and when Papa comes home from work we'll eat it. There'll be candles and presents, and everybody will sing Happy birthday, happy birthday to you, Rachel, only it's too late.

22 I'm eleven today. I'm eleven, ten, nine, eight, seven, six, five, four, three, two, and one, but I wish I was one hundred and two. I wish I was anything but eleven, because I want today to be far away already, far away like a runaway balloon, like a tiny o in the sky, so tiny-tiny you have to close your eyes to see it.

Second Read

- Reread the short story to answer these text-dependent comprehension questions.
- Write any additional questions you have about the text in your Reader/Writer Notebook.

1. **Key Ideas and Details:** What can you infer about the conflict of the story? How is it both internal and external?

2. **Craft and Structure:** How does Cisneros show the transition from one event to another?

3. **Craft and Structure:** What is the effect of a sentence that repeats short phrases such as "Not mine, not mine, not mine?" How does this sentence type help develop the story?

4. **Craft and Structure:** How does Cisneros's use of figurative language and sensory detail demonstrate Rachel's emotions?

5. **Key Ideas and Details:** What can you infer about Rachel's teacher, Mrs. Price, based on her dialogue with Rachel?

6. **Key Ideas and Details:** Summarize how the conflict is resolved. What is the effect of this incident on Rachel?

Working from the Text

7. Use the graphic organizer below to list the conflicts Rachel faces in "Eleven." Be sure to consider both Rachel's external and internal conflicts.

Conflicts (problems) Rachel faces	Is the conflict resolved?

© 2017 College Board. All rights reserved.

My Notes

WORD CONNECTIONS

Roots and Affixes

Internal and **external** derive from the Latin *interus* ("placed on the inside") and *exterus* ("placed on the outside"). The word part *inter-*, meaning "in between," is found in such words as *interior*, *interface*, and *intermission*.

The word part *exter-* (also spelled *extra-* and *extro-*) means "outside" or "beyond." It appears in words like *extreme*, *extrovert*, *extracurricular*, and *extract*.

A Day of Change: Developing the Story

My Notes

8. What is the theme of this story?

_____

_____

_____

_____

_____

_____

_____

_____

9. Focusing on the rising action and climax of the story, list events in the appropriate places on the plot diagram.

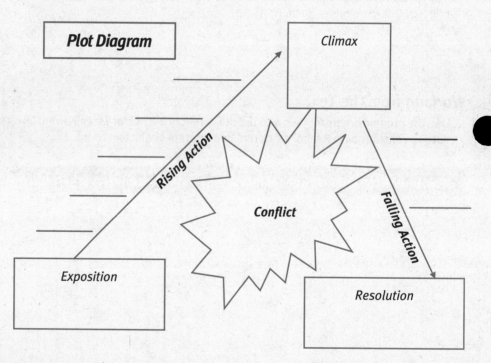

Plot Diagram

WRITING to SOURCES / **Writing Prompt**

Make up a brief dialogue between Rachel and another person in the story, focusing on one conflict from the text. Use the same exposition, but change the rising action and climax. Consider having Rachel talk to her teacher about the misunderstanding or having Rachel confront Phyllis about not claiming the red sweater. Be sure to

- Sequence events logically to focus on a conflict to develop the rising action and climax.
- Use dialogue and dialogue tags.
- Use figurative language and varied syntax.

Save this writing prompt response so that you can revisit it when generating ideas for the original short story you will create for Embedded Assessment 2.

My Notes

In the End

LEARNING STRATEGIES:
Activating Prior Knowledge, Graphic Organizer, Brainstorming, Marking the Text

Literary Terms

Personification is figurative language that gives human characteristics to an animal or nonliving thing. For example, ". . . the beam of the flashlight danced crazily . . ."

My Notes

mood: a person's overall state of mind; the way a person is feeling at a given time

stoop: stairway entrance outside of an urban residence

Learning Targets

- Analyze the resolution to a story, and transform it to create a different resolution.
- Create a thematic statement about a short story, using textual evidence.
- Identify types of figurative language and how it can be used to create mental images.

Preview

In this activity, you will read a short story to analyze its resolution, as well as the author's use of figurative language.

Setting a Purpose for Reading

- The author of "The Treasure of Lemon Brown" uses figurative language to conjure mental images that add to the drama of the story. For example, he uses **personification** to create a visualization of an eerie scene. Do a close reading of the text in which you mark the text (highlight, underline, circle, take notes) to indicate the author's use of similes, metaphors, and personification in the story.
- Circle unknown words and phrases. Try to determine the meaning of the words by using context clues, word parts, or a dictionary.

ABOUT THE AUTHOR

Walter Dean Myers (1937–2014) started writing when he was a child. He published his first book, *Where Does the Day Go?*, in 1969. During his lifetime, he wrote many books for children and young adults, two of which—*Scorpions* and *Somewhere in the Darkness*—have received Newbery Honors. His stories focus on the challenges and triumphs of growing up in a difficult environment. His memoir, *Bad Boy*, reveals how he overcame racial challenges and his own shortcomings to become a very successful author.

Short Story

"The Treasure of Lemon Brown"

by Walter Dean Myers

1 The dark sky, filled with angry, swirling clouds, reflected Greg Ridley's **mood** as he sat on the **stoop** of his building. His father's voice came to him again, first reading the letter the principal had sent to the house, then lecturing endlessly about his poor efforts in math.

2 "I had to leave school when I was thirteen," his father had said, "that's a year younger than you are now. If I'd had half the chances you have, I'd . . ."

3 Greg sat in the small, pale green kitchen listening, knowing the lecture would end with his father saying he couldn't play ball with the Scorpions. He had asked his father the week before, and his father had said it depended on his next report card. It wasn't often the Scorpions took on new players, especially fourteen-year-olds, and this was a chance of a lifetime for Greg. He hadn't been allowed to play high school ball, which he had really wanted to do, but playing for the Community Center team was the next best thing. Report cards were due in a week, and Greg had been hoping for the best. But the principal had ended the **suspense** early when she sent the letter saying Greg would probably fail math if he didn't spend more time studying.

4 "And you want to play *basketball*?" His father's brows knitted over deep brown eyes. "That must be some kind of a joke. Now you just get into your room and hit those books."

5 That had been two nights before. His father's words, like the distant thunder that now echoed through the streets of Harlem, still rumbled softly in his ears.

6 It was beginning to cool. Gusts of wind made bits of paper dance between the parked cars. There was a flash of nearby lightning, and soon large drops of rain splashed onto his jeans. He stood to go upstairs, thought of the lecture that probably **awaited** him if he did anything except shut himself in his room with his math book, and started walking down the street instead. Down the block there was an old **tenement** that had been abandoned for some months. Some of the guys had held an impromptu checker tournament there the week before, and Greg had noticed that the door, once boarded over, had been slightly ajar.

7 Pulling his collar up as high as he could, he checked for traffic and made a dash across the street. He reached the house just as another flash of lightning changed the night to day for an instant, then returned the graffiti-scarred building to the grim shadows. He vaulted over the outer stairs and pushed tentatively on the door. It was open, and he let himself in.

8 The inside of the building was dark except for the dim light that filtered through the dirty windows from the streetlamps. There was a room a few feet from the door, and from where he stood in the entrance, Greg could see a squarish patch of light on the floor. He entered the room, frowning at the musty smell. It was a large room that might have been someone's parlor at one time. **Squinting**, Greg could see an old table on its side against one wall, what looked like a pile of rags or a torn mattress in the corner, and a couch, with one side broken, in front of the window.

9 He went to the couch. The side that wasn't broken was comfortable enough, though a little creaky. From the spot he could see the blinking neon sign over the bodega on the corner. He sat awhile, watching the sign blink first green then red, allowing his mind to drift to the Scorpions, then to his father. His father had been a postal worker for all Greg's life, and was proud of it, often telling Greg how hard he had worked to pass the test. Greg had heard the story too many times to be interested now.

10 For a moment Greg thought he heard something that sounded like a scraping against the wall. He listened carefully, but it was gone.

11 Outside the wind had picked up, sending the rain against the window with a force that shook the glass in its frame. A car passed, its tires hissing over the wet street and its red taillights glowing in the darkness.

suspense: a nervous or excited feeling of uncertainty before something happens

GRAMMAR & USAGE
Possessive Pronouns
In addition to being subjects and objects, pronouns can also be **possessive**, meaning that they show possession. Possessive pronouns include *mine, hers, his, theirs, ours, and its*. Note the possessive pronouns the author uses in this text.

await: to wait for

tenement: house or apartment building in an urban area

My Notes

squint: to partly close eyes to make it easier to focus on something

In the End

WORD
CONNECTIONS

Cognates

The Spanish cognate for *imagine* is *imaginar*.

My Notes

peer: to look curiously or carefully at something

12 Greg thought he heard the noise again. His stomach tightened as he held himself still and listened intently. There weren't any more scraping noises, but he was sure he had heard something in the darkness—something breathing!

13 He tried to figure out just where the breathing was coming from; he knew it was in the room with him. Slowly he stood, tensing. As he turned, a flash of lightning lit up the room, frightening him with its sudden brilliance. He saw nothing, just the overturned table, the pile of rags and an old newspaper on the floor. Could he have been imagining the sounds? He continued listening, but heard nothing and thought that it might have just been rats. Still, he thought, as soon as the rain let up he would leave. He went to the window and was about to look when he heard a voice behind him.

14 "Don't try nothin' 'cause I got a razor sharp enough to cut a week into nine days!"

15 Greg, except for an involuntary tremor in his knees, stood stock still. The voice was high and brittle, like dry twigs being broken, surely not one he had ever heard before. There was a shuffling sound as the person who had been speaking moved a step closer. Greg turned, holding his breath, his eyes straining to see in the dark room.

16 The upper part of the figure before him was still in darkness. The lower half was in the dim rectangle of light that fell unevenly from the window. There were two feet, in cracked, dirty shoes from which rose legs that were wrapped in rags.

17 "Who are you?" Greg hardly recognized his own voice.

18 "I'm Lemon Brown," came the answer. "Who're you?"

19 "Greg Ridley."

20 "What you doing here?" The figure shuffled forward again, and Greg took a small step backward.

21 "It's raining," Greg said.

22 "I can see that," the figure said.

23 The person who called himself Lemon Brown **peered** forward, and Greg could see him clearly. He was an old man. His black, heavily wrinkled face was surrounded by a halo of crinkly white hair and whiskers that seemed to separate his head from the layers of dirty coats piled on his smallish frame. His pants were bagged to the knee, where they were met with rags that went down to the old shoes. The rags were held on with strings, and there was a rope around his middle. Greg relaxed. He had seen the man before, picking through the trash on the corner and pulling clothes out of a Salvation Army box. There was no sign of a razor that could "cut a week into nine days."

24 "What are you doing here?" Greg asked.

25 "This is where I'm staying," Lemon Brown said. "What you here for?" "Told you it was raining out," Greg said, leaning against the back of the couch until he felt it give slightly.

26 "Ain't you got no home?"

27 "I got a home," Greg answered.

28 "You ain't one of them bad boys looking for my treasure, is you?" Lemon Brown cocked his head to one side and squinted one eye. "Because I told you I got me a razor."

29 "I'm not looking for your treasure," Greg answered, smiling. "*If* you have one."

30 "What you mean, *if* I have one." Lemon Brown said. "Every man got a treasure. You don't know that, you must be a fool!"

31 "Sure," Greg said as he sat on the sofa and put one leg over the back. "What do you have, gold coins?"

32 "Don't worry none about what I got," Lemon Brown said. "You know who I am?"

33 "You told me your name was orange or lemon or something like that.

34 "Lemon Brown," the old man said, pulling back his shoulders as he did so," they used to call me Sweet Lemon Brown."

35 "Sweet Lemon?" Greg asked.

36 "Yessir. Sweet Lemon Brown. They used to say I sung the blues so sweet that if I sang at a funeral, the dead would **commence** to rocking with the beat. Used to travel all over Mississippi and as far as Monroe, Louisiana, and east on over to Macon, Georgia. You mean you ain't never heard of Sweet Lemon Brown?"

37 "Afraid not," Greg said. "What . . . happened to you?"

38 "Hard times, boy. Hard times always after a poor man. One day I got tired, sat down to rest a spell and felt a tap on my shoulder. Hard times caught up with me."

39 "Sorry about that."

40 "What you doing here? How come you don't go in home when the rain come? Rain don't bother you young folks none."

41 "Just didn't." Greg looked away.

42 "I used to have a knotty-headed boy just like you." Lemon Brown had half walked, half shuffled back to the corner and sat down against the wall. "Had them big eyes like you got. I used to call them moon eyes. Look into them moon eyes and see anything you want."

43 "How come you gave up singing the blues?" Greg asked.

44 "Didn't give it up," Lemon Brown said. "You don't give up the blues; they give you up. After a while you do good for yourself, and it ain't nothing but foolishness singing about how hard you got it. Ain't that right?"

45 "I guess so."

46 "What's that noise?" Lemon Brown asked, suddenly sitting upright. Greg listened, and he heard a noise outside. He looked at Lemon Brown and saw the old man pointing toward the window.

47 Greg went to the window and saw three men, neighborhood thugs, on the stoop. One was carrying a length of pipe. Greg looked back toward Lemon Brown, who moved quietly across the room to the window. The old man looked out, then beckoned frantically for Greg to follow him. For a moment Greg couldn't move.

Then he found himself following Lemon Brown into the hallway and up the darkened stairs. Greg followed as closely as he could. They reached the top of the stairs, and Greg felt Lemon Brown's hand first lying on his shoulder, then probing down his arm until he took Greg's hand into his own as they crouched in the darkness.

My Notes

commence: begin, start

My Notes

48 "They's bad men," Lemon Brown whispered. His breath was warm against Greg's skin.

49 "Hey! Rag man!" A voice called. "We know you in here. What you got up under them rags? You got any money?"

50 Silence.

51 "We don't want to have to come in and hurt you, old man, but we don't mind if we have to."

52 Lemon Brown squeezed Greg's hand in his own hard, gnarled fist. There was a banging downstairs and a light as the men entered.

53 They banged around noisily, calling for the rag man.

54 "We heard you talking about your treasure." The voice was slurred. "We just want to see it, that's all."

55 "You sure he's here?" One voice seemed to come from the room with the sofa.

56 "Yeah, he stays here every night."

57 "There's another room over there; I'm going to take a look. You got that flashlight?"

58 "Yeah, here, take the pipe too."

59 Greg opened his mouth to quiet the sound of his breath as he sucked it in uneasily. A beam of light hit the wall a few feet opposite him, then went out.

60 "Ain't nobody in that room," a voice said. "You think he gone or something?"

61 "I don't know," came the answer. "All I know is that I heard him talking about some kind of treasure. You know they found that shopping bag lady with that load of money in her bags."

62 "Yeah. You think he's upstairs?"

63 "HEY, OLD MAN, ARE YOU UP THERE?" Silence.

64 "Watch my back. I'm going up."

65 There was a footstep on the stairs, and the beam from the flashlight danced crazily along the peeling wallpaper. Greg held his breath. There was another step and a loud crashing noise as the man banged the pipe against the wooden banister. Greg could feel his temples throb as the man slowly neared them. Greg thought about the pipe, wondering what he would do when the man reached them—what he could do.

66 Then Lemon Brown released his hand and moved toward the top of the stairs. Greg looked around and saw stairs going up to the next floor. He tried waving to Lemon Brown, hoping the old man would see him in the dim light and follow him to the next floor. Maybe, Greg thought, the men wouldn't follow them up there. Suddenly, though, Lemon Brown stood at the top of the stairs, both arms raised high above his head.

67 "There he is!" A voice cried from below.

bash: hit with force

68 "Throw down your money, old man, so I won't have to **bash** your head in!"

69 Lemon Brown didn't move. Greg felt himself near panic. The steps came closer, and still Lemon Brown didn't move. He was an eerie sight, a bundle of rags standing at the top of the stairs, his shadow on the wall looming over him. Maybe, the thought came to Greg, the scene could be even eerier.

70 Greg wet his lips, put his hands to his mouth and tried to make a sound. Nothing came out. He swallowed hard, wet his lips once more and howled as evenly as he could.

71 "What's that?"

72 As Greg howled, the light moved away from Lemon Brown, but not before Greg saw him hurl his body down the stairs at the men who had come to take his treasure. There was a crashing noise, and then footsteps. A rush of warm air came in as the downstairs door opened, then there was only an **ominous** silence. Greg stood on the landing. He listened, and after a while there was another sound on the staircase.

ominous: showing that something bad will happen

73 "Mr. Brown?" he called.

74 "Yeah, it's me," came the answer. "I got their flashlight."

75 Greg exhaled in relief as Lemon Brown made his way slowly back up the stairs.

76 "You OK?"

77 "Few bumps and bruises," Lemon Brown said.

78 "I think I'd better be going," Greg said, his breath returning to normal. "You'd better leave, too, before they come back."

79 "They may hang around for a while," Lemon Brown said, "but they ain't getting their nerve up to come in here again. Not with crazy rag men and howling spooks. Best you stay a while till the coast is clear. I'm heading out west tomorrow, out to East St. Louis."

80 "They were talking about treasures," Greg said. "You really have a treasure?"

81 "What I tell you? Didn't I tell you every man got a treasure?" Lemon Brown said. "You want to see mine?"

82 "If you want to show it to me," Greg shrugged.

83 "Let's look out the window first, see what them scoundrels be doing," Lemon Brown said.

84 They followed the oval beam of the flashlight into one of the rooms and looked out the window. They saw the men who had tried to take the treasure sitting on the **curb** near the corner. One of them had his pants leg up, looking at his knee.

curb: raised cement border on the edge of a street

85 "You sure you're not hurt?" Greg asked Lemon Brown.

86 "Nothing that ain't been hurt before," Lemon Brown said. "When you get as old as me all you say when something hurts is, 'Howdy, Mr. Pain, sees you back again.' Then when Mr. Pain see he can't worry you none, he go on mess with somebody else."

87 Greg smiled.

88 "Here, you hold this." Lemon Brown gave Greg the flashlight.

89 He sat on the floor near Greg and carefully untied the strings that held the rags on his right leg. When he took the rags away, Greg saw a piece of plastic. The old man carefully took off the plastic and unfolded it. He revealed some yellowed newspaper clippings and a battered harmonica.

90 "There it be," he said, nodding his head. "There it be."

91 Greg looked at the old man, saw the distant look in his eye, then turned to the clippings. They told of Sweet Lemon Brown, a blues singer and harmonica player who was appearing at different theaters in the South. One of the clippings said he had been the hit of the show, although not the headliner. All of the clippings were reviews of shows Lemon Brown had been in more than fifty years ago. Greg looked at the harmonica. It was dented badly on one side, with the reed holes on one end nearly closed.

My Notes

My Notes

92 "I used to travel around and make money to feed my wife and Jesse—that's my boy's name. Used to feed them good, too. Then his mama died, and he stayed with his mama's sister. He growed up to be a man, and when the war come he saw fit to go off and fight in it. I didn't have nothing to give him except these things that told him who I was, and what he come from. If you know your pappy did something, you know you can do something too.

93 "Anyway, he went off to war, and I went off still playing and singing. 'Course by then I wasn't as much as I used to be, not without somebody to make it worth the while. You know what I mean?"

94 "Yeah." Greg nodded, not quite really knowing.

95 "I traveled around, and one time I come home, and there was this letter saying Jesse got killed in the war. Broke my heart, it truly did.

96 "They sent back what he had with him over there, and what it was is this old mouth fiddle and these clippings. Him carrying it around with him like that told me it meant something to him. That was my treasure, and when I give it to him he treated it just like that, a treasure. Ain't that something?"

97 "Yeah, I guess so," Greg said.

98 "You guess so?" Lemon Brown's voice rose an octave as he started to put his treasure back into the plastic. "Well, you got to guess 'cause you sure don't know nothing. Don't know enough to get home when it's raining."

99 "I *guess* . . . I mean, you're right."

100 "You OK for a youngster," the old man said as he tied the strings around his leg, "better than those scalawags what come here looking for my treasure. That's for sure."

101 "You really think that treasure of yours was worth fighting for?" Greg asked. "Against a pipe?"

102 "What else a man got 'cepting what he can pass on to his son, or his daughter, if she be his oldest?" Lemon Brown said. "For a big-headed boy you sure do ask the foolishest questions."

103 Lemon Brown got up after patting his rags in place and looked out the window again. "Looks like they're gone. You get on out of here and get yourself home. I'll be watching from the window so you'll be all right."

104 Lemon Brown went down the stairs behind Greg. When they reached the front door the old man looked out first, saw the street was clear and told Greg to scoot on home.

105 "You sure you'll be OK?" Greg asked.

106 "Now didn't I tell you I was going to East St. Louis in the morning?" Lemon Brown asked. "Don't that sound OK to you?"

107 "Sure it does," Greg said. "Sure it does. And you take care of that treasure of yours."

108 "That I'll do," Lemon said, the wrinkles around his eyes suggesting a smile. "That I'll do."

109 The night had warmed and the rain had stopped, leaving puddles at the curbs. Greg didn't even want to think how late it was. He thought ahead of what his father would say and wondered if he should tell him about Lemon Brown. He thought about it until he reached his stoop, and decided against it. Lemon Brown would be OK, Greg thought, with his memories and his treasure.

110 Greg pushed the button over the bell marked Ridley, thought of the lecture he knew his father would give him, and smiled.

Second Read

- Reread the short story to answer these text-dependent comprehension questions.
- Write any additional questions you have about the text in your Reader/Writer Notebook.

1. **Craft and Structure:** Explain how specific aspects of the setting create an atmosphere that fits the action at the beginning of the story.

2. **Craft and Structure:** What sensory details can you find in paragraphs 8–11? If possible, name one for each sense: taste, smell, touch, sight, and hearing.

3. **Key Ideas and Details:** The author distinguishes Greg from Lemon by the way they speak. How would you describe Lemon Brown, based on what he says? How would you describe Greg?

My Notes

In the End

4. **Key Ideas and Details:** In what ways does the introduction of the "scalawags" or the "bad men" change the relationship between Lemon Brown and Greg?

5. **Key Ideas and Details:** Literally, what is Lemon Brown's treasure? Why does it mean so much to him?

6. **Craft and Structure:** Why is the third-person point of view an effective way to tell this story? What would happen if it were told in first-person point of view? How would the story change?

Working from the Text

7. **Collaborative Discussion:** What are your initial reactions to the ending of this story? Were you surprised? If so, what surprised you?

8. Provide an example of a simile, metaphor, and the use of personification in the story. How do these examples of figurative language enhance the story?

_____

_____

_____

_____

_____

9. What is the theme of "The Treasure of Lemon Brown"? Complete this sentence:
   "The Treasure of Lemon Brown" is a story about . . ."

   _____

   _____

   _____

10. Write a theme statement, a sentence, using the theme you described.

    _____

    _____

    _____

    _____

11. Now, transform your theme statement into a question to use in a collaborative
    discussion.

    _____

    _____

    _____

    _____

12. Return to the story and mark the text to answer the following question:
    What is the portion of the story that makes up the falling action and resolution?

    _____

    _____

    _____

Check Your Understanding

WRITING to SOURCES Narrative Writing Prompt

Think of an extension to the ending of this story. What could have happened
differently to resolve the conflict? What will be different when Greg returns home?
Review the original ending of the story and transform it by writing a new ending. Be
sure to

- Focus on resolving the conflict in the falling action and resolution in order to
  convey a theme.
- Use dialogue and dialogue tags.
- Use figurative language and varied sentence structure.

My Notes

Analyzing a Story

LEARNING STRATEGIES:
Close Reading, Marking the
Text, Rereading, Think Aloud,
Visualizing, Sketching

My Notes

Learning Targets

- Analyze the theme of a short story.
- Interpret text passages and create images to represent key developments of theme and plot.

Preview

In this activity, you will read a short story and analyze its theme.

Setting a Purpose for Reading

- The short story you are about to read is a science fiction story. Science fiction is a genre in which the imaginary elements of the story could be scientifically possible. Science fiction differs from fantasy in that it is possible that the story could happen. In some respects, the imaginary elements in the next story have already happened. The story was written in 1951. Think about the developments in technology since that time. IBM introduced the personal computer in August of 1981—30 years after this story was written. As you read the story, underline clues about the setting of the story.

- Circle unknown words and phrases. Try to determine the meaning of the words by using context clues, word parts, or a dictionary.

ABOUT THE AUTHOR

Isaac Asimov (1920–1992) was a very prolific writer. He wrote nearly five hundred books on a variety of subjects—science, history, literature, medicine, but mainly science fiction. He started writing science fiction stories as a teenager. Always interested in robots, he anticipated the many uses they have today. The movie *I, Robot* was based on Asimov's writings about robots and technology. *I, Robot* was also the title of Asimov's first book of short stories.

Short Story

The Fun They Had

by Isaac Asimov

1 Margie even wrote about it that night in her diary. On the page headed May 17, 2157, she wrote, "Today, Tommy found a real book!"

2 It was a very old book. Margie's grandfather once said that when he was a little boy his grandfather told him that there was a time when all stories were printed on paper.

3 They turned the pages, which were yellow and crinkly, and it was awfully funny to read words that stood still instead of moving the way they were supposed to–on a screen, you know. And then, when they turned back to the page before, it had the same words on it that it had had when they read it the first time.

4 "Gee," said Tommy, "what a waste. When you're through with the book, you just throw it away, I guess. Our television screen must have had a million books on it and it's good for plenty more. I wouldn't throw it away."

5 "Same with mine," said Margie. She was eleven and hadn't seen as many telebooks as Tommy had. He was thirteen. She said, "Where did you find it?"

6 "In my house." He pointed without looking, because he was busy reading. "In the attic." "What's it about?" "School."

7 Margie was scornful. "School? What's there to write about school? I hate school."

8 Margie always hated school, but now she hated it more than ever. The **mechanical** teacher had been giving her test after test in geography and she had been doing worse and worse until her mother had shaken her head sorrowfully and sent for the County Inspector.

9 He was a round little man with a red face and a whole box of tools with dials and wires. He smiled at Margie and gave her an apple, then took the teacher apart. Margie had hoped he wouldn't know how to put it together again, but he knew how all right, and, after an hour or so, there it was again, large and black and ugly, with a big screen on which all the lessons were shown and the questions were asked. That wasn't so bad. The part Margie hated most was the slot where she had to put homework and test papers. She always had to write them out in a punch **code** they made her learn when she was six years old, and the mechanical teacher calculated the mark in no time.

10 The Inspector had smiled after he was finished and patted Margie's head. He said to her mother, "It's not the little girl's fault, Mrs. Jones. I think the geography sector was geared a little too quick. Those things happen sometimes. I've slowed it up to an average ten-year level. Actually, the over-all pattern of her progress is quite satisfactory." And he patted Margie's head again.

11 Margie was disappointed. She had been hoping they would take the teacher away altogether. They had once taken Tommy's teacher away for nearly a month because the history sector had blanked out completely.

12 So she said to Tommy, "Why would anyone write about school?"

13 Tommy looked at her with very **superior** eyes. "Because it's not our kind of school, stupid. This is the old kind of school that they had hundreds and hundreds of years ago." He added loftily, pronouncing the word carefully, "Centuries ago."

14 Margie was hurt. "Well, I don't know what kind of school they had all that time ago." She read the book over his shoulder for a while, then said, "Anyway, they had a teacher."

15 "Sure they had a teacher, but it wasn't a regular teacher. It was a man." "A man? How could a man be a teacher?" "Well, he just told the boys and girls things and gave them homework and asked them questions." "A man isn't smart enough." "Sure he is. My father knows as much as my teacher." "He can't. A man can't know as much as a teacher." "He knows almost as much, I betcha."

16 Margie wasn't prepared to **dispute** that. She said, "I wouldn't want a strange man in my house to teach me."

17 Tommy screamed with laughter. "You don't know much, Margie. The teachers didn't live in the house. They had a special building and all the kids went there." "And all the kids learned the same thing?" "Sure, if they were the same age."

My Notes

mechanical: created or run by a machine

code: a system of communication for a computer

superior: feeling that one is better or more knowing than another

dispute: disagree or argue

Analyzing a Story

My Notes

nonchalantly: in a confident, carefree way

18   "But my mother says a teacher has to be adjusted to fit the mind of each boy and girl it teaches and that each kid has to be taught differently."

19   "Just the same, they didn't do it that way then. If you don't like it, you don't have to read the book."

20   "I didn't say I didn't like it," Margie said quickly. She wanted to read about those funny schools.

21   They weren't even half-finished when Margie's mother called, "Margie! School!" Margie looked up. "Not yet, Mamma."

22   "Now!" said Mrs. Jones. "And it's probably time for Tommy, too."

23   Margie said to Tommy, "Can I read the book some more with you after school?"

24   "Maybe," he said **nonchalantly**. He walked away whistling, the dusty old book tucked beneath his arm.

25   Margie went into the schoolroom. It was right next to her bedroom, and the mechanical teacher was on and waiting for her. It was always on at the same time every day except Saturday and Sunday, because her mother said little girls learned better if they learned at regular hours.

26   The screen was lit up, and it said: "Today's arithmetic lesson is on the addition of proper fractions. Please insert yesterday's homework in the proper slot."

27   Margie did so with a sigh. She was thinking about the old schools they had when her grandfather's grandfather was a little boy. All the kids from the whole neighborhood came, laughing and shouting in the schoolyard, sitting together in the schoolroom, going home together at the end of the day. They learned the same things, so they could help one another on the homework and talk about it.

28   And the teachers were people...

29   The mechanical teacher was flashing on the screen: "When we add the fractions 1/2 and 1/4..."

30   Margie was thinking about how the kids must have loved it in the old days. She was thinking about the fun they had.

Second Read

- Reread the short story to answer these text-dependent comprehension questions.
- Write any additional questions you have about the text in your Reader/Writer Notebook.

1. **Key Ideas and Details:** What details of the exposition make the time of the story specific? Notice that the author has made a point of creating a specific setting and has made the main characters children. How does this help you predict the conflict?

2. **Craft and Structure:** Part of this story tells of an incident in a different time, which is called a flashback. Mark the part of the story that occurs at another time in Margie's life. What is the purpose of this flashback?

3. **Key Ideas and Details:** Does Margie's attitude toward school change by the end of the story? Explain.

Working from the Text

4. Reread the text and mark it for the following:

- Exposition
- Rising action
- Climax
- Falling action
- Resolution

Share your marked passages with a partner. With your partner, create a story board to demonstrate your understanding of the text. For each panel, include a drawing that symbolizes a key moment for that part in the plot, and include textual evidence to support the drawing.

My Notes

**INDEPENDENT
READING LINK**

Read and Connect

What sorts of conflicts have occurred in the book you are reading independently? In your Reader/Writer Notebook, compare the problems, struggles, or obstacles a character has faced with those of a character in a narrative you have read in this unit.

Analyzing a Story

My Notes

Check Your Understanding

The theme or main idea of this story is about our relationship to technology. What is Asimov suggesting about technology? Include your interpretation of Asimov's choice of title for the short story.

Sparking Ideas

Learning Targets
- Analyze picture books for images that spark writing ideas.
- Write a short story with characters, conflict, plot, dialogue, and sensory details.

1. When you hear the word *mystery*, what do you think of? What do you think makes a good mystery?

2. Chris Van Allsburg has written several books that are mysteries. Among some of his best-known books are the following:

- *The Polar Express*
- *The Mysteries of Harris Burdick*
- *The Wreck of the Zephyr*
- *Jumanji*
- *The Stranger*
- *The Garden of Abdul Gasazi*

Find copies of these or other picture books and write questions about particular pictures that intrigue you. Using one or more of the images as your inspiration, write freely to draft a story.

3. Select one of your freewrites to develop further. Before you continue to draft, plan your story. Think about your main character, such as a name, age, favorite hobby, behaviors and actions, accomplishments. Use a graphic organizer like the one below to plan your characters.

My Notes

Characterization	
Describe your main character's appearance.	What does this appearance say about your character?
Describe some of your main character's actions.	What do these actions say about your character?
Other characters	Details about these characters

Sparking Ideas

INDEPENDENT READING LINK

Investigate how the author of your independent reading book uses sensory details. Record your favorite sensory words, phrases, and sentences from this book in your Reader/ Writer Notebook.

My Notes

4. What words or phrases could you include from each sense (taste, touch, sight, smell, hearing) in your story? What vivid verbs and connotative diction help show that sense? What figurative language could you use?

_____

_____

_____

_____

_____

_____

_____

5. Consider your plot. What is the main conflict or problem? How will it be solved? How can you add a twist? How will you introduce the setting and characters? How can you build to the climax?

_____

_____

_____

_____

_____

_____

Writing Prompt: Draft a short story, adding the elements you've brainstormed as you write. Be sure to

- Sequence events logically using elements of plot.
- Use characterization and dialogue to develop conflict.
- Use language purposefully (e.g., figurative and/or sensory details and a variety of sentences).

Return to any of the texts in the unit to reinforce these elements in your writing.

Save this writing prompt response so that you can revisit it when generating ideas for the original short story you will create for Embedded Assessment 2.

Independent Reading Checkpoint

Prepare a short oral presentation about the basic elements of the plot in your independent reading book. Describe a major conflict in the story and how the author addresses it in the story's exposition, rising action, climax, and resolution.

Writing a Short Story

Assignment

Write a story using dialogue, vivid verbs, and figurative language that captures a real or imagined experience and includes characters, conflict, and a plot with exposition, climax, and resolution.

Planning and Prewriting: Take time to make a plan for your short story.

- Review the unit activities and your Reader/Writer Notebook for ideas. What activities have you completed that will help you as you create a short story with the required elements?
- What would you like your short story to be about? What prewriting strategies can you use to help you create ideas?

Drafting: Decide the structure of your story and how you will incorporate the elements of a short story.

- How will you make use of the story starters in the unit to help you create and develop a short story?
- Will you work from a plot diagram or an outline of a story idea? Is there another way you can create a structure that develops the characters and plot of your story?

Evaluating and Revising: Create opportunities to review and revise in order to make your work the best it can be.

- During the process of drafting, have you paused at points to share and respond with others to learn how well you are integrating the necessary narrative techniques into your short story?
- Is your story developing as you want it to? Are you willing to change your story if you must? Once you get suggestions, are you creating a plan to include revision ideas in your draft?
- Have you used the Scoring Guide to help you evaluate how well your draft includes the requirements of the assignment?

Checking and Editing for Publication: Confirm your final draft is ready for publication.

- How will you check for grammatical and technical accuracy?
- Have you verified spelling?

Reflection

After completing this Embedded Assessment, think about how you went about accomplishing this assignment, and answer this question: How did you make sure your final draft was the best it could be in terms of spelling, vocabulary use, and conventions for punctuating and writing dialogue?

My Notes

Technology TIP:

Use online dictionaries, thesauruses, or other resources for checking spelling and grammar in your short story.

Writing a Short Story

SCORING GUIDE

Scoring Criteria	Exemplary	Proficient	Emerging	Incomplete
Ideas	The short story • develops a focused and compelling conflict • establishes an interesting setting, character(s), and point of view • uses a variety of narrative techniques effectively to advance the plot.	The short story • presents and develops a focused conflict • establishes a setting, character(s), and point of view • uses sufficient narrative techniques to advance the plot, such as dialogue and descriptive detail.	The short story • presents an undeveloped or unclear conflict • establishes setting, character(s), and point of view unevenly • uses partial or weak narrative techniques to advance the plot.	The short story • lacks a conflict • does not establish setting, character(s), and/or point of view • uses minimal narrative techniques.
Structure	The short story • engages and orients the reader with exposition • sequences events in the plot logically and naturally to add interest or suspense • uses a variety of transitional strategies effectively and purposefully • provides a thoughtful resolution.	The short story • orients the reader with adequate exposition • sequences events in the plot logically (rising action, climax, falling action) • uses transitional words, phrases, and clauses to link events and signal shifts • provides a logical resolution.	The short story • provides weak or vague exposition • sequences events in the plot unevenly • uses inconsistent, repetitive, or basic transitional words, phrases, and clauses • provides a weak or disconnected resolution.	The short story • lacks exposition • sequences events in the plot illogically or incompletely • uses few or no transitional strategies • lacks a resolution.
Use of Language	The short story • uses connotative diction, vivid verbs, figurative language, and sensory language effectively • demonstrates command of the conventions of standard English capitalization, punctuation, spelling, grammar, and usage (including pronouns, sentence patterns, and dialogue).	The short story • uses adequate connotative diction, vivid verbs, figurative language, and sensory language • demonstrates adequate command of the conventions of standard English capitalization, punctuation, spelling, grammar, and usage (including pronouns, sentence patterns, and dialogue).	The short story • uses weak or inconsistent diction, verbs, figurative language, and sensory language • demonstrates partial or inconsistent command of the conventions of standard English capitalization, punctuation, spelling, grammar, and usage (including pronouns, sentence patterns, and dialogue).	The short story • uses limited, vague, and unclear diction and language • lacks command of the conventions of standard English capitalization, punctuation, spelling, grammar, and usage; frequent errors interfere with meaning.

The Power to Change

Visual Prompt: Plants change from one season to another and often grow in unexpected places. What trait would this plant show that you might use in your own goals for change?

Unit Overview

Where do we get the power to change? How do both internal and external forces help us see the world from a new perspective and possibly even change the course of our lives? In this unit, you will go on a journey with Salamanca Tree Hiddle, the main character of the novel *Walk Two Moons*, as she searches for her missing mother. You will travel to Paradise Falls with an elderly man who is looking for adventure and finds instead a talking dog. You will reflect and write about changes in fictional characters, in the world, and in yourself. Finally, you will conduct research and read nonfiction in order to write about how animals have the power to change our lives for the better.

The Power to Change

GOALS:
- To analyze literary elements
- To apply a variety of reading strategies to fiction and nonfiction texts
- To collaborate and communicate effectively
- To write an expository essay
- To practice using verb tenses and creating sentence variety

ACADEMIC VOCABULARY
compare
contrast
inference
prediction
communication
    (verbal/nonverbal)
synthesize

Literary Terms
topic sentence
commentary
novel
subplot
setting
literary analysis
introduction
hook
thesis statement
conclusion
nonfiction
fiction
imagery

Contents

Activities

*Texts not included in these materials.

Language & Writer's Craft

- Verb Tenses (2.2)
- Pronoun Usage and Agreement (2.4)
- Sentence Variety (2.6)
- Revising for Figurative Language (2.8)
- Parallel Structure (2.15)

MY INDEPENDENT
READING LIST

_____
_____
_____
_____
_____
_____
_____
_____
_____
_____
_____
_____
_____
_____
_____
_____
_____
_____
_____
_____

Previewing the Unit

LEARNING STRATEGIES:
Close Reading, QHT, Marking
the Text, Skimming/Scanning

My Notes

Learning Targets

- Preview the big ideas and vocabulary for the unit.
- Identify and analyze the skills and knowledge needed to complete Embedded Assessment 1 successfully.

Making Connections

In the last unit, you explored change in your own life. As part of that exploration, you learned to write narratives—both a personal narrative and a short story. In this unit, you will continue to explore change, but now you will broaden your exploration to look at change in the world around you.

Essential Questions

Based on your current knowledge, how would you answer these questions?

1. How can talking and working with others help one analyze a novel?
2. How do internal and external forces help people grow?

Developing Vocabulary

Look at the Academic Vocabulary and Literary Terms on the Contents page. Use the QHT strategy to analyze which terms you may know and which you need to learn more deeply.

Unpacking Embedded Assessment 1

Read the assignment for Embedded Assessment 1: Responding to Literature.

Your assignment is to write an expository response to the novel *Walk Two Moons*. Select one of the following prompts:

- Explain how internal or external forces cause one character from the novel to grow or change.
- Identify one subplot from the novel and explain how it relates to the main plot of the novel.
- Describe one setting from the novel and explain why it is important to a character or to the plot.
- Discuss how plot, setting, character, or conflict contributes to one of the novel's themes.

Summarize what you will need to know in order to complete this assessment successfully. With your class, create a graphic organizer to represent the skills and knowledge you will need to complete the tasks identified in the Embedded Assessment.

Forces of Change

Learning Targets

- Analyze the effect of internal and external forces on a character in a film.
- Respond to an expository writing prompt using clear organization and details from a film to support the topic.

Preview

In this activity, you will view a film and analyze the effect of internal and external forces on a character.

Setting a Purpose for Viewing

- You will next watch film clips from the movie *Up*. As you watch each clip, use the graphic organizer to take notes on the internal and external changes in Carl Fredrickson's life and on how he responds to them.

Scene	What changes does Carl Fredrickson experience?	External Forces: Events or other people that cause change	Internal Forces: Carl's own decisions or emotions that cause change
Meeting Ellie			
Scenes from Their Lives			
Construction			
Up and Away			

Forces of Change

Literary Terms

A **topic sentence** states the main ideas of a paragraph. **Commentary** is the writer's statements about the meaning and importance of the details and examples.

My Notes

_____

_____

_____

_____

_____

_____

_____

_____

_____

___ INDEPENDENT
___ READING LINK

Read and Research

As you read, think about changes that happen in real life. Some types of changes to think about are changes in the environment, changes in social issues, changes after historical events, and changes in someone's personal life. Choose a change from real life that you would like to learn more about. Research and read nonfiction texts that give you more information about this type of change. Use your Reader/Writer Notebook to take notes based on your reading and respond to any questions, comments, or reactions you might have to your reading.

Working from the Film
Expository Writing

In the last unit, you learned about narrative writing, which can be based on true incidents or made-up stories. Another form of writing is exposition, or expository writing. Expository writing is a type of writing that explains, defines, clarifies, or gives information about a topic.

1. Following is a sample expository paragraph that explains how Carl Fredrickson's life changes from external forces in the film *Up*. Mark the text as follows:
   - Circle the **topic sentence** that states the main idea.
   - Underline details and examples from the film.
   - Highlight **commentary** about how the external forces cause character change.
   - Put an asterisk (*) next to transition words.

In the film *Up*, Carl Fredrickson's life changes due to several external forces. Ellie is one of the first external forces of change in his life. She makes Carl a member of her club and doesn't really give him any choice about it. She also pushes him to walk the plank to get his balloon, which is how he breaks his arm. Although this seems like a bad thing, she really is making his life more of an adventure.

WRITING to SOURCES   Expository Writing Prompt

Work with your class to write another paragraph explaining how Carl Fredrickson's life changes from internal forces in the film *Up*. Be sure to

- Include a topic sentence that states the main idea.
- Use supporting details and examples from your graphic organizer.
- Add commentary about how the internal forces cause character change.

_____

_____

_____

_____

_____

_____

_____

_____

_____

_____

_____

_____

_____

Language and Writers Craft: Verb Tenses

Verbs show time through tenses. Incorrectly mixing tenses is a common problem in writing. The present, past, and future tenses usually are easy to keep consistent.

Examples:

Present: She *sings* in the chorus.

Past: She *sang* in the chorus.

Future: She *will sing* in the chorus.

Consistent: She *sings* in the chorus, and he *plays* in the band.

Inconsistent: She *sings* in the chorus, and he *played* in the band. (mixes present and past)

Most problems usually occur with the perfect tenses. The perfect tenses are formed by adding such common words as *can*, *do*, *may*, *must*, *ought*, *shall*, *will*, *has*, *have*, *had*, and forms of *be*.

Examples:

Present Perfect: She *has sung* in the chorus.

Past Perfect: She *had sung* in the chorus.

Future Perfect: She *will have sung* in the chorus.

As you write, be aware of your verb tenses. Here are some examples of consistent and inconsistent use of tenses.

Consistent: I *was talking* to Sarah, and I *said*, "Will you be at the party?"

Inconsistent: I *was talking* to Sarah, and I *say*, "Will you be at the party?"

Practice:

Circle the present-tense verbs in the paragraph below.

Up is the story of Carl Fredrickson, who decides to finally follow his dreams. But rather than jump in the car or take a plane, he attaches thousands of balloons to his house and floats away. "So long, boys!" he calls to some men below.

Check Your Understanding

Find the verbs in the paragraph you wrote for the previous expository writing prompt. Revise them as needed to use the correct verb tense.

GRAMMAR *&* USAGE
Literary Analysis

When writing about literature and film, use the present tense. For example, in *Up* Carl Fredrickson *attaches* balloons to his house.

My Notes

Beginning the Journey

LEARNING STRATEGIES:
Graphic Organizer, Previewing,
Note-taking

Literary Terms

A **novel** is a type of literary genre that tells a fictional story. It reveals its plot through the actions, speech, and thoughts of its characters.

My Notes

Learning Targets

- Preview the class novel by completing a graphic organizer.
- Record textual evidence in a double-entry journal while reading the class novel and analyze the textual evidence in order to add commentary and inferences about the text to the double-entry journal.

Novel Study

In this activity, you will preview the novel *Walk Two Moons* and learn how to take notes in a double-entry journal.

1. You will next begin reading Sharon Creech's **novel** *Walk Two Moons*. Just like a short story, a novel is a work of fiction. A short story tends to be written about a few characters with one major conflict. In contrast, a novel tends to include more characters and more conflicts throughout the book. Whenever you pick up a new book to read, it is a good idea to preview it. Begin with the front and back covers and the first few pages just inside the front cover.

Title	Why do you think the novel is called *Walk Two Moons*?	
	Describe the lettering used for the title (color, size, style). Does the title look interesting to you?	
Author	What do you know about the author?	
	Have you ever read any other works by this author?	
Pictures	Do you see any pictures or illustrations? If so, describe what you see.	
	Why do you think these images were selected?	
Words	Is a description of the book provided? If so, summarize it in one or two sentences.	
	Has the novel or its author won any awards? If so, what were they for?	
First Pages	What do you think the quote on the page before the Table of Contents means?	
	Pick one chapter title and explain what that chapter might be about.	

Introducing the Strategy: Double-Entry Journal

A double-entry journal is a two-column journal in which a passage is written on the left side (textual evidence) and a response to the passage is written in the right column (commentary). Responses might include asking questions of the text, forming personal opinions about the text, interpreting the text, or reflecting on the process of making meaning of the text.

2. As you read *Walk Two Moons*, you will take notes in a double-entry journal to record your thoughts and questions in response to your reading. You may respond in these ways:

- Write about an experience in your own life that relates to what is happening in the novel.
- Write your opinions about what is happening in the novel.
- Write your questions about what is happening in the novel.
- Make inferences or draw conclusions based on what is happening in the text.
- Record the definitions for tough or interesting vocabulary you come across in your reading.

Draw a horizontal line under each entry. Complete this example as you read Chapter 1 of *Walk Two Moons*.

Passage from Text	Page #	Personal Response/ Commentary
"Just over a year ago, my father plucked me up like a weed and took me and all our belongings (no, that is not true—he did not bring the chestnut tree, the willow, the maple, the hayloft, or the swimming hole, which all belonged to me) and we drove three hundred miles straight north and stopped in front of a house in Euclid, Ohio."	1	This passage reminds me of when I had to move away from my old house in the city. I was really angry that we couldn't bring the playground with us. It sounds like she really likes trees and being outdoors and that she will have to give up those things in her new home. Why is she moving, and where is her mother?

Beginning the Journey

If you are having trouble thinking of what to write, use these response starters:

- I really like (or dislike) this part because . . .
- I wonder why . . .
- I predict that . . .
- I think the character should . . .
- This reminds me of the time when I . . .
- This reminds me of a book I read (movie I watched, and so on) . . .

3. Following is an example of a blank double-entry journal form to use for the next few chapters. Copy this form into your Reader/Writer Notebook. You may need several pages for writing your thoughts while you are reading the rest of *Walk Two Moons.*

Title of Novel:

Author:

Passage from Text	Page #	Personal Response/ Commentary

Check Your Understanding

Describe how a double-entry journal is used. Also explain the difference between the text passage and the personal response or commentary.

Planting the Seeds of Character Analysis

Learning Targets

- Use knowledge of characterization to write expository literary analysis paragraphs that compare or contrast characters.
- Record textual evidence about characters in a novel and use the evidence to write commentary that explains or analyzes the characters.

Novel Study

In this activity, you will analyze the characters in *Walk Two Moons*.

1. Skim and scan Chapters 1–4 of *Walk Two Moons* to find details about the characters and add them to the graphic organizer below. Your double-entry journal may help you locate passages, since you have been noting page numbers. Remember that authors use the following techniques to develop a character:

- character's appearance
- character's actions
- what the character says
- what others say about the character

My Notes

Name	Details About Character
Sal	
Phoebe	

Planting the Seeds of Character Analysis

2. Take a closer look at the two main characters in *Walk Two Moons* by taking notes below on all the ways the author uses characterization.

Characterization Notes		
	Salamanca Tree Hiddle	Phoebe Winterbottom
What does the character look like?		
What does the character do?		
What does the character say?		
What do others say about them?		

ACADEMIC VOCABULARY

To **compare** and to **contrast** is to identify similarities and differences. Exploring ideas or objects by comparing and contrasting them is an effective way to analyze ideas.

A part of analyzing and responding to what you read is **comparing** and **contrasting** characters, settings, and incidents in a story. In writing exposition in which you compare and contrast, you will want to use transitions that help the reader see what you are comparing or contrasting. Read the examples of compare and contrast transition words and phrases in the Grammar & Usage box.

WRITING to SOURCES Expository Writing Prompt

Write an expository paragraph that compares or contrasts the two main characters in *Walk Two Moons*. Include examples from the text that show different types of characterization: appearance, actions, words, and the reactions of others. Be sure to

* Use a topic sentence.
* Include supporting details and commentary.
* Use transition words.
* Use present-tense verbs and avoid incorrect shifts in pronouns.

GRAMMAR & USAGE
Compare and Contrast
Transitions of comparison: *in the same way, likewise, as, also, similarly*

Transitions of contrast: *but, although, however, yet, nevertheless, on the other hand*

Language and Writer's Craft: Pronoun Usage and Agreement

A **pronoun** refers back to a noun or takes the place of that noun. In Unit 1, you learned about several different kinds of pronouns, including subjective, objective, intensive, and possessive. Write a brief explanation of each type.

Subjective pronoun:

Objective pronoun:

Intensive pronoun:

Possessive pronoun:

When a pronoun refers back to a noun, it is important that the noun and pronoun have certain characteristics in common. This concept is called noun-pronoun agreement, which means that each pronoun must agree in **person** and in **number** with the noun it represents.

Agreement in person: If you are writing in the first person (*I*), avoid confusing your reader by switching to the second person (*you*) or third person (*he, she, it, they*, etc.).

> **Example:** **I** sometimes get nervous because **I** don't know what other people are thinking of **me**. (NOT: **I** sometimes get nervous because **you** don't know what other people are thinking of **you**.)

Agree in number: If a pronoun takes the place of a singular noun, you must use a singular pronoun. If it takes the place of a plural noun, use a plural pronoun.

> **Example:** Just because **a man** looks old on the outside doesn't mean that **he** isn't still young at heart. (NOT: Just because a **man** looks old on the outside doesn't mean **they** aren't still young at heart.)

Check Your Understanding

Revisit the expository paragraph you wrote comparing or contrasting characters. Highlight all the pronouns you used. Check that they agree in person and in number with the nouns to which they refer. Revise your paragraphs so that your nouns and pronouns agree.

My Notes

Mapping the Journey: Plot and Subplot

Learning Targets

- Make inferences and predictions about how characters change as the plot moves toward a resolution.
- Apply understanding of plot and subplot to a discussion of the novel *Walk Two Moons*.

Novel Study

In this activity, you will make inferences about the plot of *Walk Two Moons* and its effects on the characters.

1. **Quickwrite:** How can going on a physical (external) journey change your emotional (internal) self?

2. Events in a novel or film often contribute to a character's growth or change. Sometimes the changes are immediate; at other times, you do not realize how the character has changed until the story's end. Use the graphic organizer below to record plot events and to make an **inference** or a **prediction** about how those events might affect a character.

Events in the Plot	Inferences/Predictions About Character Change

My Notes

3. There are two kinds of journeys in the book *Walk Two Moons*. Use the space below to record some of the key events from both.

- Brainstorm or illustrate events from the *physical* (external) journey Sal takes with her grandparents.
- Brainstorm or illustrate events from the *emotional* (internal) journeys Phoebe and Sal experience.

Events from physical journey:

Events from emotional journey:

Literary Terms

Subplot is a secondary plot that occurs along with a main plot.

4. Novels often have both a main plot and one or more **subplots**. The main plot focuses on a main character and has the greatest impact on the story. The subplot usually involves other characters and intersects with the main plot in some way. Which journey in *Walk Two Moons* is the main plot of the novel? Explain your reasoning.

Check Your Understanding

Discuss the plot and subplot of the book you are reading with a partner. You could also choose another book, a television show, or a movie you know well or have recently read or viewed. Be sure to express your ideas about the plot and subplot clearly. Also build on your partner's ideas during the discussion.

A Tree of One's Own: Setting

Learning Targets
- Write about how the setting of a novel relates to the theme or central idea of the text.
- Revise writing to include compound sentences.

Novel Study

In this activity, you will make connections between the setting of *Walk Two Moons* and its theme.

1. Read Sal's description of the singing tree in Chapter 16. Fill in the columns below, noting how she feels when she is at the singing tree and the textual details that help create that feeling.

Place	Time	Feeling or Mood	Details

2. Think of the singing tree on Sal's farm in Kentucky. What do the details about the tree tell you about the theme or central idea of the novel? Fill in the left column below with evidence from the text about the singing tree. Fill in the right column by making inferences about how each detail affects the theme or central idea of the novel.

Details About Singing Tree	How Details Relate to Theme or Central Idea

3. On a separate piece of paper, sketch the **setting** of Sal's singing tree. Include details from your graphic organizer that relate to the theme or central idea of the novel. Label the important details on your sketch.

WRITING to SOURCES   Expository Writing Prompt

Write a paragraph about how Sal's singing tree relates to the theme or central idea of the novel. Explain how the external setting affects Sal's internal feelings. Be sure to

- Use a topic sentence and supporting details from the novel.
- Relate each detail to the theme or central idea.
- Include commentary about how the setting makes Sal feel.
- Use transition words and demonstrate correct verb tense and correct pronoun usage.

Language and Writer's Craft: Sentence Variety

Writing that uses only one type of sentence, such as simple sentences, seems dull after a while. Using a variety of sentence types helps you keep a reader interested. One way to improve the sentence variety in your writing is to combine short, simple sentences to create compound sentences. In Chapter 16 of *Walk Two Moons*, Sharon Creech uses two kinds of compound sentences in her description of Sal's singing tree.

Independent clauses linked by a semicolon:

It was not a call; it was a true birdsong, with trills and warbles.

Independent clauses linked by a comma and a coordinating conjunction:

*I had pleaded to go along, **but** my father said he didn't think I should have to go through that.*

4. Revise the sentences below by combining independent clauses to create at least two new compound sentences.

I am proud, awestruck, and exhausted. I am at the top of Anderson Reservoir Dam. I have been hiking with my friends. I am the first one to get to the top. I look down at the swaying trees. The Guadalupe Stream is rushing down the valley. I can feel the breeze on my neck.

Check Your Understanding

Revisit the response you wrote to the prompt above. Find places where you can combine independent clauses to create compound sentences.

Literary Terms

The **setting** of a scene or story includes both where and when the action takes place. Details of setting help establish a context for the events of the story.

My Notes

_____

_____

_____

_____

_____

_____

_____

_____

_____

_____

_____

_____

_____

_____

_____

_____

GRAMMAR & USAGE
Compound Sentences

A **compound sentence** is two or more independent clauses linked by a semicolon or by a comma and a **coordinating conjunction**. The most common coordinating conjunctions are *and*, *but*, and *or*.

Questions and Discussions

LEARNING STRATEGIES:
Discussion Groups, Visualizing, Sketching, Questioning the Text

Literary Terms
Literary analysis is the study of a work of literature to evaluate and interpret elements that affect a reader's understanding or opinion of the work.

My Notes

WORD CONNECTIONS

Roots and Affixes

The word *literal* contains the root *-liter-* from the Latin word *littera*, meaning "letter." This root also appears in *literacy*, *literature*, and *alliteration*. *Interpretive* contains the root *interpret*, which means "to come to an understanding." *Universal* contains the Latin prefix *uni-*, meaning "one," and the root *-ver-*, meaning "turn." The root *-ver-* appears in *reverse*, *adversary*, *introvert*, *vertigo*, and *conversation*. The suffix *-al* indicates an adjective.

Learning Targets
- Use verbal and nonverbal communication when posing and responding to literal, interpretive, and universal questions about the novel *Walk Two Moons*.
- Identify and implement effective discussion techniques.

Novel Study
In this activity, you will strengthen your skills of literary analysis by practicing the strategy of Questioning the Text and by participating in group discussions.

Literary Analysis
For Embedded Assessment 1, you will be writing an essay responding to a prompt on the novel *Walk Two Moons*. In the past few activities, you began your reading and analysis of the novel, identifying plot and subplot, analyzing characterization, and identifying narrative elements such as setting.

In the next few activities, you will learn additional skills and strategies for a deeper **literary analysis**, skills that you will use in writing your response to literature.

Introducing the Strategy: Questioning the Text
A strategy for thinking actively and interpretively about your reading is to ask questions. As you read any text, you can ask questions that aid your understanding with different levels of ideas. Questioning helps you experience a text in depth.

- **Literal questions** (Level 1): You can answer questions on the literal level by looking to the text directly. These questions often begin with *who, what, where,* or *when*.
  Example: *What did Ellie pin onto Carl's shirt when she made him a member of her club?*

- **Interpretive questions** (Level 2): You cannot find answers to interpretive questions directly in the text; however, textual evidence points to and supports your answers.
  Example: *Why do you think Carl didn't want to move into the retirement home?*

- **Universal questions** (Level 3): These questions go beyond the text. They require you to think about the larger issues or ideas raised by a text.
  Example: *Why do people dream of traveling to strange and faraway lands?*

1. In your own words, describe each type of question.

2. Write examples of the three levels of questions, based on your reading so far of the novel *Walk Two Moons*.

Literal:

Interpretive:

Universal:

3. Your teacher will assign a section of the novel for your small group to study. As a group, prepare for your discussion by creating at least two questions for each level of questioning.

Literal:

Interpretive:

Universal:

Communicating in Discussion Groups

You have participated in discussions in the past. Think about what made them effective. What did not work so well? A discussion group works together to consider a topic, text, or question.

All members of a discussion group need to **communicate** effectively to help the group work smoothly and achieve its goals. Group members should allow opportunities for everyone to participate. With your class, create a list of guidelines to help ensure good communication.

© 2017 College Board. All rights reserved.

My Notes

ACADEMIC VOCABULARY
You may already know that to communicate is to give and receive information. **Communication** can be either **verbal**, which involves the written or spoken word, or **nonverbal**, which involves movement, gestures, or facial expressions.

Questions and Discussions

My Notes

4. Think about the communication process from the speaker's viewpoint as well as the listener's viewpoint.

As a speaker:

_____

_____

_____

_____

_____

_____

_____

As a listener:

_____

_____

_____

_____

_____

_____

_____

_____

5. All discussion groups need a process or a strategy to help them accomplish their goals. It also helps to have formal or informal roles in discussion groups. What are some of the roles that people might have, and what would they do?

_____

_____

_____

_____

_____

_____

6. Follow your teacher's directions to form a new group of students who wrote levels of questions on different sections of *Walk Two Moons*. As your new group discusses these different questions, use the graphic organizer on the next page to record key ideas. Remember to follow the communication norms for speakers and listeners as well as the discussion roles you identified with your class in questions 4 and 5. Give each other feedback on which questions were the most effective at encouraging interesting discussions and bringing out new ideas about meaning in the novel.

An Interesting Point Made by a Member of My Group	Evidence the Person Provided	My Thoughts

Check Your Understanding

- What were your strengths as a discussion group? What were your challenges, and how did you overcome them?

  _____

  _____

  _____

- Revisit the Essential Question: How can talking and working with others help one understand a novel?

  _____

  _____

  _____

My Notes

_____

_____

_____

_____

_____

_____

_____

_____

_____

_____

_____

_____

_____

Diction Detectives and "Evidence"

LEARNING STRATEGIES:
Graphic Organizer, Skimming/
Scanning

My Notes

Learning Targets
- Closely read text to analyze an author's diction to portray a character.
- Revise writing by adding figurative language.
- Use context to determine the meaning of words and phrases.

Novel Study

In this activity, you will analyze Sharon Creech's diction.

1. In Unit 1, you learned that *diction* refers to an author's word choice, which is one way an author can develop character. Skim/scan the chapters of *Walk Two Moons* that you have read, and list below some of the words Sharon Creech chooses that give Sal, Phoebe, Gram, Gramps, and the other characters their unique voices.

2. Chapter 22 is titled "Evidence" because Phoebe and Sal are both looking for clues about why their mothers went missing. With a partner or small group, read the chapter closely, looking for clues about the author's purpose for selecting specific words. Try to think about what the author was trying to show or achieve. Search for words, phrases, or passages that are especially descriptive, interesting, or even confusing. Analyze them and record your evidence in the graphic organizer below.

Page #	Word, Phrase, or Passage	Why did you choose this word, phrase, or passage?	Why do you think the author used this word, phrase, or passage?
	Word:		
	Phrase:		
	Passage:		

3. The words and sentences around a word are called its *context*. You may find clues in the context to help you determine the meaning of unfamiliar words. When Phoebe asks her father about the word *malinger*, he has her look it up in the dictionary. Read the passage below, and underline context clues that could have helped Phoebe.

Her father placed his hand on her forehead, looked deep into her eyes and said, "I'm afraid you have to go to school."

"I'm sick. Honest," she said. "It might be cancer."

"Phoebe, I know you're worried, but there's nothing we can do but wait. We have to go on with things. We can't malinger."

4. Skim/scan the paragraphs following this passage, and try to find context clues that you can use to define *frenzy, cardigan, skittish,* and *sullen*. Use a dictionary to check your definitions.

5. In Unit 1, you learned about how figurative language can enhance your own writing by forming an image in your reader's mind that will create a specific emotion or emphasize an important idea.

Look closely at the diction in Sharon Creech's figurative language. Try to walk around in her shoes (metaphorically) and deduce the reasoning behind her choices. Record examples below.

My Notes

Page #	Figurative Language	Why did you choose this word, phrase, or passage to examine?	Why do you think the author used this word, phrase, or passage?

Diction Detectives and "Evidence"

WORD CONNECTIONS

Roots and Affixes

The word **metaphor** comes from the Greek root *meta-*, meaning "after" or "beyond," and *-phor*, meaning "to carry." *Meta-* appears in *metacognitive*, *metamorphosis*, and *metabolism*.
The root *-phor-* occurs in the words *euphoria* and *phosphorescent*.

Personification has the Latin root *-person-*, from *persona*, referring to the masks representing characters in ancient dramas.

My Notes

Language and Writer's Craft: Revising for Figurative Language

Adding figurative language to your writing is one way to revise. Your use of figurative language is also part of your own style, or voice. Review the following types of figurative language that you learned in Unit 1 and then write your own example.

A *simile* is a creative comparison between two unlike things, using the word *like* or *as*:

- Her smile is as bright as the sun.
- The NBA player is as tall as a tree.

1. My example of simile:

A *metaphor* is a creative comparison between two unlike things where one thing becomes another:

- Her smile is a sunbeam warming up the room.
- The NBA player was a tree, blocking everything in its way.

2. My example of metaphor:

Personification is a kind of metaphor that gives objects or abstract ideas human characteristics:

- The sun smiled down at the girl.
- The ball bounced playfully away.

3. My example of personification:

4. Underline one idea in the paragraph below and revise it to add figurative language.

My family and I had an exhilarating time on our rafting trip in Colorado. We spent most of our days on the river, braving the rapids. Although it seemed we would never make it down the river without plunging in, the thrill was definitely worth it. Our intense experience created a stronger family bond as we pushed ourselves beyond our previously defined limits.

Check Your Understanding

Choose any piece of writing you have done in this unit. Underline several details and revise them to add figurative language.

Reporting from Paradise Falls

Learning Targets
- Learn and apply the skill of summarizing to text being read.
- Determine the theme of a film or story by analyzing details such as setting, plot, and character.
- Write and present a summary to a small group.

LEARNING STRATEGIES:
Graphic Organizer,
Summarizing, Drafting

Preview

In this activity, you will view a film and use details about setting, plot, and character to determine theme.

Earlier in this unit, you analyzed setting, plot, and character in literature, film, and your own life. Look back at those activities, and then write a brief definition of each literary term below in your own words.

Setting (Activity 2.6):

Plot (Activity 2.5):

Character (Activity 2.4):

Setting a Purpose for Viewing
- You will next watch some film clips. Working with a small group, divide the work so that one person is taking notes on each literary element as you watch the clips. Especially note changes in each element.

Setting
Plot
Character

My Notes

Reporting from Paradise Falls

Working from the Film

Summarizing involves reading text or listening to a speaker and then restating the main ideas in your own words. The purpose of a summary is to capture the essential information without using the author's or speaker's exact words.

1. Write a brief summary of your notes on setting, plot, or character.

2. Share your notes with your group, and take notes to complete the chart for the other two elements while other group members are reporting.

3. With your class, identify possible themes, or central messages, for the film *Up*. Remember that a theme should be a message, not just a topic. If *Up* is about the topic of adventure, the theme is the message the film communicates about adventure.

4. With your group, discuss plot, setting, and character in *Walk Two Moons*. Identify and discuss possible themes.

WRITING to SOURCES   Expository Writing Prompt

Write a paragraph about how the setting, plot, or characters in the film *Up* contribute to the theme. Be sure to

- Use a topic sentence that states a theme.
- Include supporting details and commentary.
- Refer to specific literary elements (theme, setting, plot, character).
- Use transitions and correct verb tense and pronoun agreement.

Making Connections and Visualizing Art

Learning Targets

- Analyze internal and external conflicts and how characters respond to conflict in a text.
- Make connections within a text, between texts, between a text and self, and between a text and the broader world.
- Synthesize the literary elements of *Walk Two Moons* in order to create a collaborative visual representation.

LEARNING STRATEGIES:
Visualizing, Graphic Organizer, Rereading, Word Maps

Novel Study

In this activity, you will analyze internal and external conflicts, make connections, and create a visual representation of *Walk Two Moons*.

Internal and External Conflicts

1. As you viewed clips from the film *Up*, you analyzed many internal and external forces that cause Carl Fredrickson to change. Whenever the main character struggles against internal and external forces, there is a *conflict* in the story.

   List one internal conflict, such as a difficult decision or emotion, that Carl Fredrickson struggles with.

   List one external conflict, such as a force of nature or another character, that Carl Fredrickson struggles against.

2. Give one of the faces below long straight hair (Sal) and the other one curly hair (Phoebe). Review your note-taking in your double-entry journal for *Walk Two Moons*. Add examples of conflict to the faces. Put at least one internal conflict inside each face and one external conflict outside each face.

3. In a collaborative group, compare and contrast your visualization of conflicts in the two characters above. Based on your analysis, discuss who is struggling more with internal conflict and who is struggling more with external conflict.

My Notes

Making Connections and Visualizing Art

Making Connections

4. An important element of literary analysis is recognizing that the events and conflicts in a text are similar to events in other texts and to those in real life. Making connections between texts and between texts and life helps you not only understand the text, but also to understand life lessons it may teach. Make connections between *Walk Two Moons*, other texts, yourself, and the world. Record your ideas in the graphic organizer.

Event from Book	Type of Connection	Explain Connection
	Text to Same Text: Make a connection to another event in the same novel.	
	Text to Different Text: Make a connection to an event in a different novel or text.	
	Text to Self: Make a connection to an event in your own life.	
	Text to World: Make a connection to an event in history or society.	

5. Making text connections also involves reflecting on what has happened in the book up to this point and predicting what will happen next. Use the graphic organizer below to connect the past to the future in *Walk Two Moons*.

What has happened previously in the book?	What do you predict will happen as the book continues?

Visualizing the Text

6. Reread the section below from Chapter 30, in which Sal talks about the power of visualization. Mark the text by highlighting or underlining every time Sal uses any form of the word *visualize*.

Once, before she left, my mother said that if you visualize something happening, you can make it happen. For example, if you are about to run a race, you visualize yourself running the race and crossing the finish line, and presto! When the time comes, it really happens. The only thing I did not understand was what if everyone visualized himself winning the race?

Still, when she left, this is what I did. I visualized her reaching for the phone. Then I visualized her dialing the phone. I visualized our phone number clicking through the wires. I visualized the phone ringing.

It did not ring.

I visualized her riding the bus back to Bybanks. I visualized her walking up the driveway. I visualized her opening the door.

It did not happen.

7. **Quickwrite:** Do you think it is possible to affect the future by picturing something happening? Explain your reasoning in the My Notes space.

8. In Chapter 32, Mr. Birkway shows the class a picture. Use the My Notes space to describe what you see when your teacher shows you this picture.

9. Discuss how talking about a picture with other people can help you see it in different ways. Do you think the same thing can happen with a novel?

10. On the following page, you will find an outline of a tree. As you read or review a chapter of *Walk Two Moons*, use the tree to take notes on different literary elements.
   - Write the *chapter title* on the trunk.
   - Describe or draw images on the tree's branches to represent different *events*.
   - Draw birds or animals in the tree to represent the *characters*, and label them with names.
   - Describe the *setting(s)* with words or images on the ground at the base of the tree.
   - Use the roots to describe *events that happened earlier* in the book.
   - In the sky above the tree, make *predictions* about what will happen next.
   - Add leaves to the tree with interesting *diction* from the chapter.

Making Connections and Visualizing Art

My Notes

11. Collaborative Group: Share your sketches and then collaborate to create a new tree outline on poster paper that **synthesizes** all of your ideas into one project. Assign a different color to each person, and provide a key so that you can see which details came from each group member.

Check Your Understanding

Writing Prompt: Reflect on visualizing and collaborating. How did sketching the tree help you understand the chapter better? How and what did you contribute to the tree that you created in your small group? What were the challenges of working with the group, and how did you deal with them? Write a response explaining your experience with visualizing and collaborating. Be sure to

- Use a topic sentence.
- Elaborate with supporting detail and commentary.
- Use transitions.
- Use a variety of sentence structures.

ACADEMIC VOCABULARY
To **synthesize** is to form by combining parts or elements into a single or unified piece.

Stepping into the Literature Circle

Learning Targets

- Analyze elements of the structure and content of a text using text evidence with a Literature Circles strategy.
- Evaluate Literature Circles as a strategy to facilitate close reading and collaborative discussion of meaning in a text.

Introducing the Strategy: Literature Circles

A Literature Circle is made up of a group that all reads the same text and then participates in a discussion of that text. Each person in the group takes on a different role, with the roles rotating to each group member. The group discussion roles are Discussion Leader, Diction Detective, Bridge Builder, Reporter, and Artist.

Literature Circle Roles

Each role within a Literature Circle group has specific responsibilities. Performance of the roles rotates so that each person in the group has an opportunity to serve in each role.

Discussion Leader: Your job is to develop a list of questions you think your group should discuss about the assigned section of the book. Use your knowledge of Levels of Questions to create thought-provoking interpretive and universal questions. Try to create questions that encourage your group to consider many ideas. Help your group explore these important ideas and share their reactions. You will be in charge of leading the day's discussion.

Diction Detective: Your job is to carefully examine the diction (word choice) in the assigned section. Search for words, phrases, and passages that are especially descriptive, powerful, funny, thought-provoking, surprising, or even confusing. List the words or phrases and explain why you selected them. Then, write your thoughts about why the author might have selected these words or phrases. What is the author trying to say? How does the diction help the author achieve his or her purpose? What tone do the words indicate?

Bridge Builder: Your job is to build bridges between the events of the book and other people, places, or events in school, the community, or your own life. Look for connections between the text, yourself, other texts, and the world. Also make connections between what has happened before and what might happen as the narrative continues. Look for the characters' internal and external conflicts and the ways these conflicts influence their actions.

Reporter: Your job is to identify and report on the key points of the reading assignment. Make a list or write a summary that describes how the setting, plot, and characters are developed in this section of the book. Consider how characters interact, major events that occur, and shifts in the setting or the mood that seem significant. Share your report at the beginning of the group meeting to help your group focus on the key ideas presented in the reading. Like that of a newspaper reporter, your report must be concise yet thorough.

My Notes

Stepping into the Literature Circle

Artist: Your job is to create an illustration related to the reading. It can be a sketch, cartoon, diagram, flow chart, or other image. It can be of a scene, an idea, a symbol, or a character. Show your illustration to the group without any explanation. Ask each group member to respond, either by making a comment or asking a question. After everyone has responded, then you may explain your picture and answer any questions that have not been answered.

Preparing for Discussion

1. Your teacher will assign roles and put you in Literature Circle groups to practice close reading and discussion of texts with a classic fairy tale. Review the directions for your role on the previous page. Also review the skills you learned in the following activities, where you were actually practicing the skills needed for each role:

   Discussion Leader (Activity 2.7)

   Diction Detective (Activity 2.8)

   Reporter (Activity 2.9)

   Bridge Builder (Activity 2.10)

   Artist (Activity 2.10)

   Create a placecard to use during the meeting. Include the role title and a symbolic visual on the front. On the back, write a brief description of your role.

Discussion Instructions

2. Keep a double-entry journal with notes that will help you prepare for your role. Remember to copy or summarize important passages on the left side of your journal. On the right-hand side

   - The Discussion Leader will keep track of questions to ask.
   - The Diction Detective will record interesting words and phrases, especially figurative language.
   - The Reporter will take notes on the setting, plot, and characters, especially shifts or changes.
   - The Bridge Builder will take notes on predictions, connections (text to self, text to text, and text to world) and conflict.
   - The Artist will take notes on how to create a visual representation.

3. Meet with the other students who are also preparing for the role you have been given. Share the notes that you took and discuss how you can use them in your Literature Circle meetings.

4. When your role is prepared, go back to your Literature Circle group. Review the guidelines for communicating in discussion groups, which you made in Activity 2.7.

Participating in a Discussion

5. At your teacher's direction, team up with another group to use the Fishbowl strategy. While the inner circle is discussing the text, the outer circle will take notes on the Discussion Group Note-taking Graphic Organizer. After the first discussion, switch places so that the inner circle becomes the outer circle for the second discussion.

6. Give each circle (inner and outer) a chance to respond to the discussion, commenting on the strengths and challenges that each group had in its analysis of the text. Fill out the Group Meeting Reflection Chart on the following page. Reflect on what you can improve on during your Literature Circle meeting for the upcoming Embedded Assessment.

My Notes

_____

_____

_____

_____

_____

_____

_____

Discussion Note-taking Graphic Organizer

An Interesting Point Made by a Member of the Discussion Group	Support the Person Provided	My Thoughts

Stepping into the Literature Circle

Group Meeting Reflection Chart

	Challenges	Goals
Speaking		
Listening		
Understanding the Text		

Check Your Understanding

Reflect on your discussion group experiences and how Literature Circle discussions contributed to your close reading of text and your ability to analyze meaning and make connections to ideas within and outside of the text.

My Notes

Circling the Moon: Literature Circle Discussion

Learning Targets

- Analyze a novel's literary elements through close reading and collaborative discussion.
- Collaboratively create a poster representing the synthesis of ideas from close reading and analysis and explain how it contributes to the text.

Preparing for Discussion

1. Work with your teacher to learn your group assignment and the role you will play in the group analysis and discussions of the final reading of *Walk Two Moons*. Then, record information about your role and your group goals below. Use the graphic organizer for your group discussions.

My Role _____

My Goal: During the Literature Circle discussion, I will be sure to

_____

_____

_____

My Group Members: _____

_____

_____

LEARNING STRATEGIES:
Literature Circles, Discussion Groups, Collaborating, Note-taking

My Notes

Discussion Note-taking Graphic Organizer

An Interesting Point Made by a Member of the Discussion Group	Support the Person Provided	My Thoughts

Circling the Moon: Literature Circle Discussion

My Notes

Creating a Synthesis Poster

2. Work collaboratively with your Literature Circle group to synthesize the analysis from your meeting(s) into a creative poster. You should include elements of each Literature Circle role as follows:

- Interesting and thought-provoking questions from the Discussion Leader
- Insightful connections or predictions made by the Bridge Builder
- Images and/or graphic organizers created by the Artist
- Key quotes identified and interpreted by the Diction Detective
- Summary statements written by the Reporter
- A title for your poster based on a theme of the novel *Walk Two Moons*

3. After observing other posters, record an important idea that stands out to you from *Walk Two Moons* for each literary element.

An important idea about a **character(s)** is...	An important idea about a **conflict** is...	An important idea about the **plot or subplot** is...
An important idea about the **setting** is...	An important idea about a **theme** is...	Other thoughts I have...

Expository Writing Prompt: Think about your collaborative group experiences during this unit and your personal response to the experience. Write a paragraph explaining how communication and collaboration with your Literature Circle group helped you understand, appreciate, and analyze the novel. Be sure to

- Use a topic sentence.
- Elaborate with supporting detail and commentary.
- Use transitions.
- Use a variety of sentence structures.
- Use correct grammar, spelling, and punctuation.

 Independent Reading Checkpoint

Look back at your independent reading notes and write a summary of what you learned about changes.

Responding to Literature

Assignment

Write an expository response to the novel *Walk Two Moons*. Choose one of the following prompts:

- Explain how internal or external forces cause one character from the novel to grow or change.

- Identify one subplot from the novel and explain how it relates to the main plot of the novel.

- Describe one setting from the novel and explain why it is important to a character or to the plot.

- Discuss how plot, setting, character, or conflict contributes to one of the novel's themes.

Planning and Prewriting: Take time to choose and make a plan for your expository response.

- Which prompt do you feel best prepared to respond to in writing?

- How have the activities in this unit and the Literature Circle roles helped prepare you for this prompt?

- How can notes from your Literature Circle discussions and the synthesis posters support your response?

Drafting: Determine the key ideas to include.

- How can your response demonstrate your understanding of literary terms such as *plot/subplot, setting, character, conflict,* or *theme*?

- What elements of an effective expository essay will you use to organize your response?

- Which details from the novel will you use to support your ideas?

Evaluating and Revising the Draft: Create opportunities to review and revise your work.

- During the process of writing, when can you pause to share and respond with others?

- What is your plan to include suggestions and revision ideas into your draft?

- How can you revise your draft to use transitions and a variety of sentence structures?

- How can the Scoring Guide help you evaluate how well your draft meets the requirements of the assignment?

Checking and Editing for Publication: Confirm that your final draft is ready for publication.

- How will you check for grammatical and technical accuracy, such as proper spelling and punctuation?

Reflection

After completing this Embedded Assessment, think about how you went about accomplishing this task, and respond to the following:

- How would you adjust or change the Literature Circle experience to help you better analyze text?

My Notes

Technology TIP:

Use a shared drive or online document storage site to share and publish your work.

Responding to Literature

SCORING GUIDE

Scoring Criteria	Exemplary	Proficient	Emerging	Incomplete
Ideas	The response • conveys original ideas by analyzing a work of literature and explaining thoroughly how one or more literary elements contribute to the overall text • develops ideas with relevant supporting details and examples.	The response • conveys focused ideas by analyzing a work of literature and explaining how one or more literary elements contribute to the overall text • develops ideas with supporting details and examples.	The response • conveys ideas unevenly or partially explains how one or more literary elements contribute to the overall text • develops ideas with insufficient or irrelevant supporting details and examples.	The response • lacks analysis or explanation of how literary elements contribute to an overall text • uses minimal supporting details and examples.
Structure	The response • introduces the main idea in an engaging manner. • uses a well-chosen organizational structure that progresses smoothly to connect ideas. • uses a variety of effective transitions purposefully. • provides a satisfying conclusion.	The response • introduces the main idea clearly • uses an organizational structure that progresses logically to connect ideas • uses appropriate transitions to clarify the relationships among ideas • provides a logical conclusion.	The response • provides a weak or unclear introduction • uses a flawed or inconsistent organizational structure • uses inconsistent, repetitive, or basic transitions • provides a weak or disconnected conclusion.	The response • lacks an introduction • has little or no organizational structure • uses few or no transitions • lacks a conclusion.
Use of Language	The response • uses literary terms such as *plot/subplot, setting, character, conflict,* or *theme* in an insightful manner • demonstrates command of the conventions of standard English capitalization, punctuation, spelling, grammar, and usage (including pronoun agreement, sentence variety, and verb tense).	The response • uses literary terms such as *plot/subplot, setting, character, conflict,* or *theme* correctly • demonstrates adequate command of the conventions of standard English capitalization, punctuation, spelling, grammar, and usage (including pronoun agreement, sentence variety, and verb tense).	The response • uses literary terms incorrectly or insufficiently • demonstrates partial or inconsistent command of the conventions of standard English capitalization, punctuation, spelling, grammar, and usage (including pronoun agreement, sentence variety, and verb tense).	The response • fails to use literary terms • lacks command of the conventions of standard English capitalization, punctuation, spelling, grammar, and usage; frequent errors obscure meaning.

Previewing Embedded Assessment 2 and Expository Writing

Learning Targets
- Analyze and summarize the components of Embedded Assessment 2.
- Explore the positive and negative connotations of change, and write a paragraph about different types of changes.

LEARNING STRATEGIES:
Graphic Organizer, Drafting, Adding, Looping

Making Connections

In the first half of the unit, you saw how people sometimes turn to nature for comfort when going through a significant change in life, just as Sal relied on a tree for comfort in *Walk Two Moons*. Similarly, in this half of the unit, you will discover how animals, a part of nature, can also play a significant role in creating positive change in a person's everyday life.

My Notes

Essential Questions

Now that you have participated in a Literature Circle, would you change your answer to the first Essential Question on how talking and working with others can help one analyze a novel? If so, how would you change your answer? If not, why not?

_____

_____

_____

Developing Vocabulary

Look in your Reader/Writer Notebook at the new Academic Vocabulary words and Literary Terms you learned in the first half of this unit. Which words do you now know well, and which do you still need to learn more about?

_____

_____

_____

Unpacking Embedded Assessment 2

Read the assignment for Embedded Assessment 2: Writing an Expository Essay.

Your assignment is to write a multiparagraph expository essay explaining how people can enhance their lives through observing and interacting with animals. What can human beings learn from animals? In what ways can they help us? In your essay, give examples from your own life, from texts you have studied in this unit, from your independent reading, or from society that help support your explanation.

In your own words, summarize what you will need to know to complete this assessment successfully. With your class, create a graphic organizer to represent the skills and knowledge you will need to complete the tasks identified in the Embedded Assessment.

Previewing Embedded Assessment 2 and Expository Writing

My Notes

1. Think about how *change* can have positive or negative connotations—the feelings and ideas associated with a word in addition to its actual meaning. Brainstorm the feelings associated with a variety of changes. As you fill in the graphic organizer below, use three different colors: one color for positive changes, another for negative changes, and a third for neutral changes.

   • In the inner circle: List words and images to represent changes that have happened in *your life*.

   • In the outer circle: List words and images to represent changes that characters have experienced in *texts you have read*.

   • Between the lines of the box and the edge of the outer circle, list words and images to represent changes that you have observed in *society* (think about changes in science/technology, entertainment, the economy, your country, or your community).

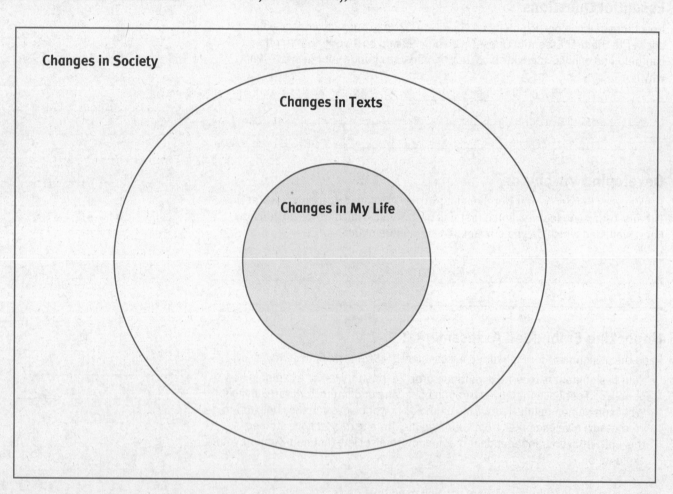

Changes in Society

Changes in Texts

Changes in My Life

2. You have now read several texts and explored different types of change. Revisit your graphic organizer about changes in society, texts, and your life. Use the information in the graphic organizer to write about what you have learned about the concept of change so far.

Consider using the following frame:

Title _____

1 We can observe changes in _____.

2 We read about changes in _____. [one word]

3 _____ is an example of a change in *Walk Two Moons*.

4 We also experience personal changes in _____.

5 _____ is an example of a personal change.

6 Changes in our country or our community are example of changes in _____ .
   [one word]

7 _____ is an example of a change in our country.

Check Your Understanding

How do these different types of changes have positive and negative connotations? Does a specific change always have the same connotation for everyone?

My Notes
_____
_____
_____
_____
_____

INDEPENDENT READING LINK

Read and Respond

With help from your teacher, librarian, and peers, find a book in which humans interact with animals. It could be a biography or autobiography. A biography is the story of another person's life. An autobiography is the story of one's own life. After you have read the book, collaborate with a partner to discuss how the interaction between humans and animals could create a positive change in a human's life.

Explaining and Interpreting Change

My Notes

Learning Targets

- Draft an expository paragraph about a change in life.
- Include key elements in an expository essay such as an introduction and supporting details.

In the next series of activities, you will practice writing an expository essay that incoporates examples from your own life, from texts, and from society or research to support your thesis on the concept of change. Think about changes in responsibilities, family relationships, friends, hobbies and interests, school, fears, physical appearance, and so on.

1. In the graphic organizer below, list each area of change as a topic on the top line inside a box. Then, on the lines below each box, write one complete sentence about the topic that could be used as a topic sentence for a paragraph. Remember that a topic sentence *controls the content of a paragraph, contains a subject, and reveals an opinion.*

Changes in Me

T.S.:

T.S.:

T.S.:

T.S.:

2. Read the following expository paragraph, and mark the text as follows:

- Underline the topic sentence.
- Scan the paragraph and put a star next to the writer's two new responsibilities.
- Circle the transitional words and phrases.
- Put an asterisk in front of the sentences that develop each of the writer's new responsibilities with commentary.

Sample Expository Paragraph

I have always had chores to do around the house, but this year I have more to do than ever before. The first thing that happened was that I got my first pet! Jeff, the gerbil, was a gift from my aunt, whose pet gerbil, Fluffy, had babies.   I got Jeff in April, and since then I have had total responsibility for his feeding and care. I have to be sure he has water and food every day. I also have to clean his cage every week and shred newspapers for the bottom of his cage. But the best part of this job is that I have to play with him every day so that he gets plenty of exercise.   My mom also expects me to take care of my little brother for a little while every day. Mainly, this means going into his room and playing with him for 30 minutes just before dinner. My mom asked me to do this so she can fix dinner without having to worry about Patrick. Patrick is only three, so I play kids' games with him like Memory, or I read a book to him, or sometimes we watch a video. During this time, I'm the only one who takes care of him. Sometimes, I have to feed him or take him to the bathroom. I like taking care of my brother, and my mom really appreciates it. Taking care of Jeff and Patrick is making me more responsible.

Expository Writing Prompt: On separate paper, draft a paragraph explaining an area of change in your life. Choose one of the areas of change from your graphic organizer. Be sure to

- Write a topic sentence that states a topic and an opinion.
- Include supporting details and commentary.
- Use transition words and a variety of sentence structures.

WORD CONNECTIONS

Roots and Affixes

The word *expository* is built on the Latin root *-pos-*, meaning "to put" or "to place." The Latin prefix *ex-* means "out" or "from." *Exposition* means "to put out" in the sense of "to make public." The suffix *-ory* makes an adjective.

My Notes

Explaining and Interpreting Change

My Notes

_____

_____

_____

_____

_____

_____

_____

_____

_____

_____

_____

3. In the spaces, mark "A" if you agree and "D" if you disagree with the statement about change.

1. _____ Change cannot be avoided.
2. _____ Change can be a good thing.
3. _____ People never really change.
4. _____ Change can ruin a friendship.
5. _____ Without change, a person cannot grow.
6. _____ Change is hard work.
7. _____ It's possible for one person to change the world.
8. _____ Change is usually uncomfortable.
9. _____ You should not try to change other people.
10. _____ Nothing ever really changes.

4. Choose one of the statements you strongly agree with, and explain why.

_____

_____

_____

Literary Terms

An **introduction** is the opening part of an essay, which should get the reader's attention and indicate the topic. The **hook** in the introduction is a compelling idea or statement designed to get the reader's attention. A **thesis statement** is a sentence in the introduction of an essay that states the writer's position or opinion on the topic of the essay.

5. Read the following sample **introduction** to an essay about change. Mark the text as follows:

- Underline the **hook**.
- Highlight the **thesis statement**.
- Circle or use a different color highlighter for the word that you think best describes the topic of the essay.

Benjamin Franklin once said, "When you're finished changing, you're finished." This means that in order to be truly alive, one must be changing and growing. I agree because every new experience can make a person change. Sometimes the change is positive, and other times it is negative. Either way, there is no avoiding change.

6. Fill out the graphic organizer on the next page by interpreting each quote, deciding if you agree or disagree, and explaining why.

_____

_____

_____

_____

_____

_____

_____

_____

_____

_____

_____

_____

Quotation	Interpretation: What does it mean?	Agree or Disagree?	Reason: Why do you agree or disagree?
"When you're finished changing, you're finished." –Benjamin Franklin			
"There's nothing wrong with change, if it is in the right direction." –Winston Churchill			
"If you don't like something, change it. If you can't change it, change your attitude." –Maya Angelou			
"Be the change you want to see in the world." –Mahatma Ghandi			
"Not everything that is faced can be changed. But nothing can be changed until it is faced." –James Arthur Baldwin			
"They say time changes things, but you actually have to change them yourself." --Andy Warhol			

Expository Writing Prompt: Choose a quote from the graphic organizer, and use it as you draft an introductory paragraph on the topic of change. Be sure to

- Include a hook.
- Write a statement about the quote.
- Include a thesis that states a strong opinion about your agreement with the quote.

Writing and Changing Together

My Notes

Learning Targets

- Draft a conclusion to an expository essay.
- Revise expository writing to include parallel structure.

1. You have already written an introduction for an expository essay and an expository paragraph about a change in your life. Work together with your class to draft an additional body paragraph about a change in a character from a book or story you have read together. Be sure to include these elements:

   - Topic sentence: A sentence that includes a subject and an opinion that works directly to support the thesis
   - Transitions: Words used to connect ideas (*for example, for instance*)
   - Supporting information: Specific examples, details, evidence, and facts
   - Commentary: Sentences that explain how the information is relevant to the thesis/topic sentence and bring a sense of closure to the paragraph

   _____

   _____

   _____

   _____

   _____

   _____

   _____

   _____

   _____

   _____

   _____

   _____

   _____

   _____

2. On a separate page, work with a partner or small group to draft another expository paragraph about a change in the world. Begin by revisiting the graphic organizer you completed in Activity 2.14. Agree on a change that has taken place in society, science/technology, entertainment, the economy, your country, or your community. Make sure you include all the elements of a body paragraph listed above.

3. With your class and your writing group, discuss the elements of an effective **conclusion**. What questions should a conclusion answer?

_____

_____

_____

Literary Terms
A **conclusion** is one or more paragraphs that bring the essay to a close and leave an impression with the reader.

4. Read through your introduction and three body paragraphs on the topic of change. Write one sentence that sums up what you said about change (the literal). Add a sentence that explains what change means to you, other people, and the world (the interpretive). Add at least one more sentence explaining why change matters (the universal).

Literal:

Interpretive:

Universal:

My Notes

5. You have now constructed all of the elements of an expository essay about change. Organize the paragraphs using the outline below, and then follow your teacher's instructions to prepare a cohesive draft before revising.

I. Introduction (See Activity 2.14)

II. Support paragraph about a change in yourself (See Activity 2.14)

III. Support paragraph about a change from a text (this activity)

IV. Support paragraph about a change from society (this activity)

V. Conclusion (this activity)

© 2017 College Board. All rights reserved.

My Notes

Introducing the Strategy: Replacing

When you revise by *replacing*, you focus on your use of language to create meaning and effect. Begin by circling words that are meaningless, boring, or awkwardly placed. For each circled word, select two new words and write them above the original word or in the margin. Use a variety of resources to find new words, including a thesaurus, your Reader/Writer Notebook, and the Word Wall. Read your sentence twice, each time with a different replacement word. Decide which word most precisely conveys your intended meaning, and cross out the other.

6. Revise the conclusion below, using the replacing strategy. Circle three words to replace, and write them underneath the paragraph. Use your vocabulary resources to select two replacement words for each circled word. Read the sentence(s) twice, each time with a different word. Circle the best option.

Change is good. Some people try not to change, but they are just wasting their time. I like change because it keeps me from being bored all the time. Try not to think about bad changes because that will just make you sad. Instead think about the good things that have happened to you, and you will realize that those are changes too.

Word 1: _____ Replacement Options: 1. _____ 2. _____
Word 2: _____ Replacement Options: 1. _____ 2. _____
Word 3: _____ Replacement Options: 1. _____ 2. _____

7. **Practice:** Look at your expository essay on change. Circle three words to replace, and use your vocabulary resources to select two replacement words for each circled word. Record your work below. Read the sentence(s) twice, each time with a different word. Circle the best option. Finally, explain how your revisions strengthen the text.

Word 1: _____ Replacement Options: 1. _____ 2. _____
Word 2: _____ Replacement Options: 1. _____ 2. _____
Word 3: _____ Replacement Options: 1. _____ 2. _____

Language and Writer's Craft: Parallel Structure

Parallel structure involves arranging words, phrases, and clauses in a series using the same grammatical structure to show that two or more similar things are of equal importance. Using parallel structure is a way of composing interesting and effective sentences. You can sometimes improve sentences by combining two or three ideas into one sentence.

The following sentences contain a series of items in parallel structure. Use these sentences as patterns to copy. Notice especially the punctuation.

- Carrie loved swimming, running, and playing tennis.
- His eyes were swollen shut, his face was red and puffy, and his nose was lopsided.
- Every day John walked in the door, threw his backpack on the chair, and opened the refrigerator.
- You may sit in the back, you may sit in the front, or you may sit anywhere in between.

8. Combine the ideas in the following sentences using parallel structure. These sentences are taken from the excerpt from *Travels with Charley* and the article "Saying Farewell to a Faithful Pal," both of which are stories about dogs that you will read later in this unit.

- Charley became a maniac. He leaped all over me. He cursed and growled. He also snarled and screamed.

  _____

  _____

- Marley chewed couches. He slashed screens. He also was a slinger of drool and a tipper of trash cans.

  _____

  _____

9. Reread your expository essay about change. Apply the revision strategies that you have learned in this unit to improve your writing.
- Combine ideas by using parallel structure or compound sentences.
- Add details, commentary, and figurative language.
- Replace words to make your language more precise, interesting, and original.

Check Your Understanding

Reflect on the changes you made to your essay and how these changes improved your writing. What will you be sure to do when you write your next expository essay?

GRAMMAR & USAGE
Commas

Use **commas** to separate words and word groups in a **series** of three or more items. Include a comma before the conjunction.
Do not use commas in a series when all items are linked by *and*, *or*, or *nor*.

My Notes

Traveling with Charley: Literary Nonfiction

pick

LEARNING STRATEGIES:
Chunking the Text, Diffusing, Visualizing

My Notes

Learning Targets

- Analyze the genre of literary nonfiction and summarize key ideas.
- Find textual evidence to support my analysis of a text.

Introducing the Strategy: Diffusing

With this strategy, you use context clues to help find the meaning of unknown words. When **diffusing**, underline words that are unfamiliar. Think of two possible substitutions (synonyms), and confirm your definition. You can confirm your definition by checking reference sources such as a dictionary or a thesaurus.

Your teacher will model how to diffuse a text, starting with the first chunk of the excerpt from *Travels with Charley*. In a small group, use context clues and dictionaries to diffuse the text of an additional chunk. Finally, meet with students who diffused the other chunks in order to share your notes and diffuse the rest of the text.

Preview

In this activity, you will read an example of literary nonfiction and write an analysis of the text.

Setting a Purpose for Reading

- *Travels with Charley* is a **nonfiction** story. As you read, mark the text by highlighting passages with strong **imagery** and description that you can picture in your head.

Literary Terms

Nonfiction text is writing that is based on facts and actual events. In contrast, **fiction** is writing that consists of imagined events.

Imagery refers to the descriptive or figurative language used to create word pictures.

ABOUT THE AUTHOR

John Steinbeck (1902—1968) was born in California. He wrote several novels and short stories but is best known for *The Grapes of Wrath*. He won the Nobel Prize in Literature in 1962. In the fall of 1960, Steinbeck decided that he had lost touch with America. He outfitted a three-quarter-ton pickup truck with a camper shell and set off from his home in New York with his French poodle, Charley, to drive cross-country. The idea was that he would travel alone, stay at campgrounds, and reconnect with the country by talking to the locals he met along the way. Steinbeck's account of his journey, *Travels with Charley: In Search of America*, became a bestseller and classic of American travel writing.

Literary Nonfiction

from Travels with Charley: In Search of America

by John Steinbeck

Chunk 1

I must confess to a laxness in the matter of National Parks. I haven't visited many of them. Perhaps this is because they enclose the **unique**, the spectacular, the **astounding**—the greatest waterfall, the deepest canyon, the highest cliff, the most stupendous works of man or nature. And I would rather see a good Brady photograph than Mount Rushmore. For it is my opinion that we enclose and celebrate the freaks of our nation and of our civilization. Yellowstone National Park is no more **representative** of America than is Disneyland.

This being my natural attitude, I don't know what made me turn sharply south and cross a state line to take a look at Yellowstone. Perhaps it was a fear of my neighbors. I could hear them say, "You mean you were that near to Yellowstone and didn't go? You must be crazy." Again it might have been the American **tendency** in travel. One goes, not so much to see but to tell afterward. Whatever my purpose in going to Yellowstone, I'm glad I went because I discovered something about Charley I might never have known.

Chunk 2

A pleasant-looking National Park man checked me in and then he said, "How about that dog? They aren't permitted in except on leash."

"Why?" I asked.

"Because of the bears."

"Sir," I said, "this is a unique dog. He does not live by tooth or fang. He respects the right of cats to be cats although he doesn't admire them. He turns his steps rather than disturb an earnest caterpillar. His greatest fear is that someone will point out a rabbit and suggest that he chase it. This is a dog of peace and tranquility. I suggest that the greatest danger to your bears will be pique at being ignored by Charley."

The young man laughed. "I wasn't so much worried about the bears," he said. "But our bears have developed intolerance for dogs. One of them might demonstrate his **prejudice** with a clip on the chin, and then—no dog."

"I'll lock him in the back, sir. I promise you Charley will cause no ripple in the bear world, and as an old bear-looker, neither will I."

"I just have to warn you," he said. "I have no doubt your dog has the best of intentions. On the other hand, our bears have the worst. Don't leave food about. Not only do they steal but they are **critical** of anyone who tries to **reform** them. In a word, don't believe their sweet faces or you might get clobbered. And don't let the dog wander. Bears don't argue."

My Notes

My Notes

Chunk 3

We went on our way into the wonderland of nature gone nuts, and you will have to believe what happened. The only way I can prove it would be to get a bear.

Less than a mile from the entrance I saw a bear beside the road, and it ambled out as though to flag me down. Instantly a change came over Charley. He shrieked with rage. His lips flared, showing wicked teeth that have some trouble with a dog biscuit. He screeched insults at the bear, which hearing, the bear reared up and seemed to me to overtop Rocinante. Frantically I rolled the windows shut and, swinging quickly to the left, grazed the animal, then scuttled on while Charley raved and ranted beside me, describing in detail what he would do to that bear if he could get at him. I was never so astonished in my life. To the best of my knowledge Charley had never seen a bear, and in his whole history had showed great **tolerance** for every living thing. Besides all this, Charley is a coward, so deep-seated a coward that he has developed a **technique** for concealing it. And yet he showed every evidence of wanting to get out and murder a bear that outweighed him a thousand to one. I don't understand it.

Chunk 4

A little farther along two bears showed up, and the effect was doubled. Charley became a maniac. He leaped all over me, he cursed and growled, snarled and screamed. I didn't know he had the ability to snarl. Where did he learn it? Bears were in good supply, and the road became a nightmare. For the first time in his life Charley resisted reason, even resisted a cuff on the ear. He became a **primitive** killer lusting for the blood of his enemy, and up to this moment he had no enemies. In a bear-less stretch, I opened the cab, took Charley by the collar, and locked him in the house. But that did no good. When we passed other bears he leaped on the table and scratched at the windows trying to get out at them. I could hear canned goods crashing as he struggled in his mania. Bears simply brought out the Hyde in my Jekyll-headed dog. What could have caused it? Was it a pre-breed memory of a time when the wolf was in him? I know him well. Once in a while he tries a **bluff**, but it is a palpable lie. I swear that this was no lie. I am certain that if he were released he would have charged every bear we passed and found victory or death.

Chunk 5

It was too nerve-wracking, a shocking spectacle, like seeing an old, calm friend go insane. No amount of natural wonders, of **rigid** cliffs and belching waters, of smoking springs could even engage my attention while that pandemonium went on.

After about the fifth **encounter** I gave up, turned Rocinante about, and retraced my way. If I had stopped the night and bears gathered to my cooking, I dare not think what would have happened.

At the gate the park guard checked me out. "You didn't stay long. Where's the dog?"

"Locked up back there. And I owe you an apology. That dog has the heart and soul of a bear-killer and I didn't know it. **Heretofore** he has been a little tender-hearted toward an underdone steak."

"Yea!" he said. "That happens sometimes. That's why I warned you. A bear dog would know his chances, but I've seen a Pomeranian go up like a puff of smoke. You know, a well-favored bear can bat a dog like a tennis ball."

Chunk 6

I moved fast, back the way I had come, and I was **reluctant** to camp for fear there might be some unofficial non-government bears about. That night I spent in a pretty

auto court near Livingston. I had my dinner in a restaurant, and when I had settled in with a drink and a comfortable chair and my bathed bare feet on the carpet with red roses, I inspected Charley. He was dazed. His eyes held a faraway look and he was totally exhausted, emotionally no doubt. Mostly he reminded me of a man coming out of a long, hard drunk—worn out, depleted, and collapsed. He couldn't eat his dinner, he refused the evening walk, and once we were in he collapsed on the floor and went to sleep. In the night I heard him whining and yapping, and when I turned on the light his feet were making running gestures and his body jerked and his eyes were wide open, but it was only a night bear. I awakened him and gave him some water. This time he went to sleep and didn't stir all night. In the morning he was still tired. I wonder why we think the thoughts and emotions of animals are simple.

Second Read

- Reread the excerpt to answer these text-dependent comprehension questions.
- Write any additional questions you have about the text in your Reader/Writer Notebook.

1. **Craft and Structure:** What is Steinbeck's point of view about national parks? How is this point of view conveyed in the text?

2. **Knowledge and Ideas:** What evidence does Steinbeck give to the ranger to convince him that his dog should be allowed in the national park?

3. **Key Ideas and Details:** What evidence from the texts supports the ranger's attitude toward bears? What evidence from the text supports Steinbeck's attitude toward bears?

4. **Craft and Structure:** Explain how the sentence "The only way I can prove it would be to get a bear" fits into the story.

5. **Key Ideas and Details:** Which details tell how Steinbeck feels at the change in Charley's behavior?

My Notes

INDEPENDENT READING LINK

Read and Respond

Use at least two of the reading strategies from this activity (Diffusing, Chunking, Visualizing) on your independent reading book. Which did you choose, and how did they help you make meaning of the text? Write about how you used these strategies on your independent reading in your Reader/Writer Notebook and/or your Independent Reading Log.

My Notes

Working from the Text

6. Underline the last line of the text. What conclusion does Steinbeck make about animals?

7. What happened in the text that led him to this conclusion? With a partner or small group, go back through the text looking for sentences or passages that support Steinbeck's conclusion. Copy a line or summarize a passage from the text:

8. Describe how the line or passage supports Steinbeck's conclusion about animals.

9. Why do you think Steinbeck brought his dog along on this trip?

Check Your Understanding

Write a paragraph about the central idea of the story. Be sure to explain how the details in the story support and elaborate on the central idea.

Reflecting on Marley: Textual Evidence

Learning Targets
- Identify and interpret textual evidence.
- Write a response to a prompt, using textual evidence to support a thesis.

Preview
In this activity, you will read a memoir and use textual evidence in response to a writing prompt.

Setting a Purpose for Reading
- You will next read a newspaper column written by John Grogan about the death of his dog Marley. Mark the text by underlining or highlighting phrases, sentences, and clauses that tell why Grogan loved his dog despite his many faults.
- Circle unknown words and phrases. Try to determine the meaning of the words by using context clues, word parts, or a dictionary.

ABOUT THE AUTHOR

John Grogan (1957 –) is a newspaper columnist and the author of the bestselling memoir *Marley and Me*, a book based on the ideas in the article you are about to read. *Marley and Me* has been adapted into a young reader's edition, several children's books, and a major motion picture. Grogan says he began writing in school because he "was so bad at everything else." In addition to *Marley and Me*, he has written articles for numerous magazines and newspapers.

Memoir

Saying Farewell
to a Faithful Pal

by John Grogan, Inquirer Columnist

1 In the gray of dawn, I found the shovel in the garage and walked down the hill to where the lawn meets the woods. There, beneath a wild cherry tree, I began to dig.

2 The earth was loose and blessedly unfrozen, and the work went fast. It was odd being out in the backyard without Marley, the Labrador retriever who for 13 years made it his business to be tight by my side for every excursion out the door, whether to pick a tomato, pull a weed, or fetch the mail. And now here I was alone, digging him this hole.

3 "There will never be another dog like Marley," my father said when I told him the news, that I finally had to put the old guy down. It was as close to a compliment as our pet ever received.

My Notes

Reflecting on Marley: Textual Evidence

gusto: hearty enjoyment

bounded: moved by leaping or jumping

despite: in spite of

WORD CONNECTIONS

Etymology

The word *hallmark* is built from the words *hall* and *mark*. *Hall* refers to Goldsmiths' Hall in London, where gold and silver were tested for purity and stamped. *Hallmark* means "a mark of excellence, quality, or purity."

optimism: the tendency to see the best in all things

4 No one ever called him a great dog—or even a good dog. He was as wild as a banshee and as strong as a bull. He crashed joyously through life with a **gusto** most often associated with natural disasters.

5 He's the only dog I've ever known to get expelled from obedience school.

6 Marley was a chewer of couches, a slasher of screens, a slinger of drool, a tipper of trash cans. He was so big he could eat off the kitchen table with all four paws planted on the floor—and did so whenever we weren't looking.

7 Marley shredded more mattresses and dug through more drywall than I care to remember, almost always out of sheer terror brought on by his mortal enemy, thunder.

CUTE BUT DUMB

8 He was a majestic animal, nearly 100 pounds of quivering muscle wrapped in a luxurious fur coat the color of straw. As for brains, let me just say he chased his tail til the day he died, apparently he was on the verge of a major canine breakthrough.

9 That tail could clear a coffee table in one swipe. We lost track of the things he swallowed, including my wife's gold necklace, which we eventually recovered, shinier than ever. We took him with us once to a chi-chi outdoor café and tied him to the heavy wrought-iron table. Big mistake. Marley spotted a cute poodle and off he **bounded**, table in tow.

10 But his heart was pure.

11 When I brought my wife home from the doctor after our first pregnancy ended in a miscarriage, that wild beast gently rested his blocky head in her lap and just whimpered. And when babies finally arrived, he somehow understood they were something special and let them climb all over him, tugging his ears and pulling out little fistfuls of fur. One day when a stranger tried to hold one of the children, our jolly giant showed a ferocity we never imagined was inside him.

12 As the years passed, Marley mellowed, and sleeping became his favorite pastime. By the end, his hearing was shot, his teeth were gone, his hips so riddled with arthritis he barely could stand. **Despite** the infirmities, he greeted each day with the mischievous glee that was his hallmark. Just days before his death, I caught him with his head stuck in the garbage pail.

LIFE LESSONS LEARNED

13 A person can learn a lot from a dog, even a loopy one like ours.

14 Marley taught me about living each day with unbridled exuberance and joy, about seizing the moment and following your heart. He taught me to appreciate the simple things—a walk in the woods, a fresh snowfall, a nap in a shaft of winter sunlight. And as he grew old and achy, he taught me about **optimism** in the face of adversity.

15 Mostly, he taught me about friendship and selflessness and, above all else, unwavering loyalty.

16 When his time came last week, I knelt beside him on the floor of the animal hospital, rubbing his gray snout as the veterinarian discussed cremation with me. No, I told her, I would be taking him home with me.

17 The next morning, our family would stand over the hole I had dug and say goodbye. The kids would tuck drawings in beside him. My wife would speak for us all when she'd say: "God, I'm going to miss that big, dumb **lug**."

lug: an awkward, clumsy fellow

18 But now I had a few minutes with him before the doctor returned. I thought back over his 13 years—the destroyed furniture and goofy antics; the sloppy kisses and utter **devotion**. All in all, not a bad run.

devotion: dedication

19 I didn't want him to leave this world believing all his bad press. I rested my forehead against his and said: "Marley, you are a great dog."

Second Read

- Reread the memoir to answer these text-dependent comprehension questions.
- Write any additional questions you have about the text in your Reader/Writer Notebook.

1. **Craft and Structure:** How do the first two sentences of the memoir contribute to the text? What is the effect of these sentences on the reader?

2. **Key Ideas and Details:** What kind of personality does Marley have? What details in the text illustrate his personality?

3. **Knowledge and Ideas:** Which evidence supports the statement that Marley's heart was pure?

4. **Craft and Structure:** In paragraphs 13 and 14, what are the connotations of the words *loopy* and *unbridled*? How do these words help the reader understand Marley?

My Notes

Reflecting on Marley: Textual Evidence

My Notes

5. **Craft and Structure:** What was the author's purpose for writing the memoir? How is the author's purpose conveyed in the text?

Working from the Text

6. Copy your textual evidence into the graphic organizer below.

Textual Evidence	Importance: What does the evidence tell you about Grogan's feelings for his dog?

WRITING to SOURCES   Expository Writing Prompt

Why do people have pets? Using John Grogan and Marley as examples, explain what human beings love about and learn from their pets. Be sure to

- Write a thesis statement (or topic sentence if the response is only one paragraph) including the topic and your opinion.
- Use textual evidence and supporting details from the newspaper column.
- Add personal commentary.

Making Connections Through Research

Learning Targets

- Closely read and analyze an autobiographical text about how animals can help people, citing text evidence to support analysis and inferences.
- Conduct research to answer questions about how animals help people.

Preview

In this activity, you will read an excerpt from an autobiography and conduct research to answer questions generated from the text.

Setting a Purpose for Reading

- Read the excerpt and star the main idea.
- Underline details that support the main idea.
- Circle unknown words and phrases. Try to determine the meaning of the words by using context clues, word parts, or a dictionary.

> **ABOUT THE AUTHOR**
> Temple Grandin (1947–) was born in Boston, Massachusetts. She is an American doctor of animal science and a professor at Colorado State University, a bestselling author, and a consultant to the livestock industry on animal behavior. As a person with high-functioning autism, Grandin is also widely noted for her work in autism advocacy. Autism is a disorder of neural development characterized by impaired social interaction and communication and by restricted and repetitive behavior.

LEARNING STRATEGIES:
KWHL, Diffusing, Visualizing

My Notes

Autobiography

"Dogs Make Us Human"
from *Animals in Translation*

by Temple Grandin and Catherine Johnson

The aborigines have a saying: "Dogs make us human." Now we know that's probably **literally** true. People wouldn't have become who we are today if we hadn't **co-evolved** with dogs.

I think it's also true, though in a different way, that all animals make us human. That's why I hope we will start to think more respectfully about animal intelligence and talent. That would be good for people, because there are a lot of things we can't do that animals can. We could use their help.

But it would be good for animals, too. Dogs first started living with people because people needed dogs and dogs needed people. Now dogs still need people, but people have forgotten how much they need dogs for anything besides love and

literally: actually, without exaggeration
co-evolved: evolved at the same time, having a close ecological relationship and acting as agents of natural selection for each other

Making Connections Through Research

practically: almost, nearly

My Notes

companionship. That's probably okay for a dog who's been bred to be a companion animal, but a lot of the bigger breeds and **practically** all of the mix breeds were built for work. Having a job to do is a part of their nature; it's who they are. The sad thing is, now that hardly anyone makes his living herding sheep, most dogs are out of a job.

It doesn't have to be that way. I read a little story on the Web site for the American Veterinary Medical Association that shows the incredible things animals are capable of doing, and would do if we gave them a chance. It was about a dog named Max who had trained himself to monitor his mistress's blood sugar levels even while she was asleep. No one knows how Max was doing this, but my guess is people must smell slightly different when their blood sugar is low, and Max had figured that out. The lady who owned him was a severe diabetic, and if her blood sugar levels got low during the night Max would wake up her husband and bug him until he got up and took care of her.

You have to think about that story for only five seconds to realize how much dogs have to offer. Dogs and a lot of other animals.

Second Read

* Reread the excerpt to answer these text-dependent comprehension questions.
* Write any additional questions you have about the text in your Reader/Writer Notebook.

1. **Craft and Structure:** What can you tell about how Grandin thinks about animals from the first two paragraphs? How do you know?

2. **Knowledge and Ideas:** What evidence does Grandin give to support the idea that animals helping humans can be good for the animals too?

3. **Key Ideas and Details:** What is the central idea of this text? Which details support the central idea?

Working from the Text

4. What questions do you have about dogs as pets after reading this text? What else would you like to know?

_____

_____

_____

_____

_____

Conducting Research

Expository writing provides information about a topic, which often means researching the topic to learn more about it and to find evidence for your writing.

5. What do you know about conducting research? What experience do you have with it? Number the lines below 1 to 6 to show a logical order for the research process.

_____ Write questions that can be answered through research.

_____ Evaluate sources.

_____ Identify the topic, issue, or problem.

_____ Communicate findings.

_____ Draw conclusions.

_____ Gather evidence and refocus when necessary.

6. Use a KWHL graphic organizer to guide your research on the topic of animals helping people. First, fill out the first two columns.

K: What do you **know** about the ways that animals help people? Try to think of at least three ways that animals can help people live better lives.

W: What do you **want** to know about the ways that animals help people?

Second, fill in the "**H**" column with the title and author of the text you just read.

Making Connections Through Research

Topic: Animals Helping People			
K Thinking about what you already KNOW helps you focus on your topic.	**W** Thinking about what you WANT to know helps you create questions to guide your research.	**H** Thinking about HOW and where you will find information helps you identify possible resources that match your questions.	**L** Thinking about what you LEARNED helps you draw conclusions in order to communicate your findings.

INDEPENDENT READING LINK

Read and Connect

Is there anything related to the research topic in your independent reading? Add information to your KWHL chart. Be sure to note any similarities and differences between the information in your research and the information in your independent reading.

7. Add to the **L** column information about what you learned from reading "Dogs Make Us Human." What did you learn about animals helping people?

8. Add to the **W** column new questions you have. In the **H** column, brainstorm how and where you will conduct research to answer your questions.

9. Follow your teacher's instructions on how to gather more research about animals helping people. As you do, complete the KWHL chart.

Check Your Understanding

After doing additional research and reading, summarize the research process you used and describe how it helped you answer the questions you wrote in your KWHL chart.

My Notes

_____

_____

_____

_____

Synthesizing Temple's Story

Learning Targets
- Analyze and summarize the main ideas in a text.
- Apply reading strategies to an autobiography and use textual evidence to respond to a writing prompt.

Preview
In this activity, you will watch a film and read excerpts from an autobiography and biography in order to synthesize information to answer a writing prompt.

Setting a Purpose for Viewing
- As you view clips from the biographical film *Temple Grandin*, use the double-entry journal below to take notes. Record descriptions, events, and observations on the left side. Add your questions, connections, predictions, responses, and commentary on the right side.

Biographical Film *Temple Grandin*	My Personal Commentary

Working from the Film
1. Write a thesis statement about the film *Temple Grandin*. Be sure to include the topic and an opinion.

LEARNING STRATEGIES:
Graphic Organizer, Marking the Text, Double-Entry Journal

My Notes

Synthesizing Temple's Story

Reading Strategies Review

2. You have used a variety of reading strategies in this unit. Rate your understanding of each strategy in the chart below. Then add one or two additional reading strategies that you are ready to use on your own. Consult the Reading Strategies section in the Resources at the end of this book for a complete list and description of all the reading strategies.

Reading Strategy	I'm still getting familiar with this strategy.	I am comfortable using this strategy with a little help.	I am ready to use this strategy on my own.
Chunking the Text			
Using Context Clues (Diffusing)			
Marking the Text			
Questioning the Text			
Graphic Organizer			
Summarizing			
Double-Entry Journal			

3. Choose two of these strategies to help you make meaning of the text you will read next.

Strategy 1: _____

Strategy 2: _____

Setting a Purpose for Reading

- As you read the text, use the strategies you listed and look for textual evidence of how animals helped the author deal with her autism.
- Circle unknown words and phrases. Try to determine the meaning of the words by using context clues, word parts, or a dictionary.

My Notes

_____

_____

_____

_____

_____

_____

Autobiography

"My Story"

from *Animals in Translation*

by Temple Grandin and Catherine Johnson

1 People who aren't autistic always ask me about the moment I realized I could understand the way animals think. They think I must have had an epiphany.

2 But it wasn't like that. It took me a long time to figure out that I see things about animals other people don't. And it wasn't until I was in my forties that I finally realized I had one big advantage over the feedlot owners who were hiring me to manage their animals: being autistic. Autism made school and social life hard, but it made animals easy.

3 I started to fall in love with animals in high school when my mother sent me to a special boarding school for gifted children with emotional problems. Back then they called everything "emotional problems." Mother had to find a place for me because I got kicked out of high school for fighting. I got in fights because kids teased me. They'd call me names, like "Retard," or "Tape recorder."

4 They called me Tape Recorder because I'd stored up a lot of phrases in my memory and I used them over and over again in every conversation. Plus there were only a few conversations I like to have, so that **amplified** the effect. I especially like to talk about the rotor ride at the carnival. I would go up to somebody and say, "I went to Nantasket Park and I went on the rotor and I really liked the way it pushed me up against the wall." Then I say stuff like, "How did you like it?" and they'd say how they liked it, and then I'd tell the story all over again, start to finish. It was like a loop inside my head, it just ran over and over again. So the other kids called me Tape Recorder.

5 Teasing hurts. The kids would tease me, so I'd get mad and smack 'em. That simple. They always started it, they liked to see me react.

6 My new school solved that problem. The school had a stable and horses for the kids to ride, and the teachers took away horseback riding privileges if I smacked somebody. After I lost privileges enough times I learned just to cry when somebody did something bad to me. I'd cry, and that would take away the aggression. I still cry when people are mean to me.

7 Nothing ever happened to the kids who were teasing.

8 The funny thing about the school was, the horses had emotional problems, too. They had emotional problems because in order to save money the headmaster was buying cheap horses. They'd been marked down because they had gigantic behavior problems. They were pretty, their legs were fine, but emotionally they were a mess. The school had nine horses altogether, and two of them couldn't be ridden at all. Half of the horses in that barn had serious **psychological** problems. But I didn't understand that as a fourteen-year-old.

9 So there we all were up at boarding school, a bunch of emotionally disturbed teenagers living with a bunch of emotionally disturbed animals. There was one horse, Lady, who was a good horse when you rode her in the ring, but on the trail

My Notes

amplified: made larger, greater, or stronger

psychological: pertaining to the mind

Synthesizing Temple's Story

she would go berserk. She would rear, and constantly jump around and prance; you had to hold her back with the bridle or she'd bolt to the barn.

10 Then there was Beauty. You could ride Beauty, but he had very nasty habits like kicking and biting while you were in the saddle. He would swing his foot up and kick you in the leg or foot, or turn his head around and bite your knee. You had to watch out. Whenever you tried to mount Beauty he kicked *and* bit—you had both ends coming at you at the same time....

11 All the horses at the school had been abused. Beauty had been kept locked in a dairy stanchion all day long. I don't know why. These were badly abused animals; they were very, very messed up.

savant: someone that knows an extensive amount about a subject

12 But I had no understanding of this as a girl. I was never mean to the horses at the school (the other kids were sometimes), but I wasn't any horse-whispering autistic **savant**, either. I just loved the horses. I was so wrapped up in them that I spent every spare moment working the barns. I was dedicated to keeping the barn clean, making sure the horses were groomed. One of the high points of my high school career was the day my mom bought me a really nice English bridle and saddle. ...

13 Boy did I take care of that saddle. I loved it so much I didn't even leave it in the tack room where it belonged. I brought it up to my **dorm** every day and kept it with me. I bought special saddle soap and leather conditioner from the saddle shop, and I spent hours washing and polishing it. ...

dorm: a building where students live and sleep

14 Animals kept me going. I spent every waking minute that I didn't have to be studying or going to school with those horses. I even rode Lady at a show. It's hard to imagine today, a school keeping a stable of emotionally disturbed and dangerous horses for its underaged students to ride. These days you can't even play dodgeball in gym class because somebody might get hurt. But that's the way it was. A lot of us got nipped or stepped on or thrown at that school, but no one was ever seriously hurt, at least not while I was there. So it worked out.

15 I wish more kids could ride horses today. People and animals are supposed to be together. We spent quite a long time evolving together, and we used to be partners. Now people are cut off from animals unless they have a dog or a cat.

Second Read

- Reread the excerpt to answer these text-dependent comprehension questions.
- Write any additional questions you have about the text in your Reader/Writer Notebook.

1. **Craft and Structure:** How does paragraph 2 contribute to the development of the text?

2. **Key Ideas and Details:** How does Grandin change as a result of her new school? How is this change explained in the text?

3. **Knowledge and Ideas:** What evidence from the text supports the idea that Grandin loved the saddle her mom gave her?

4. **Key Ideas and Details:** What does Grandin mean by saying "Animals kept me going"? What evidence from the text helps support your inference?

Setting a Purpose for Reading

- Read the excerpt and continue to use the strategies you listed and look for textual evidence of how animals helped Temple Grandin deal with her autism.
- Circle unknown words and phrases. Try to determine the meaning of the words by using context clues, word parts, or a dictionary.

Biography

Excerpt from Chapter 6
Hampshire School for
Wayward Wizards

Temple Grandin: How the Girl Who Loved Cows Embraced Autism and Changed the World
by Sy Montgomery

1 …But the memories she treasures most from high school are of the horses. All these years later, she remembers each of them by name. Bay Lady was the horse she rode most of the time: great in the ring—but halfway on the trail she'd prance and plunge. Otherwise she was the "perfect lady. " Star couldn't compete in horse shows because she had ankle problems. Circus, a big, gentle horse, died of colic, a **digestive** disease brought on by eating oat straw. Beauty was gorgeous, but he bit and kicked. Teddy was gentle enough for the littlest kids. King was an old gray horse, so well-mannered that just about anyone could ride him: then you could graduate to riding someone like Flash or Silver. Lady was hot-tempered, and her eyes were wild. "Nobody could ride that horse," Tina Henegar, another schoolmate, remembered. "But Temple could—and beautifully. She was the best."

2 Temple loved them all and could ride better than anyone.

3 It's no wonder. Horses, like autistic people, are very sensitive to detail and don't like change. That's why a horse might be frightened by a new white hat, but not a familiar black one—or might panic at the sight of a common object like a wheelbarrow in an unusual place or seen from a different angle. Temple could tell when a horse was starting to get nervous: a fearful horse swishes his tail, and the swishing becomes more rapid with **mounting** fear. But because Temple also noticed

My Notes

wayward: turned away from what is right or proper

digestive: pertaining to the process by which food is broken down by the body

mounting: increasing

the same details the horses did—like a bale of hay slightly out of place—she could make small changes to calm the animal's fear before it turned to panic.

4 Temple spent much of her time in the horse barn. She cleaned the stalls. She refilled the feed bins. She cleaned the leather bridles and saddles and other equipment, making repairs if needed. When the farrier came to hammer new shoes onto the horses' hooves, she held the reins and kept the horses calm.

5 Back at home, Temple's mother wished her daughter would study harder and get better grades instead of riding horses and mending bridles. But Temple was proud that she now had an important, responsible job in the barn. The **welfare** of nine horses depended largely on her care. To Temple, her academic classes didn't seem to matter half as much. They were "boring, boring, boring."

6 Soon she began to find it impossible to concentrate on schoolwork anyway. Now in high school, she felt that something new and terrible was happening to her. Her body was changing. The rush of new chemicals her body was producing to change her into a young woman threw Temple's unusual brain into overdrive. She started having panic attacks.

welfare: health and happiness

My Notes

Second Read

- Reread the excerpt to answer these text-dependent comprehension questions.
- Write any additional questions you have about the text in your Reader/Writer Notebook.

5. **Craft and Structure:** What is the author's point of view about Grandin's autism? How is the point of view conveyed in the text?

6. **Knowledge and Ideas:** Compare the two passages, noticing that both talk about Temple's relationship to horses and their importance in her life. Which of the two selections gives you more insight into the significance of this experience? Give textual evidence to show why you think this.

Working from the Text

WRITING to SOURCES Expository Writing Prompt

How did animals help Temple Grandin deal with the challenges of autism? Be sure to

- Write a thesis statement including the topic and your opinion.
- Use textual evidence and supporting details from both sources.
- Add personal commentary.

 Independent Reading Checkpoint

Write a brief summary of the book you've been reading independently.

Writing an Expository Essay

Assignment

Read the following quotation by John Muir, an American naturalist and writer:

> "Any glimpse into the life of an animal quickens our own and makes it so much the larger and better in every way."

Write a multiparagraph expository essay explaining how people can improve their lives through observing and interacting with animals. In your essay, give examples from your own life, from texts you have studied in this unit, from your independent reading, or from society that help support your explanation.

Planning and Prewriting: Take time to make a plan for your expository essay.

- Which prewriting strategies and graphic organizers could help you brainstorm a variety of examples from literature, experience, and research?

- Which two or three examples would be the best selections for your essay?

- How can you summarize your response to the prompt in a thesis statement?

Drafting: Determine the structure of your essay.

- How can you restate and interpret the quote in the prompt in order to introduce your thesis?

- What elements of effective support paragraphs will you use to organize your response?

- How can you conclude your essay in a way that answers the question "So what?"

Evaluating and Revising the Draft: Create opportunities to review and revise your work.

- During the process of writing, when can you pause to share and respond with others?

- What is your plan to include suggestions and revision ideas in your draft?

- How can you use strategies such as **adding** and **replacing** to revise your draft?

- How can the Scoring Guide help you evaluate how well your draft meets the requirements of the assignment?

Checking and Editing for Publication: Confirm that your final draft is ready for publication.

- How will you check for grammatical and technical accuracy, such as proper spelling and punctuation?

Reflection

After completing this Embedded Assessment, think about how you went about accomplishing this task, and respond to the following:

- How did you use a variety of examples from literature, experience, and research to support your response to the prompt?

LEARNING STRATEGIES:
Graphic Organizer, Drafting, Diffusing, Revising

My Notes

Technology TIP:

Use online search tools to research and gather information about your examples.

Writing an Expository Essay

SCORING GUIDE

Scoring Criteria	Exemplary	Proficient	Emerging	Incomplete
Ideas	The essay • responds to the prompt with a clearly focused and well-sustained main idea • integrates relevant evidence from various sources (e.g., literature, nonfiction, personal experience, research) with detail and commentary.	The essay • responds to the prompt with a focused and sustained main idea • integrates evidence from multiple sources (e.g., literature, nonfiction, personal experience, research) with commentary.	The essay • responds to the prompt with an unfocused or inconsistently sustained main idea • uses irrelevant or insufficient evidence; may lack multiple sources or provide weak commentary.	The essay • does not respond to the prompt; response is vague or confusing • uses minimal evidence and commentary.
Structure	The essay • introduces the main idea in an engaging hook and clear thesis • uses an effective multiparagraph organizational structure • uses a variety of transitions and topic sentences to create coherence and integrate ideas • provides an insightful conclusion.	The essay • introduces the main idea with a hook and thesis • uses an appropriate multiparagraph organizational structure • uses transitions and topic sentences to create coherence • provides a conclusion that connects to larger ideas.	The essay • introduces the main idea with a weak hook or thesis • uses a flawed or inconsistent organizational structure • uses transitions and topic sentences ineffectively or inconsistently • provides a weak, illogical, or repetitive conclusion.	The essay • does not include an introduction • has little or no obvious organizational structure • uses few or no transitions and topic sentences • lacks a conclusion.
Use of Language	The essay • uses precise and accurate diction to illustrate the topic • demonstrates command of the conventions of standard English capitalization, punctuation, spelling, grammar, and usage (including parallel structure, commas in a series, and semicolons).	The essay • uses diction that is appropriate to the topic and purpose • demonstrates adequate command of the conventions of standard English capitalization, punctuation, spelling, grammar, and usage (including parallel structure, commas in a series, and semicolons).	The essay • uses basic diction inappropriate to the topic or purpose • demonstrates partial or inconsistent command of the conventions of standard English capitalization, punctuation, spelling, grammar, and usage (including parallel structure, commas in a series, and semicolons).	The essay • uses diction that is vague or confusing • lacks command of the conventions of standard English capitalization, punctuation, spelling, grammar, and usage; frequent errors obscure meaning.

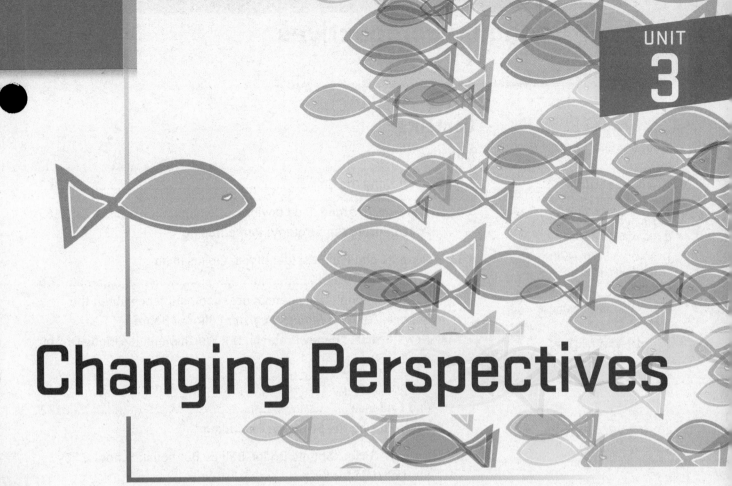

Changing Perspectives

Visual Prompt: How do you think the perspective of the single fish is different from the perspective of the rest of the fish?

Unit Overview

To change one's perspective is to change one's viewpoint, opinion, or position about something. How many times have you tried to change someone else's mind? How often do others try to change your mind? In this unit, you will learn about creating an argument and communicating to particular audiences. You will identify "hot topics" and take a stand on your opinion about one hot topic. Through analyzing informational and argumentative texts, you will see how others write and create argumentative texts. You will debate, and you will write your own argumentative text.

Changing Perspectives

GOALS:

- To analyze informational texts
- To practice nonfiction reading strategies
- To support a claim with reasons and evidence
- To engage effectively in a variety of collaborative discussions
- To write an argumentative letter
- To understand and use simple, compound, and complex sentence structures

ACADEMIC VOCABULARY

controversy
argument
claim
reasons
evidence
research
citation
plagiarism
credible
relevant
sufficient

Literary Terms
editorial
tone
formal style
rhetorical appeals
logos
pathos

Contents

Activities

Language and Writer's Craft
- Formal Style (3.6)
- Using Appositives (3.12)
- Revising by Creating Complex Sentences (3.15)

MY INDEPENDENT READING LIST

Previewing the Unit

LEARNING STRATEGIES:
Activating Prior Knowledge,
Skimming/Scanning, QHT,
Marking the Text

Learning Targets

- Preview the big ideas and academic vocabulary and literacy terms for the unit.
- Gain specific understanding of the academic vocabulary word *controversy* and its relevance in the unit.
- Identify and analyze the skills and knowledge needed to complete Embedded Assessment 1 writing assignment successfully.

Making Connections

In the last unit, you read a novel and other texts about the changes that occur throughout people's lives. You also looked at change from different perspectives: changes in your own life, changes in your community, and changes in the broader world. In this unit, you will examine arguments and how writers try to persuade others to agree with them on issues of **controversy** about which people may disagree.

Essential Questions

Based on your current knowledge, how would you answer these questions?

1. Why do we have controversy in society?

_____

_____

_____

_____

2. How do we communicate in order to convince others?

_____

_____

_____

_____

ACADEMIC VOCABULARY
A **controversy** is a public debate or dispute concerning a matter of opinion. A **controversial** issue is debatable, or an issue about which there can be disagreement.

My Notes

Developing Vocabulary

Mark the Academic Vocabulary and Literary Terms using the QHT strategy. Then, scan the Contents and find and mark a Wow activity (interesting or fun) and a Whoa activity (challenging).

Unpacking Embedded Assessment 1

Read the assignment for Embedded Assessment 1: Researching and Debating a Controversy.

> Work collaboratively to research one side of a controversy that is affecting your school, your community, or society, and then participate in a modified debate where you argue your position and incorporate a visual display for support.

Mark the text for what you will need to know in order to complete this assessment successfully. With your class, create a graphic organizer to represent the skills and knowledge you will need to complete the tasks identified in the Embedded Assessment.

INDEPENDENT READING LINK

Read and Research
You will be researching and presenting an issue for Embedded Assessment 1. If you have an idea for an issue in which you are interested, you might start finding and reading informational material about the issue. If you do not yet have an issue, you might read news articles to help you identify potential issues.

It Is Time to Argue and Convince

Learning Targets

- Infer the meanings of and explain the denotations and connotations of vocabulary words central to the unit, including the academic vocabulary word *argument*.
- Practice paraphrasing to support reading, listening, and writing skills.
- Generate a controversial topic of interest.

1. **Quickwrite:** Have you ever tried to change the mind of someone in your family? Were you successful, and if so, how did you convince the person?

_____

_____

_____

_____

2. Brainstorm all the meanings you know of the word **argument**. The concept of argumentation will become important during this unit.

Check your brainstorming in a dictionary, thesaurus, or online reference. What other definitions can you find for the word *argument*? Write them in the My Notes space.

3. What comes to mind when you hear the word *controversy*? Complete the word map graphic organizer to explore the meaning of the word.

Definition in Own Words	Personal Associations
Visual Representation	**Examples from Texts, Society, or History**

LEARNING STRATEGIES:
Think-Pair-Share, Close Reading, Marking the Text, Paraphrasing, Brainstorming, Quickwrite, Freewriting

ACADEMIC VOCABULARY
In formal speech or writing, an **argument** is a set of reasons given with the aim of persuading others that an action or idea is right or wrong. **Argumentation** is the act of formally engaging in an argument about a debatable issue.

My Notes

It Is Time to Argue and Convince

Introducing the Strategy: Paraphrasing

To paraphrase is to put a passage of text in your own words. Paraphrased material is often, but not necessarily, shorter than the original passage. Paraphrasing can help you understand what you are reading and provide support for claims in your writing. It is also a useful skill when you are listening to a speaker and you want to make notes about what the person is saying.

When you communicate your own argument about a controversy or an issue, it is essential to be able to paraphrase information. Paraphrasing involves putting a passage into your own words.

To practice paraphrasing, read and paraphrase the following quotes on controversy.

Original	My Paraphrasing
"If it matters, it produces controversy." —Jay Greene, retired NASA engineer	
"In a controversy the instant we feel anger we have already ceased striving for the truth, and have begun striving for ourselves." —Buddha	
"When a thing ceases to be a subject of controversy, it ceases to be a subject of interest." —William Hazlitt	

4. **Quickwrite:** Do you agree or disagree with any of the quotes? Explain.

5. Read the following list of claims relating to controversies from society today and place a check mark to indicate whether you agree or disagree with each one.

Anticipation Guide: Exploring Hot Topics	Agree	Disagree
Social networking should be banned at school.		
Cell phones and other electronic devices should be banned at school.		
Banning homework would hurt a student's education.		
Certain books should be banned from school.		
Junk food should be banned from schools.		
Schools should ban peanut butter.		
Kids should be banned from appearing on reality television.		
Plastic bags should be banned.		
Plastic water bottles should be banned.		
Skateboarding should be banned in public places.		
Dangerous sports such as motor racing and boxing should be banned.		
Pit bulls should be banned as pets.		
Exotic animals should be banned as pets.		
Football should be banned in middle school.		
Teenagers should be banned from playing violent video games.		

6. **Freewrite:** A controversial topic I feel strongly about is _____

_____

Check Your Understanding

Write your answers to the following:

- three things you have learned about an argument
- two hot topics that interest you, and why
- one thing you learned about paraphrasing

INDEPENDENT READING LINK

Read and Respond

Are any controversial topics represented in your independent reading book? Write about them in your Reader/Writer Notebook. Share your opinion on the topics, if you have formed one yet.

Peanuts and Pennies: Identifying Claims in an Argument

ACADEMIC VOCABULARY
In argumentation a writer makes a **claim** stating a position or opinion about a topic. To **claim** is to assert or maintain as a fact. A **claim** is the overall thesis describing the author's position on an issue.

Literary Terms
An **editorial** is a short essay in which someone speaking for a publication expresses an opinion or takes a stand on an issue. News sources—such as television, radio, magazines, newspapers, or online sources—often publish editorials for their readers.

ban: to not allow

discourage: attempt to stop an action

unenforceable: unable to make happen

Learning Targets

- Identify a writer's claim and explain the reasons presented for or against a topic.
- Write a claim stating a position or opinion about a topic.

What Is a Claim?

In argumentative writing, the author's position is known as a **claim**. The claim functions like a thesis statement in expository writing. Identifying the author's claim helps you understand the author's opinion or point of view on a topic.

Often, an author's claim appears in the opening paragraph. Sometimes the author states the claim in the middle of the text or even leaves it until the end. To identify a writer's claim, look for a statement of position or opinion that reflects what the author is trying to say about a controversial topic. A claim will be a statement that is not fact, so the author should provide reasons that support the claim.

Preview

In this activity, you will read an **editorial** and a news article and think about the claims in an argument.

Setting a Purpose for Reading

- As you read the following editorial, mark the text with an asterisk (*) next to anything you agree with and an *X* next to anything you disagree with.
- Circle unknown words and phrases. Try to determine the meaning of the words by using context clues, word parts, or a dictionary.

Editorial

Don't ban peanuts at school, *but teach about the dangers*

Des Moines Register Editorial Board

1 Waukee school officials were considering banning peanut products for all students in kindergarten through seventh grade to try to protect children with peanut allergies. The public outcry made officials change their minds. Now the district is proposing a policy that would "strongly **discourage**" the products in schools.

2 Fine. "Strongly discouraging" may help raise awareness about the danger of nut products. Just a whiff can trigger a reaction in some people with severe allergies. Schools also can do more of what they're already doing--such as having "peanut free" lunch tables.

3 And they can do what they do best: Educate. Schools should work with parents and students to help them learn about the life-threatening dangers nut products pose for some children. Schools also should provide a list of "safe" foods to send for classroom treats.

4 Banning peanut products would be **unenforceable**.

5 Are schools going to frisk a kindergartner or search the backpack of a second-grader to see if they're hiding candy with peanuts inside?

6 A student at Johnston Middle School suffered an allergic reaction to a pretzel-and-cereal trail mix from the cafeteria. It didn't even contain nuts but was exposed to peanut oils in a factory that used them in other products. Are schools supposed to investigate where prepackaged foods are manufactured and ban them if there are also nuts in the factory?

7 A ban would not ensure a child with allergies isn't exposed to harmful products. Other children will eat peanut butter for breakfast. Kids may snack on foods manufactured in a plant with peanuts.

8 The larger world isn't peanut-free. It's important that children with peanut allergies learn to protect themselves at a young age, the same way all kids with illnesses should. Children with severe asthma may need to carry inhalers. Diabetic children need candy nearby in case their blood sugar dips too low. Children with peanut allergies should have immediate access to emergency medications to counteract an allergic reaction. School staff need to be aware of students' medical conditions and know what to do in the event of an emergency.

9 A ban would offer little beyond a false sense of security.

Second Read

- Reread the editorial to answer these text-dependent questions.
- Write any additional questions you have about the text in your Reader/Writer Notebook.

1. **Craft and Structure:** How is the point of view that banning peanuts is unenforceable supported in the text?

2. **Key Ideas and Details:** Cite evidence in paragraphs 1–5 of the text that shows the editorial writer understands the dangers of peanuts at school.

3. **Craft and Structure:** What is the meaning of the word *exposed* in the second sentence of paragraph 6? Use context clues to help you determine the meaning.

4. **Key Ideas and Details:** Cite examples in the text that show an opinion about banning peanuts in school.

My Notes

_____
_____
_____
_____
_____
_____
_____
_____
_____
_____
_____
_____
_____

GRAMMAR&USAGE
Prepositions

A **preposition** links the noun or pronoun following it (its object) to another word in a sentence. The preposition, its object, and all words modifying the object make up a **prepositional phrase**. Prepositional phrases function as adjectives or adverbs. They show relationships of time, location, or direction and add specific or necessary detail in sentences. For example:

student *at Johnson Middle school* (adjective phrase modifies *student*, provides detail)

exposed *to harmful products* (adverb phrase modifies *exposed*, tells what)

Peanuts and Pennies: Identifying Claims in an Argument

Working from the Text

5. Which of these sentences from the editorial is the BEST example of a claim?

   a. Schools also should provide a list of "safe" foods to send for classroom treats. (Chunk 1)

   b. A ban would offer little beyond a false sense of security. (Chunk 2)

   c. Don't ban peanuts at school, but teach about the dangers. (Chunk 1, title)

6. Paraphrase the claim of this editorial:

7. **Quickwrite:** Explain why you agree or disagree with the claim. Then share your position with one or more classmates. Practice speaking clearly, and refer to evidence from the text to support your position.

Setting a Purpose for Reading

- The following news article presents both sides of an issue about the future of the penny. As you read, mark the reasons for (F) keeping the penny and reasons against (A) keeping the penny.

- Circle unknown words and phrases. Try to determine the meaning of the words by using context clues, word parts, or a dictionary.

ABOUT THE AUTHOR

Yunji de Nies is a journalist who has worked as a reporter, news producer, and television news anchor. While working at a TV station in New Orleans, she reported on events as Hurricane Katrina struck the area. She has also worked as a White House correspondent for ABC News. De Nies grew up in Hawaii and now works as an anchor at a local television station there.

News Article

Penny Problem:
Not Worth Metal It's Made Of

by Yunji de Nies

1 The saying goes, "See a penny, pick it up, all day long you'll have good luck."

2 But these days, the penny itself isn't having much luck. Not only is there nothing you can buy with a penny, it's literally not worth the metal it's made of.

3 With the rising cost of metals like copper and zinc, that one red cent is literally putting us in the red.

4 "It costs almost 1.7 cents to make a penny," said U.S. Mint director Ed Moy.

5 Each year, the U.S. Mint makes 8 billion pennies, at a cost of $130 million. American taxpayers lose nearly $50 million in the **process**.

6 The penny's not alone. It costs nearly 10 cents to make a nickel.

process: series of steps that lead to a result

politics: related to government and its structure

7 On Friday, Treasury Secretary Henry Paulson said he thought the penny should be eliminated, but he admitted that he didn't think it was "**politically** doable," and said he was not going to push the issue.

8 Congress held a hearing last week on a proposal to make both coins out of cheaper metals, even steel. They say it would save taxpayers more than $100 million.

9 But for now, tossing the penny altogether is not under consideration.

10 "One reason there is a lasting attachment to those coins is because they are a part of our country's history," Moy said.

11 The penny has plenty of history. It was the first U.S. coin to feature a president: Abraham Lincoln.

12 Next year, the mint plans to issue a new penny commemorating the bicentennial of Lincoln's birth.

13 That means more pennies for us to pocket.

Peanuts and Pennies: Identifying Claims in an Argument

My Notes

Second Read

- Reread the news article to answer these text-dependent questions.
- Write any additional questions you have about the text in your Reader/Writer Notebook.

8. **Craft and Structure:** What is the meaning of the word *commemorating* in paragraph 12? Use context clues to help you determine the meaning.

9. **Key Ideas and Details:** What support does the author provide for the idea that eliminating the penny is not likely to happen? Cite evidence in the text.

10. **Knowledge and Ideas:** In terms of presenting an argument and making a claim, how does this article differ from the editorial on peanuts in school?

Working from the Text

11. If you could turn this news article into an argument like an editorial, what position would you choose? Would you be for or against keeping the penny? Circle one.

    FOR (PRO)   AGAINST (CON)

12. Collaboratively paraphrase a part of the text that matches your position.

13. Collaboratively write the claim for your editorial.

_____

_____

_____

_____

_____

_____

Claims Are Debatable

A claim must be something that people could reasonably have differing opinions on. If your claim is something that is generally agreed upon or accepted as fact, then there is no reason to try to convince people.

Example of a non debatable claim: *Air pollution is bad for the environment*. This claim is not debatable. First, the word *pollution* means that something is bad or negative in some way. Further, all studies agree that air pollution is a problem; they simply disagree on the impact it will have or the scope of the problem. No one could reasonably argue that air pollution is good.

Example of a debatable claim: *At least twenty-five percent of the federal budget should be spent on limiting air pollution*. This claim is debatable because reasonable people could disagree with it. Some people might think that this is how we should spend the nation's money. Others might feel that this amount is too much to spend to limit air pollution. Still others could argue that corporations, not the government, should be paying to limit air pollution.

14. Does your claim clearly state your topic and opinion? Is your claim debatable? Share your claim with the class. Practice speaking loud enough to be heard.

Support the Sport? Creating Support with Reasons and Evidence

LEARNING STRATEGIES:
Activating Prior Knowledge, Predicting, Diffusing, Rereading, Paraphrasing, Marking the Text

ACADEMIC VOCABULARY
Reasons are the points that explain why the author is making a certain claim. **Evidence** is more specifically the facts, details, and information that support the reasons for the claim.

My Notes

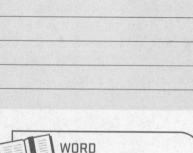

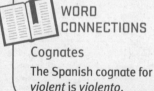

WORD CONNECTIONS

Cognates
The Spanish cognate for *violent* is *violento*.

Learning Targets
- Identify reasons and evidence in a text and analyze how they support claims.
- Participate in an effective debate by using evidence from texts, contributing ideas clearly, and responding to others' ideas.

Reasons and Evidence

A claim should be backed up with support. A writer can support his or her viewpoint with **reasons** and **evidence**. Reasons are the points or opinions the writer gives to show why his or her claim should be accepted. In writing, each reason often acts as the topic sentence of a paragraph.

Evidence is a more specific type of support. Several kinds of evidence, such as facts, statistics, examples, observations, quotations, and expert opinions, can be used to support reasons. Sometimes people believe that their reasons should be sufficient to win an argument, but arguments without evidence are just personal opinions. Argumentative speakers and writers should attempt to use both reasons and evidence to be most effective.

Preview

In this activity, you will read three news articles on sports safety and analyze the arguments in them.

Setting a Purpose for Reading
- As you read the following news article, use different colors to mark the text for the reasons and evidence provided for both sides of the argument.
- Circle unknown words and phrases. Try to determine the meaning of the words by using context clues, word parts, or a dictionary.

Online Article

Should Dodge Ball Be Banned in Schools?

by Staff of TIME for Kids

1 For years, the old playground game of dodge ball has been taking a hit. Some say it is too violent. But others say it teaches kids important skills, such as quick decision-making.

2 School districts in states including Texas, Virginia, Maine and Massachusetts banned the game in 2001. Neil Williams, a professor of physical education at Eastern Connecticut State University, even created a P.E. Hall of Shame in which dodge ball is included. "The game allows the stronger kids to pick on and target the weaker kids," he says.

3 There are other **objections** to dodge ball. A child who is hit by a ball in the first few seconds spends the remainder of the game sitting on a bench, watching others. Those who do remain in the game, according to critics, become human targets, which could lead to bullying.

objection: disagreement or disapproval

4 There are, however, those who defend the game. Rick Hanetho, founder of the National Amateur Dodge ball Association, says the game allows kids who are not good athletes to participate in a team sport. He also argues that it teaches hand-eye **coordination**, concentration and the ability to think and draw quick conclusions.

coordination: the ability of different body parts to work together smoothly

5 What's more, proponents of dodge ball say kids have a lot of fun, as long as the game is properly supervised. Gym teachers and coaches must be sure that kids follow the rules and don't aim to hurt anyone. It also helps, say dodge ball supporters, to use a soft, squishy ball.

Introducing the Strategy: Rereading

Good **readers** often reread a text as a way to make sure it makes sense and to find information they did not find during the first reading. Rereading a text two or three times may be needed to fully understand a text.

Second Read

- Reread the article to answer these text-dependent questions.
- Write any additional questions you have about the text in your Reader/Writer Notebook.

1. **Craft and Structure:** What context clues help you determine the meanings of *critics* in paragraph 3 and *proponents* in paragraph 5?

2. **Key Ideas and Details:** Summarize the claims of both sides of the issue, providing details from the text.

My Notes

Support the Sport? Creating Support with Reasons and Evidence

3. **Key Ideas and Details:** According to the article, what are some ways to minimize the violence of dodge ball?

Working from the Text

4. Use the graphic organizer to identify the components of the argument. You will need to reread the article to find reasons and evidence that support each position.

Side A	Side B
Claim:	Claim:
Reason:	Reason:
Evidence:	Evidence:
Type of evidence:	Type of evidence:

My Notes
_____
_____
_____
_____
_____
_____
_____
_____
_____
_____
_____
_____
_____

5. Take a side in the dodge ball argument, using the evidence you found in the text for either claim. Write why that evidence, in the context of the article, provides the most convincing support for whether dodge ball should be banned in school. Then brainstorm other reasons and/or evidence that might strengthen either side of the argument.

Setting a Purpose for Reading

- The following news article presents both sides of an argument on the safety of cheerleading. As you read, mark the text in two colors for the reasons and evidence provided for both sides of the argument.
- Circle unknown words and phrases. Try to determine the meaning of the words by using context clues, word parts, or a dictionary.

ABOUT THE AUTHORS
Lisa Ling is a journalist and the host of a documentary television series on cable television. She has worked as an international news reporter on television and has appeared regularly on TV talk shows discussing her reporting. Arash Ghadishah is an award-winning news producer and writer. He has produced news specials and series for ABC News and many other television and print companies. The following article was written in conjunction with a report on ABC's *Nightline* television show.

News Article

Most Dangerous "Sport" of All May Be CHEERLEADING

By Lisa Ling and Arash Ghadishah

1 Two years ago, Patty Phommanyvong was a healthy 17-year-old. Now she will never walk or talk again. She was injured while cheerleading—an athletic activity some say is now among the most dangerous for young girls.

2 Phommanyvong had never done any gymnastics before she started cheering. After just two months, her parents say, Patty's cheering partners were throwing her as high as 16 feet in the air.

3 Then she suffered an accident that stopped her breathing. Her parents claim that her school's **defibrillator** failed and the 45 minutes she went without oxygen left her with a brain injury that caused permanent **paralysis**. Today, Phommanyvong can only communicate by blinking.

4 One blink means yes. Twice means no. Maybe is multiple blinks.

5 Cheerleading has long been an iconic American pastime, and it is now more popular than ever. By one estimate, 3 million young people cheer, more than 400,000 at the high school level. And cheerleaders are no longer only on the sidelines–many cheer competitively.

6 The degree of difficulty of cheer stunts has exploded. So too has the number of accidents.

7 Cheerleading emergency room visits have increased almost sixfold over the past three decades. There were nearly 30,000 in 2008, according to the Consumer Product Safety Commission.

8 The numbers are all the more disturbing because some states don't even recognize cheerleading as a sport. That means there are no uniform safety measures and training methods.

9 Kori Johnson is the cheerleading coach at Costa Mesa High School in Southern California. She says the cheerleaders have had to step up the degree of difficulty over the years.

10 "The girls, they want to be the best," said Johnson. "They want to try harder stunts. So every year when we see new stunts we try them."

. . .

My Notes

defibrillator: a device used to apply an electric current to the heart
paralysis: inability to move

Support the Sport? Creating Support with Reasons and Evidence

intense: extreme; having great force

GRAMMAR & USAGE
Regular and Irregular Verbs

Regular verbs form the past tense and past participle by adding *-d* or *-ed*; for example: *look, looked, have looked.*

Irregular verbs do not follow this pattern. These verbs form the past tense and past participle in different ways; for example, *know, knew, have known.*

A number of irregular verbs appear in this text, such as *think, throw,* and *make.* Can you find other examples of irregular verbs? It is important to know the forms of irregular verbs so that you use them correctly. Review the forms of irregular verbs in the Grammar Handbook.

epidemic: spreading and affecting many people

Cheerleading as Competition

11 Costa Mesa High boasts a championship cheer squad.

12 Squad members say people who don't think cheerleading is a sport should just try it.

13 "They should be open-minded about it," one cheerleader said. "We throw people."

14 Like our bases are lifting like people up in the air."

15 "It's like bench-pressing a person," a second cheerleader said.

16 A third cheerleader said not everyone could keep up.

17 "We had the water polo boys stunt with us last year and they like, quit, after like an hour," she said. "They said it was really **intense**."

'It's Scary. It's Scary.'

18 Johnson is an experienced coach with safety training and cheer certifications. She says the key to avoiding major injuries is teaching stunts step by step.

19 "I would never ask them to do a stunt that they're not capable of doing and trying," said Johnson. "So we make sure they have all the basic stunting and it's like stairs. We move up the ladder."

20 But as many parents already know, injuries are now simply a part of cheerleading.

21 "It's scary. It's scary," said Lynne Castro, the mother of a Costa Mesa cheerleader. But Castro said cheerleading was too important to her daughter to stop even after she suffered a serious injury. "You see other sports figures that have injuries and they just get on with it, you know. You fix it, you rehabilitate properly, and you move forward."

22 But there's no coming back from some of the injuries cheerleaders now risk. An injury is deemed catastrophic if it causes permanent spinal injury and paralysis. There were 73 of these injuries in cheerleading, including two deaths, between 1982 and 2008. In the same time period, there were only nine catastrophic injuries in gymnastics, four in basketball and two in soccer.

. . .

23 In 2008, 20-year-old Lauren Chang died during a cheer competition in Massachusetts when an accidental kick to the chest caused her lungs to collapse.

24 "Lauren died doing what she loved, cheering and being with her friends," said Nancy Chang, her mother, soon after the accident. "We hope her death will shed light on the inherent risks of cheerleading and we hope that additional safeguards are taken."

25 "It's a national **epidemic**," said Kimberly Archie, who started the National Cheer Safety Foundation to campaign for more safety practices in cheerleading. "I think we should be extremely concerned as a nation. . . . [It's] a self-regulated industry that hasn't done a good job. If I was going to give them a report card, they'd get an F in safety."

26 Cheerleading is big business. Uniform sales alone are a multi-million-dollar industry. And there are thousands of cheer events all year across the nation, with competitors from ages 3 to 23. There are cheerleading all-star teams that do not cheer for any school but compete against one another.

27 "We don't want the kids to be hurt. We want the kids to be safe," said Tammy Van Vleet, who runs the Golden State Spirit Association, which trains cheerleading coaches and runs competitions in California. "It's our priority to make sure we provide that environment. . . . Since about 1999, the degree of difficulty in cheerleading has just exploded.

28 And we're seeing elite-level gymnasts on these cheerleading squads. And not just one athlete on the floor but 35 at a time, and [the] acrobatics and stunts that they are doing, you know, have not been matched."

29 That's why Van Vleet keeps two EMTs on site at major cheerleading **exhibitions**. But there are no uniform regulations that require such safety measures.

exhibition: public event to show something

. . .

'What Is Safe?'

30 Jim Lord is executive director of the American Association of Cheerleading Coaches and Administrators, the largest cheerleading organization in the country. "Nightline" asked him whether cheerleading is safe.

31 "That's a great question for any sport or athletics, is, 'What is safe?'" Lord said. "There's something that says, 'Well, these are cheerleaders so they shouldn't be hurt, they shouldn't have any risks, they should be on the sidelines and they shouldn't be doing anything'--when a lot of girls have selected this as their favorite athletic activity. And so I think there's that stigma, I think that goes along with it, for some reason."

32 Lord says that recognizing cheerleading as a sport would not increase safety and would only complicate managing an activity that is still not primarily competitive for most cheer squads.

33 "You can minimize the chance of having an injury, and what that comes down to [is] having a coach that's qualified," said Lord. "There's always going to be risk there, our job is to minimize that risk, especially from the catastrophic type of injury."

34 But Archie charges that the current system of recommended safety and training measures does not protect kids. Many cheer coaches only have to pass an open-book test to gain a safety certification.

35 Lord believes that cheerleading is not as dangerous as the injury **statistics** indicate. He says that cheerleading may look more dangerous than mainstream sports because there's no cheering season. Many cheerleaders practice all year, which means extended exposure to injury.

statistic: number(s) revealing information

36 Still, critics believe that until cheerleading is recognized as a sport, safety will suffer.

37 If change is coming, it is too late for the Phommanyvongs. They are suing their daughter's school, claiming that the school did not respond properly to her injury. The school declined to comment for this story.

38 "Too far," said Patty Phommanyvong's father, Say Phommanyvong. "They went too far. They should do step-by-step."

39 "Maybe we can change," said her mother, Vilay. "So I don't want it to happen to another kid."

My Notes

Support the Sport? Creating Support with Reasons and Evidence

My Notes

Second Read

- Reread the article to answer these text-dependent questions.
- Write any additional questions you have about the text in your Reader/Writer Notebook.

6. **Craft and Structure:** What kinds of evidence do the authors use in the beginning of this article to convey the idea that cheerleading is dangerous?

7. **Key Ideas and Details:** How do the comments from cheerleaders in paragraphs 13–17 contribute to the idea that cheerleading should have uniform safety and training standards?

8. **Craft and Structure:** What context clues in paragraph 21 help you determine what *rehabilitate* means? What context clues in paragraph 22 help you know that a *catastrophic* injury cannot be rehabilitated?

Working from the Text

9. Use the graphic organizer to analyze both sides of the issue. Reread if necessary.

Side A	Side B
Claim: Cheerleading IS a dangerous sport that needs to be regulated or banned.	**Claim:** Cheerleading IS NOT a dangerous sport and does NOT need to be regulated or banned.
Reason:	**Reason:**
Evidence: **Type of evidence:**	**Evidence:** **Type of evidence:**

10. Take a side in the cheerleader argument, using the evidence you found in the text for either claim. Write why that evidence provides the most convincing support for whether cheerleading is a dangerous sport and should be regulated or banned. Then brainstorm other reasons and/or evidence that might strengthen either side of the argument.

Setting a Purpose for Reading

- The following news article presents both sides of an argument on the safety of full-contact high school football. As you read, continue to mark the text for the reasons and evidence provided for both sides of the argument.

- Circle unknown words and phrases. Try to determine the meaning of the words by using context clues, word parts, or a dictionary.

ABOUT THE AUTHOR

Tina Akouris is a news writer and producer in Chicago, Illinois. She writes newscasts and manages reporters for a 24-hour news radio station. Prior to this, she was a sports reporter and columnist for the *Chicago Sun Times* newspaper for 14 years. She has written in-depth reports about high school athletics and Olympic athletes, and has also reported on one of her favorite sports, NASCAR auto racing.

My Notes

Support the Sport? Creating Support with Reasons and Evidence

concussion: injury to the brain caused by a hard blow

WORD CONNECTIONS

Cognates

The Spanish cognate for *native* is *nativo*.

self-proclaimed: a title a person gives to oneself or a group to itself

My Notes

diplomatic: sensitive to other positions or feelings

News Article

High School Football: Would a **Pop Warner Ban** Limit Concussions?

by Tina Akouris

1   When Marv Levy first started playing football, "concussions" was a word he heard about as often as "face mask."

2   The South Side native and NFL coaching legend wore a leather helmet and precious little padding. Those were the days when the Chicago Cardinals coexisted with the Bears and there was a youth football program for kids 12 and under called the Junior Bears and the Junior Cardinals.

3   As Levy matriculated through South Shore High School and Iowa's Coe College, the equipment and attitudes toward football's health hazards evolved little.

4   "You would get dinged up and just shake it off," said Levy, who coached the Buffalo Bills to four consecutive Super Bowls. "We wore leather helmets with no face guards. You were a sissy if you drank water during practice back then."

5   Levy is 86 years old. Pop Warner football, the **self-proclaimed** "largest youth football, cheerleading and dance program in the world," is 83.

6   But, when it comes to full-contact hitting in football practices—official workouts begin Wednesday for the Illinois high school season—they might not be the old-fashioned ones.

7   In June, Pop Warner instituted rule changes designed to limit players' exposure to concussions. The most significant change—limiting full-speed hitting to one-third of total practice time, when in the past there were no restrictions on full-speed hitting—was heartily endorsed by Levy.

8   "You don't need to play tackle football until you're 13 or 14, because you can learn other things about the game," Levy said. "Part of [more awareness], in my opinion, is how players are more closely monitored and there are more medical people around. They are more cautious. I think in youth football you shouldn't overdo the contact."

9   Yet, a Herald-News poll of area football coaches revealed 89 percent of respondents had no plans to change the amount of hitting they'd allow in practice compared with a year ago, and more than half say the contact allowed is unchanged over the last five years.

Hyper-awareness

10   Lincoln-Way Central football coach Brett Hefner didn't necessarily disagree with Levy, but took a more **diplomatic** approach. Every kid, he said, is different.

11   "Some are ready to handle it and other kids are not," Hefner said. "The benefits of playing at a younger age are that they understand the game more as they get older, how to position their bodies better when they tackle."

12 But are there risks associated with playing at such a young age?

13 Certainly, the football world is hyper-aware of head injuries. Chronic Traumatic Encephalopathy, a condition brought on by repeated blows to the head, has been linked to the suicide deaths of three former NFL players in the past 18 months: ex-Bears safety Dave Duerson in February 2011, ex-Falcons safety Ray Easterling in April, and ex-Chargers linebacker Junior Seau on May 2.

14 That culture of hyper-awareness, Hefner said, has led to significant changes at Lincoln-Way Central, including the presence of an athletic trainer at every practice, coaches lecturing players on concussion signs, and baseline testing at the beginning of each season for every player. Hefner said those baseline tests are used later to determine if a player has suffered a concussion.

15 "I think 15, 20 years ago, no one wanted to say anything," Hefner said. "We've been fortunate. We did have a few players have concussions last year, but everyone recovers differently.

16 "We have a better understanding of how serious they are."

17 Dr. Eric Lee, of Oak Orthopedics in Frankfort, agreed with Hefner that every child is different, and that perhaps limiting contact in practice is the way to go to avoid more concussions.

18 "It's a very controversial topic and some will say that if they don't let their child play football, then they won't let them ride a skateboard or ride a bike," said Lee, who is a volunteer physician for Lincoln-Way North, Olivet Nazarene, and the U.S. Soccer Youth National teams. "And at the freshman level, you have some kids who haven't reached their physical maturity going up against those who have."

19 Dr. Robert Cantu, co-director of Boston University's Center for the Study of Traumatic Encephalopathy, studied Duerson's brain at his brain bank and wrote a book, "Concussions and Our Kids," due out Sept. 15. One chapter advocates children not playing football until high school. Cantu fully supports Levy's opinion.

20 "We also feel that children shouldn't play (full-contact) hockey until high school and heading should be taken out of soccer," Cantu said. "Kids have poorer equipment than varsity athletes and there is less medical supervision—if any—and coaches are not well-schooled in concussion issues."

21 Lee said he sees more high school players in the south suburbs suffering head injuries during practice because of the competitive nature of football in this part of the Chicago area. Lee said a lot of players are going all out during practices to win that **coveted** starting spot.

22 Thus, Lee said, he believes taking a lot of hits out of practice is one step toward reducing head trauma.

23 "The happy medium is what Pop Warner did, with limiting the practice of contact," Lee said. "By doing that, you remove a ton of exposure to head injuries."

24 Indeed, Dr. Julian Bailes, the chairman of Pop Warner's Medical Advisory board and co-director of the NorthShore Neurological Institute, said his organization's recommendations can cut concussions by two-thirds.

25 "We can reduce 60 to 70 percent of head impact because that's what occurs at practices," Bailes told the Sun-Times in July. "This is a first step to make it safer."

26 At least one coach may take a step in another direction—perhaps not, for now, with his players, but with his 6-year-old son.

My Notes

covet: want very much

Support the Sport? Creating Support with Reasons and Evidence

28 Reavis coach Tim Zasada said it's important to teach the correct tackling technique at the high school level. Even though most coaches have the right idea in terms of how to teach players to hit, there are those at the youth football level who need to be more educated on tackling techniques.

28 And when it comes to his son, Zasada has an idea of what type of football future he wants to **implement** for his child and what other parents strongly should consider for their children.

29 "My son is 6 and is playing flag football and his friends are asking him if he will play padded football next year," Zasada said. "I have no idea what I will do with my son, but flag football in my opinion is the way to go. I see kids competing and having fun and that's what it should be about."

implement: make happen

Second Read

- Reread the article to answer these text-dependent questions.
- Write any additional questions you have about the text in your Reader/Writer Notebook.

11. **Craft and Structure:** What is the meaning of the word *hazards* in paragraph 3? Use context clues to help you determine the meaning.

12. **Key Ideas and Details:** How would you summarize the first section of the article? What is the main idea that Marv Levy and Pop Warner football support? Cite evidence to support your answer.

13. **Key Ideas and Details:** Based on the information in paragraph 13 about the suicide deaths of the NFL players, what can you infer about the nature of concussions?

14. **Key Ideas and Details:** Why is it important for children playing football and other sports to be aware of the potential for concussions? Cite evidence in the text that supports your answer.

Working from the Text

15. What is your opinion on a limit to full-speed hitting in youth football? Write your claim and reasoning in the My Notes section next to the most effective evidence in the text that supports it. Share your response in a collaborative group discussion.

Debating the Issue

> **Should youths be banned from participating in sports such as dodge ball, cheerleading, and football?**

16. **Freewrite:** Decide yes or no and write about your opinion. Be sure you have reasons and evidence marked in the texts that can support your opinion so that you are prepared for the debate.

My Notes

Support the Sport? Creating Support with Reasons and Evidence

Rules for Debate

For your debate, you will use a process called "Philosophical Chairs." This process organizes the debate and does the following:

- Helps you become aware of your own position on a topic
- Helps you practice using reasons and evidence to support your position
- Exposes you to alternative perspectives (others' positions) on a topic

How It Works

- Sit according to your position on a topic.
- Move about the room during the discussion; this symbolizes your willingness to adopt a different point of view, even if temporarily.
- Share reasons and evidence from the text to support what you say.

Rules of Engagement

- Listen carefully when others speak; seek to understand their position even if you don't agree.
- Wait for the mediator to recognize you before you speak; only one person speaks at a time. Speak clearly and loudly enough to be heard by the audience. Explicitly refer to evidence from the texts as you offer new support or elaborate on a previous point.
- If you have spoken for a side, you must wait until three other people on your side speak before you speak again.
- If you are undecided, you may sit in the available "hot seats," but for no longer than 4 minutes.

No one acknowledges any move. This is not a team game.

Self-Assessment

17. How did you do in the debate? Complete the self-assessment and set at least
one goal for improvement.

	Sometimes	Always	Never
I explicitly referred to evidence from the texts.			
I offered new support or elaborated on previous points.			
I spoke clearly, slowly, and loudly enough to be heard by the audience.			

Check Your Understanding

Complete the graphic organizer to show your final argument.

Issue: Should youths be banned from participating in sports such as dodge ball, cheerleading, and football?

Claim:

Reason 1:	**Evidence** (facts, statistics, examples, observations, quotations, expert opinion): **Source:**
Reason 2:	**Evidence** (facts, statistics, examples, observations, quotations, expert opinion): **Source:**
Reason 3:	**Evidence** (facts, statistics, examples, observations, quotations, expert opinion): **Source:**

Do Your Research: Sources, Citation, and Credibility

LEARNING STRATEGIES:
Quickwrite, Graphic Organizer,
Note-taking

My Notes

_____

_____

_____

_____

_____

_____

ACADEMIC VOCABULARY
When you **research** (verb), you locate reliable information from a variety of sources. The word *research* (noun) also describes the information found from the search.

Learning Targets
- Understand the process of research, including the importance of using credible sources and citing sources to avoid plagiarism.
- Apply my understanding of sources, citation, and credibility through discussion, note-taking, and research.

1. Read and respond to the following quotes by Bernard M. Baruch, American financial expert and presidential advisor (1870–1965):

   "Every man has a right to his opinion, but no man has a right to be wrong in his facts."

   "If you get all the facts, your judgment can be right; if you don't get all the facts, it can't be right."

   _____

   _____

   _____

   _____

   _____

2. **Quickwrite:** What is the role of **research** in presenting an argument?

   _____

   _____

   _____

   _____

3. Use the graphic organizer to review the research process and decide how comfortable you are with each step.

The Research Process	Self-Assessment		
	Very Comfortable	Somewhat Comfortable	Not Comfortable
Step 1: Identify the topic, issue, or problem.			
Step 2: Form a set of questions that can be answered through research.			
Step 3: Gather evidence and refocus when necessary.			
Step 4: Evaluate sources.			
Step 5: Draw conclusions.			
Step 6: Communicate findings.			

Sources, Citation, and Credibility

4. Take notes on the graphic organizer. Above each word, write what you already know; below the word, add words or phrases as you read and discuss.

sources	**citation**	**credibility**

ACADEMIC VOCABULARY
When you **cite** or provide a **citation**, you are following the practice of quoting or referring to sources of textual evidence. The word *cite* comes from the Latin word meaning "to set in motion." *Cite* has come to mean "to quote or refer to."

Sources

A source is any place you get valid information for your research. A source can be a document, a person, a film, a historical text, and so on. Sources are generally classified as primary or secondary.

- **Primary Source:** An account or document created by someone with firsthand knowledge or experience of an event. Letters, journal entries, blogs, eyewitness accounts, speeches, and interviews are all primary sources.

- **Secondary Source:** Documents supplied and compiled by people who do not have firsthand knowledge of an event. History textbooks, book reviews, documentary films, websites, and most magazine and newspaper articles are secondary sources.

5. Revisit the sources you have read in the unit. What kind of sources are they? When might it be effective to use primary sources to support your argument? When might it be effective to use secondary sources to support your argument?

_____

_____

_____

_____

My Notes

Do Your Research: Sources, Citation, and Credibility

ACADEMIC VOCABULARY
By citing research you avoid the mistake of **plagiarism**, which is using or imitating another person's words or ideas without giving proper credit.

My Notes

Citations

It is important to provide basic bibliographic information for sources. This practice helps you give credit to information that is not your own when you communicate your findings, and thus avoid **plagiarism**. Basic bibliographic information includes author, title, source, date, and medium of publication.

The following models show a standard format for citing basic bibliographic information for common types of sources.

- **Book**

  Last name, First name of author. *Title of Book*. City of Publication: Publisher, Year of Publication. Medium of Publication.

  Example: Henley, Patricia. *The Hummingbird House*. Denver: MacMurray, 1999. Print.

- **Film or Video Recording (DVD)**

  Title of Film. Director. Distributor, Release year. Medium.

  Example: *Star Wars Episode IV: A New Hope*. Dir. George Lucas. Twentieth Century Fox, 2006. DVD.

- **Personal Interview (Conducted by Researcher)**

  Last Name, First Name Middle Name of Person Interviewed. Personal, E-mail or Telephone interview. Day, Month (abbreviated), Year of Interview.

  Example: Jackson, Anne. Telephone interview. 6 Dec. 2012.

- **Internet Site**

  "Article or Specific Page Title." *Title of Website*. Name of Site Sponsor (if available), Date posted or last updated, if available. Medium of Publication. Day, Month (abbreviated), Year Accessed.

  Example: "Abraham Lincoln." *The White House*. Web. 16 Apr. 2013.

- **Magazine or Newspaper Article**

  Last name, First name of author. "Title of Article." *Title of Periodical*. Day Month Year: pages. Medium of publication.

  Example: Poniewozik, James. "TV Makes a Too-Close Call." *Time*. 20 Nov. 2000: 70–71. Print.

6. Suppose you are conducting research on this debatable topic: Is it ethical to keep animals in zoos? Imagine that you have used the following sources. Practice writing the basic bibliographic information for each.

Source	Bibliographic Information
You read a book on animal treatment in zoos called *Animal Attractions: Nature on Display in American Zoos,* by Elizabeth Hanson. It was published in 2002 in New York. The publishing company is Princeton University Press.	
You used information from a webpage titled *National Geographic Explore: Classroom Magazine.* The webpage's copyright date is 2001. The organization that hosts the site is National Geographic. The title of the article is "A Bear of a Job." You visited the site on January 20, 2013.	
You conducted a phone interview with a zookeeper named Nancy Hawkes from Woodland Park Zoo in Seattle, Washington, on February 7, 2013.	

Credibility

Any source you use must be **credible**. Evaluating a source's credibility will help you determine if you should use the information as part of your evidence when you communicate your findings. You can ask the following questions to determine if a source is credible:

- **Who is the author?** Credible sources are written by authors respected in their fields of study. Responsible, credible authors will cite their sources so that you can check the accuracy of and support for what they have written. (This is also a good way to find more sources for your own research.)

- **How recent is the source?** The choice to seek recent sources depends on your topic. While sources on the American Civil War may be decades old and still contain accurate information, sources on information technologies or other areas that are experiencing rapid changes need to be much more current.

- **What is the author's purpose?** Is the author presenting a neutral, objective view of a topic? Or is the author advocating one specific view of a topic? Who is funding the research or writing of this source? A source written from a particular point of view *may* be credible; however, you need to be careful that your sources don't limit your coverage of a topic to one side of a debate.

ACADEMIC VOCABULARY
To be **credible** is to be reliable, believable, and trustworthy. Evidence must be credible in order to be convincing. The **credibility** of research information and of the researchers is enhanced when sources of evidence are properly evaluated and cited.

My Notes

Do Your Research: Sources, Citation, and Credibility

My Notes

Internet Sites

Be especially careful when evaluating Internet sources! Be critical of websites where an author cannot be determined, unless the site is associated with a reputable institution such as a respected university, a credible media outlet, a government program or department, or a well-known organization. Beware of using sites like Wikipedia, which are collaboratively developed by users. Because anyone can add or change content, the validity of information on such sites may not meet the standards for academic research.

Some Internet sites may contain more credible information than others. A credible Internet source is one that contains information that is well researched, a bibliography or list of resources, and a statement of the site's purpose. One way to know whether a website is credible is through its domain suffix. The domain name is the Web address, or Internet identity. The domain suffix, typically the three letters that follow the "dot," is the category in which that Web site falls.

Domain Suffix	Definition/Description
.com	Stands for "commercial." Web sites with this suffix are created to make a profit from their Internet services. Typically these Web sites sell goods or services.
.org	Stands for "organization." Primarily used by nonprofit groups.
.net	Stands for "network." Used by Internet service providers or Web-hosting companies.
.edu	Stands for "education." Used by major universities or educational organizations and institutions.
.gov	Stands for "government." Used by local, state, and federal government sites.

7. Which of the domain suffixes listed above would provide the most credible information for research on whether it is ethical to keep animals in a zoo? Why?

_____

_____

_____

8. Which suffixes might provide the least credible information? Why?

_____

_____

_____

_____

9. Go back to the Internet source for which you recorded basic bibliographic information. Based only on the information you are given for the website, would you consider information from this Internet source to be credible? Why or why not?

_____

_____

_____

_____

Check Your Understanding

Think about the controversial topic you felt strongly about at the beginning of the unit or one you feel strongly about now. Apply what you have learned about sources, citation, and credibility as you conduct initial research on the topic. Use the graphic organizer as a guide.

Topic:		
My current position:		
Type of source:	Basic bibliographic information:	Is the source credible? Explain.
Interesting information/Notes:		

The Formality of It All: Style and Tone

Literary Terms
Tone is the attitude that a writer or speaker displays toward his or her subject.

My Notes

Learning Targets
- Analyze the purpose of formal style and tone.
- Write an original text using a formal style and tone.

Identifying Tone

1. An author of an argumentative piece uses tone as way of convincing you, the reader or listener, to adopt his or her viewpoint (to agree with his or her claim). Choose a word to describe the writer's attitude, or **tone**:

Tone Word Bank

angry	sad	sentimental
sharp	cold	upset
urgent	complimentary	condescending
boring	poignant	sympathetic
afraid	happy	confused
apologetic	childish	humorous
joyful	peaceful	mocking
sarcastic	sweet	bitter
tired	shocking	proud
giddy	serious	dramatic

Literary Terms
Formal style is a style of writing or speaking that is appropriate for formal communication such as in academics or business.

Language and Writer's Craft: Formal Style

Part of communicating effectively is using language that fits your audience and purpose. **Style** is how an author or speaker uses words and phrases to form his or her ideas and to show his or her attitude toward the subject (tone). Most often in academic settings, you should use a **formal style**.

Decide which of the following statements use formal and which use informal style.

Please refrain from talking.
Please don't talk.

Will you be attending the dance this evening?
Are you gonna go to the dance later?

You should follow the rules.
You must adhere to the guidelines.

The author of the editorial suggests discontinuing the use of plastic bags.
It says to stop using plastic bags.

What she said was totally bogus.
During the debate, the student did not provide enough evidence to support her claim.

Use the following list of characteristics of formal style to inform your writing.

My Notes

Formal Style	
DO:	**DO NOT:**
• **Use precise nouns and pronouns (no vague pronoun references).** Example: The **author** of the editorial suggests discontinuing the use of plastic bags.	• **Do not use vague pronoun references.** Example: **It** says to stop using plastic bags. (Who is "it"?)
• **Use active verbs.** Example: Please **refrain** from talking.	• **Do not use contractions.** Example: Please **don't** talk.
• **Use diction specific to the topic and precise for the audience.** Example: During the debate, the student did not provide enough **evidence** to support her **claim**.	• **Do not use slang words.** Example: What she said was **totally bogus.**

2. Why do you think formal style is important in argumentative communication?

Preview

In this activity, you will read a historical letter to analyze its style and tone, and experiment with style and tone in your own writing.

Setting a Purpose for Reading

• As you read the following letter, mark the text for precise nouns, active verbs, and diction specific to the topic and audience.

• Circle unknown words and phrases. Try to determine the meaning of the words by using context clues, word parts, or a dictionary.

The Formality of It All: Style and Tone

WORD CONNECTIONS

Content Connections

The Declaration of Independence was adopted by the Second Continental Congress in Philadelphia, Pennsylvania on July 4, 1776, more than a year into the American Revolutionary War. It declared that the thirteen American colonies were no longer a part of the British Empire and explained the reasoning for this. The document's most famous words are its second sentence: "We hold these truths to be self-evident, that all men are created equal, that they are endowed by their Creator with certain unalienable Rights, that among these are Life, Liberty and the the pursuit of Happiness."

convenient: serving a need without difficulty
reputation: general opinion regarding a person or thing
felicity: pleasing and well chosen

obnoxious: annoying, unpleasant

ABOUT THE AUTHOR

John Adams was a member of the committee appointed to draft the Declaration of Independence. Along with Lincoln's Second Inaugural Address, the Declaration of Independence stands as one of the greatest of America's official documents. Thomas Jefferson was 33 years old when he wrote the Declaration of Independence in 1776. In 1822, John Adams wrote a letter to Timothy Pickering, a politician from Massachusetts at the time, responding to Pickering's questions about the writing of the Declaration of Independence.

Historical Document

Excerpt from
"Letter on *Thomas Jefferson*"

by John Adams

1   You inquire why so young a man as Mr. Jefferson was placed at the head of the committee for preparing a Declaration of Independence? I answer: It was the Frankfort advice, to place Virginia at the head of everything. Mr. Richard Henry Lee might be gone to Virginia, to his sick family, for aught I know, but that was not the reason of Mr. Jefferson's appointment. There were three committees appointed at the same time, one for the Declaration of Independence, another for preparing articles of confederation, and another for preparing a treaty to be proposed to France. Mr. Lee was chosen for the Committee of Confederation, and it was not thought **convenient** that the same person should be upon both. Mr. Jefferson came into Congress in June, 1775, and brought with him a **reputation** for literature, science, and a happy talent of composition. Writings of his were handed about, remarkable for the peculiar **felicity** of expression. Though a silent member in Congress, he was so prompt, frank, explicit, and decisive upon committees and in conversation—not even Samuel Adams was more so—that he soon seized upon my heart; and upon this occasion I gave him my vote, and did all in my power to procure the votes of others. I think he had one more vote than any other, and that placed him at the head of the committee. I had the next highest number, and that placed me the second. The committee met, discussed the subject, and then appointed Mr. Jefferson and me to make the draft, I suppose because we were the two first on the list.

2   The subcommittee met. Jefferson proposed to me to make the draft. I said, "I will not," "You should do it." "Oh! no." "Why will you not? You ought to do it." "I will not." "Why?" "Reasons enough." "What can be your reasons?" "Reason first, you are a Virginian, and a Virginian ought to appear at the head of this business. Reason second, I am **obnoxious**, suspected, and unpopular. You are very much otherwise. Reason third, you can write ten times better than I can." "Well," said Jefferson, "if you are decided, I will do as well as I can." "Very well. When you have drawn it up, we will have a meeting."

Second Read

- Reread the letter to answer these text-dependent questions.
- Write any additional questions you have about the text in your Reader/Writer Notebook.

3. **Craft and Structure:** Based on your understanding of the Declaration of Independence, what is a synonym for *declaration*?

4. **Key Ideas and Details:** Cite details in the text that explain why Jefferson was appointed to write the Declaration of Independence.

5. **Key Ideas and Details:** What can you infer about the type of person or politician Samuel Adams was based on the letter? Cite evidence in the text in your response.

Working from the Text

6. Use the graphic organizer to help you analyze the tone and style of Adams's letter. Provide evidence from the text of Adams's specific diction and use of precise nouns and verbs.

What is the **purpose** of the letter?	What are some examples of Adams's **formal style**?

INDEPENDENT READING LINK

Read and Connect

Look for examples of formal and informal styles used in your independent reading book. In what context is each style used? Who is the speaker? Who is the audience? What is the subject under discussion? How does the tone compare to that of "Letter on Thomas Jefferson"? Record the examples and the answers to these questions in your Reader/Writer Notebook.

My Notes

The Formality of It All: Style and Tone

My Notes

What is Adams's **tone**? Is his tone appropriate for the audience and purpose? Why?

Check Your Understanding

Writing Prompt: You are trying to convince your principal to change a school rule or policy (e.g., cell phone usage, school starting time). Work collaboratively to write two letters to experiment with tone and formal style. For Letter 1, write a short letter to your principal using informal style and an inappropriate tone for the audience and purpose (refer to the "DO NOT" list). For Letter 2, transform your first letter to use formal style and an appropriate tone. Be sure to:

- State a clear claim.
- Support the claim with clear reasons and relevant evidence using credible sources.
- Pay attention to style and tone.
- Provide a concluding statement that wraps up your argument.

Be prepared to share both letters with your peers.

A Graphic Is Worth a Thousand Words

Learning Targets
- Evaluate the purpose of visual displays for communicating information.
- Create a visual display to support a claim.

Reading Graphics

Graphics come in all forms. Some provide data, while others may be photos. Every graphic tells its own story. Following these tips for reading graphics.

Tips for Reading Graphics:

- **Read the title.** It tells you what the graphic is about.
- **Read the labels.** Headings, subheadings, and numbers tell you what the graphic is about and describe the specific information given for each category of the graphic.
- **Analyze other features.** Follow arrows and lines to understand the direction or order of events of steps. Read numbers carefully, noting how amounts or intervals of time increase or decrease. If there is a key, pay attention to why different colors are used.

1. Analyze the use of visual displays you are shown. What types of visuals are used? For what purpose? Write comments in the My Notes space.

2. What conclusions can you draw from the following graph? What inferences can you make about why people are choosing to read e-books? Why does Goodreads.com use this graphic on their website?

My Notes

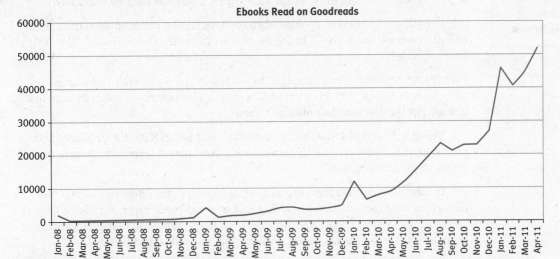

The number of people who are reading ebooks in 2011 went up **163%** over last year, and 36% up over the 4 months prior to 2011.

Source: Goodreads.com

Preview
In this activity, you will read a news article and apply visual information to ideas in it.

Setting a Purpose for Reading
- As you read the following news article, mark the text by putting an asterisk (*) next to any information that you think could be represented in a graphic.
- Circle unknown words and phrases. Try to determine the meaning of the words by using context clues, word parts, or a dictionary.

A Graphic Is Worth a Thousand Words

My Notes

ABOUT THE AUTHOR

Julie Bosman is a newspaper reporter for *The New York Times*. She has written numerous articles about presidential campaigns, the New York City Department of Education, the publishing industry, advertising, and media. Her byline has appeared in many different sections of the newspaper. Bosman grew up and went to college in Wisconsin. She was the editor in chief of the daily student newspaper at the University of Wisconsin in Madison. She now lives in New York City.

News Article

E-Readers Catch Younger Eyes and Go in Backpacks

by Julie Bosman

WORD CONNECTIONS

Cognates

The Spanish cognate for *extraordinary* is *extraordinario*.

1 Something extraordinary happened after Eliana Litos received an e-reader for a Hanukkah gift in December.

2 "Some weeks I completely forgot about TV," said Eliana, 11. "I went two weeks with only watching one show, or no shows at all. I was just reading every day."

3 Ever since the holidays, publishers have noticed that some unusual titles have spiked in e-book sales. The "Chronicles of Narnia" series. "Hush, Hush." The "Dork Diaries" series.

4 At HarperCollins, for example, e-books made up 25 percent of all young-adult sales in January, up from about 6 percent a year before—a boom in sales that quickly got the attention of publishers there.

5 "Adult fiction is hot, hot, hot, in e-books," said Susan Katz, the president and publisher of HarperCollins Children's Books. "And now it seems that teen fiction is getting to be hot, hot, hot."

6 In their infancy e-readers were adopted by an older generation that valued the devices for their convenience, portability and, in many cases, simply for their ability to enlarge text to a more legible size. Appetite for e-book editions of best sellers and adult genre fiction—romance, mysteries, thrillers—has seemed almost bottomless.

demographic: category of people in a population

7 But now that e-readers are cheaper and more plentiful, they have gone mass market, reaching consumers across age and **demographic** groups, and enticing some members of the younger generation to pick them up for the first time.

8 "The kids have taken over the e-readers," said Rita Threadgill of Harrison, N.Y., whose 11-year-old daughter requested a Kindle for Christmas.

9 In 2010 young-adult e-books made up about 6 percent of the total digital sales for titles published by St. Martin's Press, but so far in 2011, the number is up to 20 percent, a spokeswoman for the publisher said.

10 At HarperCollins Children's Books e-book sales jumped in recent weeks for titles like "Pretty Little Liars," a teenage series by Sara Shepard; "I Am Number

Four," a paranormal romance by Pittacus Lore; and "Before I Fall," a novel by Lauren Oliver. (Some sales, publishers noted, are from older people crossing over to young-adult fiction.)

11 Jon Anderson, the publisher of Simon & Schuster Children's Publishing, said some titles, like "Clockwork Angel" and books in the "Night World" series, nearly doubled their e-book sales in the four weeks after Christmas, compared with the four weeks before.

12 "We had an instant reaction—'Boy, a lot of kids got e-readers for Christmas,'" Mr. Anderson said, adding that another significant bump in sales occurred over the three-day weekend that included Martin Luther King's Birthday. "If it follows the same **trend** as adults, it's the start of an upward curve."

13 Digital sales have typically represented only a small fraction of sales of middle-grade and young-adult books, a **phenomenon** usually explained partly by the observation that e-readers were too expensive for children and teenagers.

14 Another theory suggested that the members of the younger set who were first encouraged to read by the immensely popular Harry Potter books tended to prefer hardcover over any other edition, snapping up the books on the day of their release. And **anecdotal** evidence hinted that younger readers preferred print so that they could exchange books with their friends.

15 That scene may be slowly replaced by tweens and teenagers clustered in groups and reading their Nooks or Kindles together, wirelessly downloading new titles with the push of a button, studiously comparing the battery life of the devices and accessorizing them with Jonathan Adler and Kate Spade covers in hot pink, tangerine and lime green.

16 "The young adults and the teenagers are now the newest people who are beginning to experience e-readers," said Matthew Shear, the publisher of St. Martin's Press. "If they get hooked, it's great stuff for the business."

17 It is too soon to tell if younger people who have just picked up e-readers will stick to them in the long run, or grow bored and move on.

18 But Monica Vila, who runs the popular Web site The Online Mom and lectures frequently to parent groups about Internet safety, said that in recent months she had been bombarded with questions from parents about whether they should buy e-readers for their children.

19 In a speech last month at a parents' association meeting in Westchester County, Ms. Vila asked for a show of hands to indicate how many parents had bought e-readers for their children as holiday gifts.

20 About half the hands in the room shot up, she recalled.

21 "Kids are drawn to the devices, and there's a definite desire by parents to move books into this format," Ms. Vila said. "Now you're finding people who are saying: 'Let's use the platform. Let's use it as a way for kids to learn.'"

22 Some teachers have been encouraging, too, telling their students that they are allowed to bring e-readers to school for leisure reading during homeroom and English class, for example.

23 "I didn't buy it until I knew that the teachers in middle school were allowing kids to read their books on their e-readers," said Amy Mauer-Litos, Eliana's mother, adding, "I don't know whether it's the device itself that is appealing, or the easy access to the books, but I will tell you, we've had a lot of snow days lately, and 9 times out of 10, she's in the family room reading her Nook."

My Notes

trend: general direction

phenomenon: unusual fact or situation that is difficult to explain

anecdotal: based on personal accounts rather than facts

public domain: available free for use by any person or entity

My Notes

avid: eager and dedicated

24 Some younger readers have been exploring the classics, thanks to the availability of older e-books that are in the **public domain**—and downloadable free.

25 After receiving a light gray Sony Reader from her grandparents for Christmas, Mia Garcia, a 12-year-old from Touchet, Wash., downloaded "Little Women," a book she had not read before.

26 "It made me cry," Mia said. "Then I read 'Hunger Games,'" the best-selling dystopian novel, "and it also made me cry."

27 Her 8-year-old brother, Tommy, was given an e-reader, too. "I like it because I have so many different books on it already," he said, including "The Trouble Begins at 8," a fast-paced biography of Mark Twain written for children in the middle grades.

28 Eryn Garcia, their mother, said the family used the local library—already stocked with more than 3,000 e-books—to download titles free, sparing her the usual chore of "lugging around 40 pounds of books."

29 "There's something I'm not sure is entirely replaceable about having a stack of inviting books, just waiting for your kids to grab," Ms. Garcia said. "But I'm an **avid** believer that you need to find what excites your child about reading. So I'm all for it."

Second Read

- Reread the news article to answer these text-dependent questions.
- Write any additional questions you have about the text in your Reader/Writer Notebook.

3. **Craft and Structure:** What is the meaning of the word *consumers* in paragraph 7? Use context clues to help you determine the meaning.

4. **Knowledge and Ideas:** What details in the first page of the article support the idea that e-readers are growing in popularity among teens? Does the quote from Rita Threadgill in paragraph 8 provide evidence?

5. **Knowledge and Ideas:** What information in the article could be turned into a graphic to visually develop an idea?

6. **Key Ideas and Details:** What can you infer about the rise of e-reader use by kids from the information in paragraphs 21–23?

7. **Knowledge and Ideas:** Do e-readers offer advantages for kids? Provide details from the text to support your answer.

Working from the Text

8. Write a short summary of the main ideas in this text.

_____

_____

_____

_____

_____

_____

_____

9. **Collaborative Discussion:** Revisit the graphic that appears near the beginning of this activity. What information does the graph give you that the text does not?

WRITING to SOURCES Writing Prompt

Work collaboratively to write a short argument supporting the following claim: *Schools should provide all students with e-readers.* As part of your argument, create a visual display to support the claim. Be creative but purposeful. Your argument and your visual display should help the audience better understand how the reasons and evidence support the claim. Keep these pieces in your Portfolio. On the next page you will find examples of types of graphics to consider using in your display. For your written argument, be sure to

- Provide clear reasons and evidence.
- Make a visual display that is clear and supports your argument.
- Use a formal writing style.

A Graphic Is Worth a Thousand Words

Types of Graphics

- **Line graphs** show change in quantities over time; for example, the chart on page 192 is a line graph.
- **Bar graphs** are generally used to compare quantities within categories.
- **Pie graphs** or **circle graphs** show proportions by dividing a circle into different sections (see the example below).
- **Flowcharts** show a sequence or steps.
- **Timelines** list events in chronological order.
- **Tables** use columns to present information in categories that are easy to compare.

Uses of Social Networking

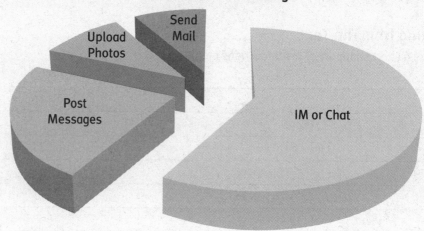

10. What other visual displays or multimedia components (images, music, sound) might be helpful for your display?

11. Present your argument and visual display to the class. Be sure to
    - State the claim clearly.
    - Check that your reasons and evidence clearly support the claim.
    - Explain how the visual supports the claim with reasons and evidence.
    - Use a formal style and a tone appropriate for the purpose and audience.

    Consider using these sentence starters when you present your explanation:
    - As you can see, . . .
    - The . . . shows that . . .
    - The . . . represents . . .

Check Your Understanding

Why are visual displays, such as charts or graphs, helpful in trying to convince an audience? Which of the visual displays you viewed was most effective? Why?

Debate It: Organizing and Communicating an Argument

Learning Targets

- Summarize the key ideas of an article about the pros and cons of social networking.
- Plan an argument about social networking by writing reasons and evidence that support my position.
- Present my position on the controversy in a debate using evidence from my research, and contributing my ideas clearly and responding to others' ideas.

1. Look at the following chart. Be sure to use the tips you learned in the last lesson about reading graphics to understand the information provided. Do you relate to any of this data? Does anything surprise you? Evaluate the effectiveness of this graphic. In what other ways could the information be shown?

LEARNING STRATEGIES:
Marking the Text,
Metacognitive Markers,
Graphic Organizer,
Debate, Paraphrasing

My Notes

How teens use social media sites

Based on teens who use social network sites or Twitter

Send instant messages or chat with a friend through the social network site	88%
Post comments on something a friend has posted	87
Post a status update	86
Post a photo or video	80
Send private messages to a friend within the social network site	76
Tag people in posts, photos, or videos	69
Play a game on a social network site	50
Median # of activities	**6**

Source: The Pew Research Center's Internet & American Life Teen-Parent survey, April 19–July 14, 2011. N = 799 for teens 12–17 and parents, including oversample of minority families. Interviews were conducted in English and Spanish.

Introducing the Strategy: Metacognitive Markers

Using metacognitive markers involves marking the text with symbols to reflect the thinking you are doing as you read. After reading, you can scan the text and use your metacognitive markers to quickly find evidence when you are talking or writing about a text. Here are the markers:

? Use a question mark for questions you have about the text.

! Use an exclamation point for a reaction to what you are reading.

* Use an asterisk for a comment about the text.

_ Use an underline to identify a key idea or detail in the text.

Debate It: Organizing and Communicating an Argument

Preview

In this activity, you will read two articles on the effects of social networking and plan an argument and participate in a debate on the subject.

Setting a Purpose for Reading

- Read the following article to explore the topic of social networking and youth. As you read, use the metacognitive markers ? (e.g., I wonder if, why, I am confused by, etc.) and ! (e.g., wow, surprising, I can relate, etc.).
- Circle unknown words and phrases. Try to determine the meaning of the words by using context clues, word parts, or a dictionary.

Article

Social Networking's
GOOD and BAD
Impacts on Kids

1 Science Daily (Aug. 6, 2011)—Social media present risks and benefits to children but parents who try to secretly monitor their kids' activities online are wasting their time, according to a presentation at the 119th Annual Convention of the American Psychological Association.

2 "While nobody can **deny** that Facebook has altered the landscape of social interaction, particularly among young people, we are just now starting to see solid psychological research demonstrating both the positives and the negatives," said Larry D. Rosen, PhD, professor of psychology at California State University, Dominguez Hills.

3 In a plenary talk entitled, "Poke Me: How Social Networks Can Both Help and Harm Our Kids," Rosen discussed potential **adverse** effects, including:

- Teens who use Facebook more often show more narcissistic **tendencies** while young adults who have a strong Facebook presence show more signs of other psychological disorders, including antisocial behaviors, mania and aggressive tendencies.

- Daily overuse of media and technology has a negative effect on the health of all children, preteens and teenagers by making them more prone to **anxiety**, depression, and other psychological disorders, as well as by making them more susceptible to future health problems.

- Facebook can be distracting and can negatively impact learning. Studies found that middle school, high school and college students who checked Facebook at least once during a 15-minute study period achieved lower grades.

4 Rosen said new research has also found positive influences linked to social networking, including:

deny: to state that something isn't true

adverse: not good, causing harm

tendency: a likelihood that a person will think or act a certain way

anxiety: a nervous mental state caused by feelings of worry, fear, and/or uncertainty

- Young adults who spend more time on Facebook are better at showing "virtual **empathy**" to their online friends.

- Online social networking can help introverted adolescents learn how to socialize behind the safety of various screens, ranging from a two-inch smartphone to a 17-inch laptop.

- Social networking can provide tools for teaching in compelling ways that engage young students.

5 For parents, Rosen offered guidance. "If you feel that you have to use some sort of computer program to **surreptitiously** monitor your child's social networking, you are wasting your time. Your child will find a workaround in a matter of minutes," he said.

empathy: ability to understand and share another person's feelings

surreptitious: secret

Second Read

- Reread the article to answer these text-dependent questions.
- Write any additional questions you have about the text in your Reader/Writer Notebook.

2. **Knowledge and Ideas:** Which adverse effect of social networking discussed in the text is supported by evidence? What is the evidence?

3. **Craft and Structure:** What is the meaning of the word *introverted* in the second bullet of paragraph 4? Use context clues to help you determine the meaning.

4. **Craft and Structure:** What does the advice from Dr. Rosen in the final paragraph tell you about the good and bad of social networking?

My Notes

Debate It: Organizing and Communicating an Argument

Working from the Text

5. Work collaboratively to examine the the main idea of the article. Use a graphic organizer similar to the one below. Write the positive effects of social networking according to the article on the left side and the negative effects on the right.

Positive	Negative

6. **Group Discussion:** Do you agree or disagree with the statement that *social networking has a negative impact on kids*? Use the following protocol to discuss your ideas with your peers.

- One participant shares.
- The other participants take turns responding directly to the person who shared.
- The first participant responds to or builds on his/her peers' comments (through reflecting and paraphrasing) and has "the last word."

Follow the same pattern until all participants have shared. As you share and respond to the discussion, keep these points in mind:

- Listen to each speaker's specific argument and claims.
- Determine whether the speaker supports his or her claims with reasons and evidence or does not clearly support claims.
- Remember to support your own argument and claim with both reasons and clear, relevant evidence.

Setting a Purpose for Reading

- As you read the following informational text, continue to use metacognitive markers to engage with the text and, as you gain more information, to support a position on the value of social networking.

- Circle unknown words and phrases. Try to determine the meaning of the words by using context clues, word parts, or a dictionary.

Informational Text

Pro and Con Arguments:
"Are social networking sites good for our society?"

Did you know?

1. Social networking and blogging sites accounted for 17% (about one in every six minutes) of all time spent on the Internet in Aug. 2009, nearly three times as much as in 2008.

2. Twitter was so important to the Iranian protests after the Iranian presidential election in June 2009 that the US State Department asked Twitter to delay a scheduled network **upgrade** that would have taken the website offline at a busy time of day in Iran. Twitter complied and rescheduled the downtime to 1:30 am Tehran time.

3. On Nov. 3, 2008, the day before the US presidential election, Democratic presidential candidate Barack Obama had 2,379,102 Facebook supporters while Republican candidate John McCain had 620,359. Obama had 833,161 MySpace friends and McCain had 217,811. Obama had 384% more Facebook supporters and 383% more MySpace friends than McCain.

4. Russians spend more time on social networking sites than people in any other country, an average of 6.6 hours per month compared to the worldwide average of 3.7 hours per month.

PRO Social Networking Sites	CON Social Networking Sites
1. Social networking sites allow people to create new relationships and reconnect with friends and family. Increased communication, even online, strengthens relationships.	1. Teens growing up with these sites may not be aware that the information they post is public and that photos and text can be retrieved even after deletion. Consequences from over-sharing personal information include vulnerability to sexual or financial

WORD CONNECTIONS

Etymology

The word *blog* was first used in the late 1990s as a shortened form of *weblog*, a website in the form of a journal. *Blog* combines the sound and meaning of two words, *web* and *log*, a system of word invention used by author Lewis Carroll in *Through the Looking Glass*. The use of *blog* was picked up by Web companies and individual Internet users and led to other derivations such as the verb *blogging*, to write short, informal posts on a blog site.

upgrade: an improvement, to a next level

My Notes

Debate It: Organizing and Communicating an Argument

WORD
CONNECTIONS

Cognates

The Spanish cognate for
predator is *depredador*.

solicitation: a request from
someone, often unwelcome

inhibition: unwillingness to act
or express freely

My Notes

PRO Social Networking Sites

2. Social networking sites allow for creative expression in a new medium. They provide free messaging, blogging, photo storage, games, event invitations, and many other services to anyone with access to a computer and the Internet.

3. Social networking sites bring people with common interests together, offer exposure to new ideas from around the world, and lower **inhibitions** to overcome social anxiety. People who have a difficulty communicating in person are more comfortable interacting via the Internet.

4. 60 million Americans received help with major life issues (changing jobs, finding a new place to live, buying a car, and caring for someone with an illness) from people in their social networks in 2006. These people said social networking sites helped them connect with friends and experts who assisted in their decisions.

5. 59% of students with access to the Internet report that they use social networking sites to discuss educational topics including career and college planning, and 50% use the sites to talk about school assignments. Some parents and teachers say that using these sites helps students improve their reading, writing, and conflict resolution skills, learn to express themselves more clearly, and meet new and different kinds of students from around the world.

CON Social Networking Sites

predators and lost job opportunities from employers finding embarrassing photos or comments.

2. Social networking sites have no way to verify that people are who they claim to be, leaving people vulnerable to **solicitations** from online predators who are able to mask their true identities. Even if the sites agree to remove sex offenders, they cannot identify all of them or stop them from creating new accounts.

3. Social networking sites make cyberbullying, a type of bullying that occurs online, easier and more public than bullying through other online activities such as email and instant messaging. A 2009 study found that 17.3% of middle school students have been victims of cyberbullying. Victims often experience a drop in grades, decreased self-esteem, and other symptoms of depression.

4. The US Marine Corps banned the use of all social media sites on its networks because the sites are "a proven haven for malicious actors and content and are particularly high risk due to information exposure, user generated content and targeting by adversaries." The entire Department of Defense is considering a ban on social networking sites because of concerns over security threats and potential computer viruses.

5. The use of social networking sites can cause personality and brain disorders in children, such as the inability to have real conversations, limited attention spans, a need for instant gratification, Attention-Deficit Hyperactivity Disorder (ADHD),

PRO Social Networking Sites

6. Social media helps low-income kids become more familiar with computers and related technology. One study showed that nearly three quarters of children from poor households have profiles on MySpace or Facebook. By using these websites, they have learned how to edit and upload photos and videos, and have become experienced in using html code to personalize their profile pages. [3]

7. Studies have shown that being part of a social network has a positive impact, including increased quality of life and a reduction in the risk of health problems. They help improve stroke recovery, memory retention, and overall well-being.

8. Social media can be a powerful tool for social change and an alternative to more traditional methods of communication. During the protests of the Iranian election in June 2009, protestors used Twitter to **circumvent** government control over phones and the media. Twitter was so important that the US State Department asked Twitter to delay a network upgrade that would have taken the website offline at a busy time of day in Iran. Twitter complied

CON Social Networking Sites

and self-centered personalities. The fast pace of the sites may rewire the brain with repeated exposure because parts of the brain used for traditional, offline activities become underused.

6. The hours per day of face-to-face socializing have declined as the use of social media has increased. People who use these sites frequently are prone to social isolation. Parents spend less time with their children and couples spend less time together even when they live in the same house, because they are using the Internet instead of interacting with each other.

7. A 2007 study found that workers using Facebook in the office were costing Australian businesses up to $4.5 billion (US) per year. [12] A Feb. 2009 report stated that social networking sites were costing UK businesses an estimated $12.5 billion (US) annually. [13] Numbers for lost revenue from lower worker productivity when employees use social networking sites in the US are not available, but one study found that two-thirds of US workers with Facebook accounts access that site during work hours.

8. A false sense of security may leave social networking site users vulnerable to security attacks such as hacking, leaking sensitive information, and sending viruses. People trust messages sent through social networking sites. However, social networks do not scan messages for

My Notes

circumvent: avoid, by getting around

Debate It: Organizing and Communicating an Argument

phishing: trick used to obtain personal information from an email account

My Notes

cookie: file added by a Web site to a personal computer containing information about the user

PRO Social Networking Sites

and rescheduled the downtime to 1:30 am Tehran time. The ability to remain anonymous helped protect people who were spreading information in real time.

9. To make social networking sites safer for children, the sites have minimum age requirements and default settings based on the user's age to protect children. MySpace, for example, requires users to be at least 14 years old, and the profiles of all users under the age of 16 are automatically set to "private" so they cannot be found during a general search.

10. Social media sites are expanding from general interest to more specific uses that benefit society. For example, sites have been created for medical purposes such as dealing with life altering diseases, alcoholism, drug addiction, weight loss, and autism. Social networking sites with a specific focus help introduce people to others who are dealing with similar issues and provide information, contacts, peer support, and encouragement.

CON Social Networking Sites

viruses or **phishing** scams, while most email accounts do scan the messages for spam and viruses through antivirus software.

9. The public nature of online profiles creates security risks about which most users are unaware. Cybercriminals can gather information to be used for identity theft from social networking profiles, such as birthdays, pet names, mothers' maiden names, names of children, and other details often used in passwords and security questions.

10. Social networking sites were created to make money, not to improve peoples' lives. These websites use networks of online friends to accumulate data about people for the purpose of selling advertising. The sites place **cookies** on the users' computers, gather information, and interests to show personalized ads.

Second Read

- Reread the informational text to answer these text-dependent questions.
- Write any additional questions you have about the text in your Reader/Writer Notebook.

7. **Key Ideas and Details:** What do the important details in the second and third paragraphs of this informational text help you understand?

8. **Craft and Structure:** Use context clues to help you determine the meaning of the word *vulnerability* in the text of paragraph 1 in the CON column. Does the word have a negative or positive connotation?

9. **Key Ideas and Details:** Based on the information in paragraphs 2 and 3 of the CON column, what can you infer about anonymity on social network sites? Provide textual evidence in your answer.

10. **Craft and Structure:** What is your understanding of the word *malicious* based on the U.S Marine Corps ban on social media discussed in paragraph 4 in the CON column?

11. **Key Ideas and Details:** Infer how social networking may improve mental health based on the evidence in paragraph 7 of the PRO column.

Debate It: Organizing and Communicating an Argument

12. **Key Ideas and Details:** Summarize the claim in paragraph 10 of the CON column. In what way is the claim supported or not supported by reasons and evidence?

Working from the Text

13. Summarize three to four key ideas from the preceding text that support your position on whether social networking is good for society.

14. Use the KWHL graphic organizer below to record information as you continue researching the topic of social networking. After reading the texts in this activity, what additional questions do you have? What reasons and evidence do you need to support your position?

Claim:

K	W	H	L
Paraphrase the ideas that stand out to you in relationship to your assigned side of the issue.	What further questions do you have?	Where could you find answers? What other credible resources could you access?	Add notes from your research.

My Notes

_____

_____

_____

_____

_____

_____

_____

_____

_____

Debate It: Organizing and Communicating an Argument

Preparing to Debate

15. Consider all of the research you have done and complete the graphic organizer to prepare for the debate. Remember, the statement you are arguing is whether you agree or disagree that social networking has a negative impact on kids.

Preparing an Argument	
Claim:	
Reason 1:	**Evidence** (*facts, statistics, examples, observations, quotations, and expert opinion*) **Source Citation:**
Reason 2:	**Evidence** (*facts, statistics, examples, observations, quotations, and expert opinion*) **Source Citation:**
Reason 3:	**Evidence** (*facts, statistics, examples, observations, quotations, and expert opinion*) **Source Citation:**
Tone:	
Language (words/phrases) to use to create a formal style:	

16. After completing your research, create a visual display (e.g., a graph or chart) that will help support your claim.

Debating the Topic

During the debate, be sure to

- State a clear claim.
- Support your claim with reasons and evidence; when necessary, offer new support or elaborate on a previous point.
- Maintain a formal style and appropriate tone.
- Speak clearly, slowly, and loudly enough to be heard by the audience.
- Listen to other speakers' claims, reasons, and evidence and distinguish between claims that are supported by credible evidence and those that are not.

Try using the following types of sentence starters when you respond to the ideas of others:

- Even though you just said that . . . , I believe that . . .
- I agree with what you said about . . . , but I think that . . .
- You make a good point about . . . , and I would add that . . .

When you are in the outer circle, create and use a chart such as the one that follows to take notes on the comments made by the inner circle. Be prepared to share your observations.

Argument FOR	Argument AGAINST

After the debate: Was your position strengthened, weakened, or changed completely as a result of the discussion? Explain.

Check Your Understanding

Respond to the Essential Question: How do you effectively communicate in order to convince someone? Add your response to your Portfolio.

 Independent Reading Checkpoint

In your Reading/Writer Notebook, write a few paragraphs describing a controversy at the center of your Independent Reading text. If you have completed the text, include how the controversy was resolved.

My Notes

Researching and Debating a Controversy

Assignment

Work collaboratively to research one side of a controversy that is affecting your school, community, or society. Then participate in a modified debate in which you argue your position and incorporate a visual display with appropriate headings and labels and/or multimedia for support.

Planning and Prewriting: Take time to make a plan for generating ideas and research questions.

- What is your issue, who does this issue affect, and what side will you be arguing?
- How can you state your position clearly as a claim?
- What questions will guide your research?

Researching: Gather information from a variety of credible sources.

- Where can you find sources, and how can you tell that the sources are credible and useful?
- Which strategies will you use to help you understand informational texts?
- How will you take notes by paraphrasing reasons and evidence and recording bibliographic information?

Preparing and Creating: Plan talking points and create a visual display.

- What kind of graphic organizer could help you select the best reasons and evidence from your research?
- How will you select talking points and create index cards for each point to support your claim?
- How will you create a visual that will enhance your talking points?
- How can the Scoring Guide help you evaluate how well you are prepared to meet the requirements of the assignment?

Speaking and Listening: Actively participate in and observe the class debates.

- How will you be sure that you and the other speakers all have the opportunity to voice your opinions?
- How will you use your visual display to support your argument?
- How will you complete a viewing guide to ensure active listening as an audience member?

Reflection

After completing this Embedded Assessment, think about how you went about accomplishing this task, and respond to the following:

- Did your position on the issue remain the same or change after the discussion? Explain your position and what caused it to remain the same or change.
- What part of preparing for the debate was your strongest (e.g., researching, organizing the argument, collaboration, creating the visual display)? Explain.
- What part of the debate was your strongest (e.g., explaining ideas, using formal language, speaking, listening)? Explain.

Technology TIP:

Use a slide presentation program such as PowerPoint or Prezi to create your visual display.

Researching and Debating a Controversy

SCORING GUIDE

Scoring Criteria	Exemplary	Proficient	Emerging	Incomplete
Ideas	The argument • shows extensive evidence of the student's ability to gather evidence, form questions to refocus inquiry, and evaluate the credibility of a variety of sources • avoids plagiarism by including properly cited bibliographic information.	The argument • provides sufficient evidence of the student's ability to gather evidence, form questions to refocus inquiry, and evaluate the credibility of multiple sources • avoids plagiarism by including basic bibliographic information.	The argument • provides insufficient evidence of the student's ability to gather evidence, form questions to refocus inquiry, and evaluate the credibility of multiple sources • includes partial or inaccurate bibliographic information.	The argument • provides little or no evidence of the student's use of a research process • lacks bibliographic information and/or information that appears to have been plagiarized.
Structure	The debater • sequences reasons and evidence to support a claim effectively • integrates visual or multimedia displays to enhance and clarify information • transitions smoothly between talking points; responds to others' ideas by contributing relevant new support and elaboration.	The debater • sequences reasons and evidence to support a claim logically • uses an appropriate visual or multimedia display to clarify information • follows protocol to transition between talking points; avoids repetition when contributing new support or elaboration.	The debater • uses flawed sequencing; supports claim ineffectively • uses a weak or unclear visual or multimedia display • transitions between talking points inconsistently; contributes primarily unrelated and/or repetitive support and elaboration to the discussion.	The debater • does not support the claim • lacks a visual or multimedia display • does not follow rules for group discussion.
Use of Language	The speaker • uses effective eye contact, volume, pacing, and clarity • demonstrates command of the conventions of standard English grammar, usage, and language • maintains a consistently appropriate style and tone.	The speaker • uses sufficient eye contact, volume, pacing, and clarity • demonstrates adequate command of the conventions of standard English grammar, usage, and language • maintains a generally appropriate style and tone.	The speaker • uses eye contact, volume, pacing, and clarity unevenly • demonstrates partial command of the conventions of standard English grammar, usage, and language • maintains an inconsistently appropriate style and/or tone.	The speaker • uses flawed or ineffective speaking skills • commits frequent errors in standard English grammar, usage, and language • uses an inappropriate style and/or tone.

Previewing Embedded Assessment 2: Preparing for Argumentative Writing

LEARNING STRATEGIES:
Graphic Organizer,
Close Reading

Learning Targets

- Analyze and summarize the skills and knowledge needed to complete Embedded Assessment 2 successfully.
- Explore rhetorical appeals used in argumentative writing.

Making Connections

In the first part of this unit, you learned about elements essential to argumentative writing: claims, reasons, and evidence. In this part of the unit, you will expand on your writing skills by writing an argumentative letter to persuade an audience to agree with your position on an issue.

Essential Questions

Reflect on your increased understanding of the Essential Questions. Based on your current understanding, how would you answer these questions now?

- Why do we have controversy in society?
- How do we communicate in order to convince others?

Developing Vocabulary

In your Reader/Writer Notebook, look at the new vocabulary you learned as you were introduced to argumentative writing in the first half of this unit. Re-sort the words below in the graphic organizer, once again using the QHT strategy. Notice which words have moved from one column to the other.

Academic Vocabulary	Literary Terms
controversy	tone
argument	formal style
claim	
reasons	
evidence	
research	
plagiarism	
credible	

Q	H	T

My Notes

Unpacking Embedded Assessment 2

Read the assignment for Embedded Assessment 2: Writing an Argumentative Letter.

> Think about a topic (subject, event, idea, or controversy) that you truly care about, and take a position on it. Write an argumentative letter to convince an audience to support your position on the topic.

In your own words, summarize what you will need to know to complete this assessment successfully. With your class, create a graphic organizer to represent the skills and knowledge you will need to complete the tasks identified in the Embedded Assessment.

Thinking About Persuasion

1. Think about times in the past when you tried to convince someone to believe or to do something. Were you successful? Write down at least four to five examples of times you tried to be persuasive and the outcome of each.

Times I Was Persuasive	Outcome

2. For each successful outcome listed above, write down the reasons that you gave that persuaded the other person. Try to list four or five examples of supporting reasons.

_____

_____

_____

_____

My Notes

Previewing Embedded Assessment 2: Preparing for Argumentative Writing

INDEPENDENT READING LINK

Read and Research

To support your learning in the second half of the unit, research and read a book, magazine articles, or news articles that explore a current "hot topic" or controversial issue.

My Notes

3. Which of the examples given in 2 above were appeals to the emotions of your listener? Which were appeals to your listener's logic—intellectual appeals?

_____

_____

_____

_____

_____

_____

4. With a group of classmates, discuss the examples you each recorded and whether those examples were appeals to emotion or to logic. Based on your examples, were emotional appeals or logical appeals more effective?

_____

_____

_____

_____

_____

_____

Looking at a Model Argumentative Letter

Learning Targets
- Read closely to identify claim, reasons, and evidence and how they support an author's purpose.
- Generate ideas and apply an organizational pattern to write an argumentative paragraph that supports a claim with sound reasons and evidence.

Preview
In this activity, you will read a student letter written in response to the argumentative prompt below and analyze and extend the argument it proposes.

Argumentative Prompt: Some state legislators believe that school libraries should not provide Internet access for students. Decide whether you agree or disagree with this position. Write a letter to convince state legislators to support your position.

Setting a Purpose for Reading
- As you read the student letter, mark the text and take notes in the margin to identify the claim, reasoning, and evidence provided.
- Circle unknown words and phrases. Try to determine the meaning of the words by using context clues, word parts, or a dictionary.
- Mark these parts of the letter: salutation, body, closing.

> **Draft**
>
> # Student Letter

Dear Legislator,

1 We live in the 21st century and see technology all around us. Americans have access to the Internet almost everywhere, at home, on cell phones, and even at school. For some students, school is the only access they have to the Internet. The web also provides many more learning opportunities and prepares us students for high school and the real world. Internet access for students in school libraries is crucial for our success.

2 Students need school access to the Internet because computers and the price for Internet service can sometimes be too costly for a family. Internet service providers, such as Quest, charge an average of fifty dollars a month. Many times teachers assign projects that students need access to computers to complete. Internet access in the school library is sometimes the only option for numerous pupils. If that only option is taken away, innocent students will be penalized for not being able to fulfill a school project.

LEARNING STRATEGIES:
Marking the Text, Brainstorming, Webbing, Writer's Checklist

My Notes

My Notes

3 When we get to high school, we will be getting prepared for the real-world that is coming to us sooner than we think. In the technology filled society that we are about to embark on, we will have to know many skills on how to best utilize a computer and the Internet. My cousin is a good example of someone who is utilizing the technology skills he learned as a teenager. He is in college and takes courses online. Taking online courses allows him to have a job and go to college at the same time. He says he spends close to 10 hours a week studying, mostly at night after his job. Knowing how to use the Internet is helping build a successful future. Students spend most of their time in school around adults that are here to teach them life skills. I believe that we can learn the most in preparation for the real world in school!

4 In conclusion, the best solution is to continue allowing school libraries to provide Internet access for students. For many, that provides the only access they have. It not only provides gateways for better learning experiences, but also readies us for the big journey that is ahead of us once we leave the comfort of middle and high school. Can you even imagine what kind of struggles would come our way if state legislators choose to terminate school Internet access?

Sincerely,

A Concerned Student

Second Read

- Reread the letter to answer these text-dependent questions.
- Write any additional questions you have about the text in your Reader/Writer Notebook.

1. **Craft and Structure:** Why does the writer believe access to the Internet is important in school? Use evidence from paragraphs 1 and 2 to describe the writer's point of view.

2. **Craft and Structure:** How does the student writer develop the argument in paragraph 3 and 4 of the letter? Use evidence from the text in your response.

Working from the Text

3. What is the writer's purpose in writing the letter? Identify the claims in the letter and explain how they support the writer's purpose.

_____

_____

_____

_____

4. Return to the letter to mark the text for formal style. Annotate the text to identify the author's tone. In My Notes, write how the author's formal style and tone help make the argument convincing, or not. Support your response with examples from the letter.

5. With the guidance of your teacher, conduct research as needed and draft another body paragraph as a new third paragraph. You will return to this body paragraph to practice revision strategies and refine your writing skills. Follow the steps below to research and draft a paragraph.

Drafting a body paragraph: Prewriting

Brainstorm evidence for the main idea (reason) of your new paragraph.

Research:

- What questions will guide your research?
- Where will you gather evidence?
- What sources will you consult?

Drafting

After conducting initial research, generate an outline for the body paragraph and then write your draft. Remember, each body paragraph should consist of

- **A topic sentence**: a sentence that consists of a subject and an opinion that works directly to support the claim (thesis)
- **Transitions**: words used to connect ideas (e.g., *for example, for instance*)
- **Supporting information**: specific evidence and details (What facts and details are most appropriate? Do you accurately synthesize information from a variety of sources?)
- **Reflective commentary**: sentences that explain how the information is relevant to the claim/thesis. (Use reflective commentary to also bring a sense of closure to the paragraph.)

My Notes

Looking at a Model Argumentative Letter

6. Draft your body paragraph in the space below.

Check Your Understanding

Create a Writer's Checklist based on what you already know you should "be sure to" do to create a successful argument.

Facts and Feelings: Rhetorical Appeals in Argumentative Writing

Learning Targets
- Identify logos and pathos used in an argument.
- Explain how evidence is relevant and sufficient to support a claim.

LEARNING STRATEGIES:
Marking the Text, Rereading,
Graphic Organizer

Rhetoric and Rhetorical Appeals

Rhetoric is the art of using words to persuade in writing and speaking. Writers use different types of rhetoric depending on their purpose and audience.

Writers of argumentative texts appeal to their audience using sound reasoning and evidence. Writers who use logical thinking that makes sense and is backed up with valid evidence (such as statistics, examples) are appealing to reason. This **rhetorical appeal** is known as **logos**.

At times, writers of argumentative texts also use evidence that appeals to feelings. When appealing to feelings, a writer uses emotional language or talks about basic values such as kindness, justice, and responsibility. This rhetorical appeal is known as **pathos**. Pathos should be used sparingly in an argument since relevant evidence is required to support a claim but an emotional appeal typically does not include evidence.

Preview

In this activity, you will read a letter and analyze how rhetorical appeals are used to support an argument.

Setting a Purpose for Reading

- As you read the letter that follows, highlight the claim. Mark the text for specific evidence that appeals to logic (logos, L) and to emotion (pathos, P).
- Circle unknown words and phrases. Try to determine the meaning of the words by using context clues, word parts, or a dictionary.

ABOUT THE AUTHOR
The Grand Council Fire of American Indians was a Native American organization whose members came from many different tribes. The organization worked for better treatment of and policies for the American Indian populations. In 1927 a political campaigner (William Hale Thompson of Chicago) used a slogan of "America First" to claim that the history taught in textbooks was biased in favor of the British. Thompson won re-election as the mayor of Chicago, and he then demanded that the city's textbooks be replaced with books that focused on the accomplishments of the ethnic groups in the United States. Members of the Grand Council Fire of American Indians used the "America First" program as an opportunity to describe how Native Americans also were misrepresented in textbooks. The president of the Council, Scott H. Peters (of the Chippewa Tribe) wrote the following letter to Chicago's newly elected mayor asking that the contributions and accomplishments of Native Americans also be included in the textbooks.

Literary Terms
Rhetorical appeals, or persuasive strategies, are used in arguments to support claims.
Logos is a rhetorical appeal that uses logical reasoning and evidence.
Pathos is a rhetorical appeal to feelings.

My Notes

Facts and Feelings: Rhetorical Appeals in Argumentative Writing

My Notes

Letter

The First Americans

by Scott H. Peters, Grand Council Fire of American Indians

December 1, 1927

To the mayor of Chicago:

1 You tell all white men "America First." We believe in that. We are the only ones, truly, that are one hundred percent. We therefore ask you, while you are teaching schoolchildren about America First, teach them truth about the First Americans.

2 We do not know if school histories are pro-British, but we do know that they are unjust to the life of our people—the American Indian. They call all white victories battles and all Indian victories massacres. The battle with Custer has been taught to schoolchildren as a fearful massacre on our part. We ask that this, as well as other incidents, be told fairly. If the Custer battle was a massacre, what was Wounded Knee?

3 History books teach that Indians were murderers—is it murder to fight in self-defense? Indians killed white men because white men took their lands, ruined their hunting grounds, burned their forests, destroyed their buffalo. White men penned our people on **reservations**, then took away the reservations. White men who rise to protect their property are called patriots—Indians who do the same are called murderers.

reservation: land in the U.S. set aside for use by Native Americans

4 White men call Indians **treacherous**—but no mention is made of broken treaties on the part of the white man. White men say that Indians were always fighting. It was only our lack of skill in white man's warfare that led to our defeat. An Indian mother prayed that her boy be a great medicine man rather than a great warrior. It is true that we had our own small battles, but in the main we were peace loving and home loving.

treacherous: not to be trusted

5 White men called Indians thieves—and yet we lived in frail skin lodges and needed no locks or iron bars. White men call Indians savages. What is civilization? Its marks are a noble religion and philosophy, original arts, stirring music, rich story and legend. We had these. Then we were not savages, but a civilized race.

6 We made blankets that were beautiful, that the white man with all his machinery has never been able to duplicate. We made baskets that were beautiful. We wove in beads and colored quills designs that were not just decorative motifs but were the outward expression of our very thoughts. We made pottery—pottery that was useful, and beautiful as well. Why not make schoolchildren acquainted with the beautiful handicrafts in which we were skilled? Put in every school Indian blankets, baskets, pottery.

7 We sang songs that carried in their melodies all the sounds of nature—the running of waters, the sighing of winds, and the calls of the animals. Teach these to your children that they may come to love nature as we love it.

8 We had our statesmen—and their oratory has never been equaled. Teach the children some of these speeches of our people, remarkable for their brilliant oratory.

9 We played games—games that brought good health and sound bodies. Why not put these in your schools? We told stories. Why not teach schoolchildren more of the wholesome proverbs and legends of our people? Tell them how we loved all that was beautiful. That we killed game only for food, not for fun. Indians think white men who kill for fun are murderers.

10 Tell your children of the friendly acts of Indians to the white people who first settled here. Tell them of our leaders and heroes and their deeds. Tell them of Indians such as Black Partridge, Shabbona, and others who many times saved the people of Chicago at great danger to themselves. Put in your history books the Indian's part in the World War. Tell how the Indian fought for a country of which he was not a citizen, for a flag to which he had no claim, and for a people that have treated him unjustly.

11 The Indian has long been hurt by these unfair books. We ask only that our story be told in fairness. We do not ask you to overlook what we did, but we do ask you to understand it. A true program of America First will give a generous place to the culture and history of the American Indian.

12 We ask this, Chief, to keep sacred the memory of our people.

Second Read

- Reread the letter to answer these text-dependent questions.
- Write any additional questions you have about the text in your Reader/Writer Notebook.

1. **Craft and Structure:** What is the speaker's tone? What words or phrases in the opening paragraphs reflect this tone?

2. **Craft and Structure:** How does the author use the words "murderer" and "savage" to appeal to both the logic and emotions of the reader? Provide text evidence in your response.

My Notes

Facts and Feelings: Rhetorical Appeals in Argumentative Writing

3. **Key Ideas and Details:** In paragraphs 3–5, how does the author respond to negative perceptions of Indians?

4. **Key Ideas and Details:** What evidence does the author include to show that Native Americans are a civilized race?

5. **Craft and Structure:** What is the purpose of this speech, and how is it conveyed in the text?

Working from the Text

6. Reread the letter. Use the graphic organizer to record examples of the writer's use of rhetorical appeals.

Title: *The First Americans*
Appeals to Reason—logos *(facts, statistics, examples, observations, quotations, and expert opinions)*
Examples:

Appeals to Feelings–pathos (*emotional language; mention of basic values*)

Examples:

7. Choose one piece of evidence and discuss how it is both **relevant** and **sufficient** to support the claim of the letter.

_____

_____

_____

_____

_____

_____

_____

ACADEMIC VOCABULARY
In order to be convincing, evidence must be both **relevant** or closely connected to the matter at hand, and **sufficient**, or enough for the purpose of supporting a claim or reason.

8. Revisit and reread another text you have previously read in this unit. Analyze that text for rhetorical appeals. Then, complete the graphic organizer on the next page.

Facts and Feelings: Rhetorical Appeals in Argumentative Writing

My Notes

Title:
Appeals to Reason: logos *(facts, statistics, examples, observations, quotations, and expert opinions)*
Examples:

Appeals to Feelings: pathos *(emotional language; mention of basic values)*
Examples:

Check Your Understanding

Which text do you find most convincing? Explain how that author incorporated rhetorical appeals to create the argument. Did the argument of that text use one kind of appeal—logos or pathos—more than the other?

_____

_____

_____

_____

_____

_____

Citing Evidence

Learning Targets

- Record information about credible sources, cite them accurately, and paraphrase relevant information.
- Use appositives to give specific information about sources.

1. What does it mean to "give credit" when writing an argumentative text? How does this help writers avoid plagiarism? What does "giving credit" have to do with logos?

_____

_____

_____

_____

LEARNING STRATEGIES:
Metacognitive Markers

My Notes

Citing Sources

When using information gained from research, it is important to cite the sources of that information to avoid plagiarism. Remember that plagiarism is using someone else's work without giving them credit.

For argumentative writing, citing sources also builds credibility with an audience and adds authority to evidence.

You can incorporate research material in your writing in two ways:

- **Direct quotations** are word-for-word quotes from the source. The source must be named. Direct quotations are usually short.
- **Paraphrasing** involves putting a passage from source material into your own words. A paraphrase must also be attributed to the original source. Paraphrased material is usually shorter than the original passage, taking a somewhat broader portion of the source and condensing it slightly.

Tips for Citing Sources

Follow these tips for citing sources to avoid plagiarism and to improve the organization of your writing:

- Use a statement that credits the source; e.g., "According to Dr. Martin Luther King, Jr., ..."
- Put quotation marks around any unique words or phrases that you cannot or do not want to change; e.g., "'savage inequalities' exist throughout our educational system."
- If you are having trouble paraphrasing, try writing your paraphrase of a text without looking at the original, relying only on your memory and notes.
- Check your paraphrase against the original text. Correct any errors in content accuracy, and be sure to use quotation marks to set off any exact phrases from the original text. Check your paraphrase against sentence and paragraph structure, as copying those is also considered plagiarism.

Citing Evidence

Language and Writer's Craft: Using Appositives

An appositive is a noun and any accompanying modifiers that are placed close to another noun to identify it.

Example: My friend **Sean** is an expert on baseball.

In this sentence the appositive *Sean* identifies the noun "my friend."

An appositive can be a single word, as in the example above, or a phrase. Appositive phrases are usually set off by commas, parentheses, or dashes.

Example: Mary Southard, **director of volunteers at the children's hospital**, reports that over fifty new volunteers signed up this year.

This appositive phrase identifies Mary Southard as someone who has knowledge (and credibility) of the number of new volunteers.

When you cite sources in an argument, use appositives and appositive phrases to give more precise information about a source. This information strengthens your appeal to logos.

2. Combine the following parts to create a sentence with an appositive phrase. Pay attention to your punctuation.
- president and publisher of HarperCollins Children's Books
- Susan Katz
- explains that teen fiction is "hot" right now to people who read on e-books

3. Read the passage below from the last activity. Think about the main idea.

Tell your children of the friendly acts of Indians to the white people who first settled here. Tell them of our leaders and heroes and their deeds. Tell them of Indians such as Black Partridge, Shabbona, and others who many times saved the people of Chicago at great danger to themselves. Put in your history books the Indian's part in the World War. Tell how the Indian fought for a country of which he was not a citizen, for a flag to which he had no claim, and for a people that have treated him unjustly.

—From *The First Americans*

4. Now write a sentence that briefly summarizes the passage, including the name of the author (Scott H. Peters) and an appositive phrase to give more information about the author.

5. Imagine you were the author of the letter *The First Americans* and you wanted to add some evidence of Native Americans' contribution to World War I. Find a credible digital or print source of this information and paraphrase the information you find most relevant to include in the letter.

Revising to Add Appeals: Return to the body paragraph you wrote for the model argumentative letter in Activity 3.10. Mark the text for appeals to logos you used. Revise the paragraph as needed to add appeals to logos and strengthen your reasons and evidence. Be sure to

- Support your claim with valid evidence (statistics, examples, quotations).
- Cite sources from your research as needed to strengthen the logic of your argument.
- Use at least one appositive phrase to give more precise information about a source.

Add this writing piece to your Portfolio.

Check Your Understanding

Explain the relationship between citing sources and appealing to logos. Then, describe one revision you made to your letter and why you made it.

My Notes

**INDEPENDENT
READING LINK**

Read and Discuss

Discuss with a partner how the author of your independent reading book gives credit to his or her sources. If you wanted more information on one of the sources cited, discuss how would you know where to look. Record answers in your Reader/Writer Notebook.

Playing with Persuasive Diction: Appealing to Pathos

LEARNING STRATEGIES:
Skimming, Marking the
Text, Looping

Learning Targets
- Identify and analyze examples of persuasive diction.
- Match style and purpose in writing by applying looping and persuasive diction to add pathos.

What's in a Word?

Consider how similar words can make you feel different ways. Would you rather be called *youthful* or *immature*? Would you rather be considered *curious* or *nosy*? Word choice, or diction, is an important aspect of argumentative writing. Because words can carry an emotional impact, each one represents an opportunity for the writer to convince his or her audience.

Learning from Advertisements

1. As you skim through ads, record words that stand out for their emotional meaning (strong connotative diction).

2. Sort the adjectives and verbs you find by adding them to the list below:

Power Adjective List:

amazing, authentic

best

convenient, critical

dependable

easy

free

guaranteed

healthy

important, improved, instant

limited, lucky

new

powerful

secure

tested

unique, unlimited, unreal, unsurpassed

vital

wonderful

My Notes

Power Verb List:

abolish, achieve, act, adopt, anticipate, apply, assess

boost, break, bridge, build

capture, change, choose, clarify, comprehend, create

decide, define, deliver, design, develop, discover, drive

eliminate, ensure, establish, evaluate, exploit, explore

filter, finalize, focus, foresee

gain, gather, generate, grasp

identify, improve, increase, innovate, inspire, intensify

lead, learn

manage, master, maximize, measure, mobilize, motivate

overcome

penetrate, persuade, plan, prepare, prevent

realize, reconsider, reduce, replace, resist, respond

save, simplify, solve, stop, succeed

train, transfer, transform

understand, unleash

win

Introducing the Strategy: Adding by Looping

Looping is one way to add emotional appeal (pathos) to your writing. With looping, you underline an important sentence or a particular word or phrase. You then write a few more sentences to add new ideas. Repeating the process with the new sentences allows you to keep adding ideas to your writing.

3. Imagine you have drafted the following note to your family trying to convince them where to go on vacation. Underline an important sentence, phrase, or word, and then write two more sentences on the next page. Be sure to appeal to pathos by using power adjectives and verbs in your new sentences.

Dear Family

I would like to go to Colorado for our family vacation. We could go on a rafting trip there! I have heard that rafting is an exhilarating experience. My friend's family went last summer, and she described plunging down rapids and paddling against intense currents. Going rafting together would be exciting and would probably make our family bond even stronger.

Thank you for considering it.

Your daughter

My Notes

Playing with Persuasive Diction: Appealing to Pathos

My Notes

Your two new sentences:

a. _____

_____

_____

_____

b. _____

_____

_____

_____

Check Your Understanding

Respond to the following questions about the note you just revised:

• What is the relationship between persuasive diction and appealing to pathos?

• What power adjectives and verbs did you add that were especially effective?

• If you were going to improve the practice paragraph even more, what would you do? What do you notice it is missing? Explain.

Revising for Persuasive Diction: Return to the body paragraph you wrote and revised for the model argumentative letter (Activity 3.10). Revise the paragraph for persuasive diction. To properly add pathos to the development of your argument, be sure to

• Mark the text for appeals to pathos you may have already used.

• Add emotional appeals that support your logical appeals for a balance that fits your purpose and audience.

• Use looping to revise by adding new ideas and persuasive diction (power verbs and adjectives).

INDEPENDENT READING LINK

Read and Respond

Find at least five words or phrases that carry strong emotional meaning in your independent reading book. Write them in your Reader/Writer Notebook and set a goal to use them in your own writing.

Writing an Introduction and a Conclusion

LEARNING STRATEGIES:
Marking the Text, Rereading

Learning Targets

- Write an argument to support a claim with clear reasons and evidence.
- Write effective introductions and conclusions to an argument.

Timed Writing

On a separate piece of paper, write a response to one of the prompts below or to one your teacher provides. Consider audience and purpose as you plan your draft. Remember to apply your knowledge of how to write a claim and support it with relevant reasons and evidence. If possible, use a word-processing program to create your draft and develop your keyboarding skills. If writing by hand, double-space your draft to provide room for revision.

Argumentative Writing Prompt: Write a letter to argue for one of the following:

- Convince a family member of something you would like to do over the summer.
- Convince your principal or a teacher to change a school rule or policy.
- Convince a friend of something you would like to do together over the weekend.

1. Now that you have drafted your letter, analyze the beginning and ending of your text. Explain how you started and ended your letter.

_____

_____

_____

My Notes

Introductions and Conclusions

Review the guidelines below about writing an introduction and a conclusion. Mark the text for new or important information as you read.

An **introduction** contains the following:

- **A hook**. Can you think of an event, a question, or a real-life story (called an anecdote) to hook your reader?
- **A connection between the hook and the claim**. How does your hook relate to your claim?
- **The claim**. Your viewpoint on an issue is important to you; what is it?

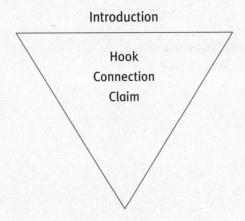

Introduction

Hook
Connection
Claim

Writing an Introduction and a Conclusion

My Notes

A **conclusion** contains the following:

- A **summary** of the most important reason for the argument
- A **call to action** restating what you want the reader to believe or do

It is important to end an argument in a convincing way. You might conclude your argument by summarizing your most important reason. However, an especially effective conclusion is a call to action in which you state for the last time what the reader should believe or do. It is also interesting and effective to revisit the idea in your hook at some point in your conclusion.

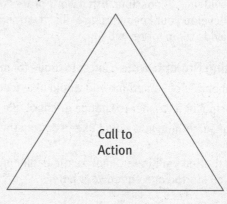

Call to
Action

Conclusion

2. Return to the sample argumentative letter in Activity 3.10 and reread its introduction and conclusion. Mark the text for the components of an effective introduction and conclusion. Make notes about any revisions that you would consider to improve the beginning and ending of the letter.

Revising Your Letter: Return to the letter you drafted for the timed writing in this activity and revise by looping, adding, deleting, and replacing to improve its introduction, body paragraphs, and conclusion. Be sure to

- Inform your audience of the purpose and introduce your claim clearly in the introduction.
- Revise the body paragraphs to make your reasons and evidence stronger.
- Revise the ending to make sure your letter connects to the claim, reasons, and evidence in the argument you have presented.
- Check that words are spelled correctly and that you are using correct grammar and punctuation.

Check Your Understanding

Complete the following statements.

An introduction **does** ...

An introduction **does not** ...

A conclusion **does** ...

A conclusion **does not** ...

Saying Too Much or Too Little?

Learning Targets

- Identify and use transitions to improve the coherence of writing.
- Revise writing by using transitions, deleting, and creating complex sentences to clarify claims, reasons, and evidence.

Giving and Interpreting Directions

You will work in pairs to give directions and draw a picture. One person will give directions while the other person listens and follows the directions to draw a picture.

1. As the person giving directions, think about what you will say and the best way to communicate what is to be drawn by your partner. Make any notes below.

2. As the person following the directions, was your drawing successful? What did your partner say that helped you draw correctly? What additional information would have been helpful?

Revising for Coherence

As you learned in the preceding exercise, explaining clearly makes a difference in how well your audience understands your meaning. In Unit 1, you learned that the term *coherence* refers to the logical organization of an essay. A coherent essay ties ideas together to flow smoothly from one sentence to the next and from one paragraph to the next, making the essay easy to follow for the reader.

An effective way to revise for coherence is to use transitions, both within and between paragraphs. Transitions help you move from one sentence or thought to another.

Certain words and phrases in the English language are typical transitions. These transitions are outlined in the table on the next page. Read the information in the table, and place a star (*) next to the words or phrases you used or heard in the drawing activity.

LEARNING STRATEGIES:
Visualizing, Rereading, Marking the Text, Adding, Replacing, Deleting

My Notes

Saying Too Much or Too Little?

Transitions That ...	Transitional Signal Words and Phrases
Add ideas	*in addition, furthermore, moreover, further, besides, too, also, and then, then too, again, next, secondly, equally important*
Compare or contrast	*similarly, likewise, in comparison, in a like manner, however, in contrast, conversely, on the other hand, but, nevertheless, and yet, even so, still*
Show examples	*for example, for instance*
Reinforce an idea	*indeed, in fact, as a matter of fact, to be sure, of course, in any event, by all means*
Indicate results	*as a result, as a consequence, consequently, therefore, thus, hence, accordingly*
Express a sequence of ideas	*first, second, soon after, then, previously, meanwhile, in the meantime, later, at length, after a while, immediately, next*
Show proximity	*here, nearby, at this spot, near at hand, in this area, on the opposite side, across from, not far from*
Conclude	*finally, in short, in other words, to sum up, in conclusion, in the end*

My Notes

3. Return to the student sample argumentative text in Activity 3.10 and read it for organization and coherence. Mark the text for transitional words and phrases. Make notes about any revisions that you think would improve coherence.

Revising for Coherence: Return to the letter you drafted and revised for the timed writing prompt in Activity 3.14. Revise to improve its coherence. Be sure to

- Use adding or replacing to incorporate transitional words and phrases.
- Use words and/or phrases to clarify the relationships between your ideas, specifically your claims, reasons, and evidence.
- Read your revised piece to a peer for feedback on its coherence.

Introducing the Strategy: Deleting

When you revise by **deleting**, you identify irrelevant, repetitive, or meaningless words and remove them from your writing. When you delete a word, phrase, or sentence, reread the section aloud to make sure that it still makes sense after your deletion. Deleting sentences or parts of sentences can improve overall coherence in your writing.

Revising by Deleting

4. Revise the paragraph below. Identify words and sentences that are irrelevant, repetitive, or meaningless, and delete them by drawing a line through them. Then write your new paragraph in the space below.

My family and I had a great time on our fun rafting trip. We went to Colorado. Colorado is called the Rocky Mountain State. The rafting was really very exciting and scary. The weather was a little cold, so we all got sick on our way home.

5. Why did you delete the words and/or sentences you did?

_____

_____

_____

6. Return to the student sample argumentative letter from Activity 3.10. Reread it to see if any part is irrelevant, repetitive, or meaningless. Make notes about any sentences that you would consider deleting and why.

_____

_____

_____

Saying Too Much or Too Little?

My Notes

7. Return to the letter you revised for the timed writing in Activity 3.14. Read it for coherence and for possible sentences or ideas to delete. Be sure to

- Read for coherence to help you decide whether deleting (or adding) ideas would improve the flow of the letter.

- Identify and remove irrelevant, repetitive, or meaningless ideas.

- Check your letter for correct spelling, grammar, and punctuation.

- Select a part of your letter that you revised by deleting. Read the "before" and "after" versions to a peer to get feedback.

Language and Writer's Craft: Revising by Creating Complex Sentences

Sentence variety is another important aspect of good writing. Varying the types of sentences you use helps keep your audience interested. One way to create sentence variety is by revising to create complex sentences.

A **complex sentence** shows a close relationship between two ideas. It is made up of a **dependent clause** and an **independent clause**.

- A dependent clause cannot stand alone as a sentence. For example, *because I feel strongly about this subject* is a dependent clause.

- An independent clause can stand alone as a sentence. For example, *I have decided to write a letter to share my thoughts* stands alone as a complete thought.

- A complex sentence combines a dependent and an independent clause. For example, *Because I feel strongly about this subject, I have decided to write a letter to share my thoughts*.

Dependent clauses are easy to identify because they almost always start with a "dependent marker" such as those in the list below.

after	as though	in order that	unless
although	because	provided that	whereas
as if	before	since	while

Revising by Creating Complex Sentences

8. Revise the paragraph below by combining sentences to create complex sentences. Use a dependent marker to connect the dependent and independent clauses.

We should go to the movies on Saturday. The weather will be lousy. The test we had today was tough. A movie will be a good way to unwind. The new *Hunger Games* installment is out. I know you're a big fan of the books. This will convince you to see all the films in the series, too. I may be able get my brother to drive us. He wants to see it anyway.

Check Your Understanding

Explain three ways you can revise your writing to improve its coherence.

Preparing to Write an Argument

Learning Targets
- Reflect on personal argumentative writing skills.
- Assess strengths and weaknesses and plan how to address them in future writing.

1. Use the graphic organizer to help you reflect on what you have learned about argumentative writing and revising—and how you will use your knowledge to complete Embedded Assessment 2.

Argumentative Letter Reflection and Planning		
Scoring Criteria	**Reflection**	**Planning**
Paraphrase the specific evaluation criteria from the Scoring Guide.	Self-assess by describing an area of strength and an area of weakness for you.	How can you use this information to help you write your argumentative letter? What do you plan to do? Be specific.
Ideas	Strength: Weakness:	
Structure	Strength: Weakness:	
Use of Language (including conventions)	Strength: Weakness:	

2. In order of importance, write the three areas you most need help with.

_____

_____

_____

 Independent Reading Checkpoint

Make a short oral presentation about a character or person in your Independent Reading text who was able to successfully convince others of something. Include how the person was successful in convincing others. Did he make an argument using reasons and evidence, or communicate in a different way?

Writing an Argumentative Letter

Assignment

Think about a topic (subject, event, idea, or controversy) that you truly care about and take a position on it. Write an argumentative letter to convince an audience to support your position on the topic.

Planning and Prewriting: Take time to make a plan for generating ideas and research questions.

- What is a relevant topic that you care about and can take a position on?

- How can you use a prewriting strategy such as prewriting or webbing to explore your ideas?

- What questions will guide your research?

Researching: Gather information from a variety of credible sources.

- Where can you find sources, and how can you tell that the sources are credible and useful?

- Which strategies will you use to help you understand informational texts?

- How will you take notes by paraphrasing reasons and evidence and recording bibliographic information?

Drafting: Write an argumentative letter that is appropriate for your task, purpose, and audience.

- How will you select the best reasons and evidence from your research?

- Who is the audience for your letter, and what would be an appropriate tone and style for this audience?

Evaluating and Revising the Draft: Create opportunities to review and revise your work.

- During the process of writing, when can you pause to share with and respond to others?

- What is your plan to add suggestions and revision ideas into your draft?

- How can you revise your draft to improve your diction and syntax?

- How can the Scoring Guide help you evaluate how well your draft meets the requirements of the assignment?

Checking and Editing for Publication: Confirm that your final draft is ready for publication.

- How will you check for grammatical and technical accuracy?

Reflection

After completing this Embedded Assessment, think about how you went about accomplishing this task, and respond to the following:

- What were the strongest elements of your argument?
- How did you use emotional appeals to connect with your audience?

My Notes

Technology TIP:

Use a word-processing program to help you format your letter correctly and to make it easy to make corrections for preparing a publishable draft.

Writing an Argumentative Letter

SCORING GUIDE

Scoring Criteria	Exemplary	Proficient	Emerging	Incomplete
Ideas	The letter • supports a claim with compelling reasons, evidence, and commentary, including relevant facts, details, quotes, paraphrases, and rhetorical appeals (pathos, logos) • avoids plagiarism by including proper and thorough citations.	The letter • supports a claim with sufficient reasons, evidence, and commentary, including adequate facts, details, quotes, paraphrases, and rhetorical appeals (pathos, logos) • avoids plagiarism by including basic citations.	The letter • has an unclear or unfocused claim and/or insufficient support such as unrelated, weak, or inadequate facts, details, quotes, paraphrases, and rhetorical appeals (pathos, logos) • includes partial or inaccurate citations.	The letter • has no obvious claim or provides minimal or inaccurate support • lacks citations and/or appears plagiarized.
Structure	The letter • follows an effective organizational structure, including an engaging introduction and a thoughtful conclusion • uses a variety of effective transitional strategies to create coherence.	The letter • follows a logical organizational structure, including an introduction with a hook and a conclusion that follows from the argument presented • uses transitional strategies to clarify and link ideas.	The letter • follows a flawed or uneven organizational structure; may have a weak introduction and/or conclusion • uses basic transitional strategies ineffectively or inconsistently.	The letter • has little or no organizational structure • uses few or no transitional strategies.
Use of Language	The letter • uses persuasive and connotative diction • demonstrates command of the conventions of standard English capitalization, punctuation, spelling, grammar, and usage • maintains an engaging and appropriate style and tone.	The letter • uses some persuasive and/or connotative diction • demonstrates adequate command of the conventions of standard English capitalization, punctuation, spelling, grammar, and usage • maintains an appropriate style and tone.	The letter • uses basic or weak diction • demonstrates partial command of the conventions of standard English capitalization, punctuation, spelling, grammar, and usage • maintains an inconsistently appropriate style and/or tone.	The letter • uses confusing or vague diction • lacks command of the conventions of standard English capitalization, punctuation, spelling, grammar, and usage; frequent errors obscure meaning • has an inappropriate style and/or tone.

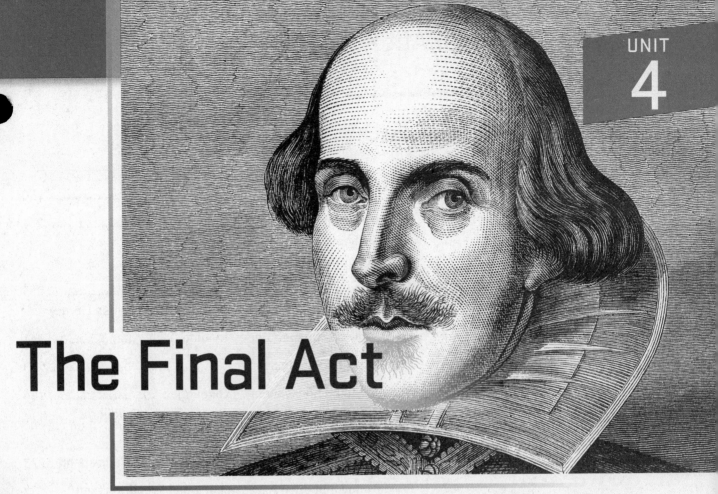

The Final Act

Visual Prompt: Who is this man? What clues do you see in how he is dressed? Predict how this image might relate to this last unit of study.

Unit Overview

Unit 4 introduces and gives you the opportunity to find out more about William Shakespeare, his society, and his language. The unit also extends your presentation skills and prepares you to collaborate with your classmates to perform scenes from one of Shakespeare's comedies, *The Taming of the Shrew*.

The Final Act

pick

GOALS:

- To analyze and understand the relationships among setting, characterization, conflict, and plot
- To research a drama from a different time period
- To rehearse and present an engaging performance of a drama
- To revise for effective sentence variety

ACADEMIC VOCABULARY
source
bibliography
evaluate
annotate

Literary Terms
rhythm
iambic pentameter
tableau
limerick
rhyme scheme
oral interpretation
inflection
rate
drama
free verse
alliteration

My Notes

Contents

Activities

*Texts are not included in these materials.

Language and Writer's Craft
- Choosing Sentence Structure (4.3)
- Pronoun Usage (4.9)

MY INDEPENDENT READING LIST

_____
_____
_____
_____
_____
_____
_____
_____
_____
_____
_____
_____
_____
_____
_____
_____
_____
_____
_____
_____
_____
_____
_____
_____

Previewing the Unit

My Notes

Learning Targets

- Preview the big ideas and vocabulary for the unit.
- Identify and analyze the skills and knowledge needed to complete Embedded Assessment 1 successfully.

Making Connections

So far this year, you have read poetry, short stories and other narratives, news articles and informational texts, and historical letters. In this unit, you will encounter another historical text: scenes from one of William Shakespeare's comedies. In the first part of the unit, you will learn about Shakespeare and why his writing is still alive after more than 400 years. In the last part of the unit, you will study and perform a Shakespearean scene.

Essential Questions

Based on your current knowledge, how would you answer these questions?

1. How can research shape one's understanding of a literary text?
2. How is reading a text similar to and different from viewing and performing a text?

Developing Vocabulary

Use a QHT chart to sort the Academic Vocabulary and Literary Terms from the Contents page into the columns *Q, H,* and *T.* Remember that *Q* means you have questions about the meaning of the word because it is unfamiliar; *H* means you have heard of the word, so it is familiar; and *T* means you can teach the word to your classmates because you know it so well. One academic goal is to move all words to the *T* column by the end of the unit.

Unpacking Embedded Assessment 1

Read the assignment and Scoring Guide for Embedded Assessment 1.

Work collaboratively to conduct research, synthesize findings, and present a topic relating to Shakespeare and his play *The Taming of the Shrew.* Your presentation should be five minutes in length, and speaking parts should be divided equally. If possible, incorporate multimedia elements, including video and sound, into your presentation.

With your class, paraphrase the expectations from the Scoring Guide and create a graphic organizer to use as a visual reminder of the required concepts (what you need to know) and skills (what you need to do). After each activity, use this graphic to guide reflection about what you have learned and what you still need to learn in order to be successful on the Embedded Assessment.

INDEPENDENT READING LINK

Read and Discuss

This unit focuses on dramas (plays). To identify an independent reading title for this unit, gather several examples of plays that look interesting to you. Preview each text, and then decide which you want to read. Discuss your choice with a partner. Create a reading plan for the text you have chosen, including when and where you will read and how often.

Shakespeare in School

Learning Target

- Create and write an argument, introducing and organizing claims clearly, supporting claims with clear reasons and relevant evidence, and demonstrating an understanding of the topic.
- Participate in a class debate, evaluating other speakers' arguments to be sure their claims are supported by reasons and evidence.

Preview

In this activity, you will read an article and participate in a class debate about teaching Shakespeare in school.

Setting a Purpose for Reading

- As you read the article, mark the text using two different colors to indicate support for the pro and con sides of the controversy.
- Circle unknown words and phrases. Try to determine the meaning of the words by using context clues, word parts, or a dictionary.

ABOUT THE AUTHOR
Laura Clark is a British journalist. She is the education correspondent for the British newspaper *Daily Mail*.

LEARNING STRATEGIES:
Brainstorming, Diffusing, Marking the Text, Debating

My Notes

Article

Shakespeare dumbed down in comic strips for bored pupils

by Laura Clark

1 Shakespeare's plays are being rewritten as comic strips for pupils who find his poetry boring, it **emerged** today.

2 Thousands of teenagers are to study cartoon versions of famous plays such as *Macbeth*, which reduce finely-crafted passages to snappy phrases.

3 The publishers hope the comics—illustrated by artists who have worked on the Spiderman series—will inspire disaffected readers with a love of the **Bard's** plays.

4 But the Queen's English Society warned that "dumbed down" versions could backfire by allowing pupils to avoid tackling the language and themes of the originals.

5 The firm behind the initiative, Classical Comics, will launch its first comic book plays next term.

6 They are targeted at older primary pupils and teenagers and have already won the backing of the National Association for the Teaching of English.

7 Three versions of each play will be produced to help teachers cater to children of differing literacy abilities.

WORD CONNECTIONS

The Spanish cognate for *comic* is *cómic*.

emerged: developed

bard: a poet; "the Bard" is a nickname for Shakespeare

8 The first uses Shakespeare's own words, the second translates them into plain English, and the third is a "quick text" version and uses as few words as possible.

9 The firm hopes to print 10,000 copies of each version of its first comic play, *Henry V*.

10 *Macbeth* should be ready next year and there are also plans in the pipeline for *Romeo and Juliet*, as well as classic novels including *Jane Eyre* and *Great Expectations*.

11 The firm hopes **eventually** to publish comic strip versions of all Shakespeare's plays.

12 Dr. Bernard Lamb, chairman of the London branch of the Queen's English Society, said: "Pupils may just enjoy the cartoons and not connect it with Shakespeare and they won't be much of a contribution to education.

13 "I am sure they are already well-versed in cartoon characters and comic strips, so it would be good for them to get away from that and study something a bit more serious.

14 "A lot of the beauty of Shakespeare is in the language more than the plot.

15 Dr. Lamb added: "There is so much dumbing down all round. Students are unaware of what language is appropriate in different circumstances. I have had students in degree exams using 'eight' for 'ate.'"

16 But Clive Bryant, chairman of Classical Comics, insisted the shortened versions of his plays would give youngster a "leg up" to enjoying the originals.

17 "We want to make Shakespeare as energetic and colourful as Spiderman" he told the Times Educational Supplement.

18 "Teachers tell us they are desperate for something exciting to use in the classroom, but if you ask kids about Shakespeare the word they usually come back with is 'boring'.

19 "We're trying to break down the barriers so they can get interested."

20 Ian McNeilly, director of the National Association for the Teaching of English, said: "This is a fun way of getting into the stories.

21 "Plays are not meant to be read, but to be seen. The illustrations in these books are an easy way of following what is going on.

22 "The **genius** of Shakespeare is in the language, but for some students understanding it can be a struggle. It will be useful for teachers to have three different versions of the text."

Source: www.dailymail.co.uk, August 7, 2007

Second Read

- Reread the article to answer these text-dependent questions.
- Write any additional questions you have about the text in your Reader/Writer Notebook.

eventually: at some later time

genius: distinctive character or spirit

1. **Craft and Structure:** What does the phrase "dumbed down" mean in the title? What words in the passage give a clue to the meaning of the phrase?

2. **Craft and Structure:** Based on the context surrounding the word *initiative* in paragraph 5, what is its meaning? What words in the paragraph help identify its meaning?

3. **Key Ideas and Details:** What does paragraph 8 say about how the quick text will differ from the original text?

4. **Key Ideas and Details:** What does Dr. Bernard Lamb say in paragraph 12 about why it is not a good idea to use cartoon/comics to teach Shakespeare?

5. **Integration of Knowledge and Ideas:** Which evidence supports the claim that a comic book is an appropriate way to present a classic play?

Working from the Text

6. Use the frame below to write and support a claim for your side of the controversy.

Teachers [*should/should not*] expect students to read original versions of Shakespeare's plays because [*paraphrase two reasons from the text and provide one based on personal experience*].

• Reason 1:

• Reason 2:

• Reason 3:

Shakespeare in School

© 2017 College Board. All rights reserved.

My Notes

7. Participate in a class debate. Be sure to

- Express ideas clearly, using appropriate eye contact, adequate volume, and clear pronunciation.
- Use evidence from the text and from personal experience to support your argument.
- Listen to other speakers and evaluate their claims to be sure they are supported by reasons and evidence.

Check Your Understanding

As you listened to your classmates present their claims in the argument and present evidence, which specific claims were supported by reasons and evidence? Which specific claims were not supported? How did you decide which claims were supported by relevant evidence and which were not?

Learning Targets
- Analyze information about Shakespeare and his society in response to research questions.
- Write an explanatory text explaining research and provide basic bibliographic information about sources.
- Use varied sentence structure in writing.

Preview
In this activity, you will read an informational text and other **sources** to answer research questions.

Setting a Purpose for Reading
- As you read, underline words and phrases that answer the research question, *Who* was Shakespeare?
- Circle unknown words and phrases. Try to determine the meaning of the words by using context clues, word parts, or a dictionary.

LEARNING STRATEGIES
Shared Reading, Diffusing, Paraphrasing, Summarizing, Note-taking, Brainstorming, Drafting

ACADEMIC VOCABULARY
When you refer to a **source** in research, you are referring to a place from which information comes or is obtained. **Sources** must be evaluated and cited to avoid plagiarism.

Informational Text

Shakespeare's Life

from The British Library

The Key Dates

1564 Shakespeare born in Stratford-upon-Avon.

1594 Joins Lord Chamberlain's Men. *Titus Andronicus*, first quarto, published.

1599 Globe playhouse built.

1603 Death of Elizabeth I. Accession of James I.

1613 Shakespeare's writing career over.

1616 Shakespeare dies in Stratford-upon-Avon.

1623 Publication of the First Folio.

1642 Civil War closes the theatres.

1660 Theatres reopen with restoration of Charles II.

1769 Garrick's Shakespeare Jubilee in Stratford-upon-Avon.

1780 Garrick's library arrives in British Museum.

1828 George III's library arrives in British Museum.

1858 Quartos purchased from Halliwell-Phillipps.

2003 93 British Library Shakespeare quartos digitised.

2009 Digital Shakespeare quarto editions completed (107 quartos in total).

Shakespeare and His Society

GRAMMAR & USAGE
Subordinating Conjunctions

A **subordinating conjunction** introduces a dependent clause. Many transition words are subordinating conjunctions, such as *because, although, while, since,* and *if.* Find additional examples of subordinating conjunctions and study how the writer uses them to transition from one idea to another.

My Notes

_____
_____
_____
_____
_____
_____
_____
_____
_____

regulated: controlled

copyright: the exclusive rights to a literary, artistic, or musical work

Who was William Shakespeare?

1   Shakespeare was born in Stratford-upon-Avon, Warwickshire, in 1564. Very little is known about his life, but by 1592 he was in London working as an actor and a dramatist. Between about 1590 and 1613, Shakespeare wrote at least 37 plays and collaborated on several more. Many of these plays were very successful both at court and in the public playhouses. In 1613, Shakespeare retired from the theatre and returned to Stratford-upon-Avon. He died and was buried there in 1616.

What did he write?

2   Shakespeare wrote plays and poems. His plays were comedies, histories and tragedies. His 17 comedies include *A Midsummer Night's Dream* and *The Merry Wives of Windsor.* Among his 10 history plays are *Henry V* and *Richard III.* The most famous among his 10 tragedies are *Hamlet, Othello,* and *King Lear.* Shakespeare's best-known poems are *The Sonnets,* first published in 1609.

What are the quartos?

3   Shakespeare's plays began to be printed in 1594, probably with his tragedy *Titus Andronicus.* This appeared as a small, cheap pamphlet called a quarto because of the way it was printed. Eighteen of Shakespeare's plays had appeared in quarto editions by the time of his death in 1616. Another three plays were printed in quarto before 1642. In 1623 an expensive folio volume of 36 plays by Shakespeare was printed, which included most of those printed in quarto.

Why are the quartos important?

4   None of Shakespeare's manuscripts survives, so the printed texts of his plays are our only source for what he originally wrote. The quarto editions are the texts closest to Shakespeare's time. Some are thought to preserve either his working drafts (his foul papers) or his fair copies. Others are thought to record versions remembered by actors who performed the plays, providing information about staging practices in Shakespeare's day.

Shakespeare in Print

5   By the time Shakespeare began creating his plays, the London book trade was well established and growing steadily. Printing was **regulated** by the ecclesiastical authorities and the Stationers' Company, although the regulations were not always enforced. The printers, booksellers, and publishers who ran London's book trade were almost all stationers.

6   Printed plays formed a very small part of the book trade. Relatively few plays got into print. They did not sell in large numbers, and were not particularly profitable. The companies of players were not necessarily reluctant to have their plays printed, but the uncertainty of profits may well have deterred publishers. The dramatists themselves were unlikely to make money from the printing of their plays. There was no law of **copyright** to protect their interests. Once a manuscript play had been sold to a publisher, and he had paid for its approval and licensing for printing, he had sole rights over the work.

7 Several of Shakespeare's plays, including *Richard II* and *Richard III,* were popular enough to be printed in several editions. From 1598, with *Love's Labour's Lost,* his name began to be added to their title-pages as a selling point. Scholars have long held that Shakespeare had no interest in the printing of his plays, but this is now being challenged.

Shakespeare's Theatre

8 Shakespeare began his career not long after the first public playhouses were established in London. His earliest plays were given at the Theatre, an open-air playhouse in Shoreditch. Many of his plays were written for the Globe, rebuilt from the timbers of the Theatre on Bankside. A number of Shakespeare's later plays were created for the very different surroundings of the indoor playhouse at Blackfriars.

9 Shakespeare, a player as well as a dramatist, belonged to a company of players. His company, the Lord Chamberlain's Men (from 1603 the King's Men) competed with others, notably the Admiral's Men, for audiences. Like most leading players, Shakespeare was a sharer in his company and was able to enjoy its profits. He also had to suffer its losses—for example, when the first Globe burnt down in 1613. His plays were created with his company's players in mind. Such players as the tragedian Richard Burbage and clowns like William Kemp influenced the roles within Shakespeare's plays.

10 Shakespeare's theatre came to an end in 1642. In that year, on the eve of the Civil War, all the playhouses were closed by order of Parliament. Those which were still structurally sound were either converted into **dwellings**, or demolished so that their timbers could be reused elsewhere. The players could no longer perform their plays in public.

Source: The British Library (http://www.bl.uk/treasures/shakespeare), accessed May 16, 2013.

Second Read

- Reread the informational text to answer these text-dependent questions.
- Write any additional questions you have about the text in your Reader/Writer Notebook.

1. **Key Ideas and Details:** What does paragraph 1 say about Shakespeare's life?

2. **Craft and Structure:** What does the word *manuscript* mean in paragraph 4? Which phrase in the sentence helps you understand the meaning of the word?

My Notes

dwelling: a place to live

Shakespeare and His Society

3. **Key Ideas and Details:** How do the details in the fourth paragraph show that the quartos are important?

4. **Craft and Structure:** Which details from the section *Shakespeare in Print* contribute to the development of the ideas in the text, and how?

Working from the Text

5. As you reread the informational text, take notes using a graphic organizer like the one below. In the left column, paraphrase, summarize, and quote information that answers the following research questions: *Who* was Shakespeare? *What* did he accomplish? *When* did he live? *Where* did he live? *Why* is he still known today? *What* was society like when Shakespeare was writing *The Taming of the Shrew*? In the middle column, categorize or classify the information as it relates to Shakespeare's life, his society, his plays, or his impact. In the right column, form additional research questions of interest to you.

	Information (paraphrased, summarized, or quoted)	Categories of Information (Shakespeare's life, society, plays, or impact)	New Research Questions
1			
2			

6. Look at the source of the informational text. Why do you think this source is credible?

7. Brainstorm how you could use multimedia to clarify ideas and add interest to a presentation of this information (e.g., graphics, images, music/sound).

8. Writers create a **bibliography** to give full credit to the sources from which they take information. Record basic bibliographic information for the text you read in Activity 4.2 and in this activity. Note that online information may not have a publication date, in which case use the date on which you accessed the information from the Internet.

Source 1:

Author:

Title:

Source:

Date of Publication:

Source 2:

Author:

Title:

Source:

Date of Publication:

ACADEMIC VOCABULARY
Creating a **bibliography**, which is a list of source materials used to prepare a research paper or presentation, is an important part of a researcher's responsibility.

WORD CONNECTIONS

The word *cite* comes from the Latin word meaning "to set in motion." *Cite* has come to mean "to quote or refer to."

My Notes

INDEPENDENT READING LINK

Read and Research
Search for an informational text that gives information about the author of the play that you are reading independently. Take notes on the reading and then write a paragraph about whether or not you think the source is credible.

Shakespeare and His Society

Language and Writer's Craft: Choosing Sentence Structure

You may have learned already about simple, compound, and complex sentences. Writers use a variety of sentence types to keep the reader's interest and to convey ideas most effectively.

Following is a review of the types of sentences you have learned about. As you write—and as you review and revise your writing—choose the type of sentence that is most appropriate for the ideas you want to communicate. Remember to use a variety of well-structured sentences.

Sentence Type	Definition	Example
Simple	A simple sentence has one independent clause (a subject-verb combination).	Dogs howled. The neighborhood dogs howled nervously.
Compound	A compound sentence contains two independent clauses joined by a semicolon **or** by *and, or, nor, for, but,* or *yet* and a comma.	The neighborhood dogs howled nervously, but the cat slept undisturbed in the house.
Complex	A complex sentence contains an independent clause and a dependent clause (often signaled by a marker such as *because, while, although, unless, until,* etc.).	While the fireworks rocketed into the air, the neighborhood dogs howled nervously.

Check Your Understanding

WRITING to SOURCES   Expository Writing Prompt

Explain what you learned about Shakespeare through research. Remember to use transitional words and phrases, and a variety of types of sentences to clarify the relationships among ideas and concepts in an informative/explanatory text. Be sure to

- Establish a controlling idea.
- Organize information by classifying or categorizing the information with headings.
- Provide relevant information and examples.
- Use academic vocabulary and/or literary terms to maintain a consistent and formal style and tone.
- Revise to improve transitions and to add variety in sentence types.
- Provide a strong conclusion that follow from the information presented.

Use your final essay to present to the class what you learned about Shakespeare through research.

Researching to Deepen Understanding

Learning Targets
- Research additional information about Shakespeare and his society using multiple print and digital sources that have been evaluated for their credibility.
- Write an explanatory text integrating information gained through research.

Conducting Research

1. Use your notes from the previous activity to help you brainstorm ideas for research.

   Topics to Research:

2. Select a research topic and work collaboratively in your expert groups to develop thoughtful questions to guide your research.

   Research Questions:

3. Identify potential sources (print and/or online).
   - Which sources are best for your topic?
   - Where can you find them?

4. **Evaluate** your sources by determining their credibility and usefulness.
   - Can you trust the source of information? Why or why not?
   - How does the source address your research question(s)?

5. Use reading strategies to make meaning of the informational texts.
   - Which strategies work best for you when you read informational texts?
   - What will you do if you do not understand the reading?

6. Take notes using a double-entry journal. In the left column, paraphrase, summarize, and quote information that answers your research questions. In the right column, form a response to the information (statements and/or questions). Think about the following:
   - When should you paraphrase or summarize?
   - When should you directly quote?
   - What makes an effective response?

LEARNING STRATEGIES
Brainstorming, Collaborative Discussion, Diffusing, Marking the Text, Paraphrasing, Summarizing, Note-taking, Drafting

My Notes

ACADEMIC VOCABULARY
When you **evaluate**, you examine and judge carefully in order to determine the value of something, such as an idea, a comment, or a source.

INDEPENDENT READING LINK

Read and Research

In order to practice identifying sources, plan a research project about the play you are reading independently. Find several sources that contain information on the play. The sources could be reviews, critiques, or informational articles. Evaluate each source for credibility and write several sentences about why each source would be appropriate for your research project.

Researching to Deepen Understanding

My Notes

7. Print, copy, and/or record multimedia sources to clarify ideas and add interest to your presentation (e.g., graphics, images, music/sound).

   • Where can you find effective multimedia sources?

   • How will the selected multimedia sources support your audience's understanding of key information about your topic?

8. Record basic bibliographic information for each of your sources (author, title, source, date of publication, type: print or online) on note cards or in your Reader/Writer Notebook.

Source #:

Author:
Title:
Source:
Date of Publication:
Type (print or online):

9. Continue to research until you thoroughly answer your research questions.

   • Have you learned enough about your topic to create a presentation and communicate your ideas to an audience?

   • Do you feel confident answering questions about your topic?

Check Your Understanding

WRITING to SOURCES Expository Writing Prompt

Explain what you have learned about Shakespeare through research. Be sure to

• Write to answer your research questions by drawing on several sources.

• Assess the credibility of your sources and provide bibliographic information for each the sources you choose.

• Provide relevant information and examples from multiple sources, making sure to quote or paraphrase information to avoid plagiarism.

• Use academic vocabulary and/or literary terms to maintain a consistent and formal style and tone.

• Revise as needed to improve the organization of ideas and to add transitions and/or to use a variety of sentence types.

Planning to Present Research

Learning Targets
- Synthesize research about Shakespeare and his society.
- Create a multimedia presentation on Shakespeare and his society.

1. Present your information in your jigsaw group, and listen to comprehend while others present. Use your written response from the previous activity to guide your presentation about your topic.

When you are the speaker:
- Come to the discussion prepared.
- Use appropriate eye contact, adequate volume, and clear pronunciation.
- Form and respond to specific questions relating to the topic under discussion.

When you are the listener:
- Take notes and ask questions for clarification after each speaker presents in order to understand their ideas.
- Challenge your group to explore ideas and think about the topic on a deeper level.
- Evaluate the strength of ideas to provide constructive feedback and offer suggestions to strengthen ideas when necessary.

Check Your Understanding

Work collaboratively in your jigsaw group to synthesize information by putting different pieces of your research together to form a coherent whole. Use the questions below to guide the process:
- What conclusion(s) can you draw about Shakespeare and his society?
- How can you organize and sequence (order) your information to make your conclusions clear to others (e.g., use headings and transitions). Use the mapping strategy to show your thinking.
- How can you use multimedia and/or visual displays to clarify ideas and add interest?

WORD CONNECTIONS

Roots and Affixes

The word ***collaborate*** contains the Latin root *-labor-*, meaning "work" and the prefix *co-* or *col-* meaning "together" or "with." Knowing the Latin root *-labor-* can also help you understand the meaning of the word *elaboration* (the process of working something out in detail). Knowing the Latin prefix *col-* can also help you understand the meaning of *collect* (to gather together).

My Notes

Understanding Shakespeare's Language

LEARNING STRATEGIES
Summarizing, Collaborative Discussion, Chunking, Diffusing, Marking the Text, Note-taking, Drafting

ACADEMIC VOCABULARY
When you **annotate** (*verb*) or make **annotations** (*noun*), you are writing notes to explain or present ideas that help you and others understand a text.

WORD CONNECTIONS

Cognates

The Spanish cognate for *annotate* is *anotar*.

My Notes

immense: huge

Learning Target
- Explain unique aspects of Shakespeare's language (orally and in writing).
- Annotate an essay to identify details that convey the central idea.

Preview
In this activity, you will read an essay and think about the central idea.

Setting a Purpose for Reading
- As you read the essay, underline words and phrases that tell what is unique and challenging about Shakespeare's language.
- **Annotate** and highlight unknown words and phrases. Try to determine the meaning of the words by using context clues, word parts, or a dictionary.

ABOUT THE AUTHORS
Barbara A. Mowat is director of academic programs at the Folger Shakespeare Library, executive editor of *Shakespeare Quarterly,* chair of the Folger Institute, and author of *The Dramaturgy of Shakespeare's Romances* and of essays on Shakespeare's plays and on the editing of the plays.

Paul Werstine is professor of English at Kings's University College at The University of Western Ontario, Canada. He is general editor of the New Variorum Shakespeare and author of many papers and articles on the printing and editing of Shakespeare's plays.

Essay

"Reading Shakespeare's Language"
The Taming of the Shrew

by Barbara A. Mowat and Paul Werstine (editors)

1   For many people today, reading Shakespeare's language can be a problem–but it is a problem that can be solved. [It requires] developing the skills of untangling unusual sentence structures and of recognizing and understanding poetic compressions [combining], omissions [cutting], and wordplay. And even those skilled in reading unusual sentence structures may have occasional trouble with Shakespeare's words. Four hundred years have passed between his speaking and our hearing. Most of his **immense** vocabulary is still in use, but a few of his words are not, and, worse, some of his words now have meanings quite different from those they had in the sixteenth century. When reading on one's own, one must do what each actor does: go over the lines (often with a dictionary close at hand) until the puzzles are solved and the lines yield up their poetry and the characters speak in words and phrases that are, suddenly, rewarding and wonderfully memorable.

Shakespeare's Words

2 Some words are strange not because of the changes in language over the past centuries but because these are words that Shakespeare is using to build a dramatic world that has its own space and time. In the opening scenes of the main body of the play, the setting in Italy and the story's focus on **wooing** are created through repeated [local references and phrases].

3 The most problematic words are those that we still use but that we use with a different meaning. The word *heavy* has the meaning of "distressing," *brave* where we would say "splendid," *idle* where we would say "silly," and *curst* where we would say "bad-tempered." Such words will be explained in the notes to the text, but they, too, will become familiar as you continue to read Shakespeare's language.

Shakespearean Wordplay

4 Shakespeare plays with language so often and so variously that entire books are written on the topic. Here we will mention only two kinds of wordplay, puns and metaphors. A pun is a play on words that sound the same but that have different meanings. The first scene between Kate and Petruchio (2.1.190–293) is built around a whole series of puns, beginning with puns on the name Kate. In all of Shakespeare's plays, one must stay alert to the sounds of words and to the possibility of double meanings. In *The Taming of the Shrew,* many scenes are funny only if we hear the puns.

5 A metaphor is a play on words in which one object or idea is expressed as if it were something else, something with which it shares common features. *The Taming of the Shrew* is not rich in metaphoric language, but metaphor is used in a powerful and significant way.

Shakespeare's Sentences and Syntax

6 In an English sentence, meaning is quite dependent on the place given each word. "The dog bit the boy" and "The boy bit the dog" mean very different things, even though the individual words are the same. [Therefore,] unusual arrangements of words can puzzle a reader. Shakespeare frequently shifts his sentences away from "normal" English arrangements–often to create the rhythm he seeks, sometimes to use a line's poetic rhythm to **emphasize** a particular word, sometimes to give a character his or her own speech patterns or to allow the character to speak in a special way.

7 In reading for yourself, do as the actor does. That is, when you become puzzled by a character's speech, check to see if words are being presented in an unusual sequence. Look first for the placement of the subject and the verb. Shakespeare often places the verb before the subject (e.g., instead of "He goes," we find "Goes he"). More problematic is Shakespeare's frequent placing of the object before the subject and verb. "For how I firmly am resolved you know" (1.1.49), where the normal sentence order would be: "For you know how I am firmly resolved.") Inversions (words in reversed order) serve primarily to create the poetic rhythm of the lines, called iambic pentameter.

8 Often in his sentences words that would normally appear together are separated from each other. (Again, this is often done to create a particular rhythm or to stress a particular word.)

wooing: seeking affection

Literary Terms
Rhythm is the pattern of stressed and unstressed syllables in spoken or written language, especially in poetry.

Literary Terms
Iambic pentameter is the most common meter (rhythm) in English verse (poetry). It consists of a line ten syllables long that is accented (stressed) on every second beat. An iamb consists of two syllables (an unstressed followed by a stressed). Think of an iamb as a heartbeat: ker-THUMP. Each line written in iambic pentameter contains five heartbeats.

emphasize: to stress

WORD CONNECTIONS

Cognates

The Spanish cognate for *rhythm* is *ritmo.*

Understanding Shakespeare's Language

Implied Stage Action

9 Finally, in reading Shakespeare's plays you should always remember that what you are reading is a performance script. The dialogue is written to be spoken by actors who, at the same time, are moving, gesturing, picking up objects, weeping, shaking their fists. Some stage action is described in what are called "stage directions"; some is suggested within the dialogue itself. Learn to be alert to such signals as you stage the play in your imagination.

[Conclusion]

10 It is immensely rewarding to work carefully with Shakespeare's language so that the words, the sentences, the wordplay, and the implied stage action all become clear—as readers for the past [five] centuries have discovered. The joy of being able to stage one of Shakespeare's plays in one's imagination, to return to passages that continue to yield further meanings (or further questions) the more one reads them—these are pleasures that certainly make it worth considerable effort to "break the code" of Elizabethan poetic drama and let free the remarkable language that makes up a Shakespeare text.

Second Read

- Reread the essay to answer these text-dependent questions.
- Write any additional questions you have about the text in your Reader/Writer Notebook.

1. **Craft and Structure:** How does the first paragraph of the essay classify the challenging parts of Shakespeare's language into *syntax* and *diction?* How does this contribute to the development of ideas in the essay?

2. **Key Ideas and Details:** How is the idea that some of Shakespeare's words are no longer used the same way illustrated in the third paragraph?

3. **Craft and Structure:** What is the connotative meaning of the word *puzzled* in paragraph 7?

4. **Integration of Knowledge and Ideas:** What claim does the author make in the conclusion? What reasons and evidence does the author use to support the claim?

Working from the Text

5. Summarize the key information by answering each of the following questions:

- What did you learn about Shakespeare's diction (word choice)?

- What did you learn about Shakespeare's syntax (sentence structures)?

- What did you learn about implied stage action?

My Notes

Understanding Shakespeare's Language

My Notes

Analyzing Shakespeare's Language

6. Following are types of figurative language and words that are rhetorical devices. Your teacher will assign a word to you. Create and present a Word Wall card for your assigned poetic or rhetorical device to guide analysis of Shakespeare's language. You may need to consult references to find examples or create your own original examples.

Language Type	Definition
Types of Figurative Language	Imaginative language that is not meant to be interpreted literally
Hyperbole	extreme exaggeration used for emphasis, often used for comic effect
Simile	a comparison between two unlike things using the word *like* or *as* (X is *like* Y).
Metaphor	a comparison between two unlike things in which one thing is said to be another (X = Y)
Personification	a kind of metaphor that gives objects or abstract ideas human characteristics
Pun	the humorous use of a word or words to suggest another word with the same sound but a different meaning
Types of Rhetorical Devices	A rhetorical device is a use of language that is intended to have an effect on its audience.
Rhetorical Question	a question asked to emphasize a point or create an effect; no answer is expected
Parallel Structure	using the same pattern of words (words, phrases, or clauses) to show that two or more ideas have the same level of importance
Repetition	key words or phrases that are repeated for emphasis or effect

Sample Word Wall card:

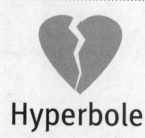

Hyperbole

an exaggeration for effect (Definition)

I could sleep for days. (Example 1)

I can't live without you. (Example 2)

You are breaking my heart. (Example 3)

7. Following are quotations from some of Shakespeare's most famous works. Work collaboratively in your expert group to analyze your assigned quotes. Diffuse the text when necessary, and mark the text to indicate specific examples of Shakespeare's use of diction, syntax, and rhetorical devices.

Model Analysis

"The King's name is a tower of strength."	metaphor; just saying the King's name creates a sense of strength
"Yet I do fear thy nature; It is too full o' the milk of human kindness."	metaphor; he is naturally kind hearted

Group 1

Sonnet 18: "Shall I compare thee to a summer's day? Thou art more lovely and more temperate:"	
Hamlet: "I will speak daggers to her, but use none." (Act III, Scene II)	
Hamlet: "When sorrows come, they come not single spies, but in battalions." (Act IV, Scene V)	
As You Like It: "All the world's a stage, and all the men and women merely players. They have their exits and their entrances; And one man in his time plays many parts." (Act II, Scene VII)	
The Taming of the Shrew: "Out of the jaws of death." (Act III, Scene IV)	

My Notes

Understanding Shakespeare's Language

Group 2

Romeo and Juliet: "It is the east, and Juliet is the sun." (Act II, Scene II)	
Romeo and Juliet: "It seems she hangs upon the cheek of night like a rich jewel in an Ethiope's ear." (Act I, Scene V)	
Romeo and Juliet: "See, how she leans her cheek upon her hand! O that I were a glove upon that hand, that I might touch that cheek!" (Act II, Scene II)	
The Merchant of Venice: "But love is blind, and lovers cannot see."	
Measure for Measure: "Our doubts are traitors, and make us lose the good We oft might win, by fearing to attempt." (Act I, Scene IV)	

Group 3

King Henry IV, Part II: "He hath eaten me out of house and home." (Act II, Scene I)	
Richard III: "Now is the winter of our discontent / Made glorious summer by this sun of York;"	
Julius Caesar: "Friends, Romans, countrymen, lend me your ears; I come to bury Caesar, not to praise him." (Act III, Scene II)	
Julius Caesar: "A dish fit for the gods." (Act II, Scene I)	
Julius Caesar: "Cowards die many times before their deaths; / "The valiant never taste of death but once." (Act II, Scene II)	

Group 4

All quotes from Macbeth:	
"There's daggers in men's smiles." (Act II, Scene III)	
"All the perfumes of Arabia will not sweeten this little hand." (Act V, Scene I)	
"When shall we three meet again? In thunder, lightning, or in rain? When the hurlyburly's done, When the battle's lost and won." (Act I, Scene I)	
"If chance will have me king, why, chance may crown me." (Act I, Scene III)	
"Look like the innocent flower, but be the serpent under 't." (Act I, Scene V)	

Group 5

Macbeth: "Out, out, brief candle! Life's but a walking shadow, a poor player That struts and frets his hour upon the stage And then is heard no more . . ." (Act V, Scene V)	
King Lear: "How sharper than a serpent's tooth it is To have a thankless child!" (Act I, Scene IV)	
Othello: "I will wear my heart upon my sleeve . . ." (Act I, Scene I)	
Twelfth Night: "Be not afraid of greatness: some are born great, Some achieve greatness and some have greatness Thrust upon them." (Act II, Scene V)	
Titus Andronicus: "These words are razors to my wounded heart." (Act I, Scene I)	

Understanding Shakespeare's Language

My Notes

8. Present your analysis in your jigsaw group. Listen to comprehend and take notes while others present.

When you are the speaker:
- Come to the discussion prepared.
- Use appropriate eye contact, adequate volume, and clear pronunciation.
- Form and respond to specific questions relating to the topic under discussion.

When you are the listener:
- Understand ideas by taking notes and asking questions for clarification after each speaker presents.
- Explore ideas by challenging your group to think about the topic on a deeper level.

Check Your Understanding

WRITING to SOURCES Expository Writing Prompt

Explain what you learned about Shakespeare's use of language. Include information that describes Shakespeare's use of figurative language, word relationships, and nuances in word meaning. Be sure to

- Establish a controlling idea.
- Provide relevant information and examples.
- Use academic vocabulary and/or literary terms in your writing to maintain a consistent and formal style and tone.
- Include transitions and a variety of sentence types.

Revise as needed to add transitions and replace simple sentences with a variety of sentence types.

 Independent Reading Checkpoint

Write a comparison of the use of language in the the play you are reading independently to Shakespeare's use of language.

Researching and Presenting Shakespeare

Assignment

Work collaboratively to conduct research, synthesize findings, and present a topic relating to Shakespeare and his play *The Taming of the Shrew*. Your presentation should be five minutes in length, and speaking parts should be divided equally. If possible, incorporate multimedia elements, including video and sound, into your presentation.

Planning and Prewriting: Take time to make a plan for generating ideas and research questions.

- How will you select a topic related to Shakespeare and the comedy *The Taming of the Shrew*?
- What questions will guide your research?
- How will you ensure that each group member is researching a different aspect of your topic?

Researching: Gather information from a variety of relevant sources.

- Where can you find sources, and how can you tell that the sources are relevant and useful?
- How will you take notes by paraphrasing information and recording bibliographic information?
- How will you use research to gather visuals and other multimedia?

Preparing and Creating: Organize talking points and create a multimedia presentation.

- What strategy will you use to organize information?
- How will you be sure that ideas are presented clearly with an introduction, transitions, and a conclusion?
- How will you integrate multimedia and visuals to clarify and add interest?

Evaluating and Rehearsing: Create opportunities to review and rehearse your presentations.

- When can you present to a group of your peers to get feedback and suggestions for improvement?
- How can the Scoring Guide help you evaluate how well prepared you are to meet the requirements of the assignment?

Speaking and Listening: Participate effectively as both a presenter and audience member.

- How will you use volume, eye contact, and pronunciation to engage your audience?
- How will you take notes during the other students' presentations?

Reflection

After completing this Embedded Assessment, think about how you went about accomplishing this task, and respond to the following questions:

- What did you learn about Shakespeare and his times that will help you understand the play *The Taming of the Shrew*?
- Which of the class presentations were the most engaging, and why?

My Notes

Technology TIP:

Use a presentation tool such as PowerPoint or Prezi to organize the multimedia and visual aspects of your presentation.

Researching and Presenting Shakespeare

SCORING GUIDE

Scoring Criteria	Exemplary	Proficient	Emerging	Incomplete
Ideas	The presentation • supports a clearly focused main idea with relevant descriptions, facts, and details synthesized from a variety of sources • includes a correct and complete bibliography or works cited page.	The presentation • supports a main idea with sufficient descriptions, facts, and details synthesized from multiple sources • includes a bibliography or works cited page that follows a standard format.	The presentation • has an unclear, unfocused, or insufficiently supported main idea; may rely too heavily on a single source for information • includes a partial or inaccurate bibliography or works cited page.	The presentation • does not include a main idea or shows little or no evidence of research • lacks a bibliography or works cited page.
Structure	The presentation • demonstrates strong evidence of collaboration • sequences ideas effectively, including an engaging introduction, clear headings, smooth transitions, and a logical conclusion • integrates a variety of multimedia to enhance ideas.	The presentation • demonstrates adequate evidence of collaboration • sequences ideas logically, including an introduction, headings, transitions, and a concluding section/statement • uses multimedia to clarify ideas and add interest.	The presentation • demonstrates uneven or ineffective collaboration • uses flawed sequencing; may lack one or more of the following: an introduction, headings, transitions, and a concluding section/statement • uses multimedia ineffectively.	The presentation • demonstrates a failure to collaborate • has little or no discernable structure • lacks multimedia support.
Use of Language	The presenter • uses effective eye contact, volume, pacing, and clarity • demonstrates command of the conventions of standard English grammar, usage, and language, including a variety of syntax • maintains a consistently formal style and tone, including the consistent use of academic vocabulary and literary terms.	The presenter • uses appropriate eye contact, volume, and pronunciation • demonstrates adequate command of the conventions of standard English grammar, usage, and language, including a variety of syntax • maintains a generally formal style and tone, including the use of some academic vocabulary or literary terms.	The presenter • uses eye contact, volume, and pronunciation unevenly • demonstrates partial command of the conventions of standard English grammar, usage, and language; uses little variety of syntax • maintains an inconsistently formal style and/or tone and uses limited academic vocabulary or literary terms.	The presenter • uses flawed or ineffective speaking skills • makes frequent errors in standard English grammar, usage, and language • uses an inappropriate style and/or tone.

Previewing Embedded Assessment 2 and Preparing for a Performance

ACTIVITY
4.7

Learning Targets
- Identify the knowledge, skills, and vocabulary needed to complete Embedded Assessment 2 successfully.
- Preview and practice the skills needed for a class performance.

LEARNING STRATEGIES
QHT, Close Reading,
Paraphrasing, Graphic
Organizer

Making Connections
In the first part of this unit you learned how to do research, and you presented your research on a topic related to Shakespeare's *The Taming of the Shrew*. In the second part of the unit, you will learn how to perform a scene from a literary work.

Essential Questions
Reflect on your understanding of the first Essential Question. How can research shape one's understanding of a literary text? How would you answer that question at this point in the unit?

Developing Vocabulary
1. Resort the following Academic Vocabulary and Literary Terms using the QHT strategy.

Academic Vocabulary	Literary Terms
source bibliography evaluate	rhythm iambic pentameter

Q (unfamiliar)	H (familiar)	T (very familiar)

2. Compare this sort with your original sort. How many words have changed category? How many have stayed the same?

3. Select a word from the chart and write a concise statement about your learning. How has your understanding of the word changed over the course of this unit?

© 2017 College Board. All rights reserved.

Unit 4 • The Final Act   **275**

Previewing Embedded Assessment 2 and Preparing for a Performance

My Notes

Unpacking Embedded Assessment 2

Read the assignment for Embedded Assessment 2: Performing Shakespeare.

> Work collaboratively to prepare and present a Reader's Theater performance of a scene from Shakespeare's play *The Taming of the Shrew*. Your performance should have a clear beginning, middle, and end.

Work with your class to paraphrase the expectations and create a graphic organizer to use as a visual reminder of the required concepts (what you need to know) and skills (what you need to do). Copy the graphic organizer for future reference. After each activity, use this graphic to guide reflection about what you have learned and what you still need to learn in order to be successful on the Embedded Assessment.

4. **Quickwrite:** How has your understanding of Shakespeare changed since the beginning of this unit?

Performance Practice

5. Choose a poem that you like or that your teacher suggests. Read the poem several times to yourself and then read it aloud to your classmates. Reflect on the experience by answering the following questions:

- What was enjoyable about reading the poem?

- What was difficult about reading the poem? How might you work to improve in this area for the next performance?

INDEPENDENT READING LINK

Read and Research

To support your learning in the second half of the unit, identify another play that looks interesting to you. You might choose a play by William Shakespeare as a way to become familiar with Shakespeare's work and language. Discuss your choice with a partner. Create a reading plan for the text you have chosen.

Learning Targets
- Explain how a text's structure contributes to the development of the theme in a written response.
- Analyze an author's use of diction to create meaning and tone.

Preview
In this activity, you will read a short story and think about the theme.

Setting a Purpose for Reading
- As you read the short story, underline words and phrases that suggest emotion.
- Draw a star next to any evidence that the characters' attitudes are changing.
- Circle unknown words and phrases. Try to determine the meaning of the words by using context clues, word parts, or a dictionary.

LEARNING STRATEGIES:
Previewing, Predicting, Marking the Text, Summarizing, Collaborative Discussion, Close Reading, Rereading, Brainstorming, Drafting

ABOUT THE AUTHOR
Judith Viorst is a journalist and an author who writes fiction and nonfiction for both adults and children. Her well-known and loved children's classic *Alexander and the Terrible, Horrible, No Good, Very Bad Day* and its sequels are based on the adventures of her own three sons.

WORD CONNECTIONS

Etymology
The word *southpaw* is baseball slang for a left-handed pitcher. Originally baseball diamonds were laid out with home plate to the west, so left-handed pitchers' pitching arms would be facing south when they stood on the pitching mound.

Short Story

by Judith Viorst

Inning 1
Dear Richard,
Don't invite me to your birthday party because I'm not coming. And give back the Disneyland sweatshirt I said you could wear. If I'm not good enough to play on your team, I'm not good enough to be friends with.

> Your former friend,
>
> Janet

P.S. I hope when you go to the dentist he finds 20 cavities.

My Notes

_____

_____

_____

_____

_____

_____

_____

_____

_____

_____

_____

_____

_____

Play Ball: Analyzing a Game of Life

Dear Janet,

Here is your stupid Disneyland sweatshirt, if that's how you're going to be. I want my comic books now—finished or not. No girl has ever played on the Mapes Street baseball team, and as long as I'm captain, no girl ever will.

> Your former friend,
>
> Richard

P.S. I hope when you go for your checkup you need a tetanus shot.

Inning 2

Dear Richard,

I'm changing my goldfish's name from Richard to Stanley. Don't count on my vote for class president next year. Just because I'm a member of the ballet club doesn't mean I'm not a terrific ballplayer.

> Your former friend,
>
> Janet

P.S. I see you lost your first game 28–0.

Dear Janet,

I'm not saving any more seats for you on the bus. For all I care you can stand the whole way to school. Why don't you just forget about baseball and learn something nice like knitting?

> Your former friend,
>
> Richard

P.S. Wait until Wednesday.

Inning 3

Dear Richard,

My father said I could call someone to go with us for a ride and hot-fudge sundaes. In case you didn't notice, I didn't call you.

> Your former friend,
>
> Janet

P.S. I see you lost your second game, 34–0.

Dear Janet,

Remember when I took the laces out of my blue-and-white sneakers and gave them to you? I want them back.

> Your former friend,
>
> Richard

P.S. Wait until Friday.

Inning 4

Dear Richard,
Congratulations on your unbroken record. Eight straight losses, wow! I understand you're the laughing stock of New Jersey.

> Your former friend,
>
> Janet

P.S. Why don't you and your team forget about baseball and learn something nice like knitting maybe?

Dear Janet,
Here's the silver horseback riding trophy that you gave me. I don't think I want to keep it anymore.

> Your former friend,
>
> Richard

P.S. I didn't think you'd be the kind who'd kick a man when he's down.

Inning 5

Dear Richard,
I wasn't kicking exactly. I was kicking back.

> Your former friend,
>
> Janet

P.S. In case you were wondering, my batting average is .345.

Dear Janet,
Alfie is having his tonsils out tomorrow. We might be able to let you catch next week.

> Richard

Inning 6

Dear Richard,
I pitch.

> Janet

Dear Janet,
Joel is moving to Kansas and Danny sprained his wrist. How about a permanent place in the outfield?

> Richard

My Notes

Play Ball: Analyzing a Game of Life

Inning 7

Dear Richard,
I pitch.

Janet

Dear Janet,
Ronnie caught the chicken pox and Leo broke his toe and Elwood has these stupid violin lessons. I'll give you first base, and that's my final offer.

Richard

Inning 8

Dear Richard,
Susan Reilly plays first base, Marilyn Jackson catches, Ethel Kahn plays center field, I pitch. It's a package deal.

Janet

P.S. Sorry about your 12-game losing streak.

Dear Janet,
Please! Not Marilyn Jackson.

Richard

Inning 9

Dear Richard,
Nobody ever said that I was unreasonable. How about Lizzie Martindale instead?

Janet

Dear Janet,
At least could you call your goldfish Richard again?

Your friend,
Richard

Second Read

- Reread the short story to answer these text-dependent questions.
- Write any additional questions you have about the text in your Reader/Writer Notebook.

1. **Craft and Structure:** How does the author develop the point of view of this story?

2. **Key Ideas and Details:** What is the main idea of the section *Inning 2?* Which details in this section support the main idea?

3. **Key Ideas and Details:** How is Richard's baseball team doing in *Inning 4?* Support your answer with text evidence.

4. **Key Ideas and Details:** Which sentence in *Inning 5* shows that Richard is changing his mind?

5. **Key Ideas and Details:** In *Inning 9,* how can you tell that Richard's tone has changed since the beginning of the story?

My Notes

Play Ball: Analyzing a Game of Life

GRAMMAR & USAGE
Adjectives and Predicate Adjectives

An **adjective** describes a noun or a pronoun and answers the questions *what kind, which one, how many,* or *how much.* **Predicate adjectives** are adjectives that follow the verb *to be* or linking verbs, as in the sentences below:
The bear is furry.
The girl seems lonely.
The water looks calm.

GRAMMAR & USAGE
Adverbs

An **adverb** answers the question *how* or *in what way.* The suffix *-ly* may be added to adjectives to form adverbs. Note how the following adjectives become adverbs:
proud + ly = proudly
angry + ly = angrily
regretful + ly = regretfully

My Notes

_____
_____
_____
_____
_____
_____
_____
_____
_____

Working from the Text
Literacy Center Reading

For this activity, you will analyze the story and participate in collaborative work and discussion.

First Base: Use precise adjectives to describe tone.

You might say that the two characters in "The Southpaw" express a *mad* or *angry* tone in the first half of the story, but these words are not precise. Reread your assigned letters (see below) and discuss each letter's tone with your group members. Using classroom resources such as a thesaurus, tone list, and Word Wall, brainstorm a list of synonyms for the identified tone and order them from least intense to most intense. Then, agree upon and record a precise adjective in the My Notes section next to each assigned letter. Leave your brainstorming notes for other groups to use as a resource.

Group 1: Letters 1–4
Group 2: Letters 13–18
Group 3: Letters 9–12
Group 4: Letters 5–8

Note: Groups 1, 3, and 4 should first review the previous responses and revise to identify a more accurate or precise tone.

Second Base: Use adverbs to communicate tone.
Adverbs can also describe a character's tone. Next to each character's name in your assigned letters, record a verb and precise adverb that capture the writer's emotions. For example, a character could <u>state</u> *proudly*, <u>demand</u> *angrily*, or <u>explain</u> *regretfully*. Use classroom resources such as a dictionary, adverb list, or Word Wall to expand your options.

Group 1: Letters 5–8
Group 2: Letters 1–4
Group 3: Letters 13–18
Group 4: Letters 9–12

Third Base: Summarize the point of view.

Reread your assigned letters (see below). In the My Notes section, concisely summarize each set of notes by explaining each character's point of view and how it is created.

Group 1: Letters 9–12
Group 2: Letters 5–8
Group 3: Letters 1–4
Group 4: Letters 13–18

Note: Groups 2, 3, and 4 should first review the previous responses and revise if they can write a more accurate or concise summary.

Home Base: Make a connection between conflict and plot.

Think of the exchange of letters in the story as a baseball scoreboard. The first two letters between Janet and Richard are Inning 1, letters 3 and 4 are Inning 2, and so on.

For each pair of assigned letters, decide who "wins" the argument. Write a "1" in his or her box and a "0" in the other character's box. Explain your thinking in the My Notes section, and discuss the connection between conflict and plot.

	Inning 1 (1–2)	Inning 2 (3–4)	Inning 3 (5–6)	Inning 4 (7–8)	Inning 5 (9–10)	Inning 6 (11–12)	Inning 7 (13–14)	Inning 8 (15–16)	Inning 9 (17–18)
Janet									
Richard									

Group 1: Letters 13–18   Group 3: Letters 5–8

Group 2: Letters 9–12   Group 4: Letters 1–4

Check Your Understanding

It should now be clear that writers of literary texts purposefully use structure and language to develop a story. Describe how this story unfolds and how the two characters change as they resolve their conflict. How does the tone change with each set of letters?

WRITING to SOURCES   Expository Writing Prompt

Think about the characters, conflict, and plot.

Explain the theme of the story, and identify the details that show the theme. Be sure to

- Establish a central idea.
- Support the central idea with textual evidence from the story (relating to characters, conflict, and/or plot) and thoughtful analysis.
- Use precise diction (e.g., specific literary terms) to create a formal tone.

My Notes

Drama Games: Connecting the Mind and Body

Learning Target

- Collaborate and perform a series of drama games to explore how tone, facial expressions, eye contact, and other elements contribute to the overall success of a performance.

Introducing the Strategy: Drama Games

Games can be a fun way to learn. Drama games are a form of role playing. Performing a role helps you make meaning of a text and understand it from the viewpoint of both a reader and a performer. Drama games require imagination, teamwork, and rehearsal. They also require a sharing of ideas to help make a text come alive in a visual way.

WORD CONNECTIONS

Roots and Affixes

Pantomime contains the Greek roots *-mime-*, meaning "mimic," and *pan,* meaning "all" or "entirely." Knowing the Greek root *-mime-* can also help you understand the meaning of the word *mimetic* (characterized by imitation). Knowing the Greek prefix *pan-* can also help you understand the meaning of the word *panacea* (a remedy for all disease or ills).

Game 1: Accept-Change-Pass

1. Stand up and form a circle of four to five students.
2. The student whose birthday is closest to today's date becomes the first actor. He or she should hold up an imaginary box and pull out an imaginary object.
3. After setting the box down, the actor should pretend to use the object without speaking or making a sound. Each person in the group should have a chance to try to identify the object.
4. Once someone correctly identifies the object, the actor should place the object back in the box, pick the box up, and pass it to his or her left.
5. Repeat the process until all group members have had a chance to play the actor's role.

Game 2: Shadowing

1. Stand up, form pairs, and label yourselves *Y* and *Z*.
2. After your teacher calls out an action, the *Y* students should begin to silently pantomime the action while the *Z* students copy them. Students *Y* and *Z* should look like reflections in a mirror.
3. At the signal, switch roles. This time the *Z* students should choose their own actions to pantomime as the *Y* students copy their actions.

My Notes

Game 3: The Cycle of Life

1. Stand up and form a circle of four to five students.
2. Plan a **tableau** and then brainstorm ways to role-play the five stages of humans: infancy, childhood, adolescence, adulthood, and old age. Use sounds—but no words—and imaginative props to enhance your performance.
3. After planning and rehearsing, return to your seat.
4. When it is your group's turn, form a tableau of ages, mixing up the order. Freeze for a count of ten and then come to life, one by one, with sounds and props. After you perform your role, the class will guess which age you represent.

Literary Terms

A **tableau** is a purposeful arrangement of characters frozen as if in a painting or a photograph. The arrangement should convey information about the characters and their relationships.

Game 4: The Tone Game

In order to effectively deliver lines in a drama, you must accurately express your character's tone of voice. As you know, delivery rate, inflection, and facial expressions help to communicate tone. Because this is such a key part of a performance, it is important to practice speaking with different tones to get feedback from an audience.

1. When it is your turn, select a line and one of the tones below. Do your best to deliver the line effectively to others in your group. They should be able to identify the tone right away. Remember that facial expressions and eye contact help to communicate tone.

2. If your audience cannot guess your intended tone, revise your approach and try again.

I am going home now! **Tone: angry**	**I need to eat something!** **Tone: urgent**	**I need a break.** **Tone: playful**
I am going home now. **Tone: sad**	**I need to eat something!** **Tone: joyful**	**I need a break!** **Tone: angry**
I am going home now! **Tone: excited**	**I need to eat something.** **Tone: depressed**	**I need a break.** **Tone: sarcastic**
I am going home now. **Tone: indifferent**	**I need to eat something.** **Tone: nervous**	**I need a break.** **Tone: indifferent**
I am going home now. **Tone: bored**	**I need to eat something.** **Tone: indifferent**	**I need a break.** **Tone: bored**

My Notes

Drama Games: Connecting the Mind and Body

My Notes

Language and Writer's Craft: Pronoun Usage

Correct language use is just as important in speaking as in writing. As you complete writing and speaking assignments in this unit, be aware of how you are using pronouns and follow these rules:

- Recognize and correct inappropriate shifts in noun/pronoun agreement (for example, "The student carried his/her backpack." not "The student carried their backpack.")

- Avoid vague pronouns when referring to characters or to actions (for example, "Smith and Jones are the new employees. Smith works in the garden department." not "Smith and Jones are the new employees. She works in the garden department.")

- Use pronouns in the proper case: subjective, objective, and possessive.

- Use intensive pronouns (such as *themselves, ourselves, myself*) correctly.

Check Your Understanding

1. Make up a sentence of your own that communicates a specific tone. Use descriptive words to express your tone. Share with your group to see if they can infer the tone.

2. Why is teamwork a necessary part of any dramatic performance?

3. How does imagination relate to performance?

4. Why is it important to plan and rehearse facial expressions and movement prior to a performance?

5. How do sound and props enhance a performance?

INDEPENDENT READING LINK

Read and Respond

Select, rehearse, and role-play a character's lines from the play you are reading independently. Then tell the class how performing lines from the play helped your understanding of the plot, theme, and characters.

Lear's Limericks: Playing with Rhythm and Rhyme

Learning Target
- Analyze how parts of a limerick fit into the overall structure and develop theme.
- Rehearse a limerick and present a practiced oral interpretation of the poem, demonstrating command of rhyme, rhythm, inflection, and rate.

LEARNING STRATEGIES:
Diffusing, Summarizing, Marking the Text, Rereading, Rehearsal, Oral Reading

Introducing the Strategy: Oral Interpretation
An **oral interpretation** is reading aloud a literary text with expression. The purpose is to share with an audience the reader's personal insight into a text through voice, fluency, tone, and purpose. The oral interpretation requires careful analysis of a text to determine appropriate **rate** (speed), **inflection** (emphasis on specific words for effect), and **tone** (speaker's attitude toward the subject). It also requires appropriate eye contact and facial expressions to show an understanding of the meaning of the text.

Literary Terms
An **oral interpretation** is a way of expressing the meaning of a written text to others. The reader uses fluency, tone of voice, speed, and inflection to convey meaning or interpret the text.

Preview
In this activity, you will read a selection of limericks and present an interpretation of one of them to the class.

Setting a Purpose for Reading
- **Limericks** are a form of poetry with a specific **rhyme scheme**. Limericks usually have three long lines that end in words that rhyme and two shorter lines that rhyme. A rhythm is created when reading limericks by stressing the rhyming words. As you read the limericks, underline words and phrases that show rhyme and rhythm.
- Circle unknown words and phrases. Try to determine the meaning of the words by using context clues, word parts, or a dictionary.

Literary Terms
A **limerick** is a light, humorous, nonsensical verse of five lines, usually with a **rhyme scheme**, or rhyming pattern, of a-a-b-b-a. In poetry, rhythm refers to the pattern or flow of sound created by the arrangement of stressed and unstressed syllables. Many types of poems, such as limericks, have a specific rhythm.

ABOUT THE AUTHOR
Although Edward Lear (1812–1888) was an artist and illustrator, he is remembered mainly for his limericks and nonsense poetry. He began writing his nonsense verses as he was trying to become established as an artist. Eventually he used his artistic skills to illustrate his own humorous works.

My Notes

GRAMMAR & USAGE
Punctuation Conventions

Commas (,) and **semicolons** (;) signal a brief pause, so slow down the rate of speaking. The **dash** (—) is used to emphasize the content that follows, so read the content with inflection. **Exclamation points** (!) indicate that the speaker feels strong emotion (e.g., excitement, concern, or surprise), so read the content with louder volume, a faster rate, and a higher inflection.

My Notes

Literary Terms
Inflection is the emphasis a speaker places on words through changes in pitch or volume. The **rate** is the speed at which a speaker delivers words.

Limericks

from a book of nonsense

by Edward Lear

1 There was an Old Man with a beard,
   Who said, "It is just as I feared! —
   Two Owls and a Hen,
   Four Larks and a Wren,
   Have all built their nests in my beard!"

2 There was an Old Man with a nose,
   Who said, "If you choose to suppose
   That my nose is too long,
   You are certainly wrong!"
   That remarkable Man with a nose.

3 There was an Old Man on a hill,
   Who seldom, if ever, stood still;
   He ran up and down,
   In his Grandmother's gown,
   Which adorned that Old Man on a hill.

4 There was a Young Lady whose chin
   Resembled the point of a pin;
   So she had it made sharp,
   And purchased a harp,
   And played several tunes with her chin.

5 There was an Old Man of Kilkenny,
   Who never had more than a penny;
   He spent all that money
   In onions and honey,
   That wayward Old Man of Kilkenny.

6 There was an Old Man in a boat,
   Who said, "I'm afloat! I'm afloat!"
   When they said, "No! you ain't!"

He was ready to faint,

That unhappy Old Man in a boat.

7 There was an old man from Nantucket, Who kept all his cash in a bucket.

His daughter named Nan

Ran away with a man.

And as for the bucket, Nantucket.

Second Read

- Reread the limericks to answer these text-dependent questions.
- Write any questions you have about the text in your Reader/Writer Notebook.
1. Choose two limericks to compare with one another. How are the rhyme and rhythm similar or different in each? How do the two limericks relate to each other, and the collection in general?

2. What does the title of the collection tell you about the theme of the limericks? Which details in the limericks relate to the title?

Working from the Text

1. You will perform an assigned limerick for your group or class. Copy your poem onto a separate piece of paper or large index card. This will become your cue card during your performance. Mark the text to help you perform it by doing the following:
   - Use one color to highlight the three end words that rhyme with each other. Use a second color for the other two end words that rhyme.
   - Look at the punctuation to help guide your **inflection** and **rate** for your oral delivery. Highlight or note places where you should go slower or faster.
   - Count and record the number of syllables per line. Then, circle the stressed syllables or mark them with a third color.
2. Read your limerick aloud to yourself and follow your markings for rate, inflection, and tone. Make adjustments as needed.
3. Memorize your limerick and rehearse your oral interpretation. Practice delivering your poem. Be sure to use the following:
   - Effective rate, inflection, and tone.
   - Appropriate facial expressions and eye contact.
4. When it is your turn, perform your oral interpretation of a limerick.

Check Your Understanding

Listen to your classmates' performances. What do you notice about the rate, inflection, and tone of each performance? Decide which performances were best, and write an explanation for the elements of performance used and how they affected the oral interpretation.

My Notes

INDEPENDENT READING LINK

Read and Recommend

Think about the play you are reading independently. Based on what you have read so far, would you recommend the play to a classmate? Write a note to a classmate explaining why or why not.

Planning and Presenting a Reader's Theater

LEARNING STRATEGIES:
Close Reading, Marking the Text, Summarizing, Rereading, Graphic Organizer, Rehearsal, Brainstorming, Role Playing

Literary Terms
A **drama** is also called a play. It is a genre of literature that is intended to be performed before an audience.

My Notes

Learning Targets
- Describe how a drama's plot unfolds in a series of episodes as well as how the characters respond or change as the plot moves toward a resolution.
- Determine the meaning and impact of specific words on a text.
- Analyze and rehearse a drama and present it as a Reader's Theater.

Preview
In this activity, you will read a **drama** and deliver a Reader's Theater performance.

Setting a Purpose for Reading
- As you read the drama, underline words and phrases that relate to the story's plot, conflict, and theme.
- Circle unknown words and phrases. Try to determine the meaning of the words by using context clues, word parts, or a dictionary.

ABOUT THE AUTHOR
Aaron Shepard has written numerous award-winning books and stories. He specializes in folk tales and other forms of traditional literature. Mr. Shepard wrote his first story in fourth grade. From there, he went on to write multiple poems, essays, and stories. He has performed professionally in Reader's Theater and currently is a full-time writer who expresses this thought about writing: "With researching, writing, and revising, a story can take me years to finish—or you might say that it's never finished at all."

Drama

The Millionaire Miser

by Aaron Shepard

Cast of Characters:

NARRATOR 1

NARRATOR 2

NARRATOR 3

NARRATOR 4

SUSHIL—the miser

BOY

NIRMALA—the miser's wife

SAKKA—The King of Heaven

MAN

WOMAN

RAJAH—The Prince or Ruler

(SERVANT, OTHER TOWNSPEOPLE, CHILDREN)

How to Say the Names:

Sushil | SOO-shil

Nirmala | NEER-ma-la

Sakka | SOK-a

1 **NARRATOR 1:** Sushil was a miser. Though his treasure house was full, he was too stingy to give away even the smallest coin.

2 **NARRATOR 4:** And since food cost money, he ate almost nothing, and starved his family and servants besides.

3 **NARRATOR 2:** One morning, as Sushil took his daily walk through town, he saw a boy eating a sweet rice dumpling.

4 **BOY:** (*makes loud sounds of enjoyment as he eats*)

5 **NARRATOR 3:** Sushil's mouth watered as he made his way home. He said to himself,

6 **SUSHIL:** If only I could ask my wife to make me a sweet dumpling. But if *I* wanted one, so would my *wife*. And if my wife wanted one, so would the children. And if the children wanted one, so would the servants. So I had better just keep quiet.

7 **NARRATOR 1:** When Sushil arrived home, he said nothing about a dumpling. But he wanted one so badly, he felt weak. His legs shook, and he had to go to bed.

8 **NARRATOR 4:** His wife, Nirmala, came to him. She asked,

9 **NIRMALA:** What is wrong, my husband?

10 **NARRATOR 2:** Sushil lay groaning and clenched his teeth.

11 **NIRMALA:** Is there something you want?

12 **NARRATOR 3:** Sushil's face grew red, then purple. At last he squeaked,

13 **SUSHIL:** I would like a sweet rice dumpling.

14 **NIRMALA:** *That* is no problem. We are wealthy enough. Why, I will make sweet dumplings for the whole town!

15 **SUSHIL:** (*gasps*)

16 **NARRATOR 1:** Sushil gasped in horror.

17 **SUSHIL:** You will make a **pauper** of me!

18 **NIRMALA:** Well then, I will make dumplings for our family and servants.

19 **SUSHIL:** Why would the servants need any?

20 **NIRMALA:** Then I will make them for us and the children.

21 **SUSHIL:** I am sure the children can do without.

22 **NIRMALA:** Then I will make one for you and one for me.

23 **SUSHIL:** Why would *you* want one?

24 **NARRATOR 4:** Nirmala sighed and went out.

25 **NARRATOR 2:** After a while, she returned with a single sweet dumpling.

26 **NARRATOR 3:** Then she looked on as Sushil, moaning with delight, devoured every crumb.

WORD CONNECTIONS

Roots and Affixes

The word *script* comes from the Latin word *scribere*, meaning "to write." The roots -*script*- and -*scrib*- both mean "write" and appear in many English words. Knowing these Latin roots can also help you understand the meaning of the words *scribble* (to write quickly or carelessly), *scripture* (sacred writings), *describe* (to give an account using written or spoken words), and *manuscript* (an original text of an author's work).

My Notes

pauper: a very poor person

Planning and Presenting a Reader's Theater

27 SUSHIL: (*makes loud sounds of enjoyment as he eats*)

***

28 NARRATOR 1: Now, it happened that all this was seen by Sakka, the King of Heaven, who was sitting on his marble throne in his thousand-mile-high palace.

millennia: a thousand years

29 SAKKA: (*appalled, looking down to earth*) Not in seventy-seven **millennia** have I ever seen such a miser! I will teach this fellow not to be so stingy.

30 NARRATOR 4: So the god waited till the next day, when Sushil left on his morning walk. Then he made himself look just like Sushil and came down to earth.

31 NARRATOR 2: Sakka walked into Sushil's house as if he were Sushil himself.

32 NARRATOR 3: In Sushil's own voice he told a servant,

33 SAKKA: (*imitating Sushil*) Run through the town and invite everyone you see. Today Sushil will share his wealth!

34 SERVANT: (*excitedly bows and runs off*)

35 NARRATOR 1: When Nirmala heard these words, she cried,

36 NIRMALA: Husband, can this be true? Heaven be praised for your change of heart!

37 NARRATOR 4: Then she helped him open the treasure house.

38 TOWNSPEOPLE (including WOMAN, MAN, BOY): (*enter*)

39 NARRATOR 2: Soon the people of the town arrived. The pretend Sushil told them,

40 SAKKA: Take what you will! And if anyone who looks like me tries to stop you, drive away the scoundrel!

41 MAN: Thanks to Lord Sushil!

42 WOMAN: The most generous man alive!

43 NARRATOR 3: They rushed into the treasure house and loaded themselves with gold, silver, diamonds, and pearls.

44 NARRATOR 1: Just then, the real Sushil came home.

45 NARRATOR 4: When he saw his treasure being carried out the gate, he screamed,

46 SUSHIL: Robbers! Thieves! Put that back! How dare you!

47 NARRATOR 2: But the townspeople said,

48 BOY: This must be the one that Lord Sushil warned us about!

49 NARRATOR 3: And they chased Sushil halfway across town.

50 WOMAN: (*chasing Sushil*) Be off with you!

51 MAN: (*chasing Sushil*) And don't show your face again!

My Notes

WORD CONNECTIONS

Cognates
The Spanish cognate for *generous* is *generoso.*

52 NARRATOR 1: The crowd turned back. Sushil rushed on to the court of the Rajah.

53 SUSHIL: (*arriving out of breath, speaking frantically*) Your Majesty, the people of the town are taking all I own!

54 RAJAH: But your own servant invited them!

55 NARRATOR 4: ... said the Rajah.

56 RAJAH: I heard him myself. Did you not give the order?

57 SUSHIL: Never! If the order was given, I beg you to bring the one who gave it!

58 NARRATOR 2: So the Rajah sent a messenger.

59 NARRATOR 3: Soon came Sakka, still pretending to be Sushil, along with Nirmala and the children. The children stared wide-eyed at the two Sushils, and Nirmala nearly fainted.

60 SUSHIL: Impostor!

61 SAKKA: Deceiver!

62 RAJAH: (*bewildered, looking from one to the other*) I cannot tell the difference between you!

63 NARRATOR 1: ... said the Rajah. He turned to Nirmala.

64 RAJAH: Can *you* say which is the true Sushil?

65 NARRATOR 4: Nirmala looked at both men.

66 NIRMALA: Your Majesty, may I ask them a question?

67 RAJAH: Certainly.

68 NARRATOR 2: Nirmala turned to Sakka.

69 NIRMALA: Is it better to be generous to yourself, to your family, to your servants, or to your neighbors?

70 SAKKA: It is best to be generous to all! When you are generous, others also grow generous, and everyone is wealthier.

71 NARRATOR 3: Then Nirmala turned to Sushil.

72 NIRMALA: Is it better to be generous to yourself, to your family, to your servants, or to your neighbors?

73 SUSHIL: To none! It is a waste of wealth that can never be regained!

74 NARRATOR 1: Nirmala took a deep breath. She gathered the children, then drew close to Sakka.

75 NIRMALA: This is the true Sushil, Your Majesty.

76 SUSHIL: But, Nirmala! My wife! My children!

77 NARRATOR 4: At that, the god stepped forward. With a blinding flash of light, he changed back to his own shape.

My Notes

Planning and Presenting a Reader's Theater

78 **SAKKA:** Your Majesty, I am not Sushil but Sakka. I came down from Heaven to teach this man a lesson!

79 **NARRATOR 2:** He turned to the trembling and downcast Sushil.

80 **SAKKA:** Do you see? You are so stingy, even your wife and children deny you!

81 **SUSHIL:** (*moans*)

82 **SAKKA:** There is but one hope for you. Will you stop being such a miser?

83 **SUSHIL:** (*hesitantly*) Well … maybe I could be a *little* more generous.

84 **SAKKA:** (*sternly*) A *little* more?

85 **SUSHIL:** Well … maybe a little *more* than a little more.

86 **SAKKA:** You had better be a *lot* more generous. Or I'll be back!

87 **NARRATOR 3:** And with another flash of light, he vanished.

88 **RAJAH:** (*to Sushil*) Well!

89 **NARRATOR 1:** … said the Rajah to Sushil.

90 **RAJAH:** It seems you indeed have been taught a good lesson!

91 **SUSHIL:** I suppose so, Your Majesty.

92 **NARRATOR 4:** He turned shyly to Nirmala and held out his hand.

93 **SUSHIL:** (*questioningly*) Wife?

94 **NARRATOR 2:** Nirmala took it.

95 **NIRMALA:** (*smiling at him*) Husband! Oh, Sushil, let us celebrate! I have an idea. Let us make sweet rice dumplings for the entire town!

96 **SUSHIL:** (*gasps*)

97 **NARRATOR 3:** Sushil gasped in horror.

98 **NARRATOR 1:** His legs shook.

99 **NARRATOR 4:** He groaned and clenched his teeth.

100 **NARRATOR 2:** His face grew red, then purple.

101 **NARRATOR 3:** Then he squeaked,

102 **SUSHIL:** All right!

Second Read

- Reread the drama to answer these text-dependent questions.
- Write any additional questions you have about the text in your Reader/Writer Notebook.

1. **Craft and Structure:** What are some examples of text features in "The Millionaire Miser?" How do they fit into the overall structure of the text?

2. **Key Ideas and Details:** What do details from Nirmala's conversation with Sushil beginning at paragraph 9 reveal about her character? How does this exchange advance the plot of the drama?

3. **Craft and Structure:** What instruction does Sakka give to Sushil's servant in paragraph 33? How does this instruction advance the plot of the drama?

4. **Craft and Structure:** What does the word *impostor* mean in paragraph 60? Which words from the text help you understand the meaning of the word?

5. **Key Ideas and Details:** What does the text say about how Nirmala made her choice between the two men? How does this choice advance the plot of the drama?

Planning and Presenting a Reader's Theater

6. **Craft and Structure:** How do the words *trembling* and *downcast* in paragraph 79 impact the meaning and tone of the story? Which details from the story support your interpretation of these words?

7. **Key Ideas and Details:** At the end of the story, how does Sushil feel about Nirmala making dumplings for the entire town? Which details in the drama show the reader how Sushil feels?

Working from the Text

8. What is the meaning of the word "miser?" What other words mean the same thing?

9. In your groups, summarize the plot in two or three sentences, being sure to mention the main characters, the conflict, and the resolution to the conflict.

10. What is the story's theme? Choose details from the text (e.g., events) and explain how they contribute to the development of the theme.

11. Compare and contrast poems and stories. How would this fable change if it were written as a poem? Consider ideas, organization, language, and conventions.

Reader's Theater Performance

With your group, you will next prepare to perform this drama for your classmates. **Reader's Theater** is different from ordinary drama because instead of moving around on a stage, each group begins by standing together with backs facing the audience. When it is time to deliver lines, each character, in turn, will face the audience to deliver his or her lines. Each group must figure out a way to indicate the end of the performance.

12. You will be responsible for preparing to read a role in the play. Complete a close reading of the drama. Mark the text by highlighting punctuation, *italicized* words, and strong connotative diction (word choices) spoken by your character, and decide how these determine the tone of voice you will use. Write a precise word next to each of your character's lines to describe the tone. Also, note how you can use rate, inflection, and facial expressions to support the tone.

13. As you reread the play, use the graphic organizer on the next page to record your character analysis. Some categories may not apply, depending on your character.

My Notes

Planning and Presenting a Reader's Theater

Character Name	Analysis	Textual Evidence
Appearance		
Actions		
Words / Tone		
Thoughts and Feelings		
Others' Reactions		

14. Write a statement of interpretation about your character, based on the information in the graphic organizer.

15. Remember that props are used to clarify or add interest to a performance. Brainstorm and record creative yet simple prop ideas next to your character's lines.

16. Work collaboratively to rehearse role playing in a Reader's Theater. You do not need to memorize your lines, but you should know your part well.

- Brainstorm ideas for placement of characters in the line. Place people purposefully for effect.
- Practice delivering your lines fluently, with effective rate, inflection, and tone.
- Practice using facial expressions and eye contact appropriate for your lines.
- Practice using a prop to clarify or add interest.
- Decide how to signal the conclusion of the performance.

17. Rehearse until you feel confident that your presentation has a strong beginning, middle, and end.

18. After your performance, reflect on the following questions:

- Are you satisfied with your performance? Explain.
- You saw how other students performed your character. If you were to perform this character again, what would you do differently?
- What helped you plan and prepare your performance? Explain.
- How did your reading and performance skills improve? What do you still need to work on?

Check Your Understanding

As a member of the audience, listen to other students and evaluate their performances.

- Who was most successful at conveying an appropriate tone? Why?
- Who was the most believable character? What did this student do well?
- What can students do to create a more believable character?
- Who had the most effective prop? Explain.
- How do props affect your perception of the performance and the character?

Writing Prompt: Write a paragraph comparing and contrasting the experience of reading the drama and viewing the live version of the text. Be sure to contrast what you saw and heard in your mind when reading the text to what you observed when you watched the groups perform the same text.

A Poetic Performance

LEARNING STRATEGIES:
Diffusing, Summarizing, Choral Reading, Marking the Text, Rereading, Brainstorming, Rehearsal

Literary Terms
Free verse is poetry that does not follow any regular pattern, rhythm, or rhyme.

My Notes

Learning Target
- Analyze a poem for details, theme, and meaning. Then use the analysis to creatively present the poem to the class, using the appropriate rate, inflection, and tone.

Preview
In this activity, you will read a poem and prepare for a choral reading.

Setting a Purpose for Reading
- As you read the **free verse** poem, underline punctuation to show when to slow down or pause during your oral delivery.
- Circle unknown words and phrases. Try to determine the meaning of the words by using context clues, word parts, or a dictionary.

ABOUT THE AUTHOR
Of Mexican American heritage, Gary Soto grew up in Fresno, California. In high school, he discovered a love of reading and knew he wanted to be a writer. He started writing while in college. His poems, short stories, and novels capture the vivid details of everyday life and have won numerous awards and prizes.

Poetry

Oranges

by Gary Soto

The first time I walked
With a girl, I was twelve,
Cold, and weighted down
With two oranges in my jacket.
5 December. Frost cracking
Beneath my steps, my breath
Before me, then gone,
As I walked toward
Her house, the one whose
10 Porch light burned yellow
Night and day, in any weather.
A dog barked at me, until
She came out pulling
At her gloves, face bright
15 With rouge. I smiled,
Touched her shoulder, and led

Her down the street, across
A used car lot and a line
Of newly planted trees,

20 Until we were breathing
Before a drugstore. We
Entered, the tiny bell
Bringing a saleslady
Down a narrow aisle of goods.

25 I turned to the candies
Tiered like bleachers,
And asked what she wanted—
Light in her eyes, a smile
Starting at the corners

30 Of her mouth. I fingered
A nickel in my pocket,
And when she lifted a chocolate
That cost a dime,
I didn't say anything.

35 I took the nickel from
My pocket, then an orange,
And set them quietly on
The counter. When I looked up,
The lady's eyes met mine,

40 And held them, knowing
Very well what it was all
About.
        Outside,
A few cars hissing past,
Fog hanging like old

45 Coats between the trees.
I took my girl's hand
In mine for two blocks,
Then released it to let
Her unwrap the chocolate.

50 I peeled my orange
That was so bright against
The gray of December
That, from some distance,
Someone might have thought

55 I was making a fire in my hands.

My Notes

A Poetic Performance

Second Read

- Reread the poem to answer these text-dependent questions.
- Write any additional questions you have about the text in your Reader/Writer Notebook.

1. **Key Ideas and Details:** What is the theme of the poem? Support your answer with details from the poem.

2. **Craft and Structure:** Which words in the first stanza of the poem contribute to the theme?

3. **Key Ideas and Details:** Which words in the poem show that the author likes the girl?

4. **Key Ideas and Details:** Which details in lines 30–42 help to convey the theme of the poem?

Setting a Purpose for Reading

- As you read the poem, underline words and phrases that describe the Jabberwocky.

ABOUT THE AUTHOR

As one of eleven children, Lewis Carroll (1832–1898) became adept at entertaining himself and his siblings with fantastic stories. Born as Charles Dodgson, Carroll published his stories under a pen name. Carroll is best known for *Alice's Adventures in Wonderland* and *Through the Looking-Glass and What Alice Found There*. His books have become classics that children throughout the world enjoy.

My Notes

Poetry

Jabberwocky

by Lewis Carroll

'Twas brillig, and the slithy toves
Did gyre and gimble in the wabe:
All mimsy were the borogoves,
And the mome raths outgrabe.

5 'Beware the Jabberwock, my son!
The jaws that bite, the claws that catch!
Beware the Jubjub bird, and shun
The frumious Bandersnatch!'
He took his vorpal sword in hand:

10 Long time the manxome foe he sought –
So rested he by the Tumtum tree,
And stood a while in thought.
And, as in uffish thought he stood,
The Jabberwock, with eyes of flame,

15 Came whiffling through the tulgey wood,
And burbled as it came!
One two! One two! And through and through
The vorpal blade went snicker-snack!
He left it dead, and with its head

20 He went galumphing back.
'And hast thou slain the Jabberwock?
Come to my arms, my beamish boy!
Oh frabjous day! Callooh! Callay!'
He chortled in his joy.

A Poetic Performance

My Notes

25 'Twas brillig, and the slithy toves
    Did gyre and gimble in the wabe:
    All mimsy were the borogoves,
    And the mome raths outgrabe.

Second Read

- Reread the poem to answer these text-dependent questions.
- Write any additional questions you have about the text in your Reader/Writer Notebook.

5. **Craft and Structure:** Which nonsense words from lines 20–24 remind you of other words that you know? How do these words impact the meaning of the poem?

Literary Terms

Alliteration is the repetition of consonant sounds at the beginnings of words that are close together. For example: Lucie loves lions and lollipops. Kind-hearted Kate helped Henry with his homework.

WORD CONNECTIONS

Word Relationships

Looking for the relationships among words can help you make meaning. For example, *fly*, *flying*, and *flight* have similar meanings. Other relationships may be shown with different words that have similar meanings. What do *copying*, *scribblers*, and *signing* have in common?

Setting a Purpose for Reading

- As you read the poem, underline words and phrases that show **alliteration**.
- Circle unknown words and phrases. Try to determine the meaning of the words by using context clues, word parts, or a dictionary.

ABOUT THE AUTHOR

Paul Fleischman, who writes historical fiction and drama as well as poetry, loves to make a connection between writing and music, as he does in "Fireflies." He won the Newbery Medal in 1989 for *Joyful Noise: Poems for Two Voices*.

Poetry

Fireflies
A Poem for Two Voices

by Paul Fleischman

Light	Light
	is the ink we use
Night	Night
is our parchment	
	We're fireflies
fireflies	flickering
flitting	
	flashing
fireflies	
glimmering	fireflies
	gleaming
glowing	
Insect calligraphers	Insect calligraphers
practicing penmanship	
	copying sentences
Six-legged scribblers	Six-legged scribblers
of vanishing messages,	
	fleeting graffiti
Fine artists in flight	Fine artists in flight
adding dabs of light	
	bright brush strokes
Signing the June nights	Signing the June nights
as if they were paintings	as if they were paintings
	We're
flickering	fireflies
fireflies	flickering
fireflies.	fireflies.

My Notes

Second Read

- Reread the poem to answer these text-dependent questions.
- Write any additional questions you have about the text in your Reader/Writer Notebook.

A Poetic Performance

6. **Craft and Structure:** What are some examples of figurative language in the poem? What types of figurative language are used?

Working from the Text

7. What are the differences between fixed form poetry (like limericks) and free verse poetry? How does each type of poetry affect how the author expresses ideas? What are the benefits of each type of poetry?

8. How might alliteration strengthen a poem or performance?

Introducing the Strategy: Choral Reading

Choral reading is reading text aloud in groups to present an interpretation of a text. This strategy can be used to develop reading fluency; to practice phrasing, pacing, and reading dialogue; and to show how a character's emotions are captured through vocal emphasis and tone.

9. Your teacher will assign one of the three poems to your group for choral reading. For your poem:

- Copy the poem onto a separate piece of paper or large index cards. These will become your cue card(s) during your performance.
- Work to make meaning of your poem by *diffusing* the text. Summarize the poem on the back of the card and state the main idea.
- Analyze the structure of the poem and plan your choral reading. Mark the text, deciding how you could divide up the poem for two to three voices. You may also want some lines to be read by more than one speaker at the same time. Why should you emphasize these words in the poem?
- Highlight the punctuation to show when to slow down or pause during your oral delivery.
- Highlight alliteration in the poem. Decide how you will use this feature in your oral delivery.
- Remember that a performance requires careful analysis to determine appropriate rate (speed), inflection (emphasis on specific words for effect), and tone (speaker's attitude toward the subject). It also requires appropriate eye contact and facial expressions, which should be consistent with the other elements. Reread the text and record your analysis of these five elements of performance next to your poem.
- Props can be used to clarify ideas and add interest. Brainstorm creative yet simple ideas for props. Record your ideas for props next to appropriate lines in the poem.

10. Parts of this poem can be read by two voices at the same time. Words in blue that can be spoken by the two speakers together. Mark the rest of the poem to decide how you would have two people read lines at the same time.

11. Prepare to deliver your choral reading. Reread your lines aloud multiple times to improve your fluency.

12. Rehearse your performance with your partner or group. As you rehearse:

- Deliver a choral reading of your poem until it is smooth and effective.
- Practice your lines with an effective rate, inflection, and tone.
- Use facial expressions and eye contact appropriate for your lines.
- Practice delivering your poem with props.

When it is your turn, perform your poem.

Check Your Understanding

As your classmates deliver their choral readings, listen closely to comprehend the tone and meaning of each poem. Also evaluate each speaker's rate and inflection for how they added to your understanding. Use the graphic organizer below to compare and contrast the experience of reading the poems to hearing and seeing them performed. Be sure to include responses to these questions in your comparison:

- What was your understanding of the poem from reading it alone?
- How did your understanding change during group discussions and preparing for a choral reading?
- How did listening to a live performance change how you visualized the scene from the poem?

Reading Poem   **Listening to Performance**

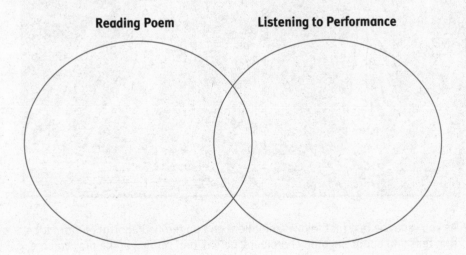

INDEPENDENT READING LINK

Read and Discuss

Choose lines from the play you are reading independently to rehearse and deliver to a partner. Focus on communicating meaning through your delivery rate, inflection, tone, facial expressions, and eye contact. Then discuss with your partner how reading lines aloud changed your understanding of the play.

My Notes

Previewing the Play

LEARNING STRATEGIES:
Diffusing, Marking the Text,
Paraphrasing, Summarizing,
Role Playing

My Notes

Learning Targets

- Analyze visual and informational texts and make predictions about the characters, plot, and conflict of a drama.
- Analyze dialogue and cite textual evidence to understand and explain character and plot.

The Taming of the Shrew

1. Look closely at this illustration of a scene from *The Taming of the Shrew*. What does this picture communicate about the play's setting, characters, conflict, and plot?

2. As you read the text that follows, highlight and underline important information that tells you about the plot, characters, action, and conflict of the play you are to read.

Plot Summary: *The Taming of the Shrew*

Shakespeare wrote the comedy *The Taming of the Shrew* toward the beginning of his career (1590). The play is set in Padua, Italy, where a wealthy old man, Baptista, has two daughters of marriageable age. His younger daughter, Bianca, is beautiful and well-mannered, so men such as Gremio and Hortensio, suitors for her hand in marriage, are attracted to her. His older daughter, Katherine, is also beautiful, but she is ill-tempered and a shrew (a woman of violent temper), so men are not as attracted to her. Baptista will not allow Bianca to get married until someone marries Katherine. Petruchio, an arrogant young man from Verona, decides he will marry Katherine for her money—whether she likes it or not—and her father agrees to the match. Petruchio then manages to woo and win Kate's heart and obedience so that they live happily ever after.

My Notes

Cast of Characters

Character	Pronunciation	Description
Baptista Minola	[bap-TEES-tuh]	Katherine and Bianca's father, a wealthy old man
Katherine	[kat-ah-REE-nuh]	Baptista's older daughter; the shrew
Bianca	[bee-AN-kuh]	Baptista's younger daughter
Petruchio	[peh-TROOK-ee-oh]	A young man from Verona who wants to marry Katherine
Grumio	[GROOM-ee-oh]	Petruchio's servant
Lucentio	[loo-CHEN-see-oh]	A rich young man from Pisa who wants to marry Bianca (later disguised as the teacher Cambio)
Tranio	[TRAH-neeoh]	Lucentio's servant (later disguised as Lucentio)
Biondello	[bee-yawn-DELL-oh]	Lucentio's servant
Hortensio	[hor-TEN-see-oh]	A young man who wants to marry Bianca (later disguised as the teacher Litio); friend of Petruchio
Gremio	[GREEM-ee-oh]	A rich and ridiculous old man who wants to marry Bianca

3. Define *comedy* as the opposite of *tragedy*.

4. Why do you think "taming" a shrew would be a comedy?

Previewing the Play

Introducing the Conflict

5. Read the following scene from Act I of *The Taming of the Shrew*. As you read, look at the underlined words and their meaning in modern English.

Hortensio: (a young man who wants to marry Bianca) . . . Signior Gremio; but a word, I pray. Though the nature of our <u>quarrel</u> yet never <u>brooked parle</u>, know now, upon <u>advice</u>, it <u>toucheth</u> us both (that we may yet again have access to our fair mistress and be happy rivals in Bianca's love) to <u>labor and effect</u> one thing specially.	I pray = please; may I ask quarrel = reason for hostility brooked parle = allowed for discussion advice = careful consideration toucheth = concerns labor and effect = strive for and achieve
Gremio: (a rich old man who wants to marry Bianca) What's that, I pray?	
Hortensio: <u>Marry</u>, sir, to get a husband for her sister.	Marry = listen, I agree, well, indeed
Gremio: A husband? a devil!	
Hortensio: I say "a husband."	
Gremio: I say "a devil." <u>Think'st thou</u>, Hortensio, though her father be very rich, any man is so very a fool to be married to hell?	Think'st thou = do you imagine
Hortensio: <u>Tush</u>, Gremio. Though it pass your patience and mine to endure her loud <u>alarums</u>, why, man, there be good fellows in the world, an a man could <u>light on</u> them, would take her with all faults, <u>and</u> money enough.	Tush = an exclamation of disapproval alarums = noises; disturbances light on = find and = if (there were)
Gremio: I cannot tell; but I <u>had as lief</u> take her <u>dowry</u> with this condition: to be <u>whipped at the high cross</u> every morning.	had as lief = would just as soon dowry = the money, goods, or estate that a wife brings to her husband at marriage whipped at the high cross = an allusion (reference) to a cruel mode of punishment
Hortensio: <u>Faith</u>, as you say, there's small choice in rotten apples. But, come; since this <u>bar in law</u> makes us friends, it shall be so far forth friendly maintained till by helping Baptista's eldest daughter to a husband we set his youngest free for a husband, and then <u>have to't afresh</u>. Sweet Bianca! <u>Happy man be his dole!</u> He that runs fastest gets the ring. How say you, Signior Gremio?	Faith = an emphatic expression used to confirm an idea bar in law = legal barrier (Baptista's "law") have to't afresh = compete (become rivals) again Happy man be his dole! = may the man find happiness
Gremio: I am agreed; and <u>would I had</u> given him the best horse in Padua to begin his <u>wooing</u> that would thoroughly woo her, wed her, and rid the house of her! Come on.	would I had = I wish I had wooing = trying to win a woman to marriage
Gremio and Hortensio exit	

6. With a partner, reread the dialogue in the scene carefully. Paraphrase the text to show your understanding of this scene.

7. Reread the lines of your assigned character, mark the punctuation, and annotate the text to show how the punctuation affects an oral delivery (i.e., rate, inflection, volume, tone). Role-play with a partner. Be sure to focus on all elements of your oral delivery.

Check Your Understanding

Briefly summarize the excerpt on the preceding page. What does the dialogue reveal about Katherine? What does the dialogue reveal about Baptista? What conflict is being set up?

My Notes

Guided Reading of *The Taming of the Shrew*

LEARNING STRATEGIES:
Previewing, Sketching, Visualizing, Predicting, Rereading, Close Reading, Marking the Text, Rehearsal, Oral Interpretation

My Notes

Learning Target

- Analyze how the plot of *The Taming of the Shrew* unfolds and how the characters respond as the plot moves forward.
- Analyze and rehearse an excerpt from *The Taming of the Shrew* to present an oral interpretation of the scene with attention to rate, rhythm, inflection, and tone.

Preview

In this activity, you will read a drama and present an oral interpretation of a scene.

Setting a Purpose for Reading

- As you read the drama, underline words and phrases that show Shakespeare's use of diction, syntax, and rhetorical devices.
- Circle unknown words and phrases. Try to determine the meaning of the words by using context clues, word parts, or a dictionary.

ABOUT THE AUTHOR
William Shakespeare was an important English poet and dramatist. Although Shakespeare wrote in the late 1500s and early 1600s, his writings continue to be analyzed, performed, and enjoyed throughout the world.

Drama

THE TAMING OF THE Shrew

by William Shakespeare

Chunk 1

Act I, Scene II

> Padua. Before HORTENSIO'S house
> *Enter* PETRUCHIO *and his man* GRUMIO, *and* HORTENSIO
>
> **Hortensio:** Petruchio, shall I then come roundly to thee
> And wish thee to a shrewd ill-favour'd wife?
> Thou'dst thank me but a little for my counsel.
> And yet I'll promise thee she shall be rich,
> And very rich : but thou'rt too much my friend,
> And I'll not wish thee to her.
>
> **Petruchio:** Signior Hortensio, 'twixt such friends as we
> Few words suffice; and therefore, if thou know
> One rich enough to be Petruchio's wife,
> As wealth is burden of my wooing dance,
> Be she as foul as was Florentius' love,

As old as Sibyl, and as curst and shrewd
As Socrates' Xanthippe or a worse,
She moves me not, or not removes, at least
Affection's edge in me, were she as rough
As are the swelling Adriatic seas.
I come to wive it wealthily in Padua;
If wealthily, then happily in Padua.

Grumio: Nay, look you, sir, he tells you flatly what his
mind is. Why, give him gold enough and marry him to
a puppet or an aglet-baby, or an old trot with ne'er
a tooth in her head, though she have as many diseases
as two and fifty horses. Why, nothing comes amiss,
so money comes withal.

Hortensio: Petruchio, since we are stepp'd thus far in,
I will continue that I broach'd in jest.
I can, Petruchio, help thee to a wife
With wealth enough, and young and beauteous;
Brought up as best becomes a gentlewoman;
Her only fault, and that is faults enough,
Is that she is intolerable curst,
And shrewd and froward so beyond all measure
That, were my state far worser than it is,
I would not wed her for a mine of gold.

Chunk 2

Petruchio: Hortensio, peace. Thou know'st not gold's effect.
Tell me her father's name, and 'tis enough;
For I will board her though she chide as loud
As thunder when the clouds in autumn crack.

Hortensio: Her father is Baptista Minola,
An affable and courteous gentleman;
Her name is Katherine Minola,
Renown'd in Padua for her scolding tongue.

Petruchio: I know her father, though I know not her;
And he knew my deceased father well.
I will not sleep, Hortensio, till I see her;
And therefore let me be thus bold with you
To give you over at this first encounter—
Unless you will accompany me thither.

Grumio: [*to Hortensio*] I pray you, sir, let him go while
the humour lasts. O' my word, and she knew him as well as I do, she
would think scolding would do little good upon him.
She may perhaps call him half a score knaves or so.
Why, that's nothing; an he begin once, he'll rail in
his rope-tricks. I'll tell you what, sir: an she
stand him but a little, he will throw a figure in

My Notes

Guided Reading of *The Taming of the Shrew*

her face, and so disfigure her with it that she
shall have no more eyes to see withal than a cat.
You know him not, sir.

. . . Enter Gremio and Lucentio (disguised as Cambio)
Hortensio: Gremio, 'tis now no time to vent our love.
Listen to me, and if you speak me fair
I'll tell you news indifferent good for either.
[Presenting Petruchio.] Here is a gentleman whom by chance I met,
Upon agreement from us to his liking,
Will undertake to woo curst Katherine,
Yea, and to marry her, if her dowry please.

Gremio: So said, so done, is well.
Hortensio, have you told him all her faults?

Petruchio: I know she is an irksome brawling scold.
If that be all, masters, I hear no harm.

Chunk 3
Gremio: No, sayst me so, friend? What countryman?

Petruchio: Born in Verona, old Antonio's son.
My father dead, my fortune lives for me,
And I do hope good days and long to see.

Gremio: Oh, Sir, such a life with such a wife were strange.
But if you have a stomach, to't, i' a God's name!
You shall have me assisting you in all.
But will you woo this wild-cat?

Petruchio: Will I live?

Grumio: Will he woo her? Ay, or I'll hang her.

Petruchio: Why came I hither but to that intent?
Think you a little din can daunt mine ears?
Have I not in my time heard lions roar?
Have I not heard the sea, puffed up with winds,
Rage like an angry boar chafed with sweat?
Have I not heard great ordnance in the field,
And heaven's artillery thunder in the skies?
Have I not in a pitched battle heard
Loud 'larums, neighing steeds, and trumpets' clang?
And do you tell me of a woman's tongue,
That gives not half so great a blow to hear
As will a chestnut in a farmer's fire?
Tush! tush! fear boys with bugs.

Grumio: For he fears none.

Act II, Scene I

Padua. BAPTISTA'S house
Enter KATHERINE and BIANCA (with her hands tied)

Bianca: Good sister, wrong me not, nor wrong yourself,
To make a bondmaid and a slave of me.
That I disdain; but for these other goods—
Unbind my hands, I'll pull them off myself,
Yea, all my raiment, to my petticoat,
Or what you will command me will I do,
So well I know my duty to my elders.

Chunk 4

Katherine: Of all thy suitors here I charge thee tell
Whom thou lov'st best. See thou dissemble not.

Bianca: Believe me, sister, of all the men alive
I never yet beheld that special face
Which I could fancy more than any other.

Katherine: Minion, thou liest. Is't not Hortensio?

Bianca: If you affect him, sister, here I swear
I'll plead for you myself but you shall have him.

Katherine: O then, belike, you fancy riches more:
You will have Gremio to keep you fair.

Bianca: Is it for him you do envy me so?
Nay, then you jest; and now I well perceive
You have but jested with me all this while.
I prithee, sister Kate, untie my hands.

Katherine: [*Strikes her*] If that be jest, then all the rest was so.
Enter BAPTISTA

Baptista: Why, how now, dame! Whence grows this insolence?
Bianca, stand aside—poor girl, she weeps!
[*He unties her hands.*] [*to Bianca*] Go ply thy needle; meddle not with her.
[*to Katherine*] For shame, thou hilding of a devilish spirit,
Why dost thou wrong her that did ne'er wrong thee?
When did she cross thee with a bitter word?

Chunk 5

Katherine: Her silence flouts me, and I'll be revenged! [*She flies after*
BIANCA.]

Baptista: What, in my sight? Bianca, get thee in.
Exit BIANCA

Katherine: What, will you not suffer me? Nay, now I see
She is your treasure, she must have a husband;
I must dance bare-foot on her wedding-day,
And, for your love to her, lead apes in hell.
Talk not to me; I will go sit and weep
Till I can find occasion of revenge.

Exit KATHERINE

My Notes

Baptista: Was ever gentleman thus grieved as I?
But who comes here?
Enter GREMIO, *with* LUCENTIO *in the habit of a mean man;* PETRUCHIO, *with* HORTENSIO *as a musician; and* TRANIO, *as* LUCENTIO, *with his boy,* BIONDELLO, *bearing a* lute *and* books

Gremio: Good morrow, neighbor Baptista.

Baptista: Good morrow, neighbor Gremio.
God save you, gentlemen.

Petruchio: And you, good sir. Pray, have you not a daughter
Called Katherine, fair and virtuous?

Baptista: I have a daughter, sir, called Katherine.

Gremio: [*to Petruchio*] You are too blunt; go to it orderly.

Petruchio: You wrong me, Signior Gremio; give me leave.
I am a gentleman of Verona, sir,
That, hearing of her beauty and her wit,
Her affability and bashful modesty,
Her wondrous qualities and mild behavior,
Am bold to show myself a forward guest
Within your house, to make mine eye the witness
Of that report which I so oft have heard . . .

Second Read

- Reread the drama to answer these text-dependent questions.
- Write any additional questions you have about the text in your Reader/Writer Notebook.

1. **Key Ideas and Details:** What does Hortensio want in Chunk 1 of the text? What does he say to Petruchio to try to get what he wants?

2. **Craft and Structure:** How does Hortensio use figurative language to describe Katherine in Chunk 1 of the text? What effect does this language have?

3. **Key Ideas and Details:** How does Petruchio react to Hortensio's warnings in Chunk 2 of the text? What does this show about Petruchio's personality?

4. **Key Ideas and Details:** How does Bianca feel about all of her suitors in Chunk 4 of the text? How is this conveyed in the text?

5. **Craft and Structure:** How does Katherine use figurative language to describe Bianca when she is speaking to her father in Chunk 5 of the text? What effect does this language have?

6. **Key Ideas and Details:** How does Baptista react in Chunk 5 of the text when Petruchio asks if he has a fair and virtuous daughter named Katherine? What does this show about Baptista?

Working from the Text

7. What unique features of a drama did you note in *The Taming of the Shrew*?

8. Conduct a close reading to analyze your assigned character based on what the text says explicitly as well as what you infer from the text. Record your analysis and evidence in the graphic organizer.

Guided Reading of *The Taming of the Shrew*

Character Name	Analysis	Textual Evidence
Appearance		
Actions		
Words and Tone		
Thoughts and Feelings		
Others' Reactions		

INDEPENDENT READING LINK

Read and Respond

Complete the following for the play you have chosen.

- Sketch a tableau that shows the relationships among characters in the play.

- Analyze the diction, syntax, and rhetorical devices used by the writer for effect. Do you notice any patterns?

- Analyze your favorite character.

- Determine the central idea or theme of the play.

9. How does Shakespeare develop the point of view of each character in the scene?

10. What is the theme or central idea of the scene? How does Shakespeare convey this idea?

Plan a Performance

11. Now that you have a deeper understanding of your character and the scene, plan a performance.

- Annotate the text to indicate how you would *orally* deliver each of your lines: Determine an accurate and effective rate, rhythm, inflection, and tone.

- Annotate the text to indicate how you would *physically* deliver each of your lines: Determine accurate and effective eye contact, facial expressions, and movement.

- Complete the graphic organizer below to indicate how you could enhance the delivery of your lines through the use of objects and background sound or images.

Element of Performance	Description	Explanation
Props		
Sound or Images		

12. Set goals for your oral interpretation and rehearse until your group feels confident that you have met your goals. Remember, Shakespeare's lines are often written in iambic pentameter (10 unstressed/stressed beats per line). As you discuss your scene and rehearse, keep the following in mind:

- Understand ideas: Ask questions for clarification when necessary.
- Explore ideas: Challenge your classmates to think in a different way or on a deeper level.
- Reflect on the strength of ideas under discussion. Offer ideas to strengthen the presentation.

13. When it is your turn, deliver your presentation. After your presentation, reflect on your performance and what you may need to do to prepare for the performance for the Embedded Assessment.

Check Your Understanding

As each group performs, write a summary of your interpretation of the scene. Listen carefully to comprehend meaning, and use verbal and visual clues to help you understand the performance.

My Notes

One Text, Two Perspectives

Learning Target

- Analyze scenes from a film version of Shakespeare's *The Taming of the Shrew* and explain how the play and the film are similar and different.

1. As you view scenes from the play, compare and contrast Shakespeare's play with the 1967 film version. Take notes in the graphic organizer below.

	The Play	The Film
Setting		
Characters		
Conflict/Plot		
Theme		

2. Compare and contrast the experience of reading a drama to viewing a film version of the text.

Check Your Understanding

WRITING to SOURCES   Expository Writing Prompt

Explain how Shakespeare's and the director's approach to the same topic and theme are similar and different. Be sure to

- Establish a controlling, or central, idea.
- Organize information using the compare/contrast strategy.
- Provide relevant information and examples.
- Use literary terms and/or academic vocabulary to inform or explain.

 Independent Reading Checkpoint

Think about the play you have been reading independently and write a paragraph about how you would adapt the play to film.

My Notes

Performing Shakespeare

Assignment

Work collaboratively to prepare and present a Reader's Theater performance of a scene from Shakespeare's play *The Taming of the Shrew*. Your performance should have a clear beginning, middle, and end.

Planning: Take time to make a plan for your performance.

- Who will be the members of your group, and what will you name your acting company?
- How will you choose a director and divide the lines fairly among the actors?

Analyzing: Read your script carefully for understanding and character analysis.

- How can you work collaboratively to make meaning of the text?
- How will you (as an actor) work independently to further analyze your character?
- How will you (as the director) support the actors in their character analysis?

Preparing and Rehearsing: Create and revise a performance plan.

- How will you (as an actor) learn your lines and create cue cards to aid memorization and performance?
- How will you (as the director) draft an introduction and conclusion and help the actors to prepare?
- How will you work collaboratively to revise and polish your performance plan?

Evaluating and Performing: Create opportunities to review and rehearse your presentations.

- How can the Scoring Guide help you evaluate how well you are prepared to meet the requirements of the assignment?
- How will you use oral, physical, and visual elements to engage your audience?
- How will you take notes during the other students' presentations to compare and contrast their interpretations with your own?

Reflection

After completing this Embedded Assessment, think about how you went about accomplishing this task, and respond to the following:

- How did students perform the same characters differently? Which choices did you think were most effective and engaging?
- If you were to perform a Shakespearean scene again, what would you do differently?

My Notes

Technology TIP:

If possible, videotape one of your rehearsals in order to review and refine your performance.

Performing Shakespeare

Group 1

Act II, Scene I: Padua. BAPTISTA'S *house*

Exit all but PETRUCHIO . . .
[Enter KATHERINE]

Petruchio: Good morrow, Kate—for that's your name, I hear.

Katherine: Well have you heard, but something hard of hearing:
They call me Katherine that do talk of me.

Petruchio: You lie, in faith, for you are call'd plain Kate,
And bonny Kate, and sometimes Kate the curst;
But, Kate, the prettiest Kate in Christendom,
Kate of Kate Hall, my super-dainty Kate,
For dainties are all Kates, and therefore, Kate,
Take this of me, Kate of my consolation—
Hearing thy mildness prais'd in every town,
Thy virtues spoke of, and thy beauty sounded,
Yet not so deeply as to thee belongs,
Myself am mov'd to woo thee for my wife.

Katherine: Mov'd! in good time! Let him that mov'd you hither
Remove you hence.

Petruchio: Alas, good Kate, I will not burden thee!
For, knowing thee to be but young and light—

Katherine: Too light for such a swain as you to catch;
And yet as heavy as my weight should be.

Petruchio: Should be! should—buzz!

Katherine: Well ta'en, and like a buzzard.

Petruchio: O, slow-wing'd turtle, shall a buzzard take thee?

Katherine: Ay, for a turtle, as he takes a buzzard.

Petruchio: Come, come, you wasp; i' faith, you are too angry.

Katherine: If I be waspish, best beware my sting.

Petruchio: My remedy is then to pluck it out.

Katherine: Ay, if the fool could find it where it lies.

Petruchio: Who knows not where a wasp does wear his sting?

Katherine: In his tongue.

Petruchio: Whose tongue?

Katherine: Yours, if you talk of tales; and so farewell.

Petruchio: Nay, come again, Good Kate; I am a gentleman.

Katherine: That I'll try. *[She strikes him]*

Petruchio: I swear I'll cuff you, if you strike again.

Katherine: So may you lose your arms.
If you strike me, you are no gentleman;
And if no gentleman, why then no arms.

Group 2

Petruchio: Nay, come, Kate, come; you must not look so sour.

Katherine: It is my fashion, when I see a crab.

Petruchio: Why, here's no crab; and therefore look not sour:

Katherine: There is, there is.

Petruchio: Then show it me.

Katherine: Had I a glass I would.

Petruchio: What, you mean my face?

Katherine: Well aim'd of such a young one.

Petruchio: Now, by Saint George, I am too young for you.

Katherine: Yet you are wither'd.

Petruchio: 'Tis with cares.

Katherine: I care not.

Petruchio: Nay, hear you, Kate—in sooth, you scape not so.

Katherine: I chafe you, if I tarry; let me go.

Petruchio: No, not a whit; I find you passing gentle.
'Twas told me you were rough, and coy, and sullen,
And now I find report a very liar;
For thou art pleasant, gamesome, passing courteous,
But slow in speech, yet sweet as springtime flowers.
Thou canst not frown, thou canst not look askance,
Nor bite the lip, as angry wenches will,
Nor hast thou pleasure to be cross in talk;
But thou with mildness entertain'st thy wooers;
With gentle conference, soft and affable.
Why does the world report that Kate doth limp?
O sland'rous world! Kate like the hazel-twig
Is straight and slender, and as brown in hue
As hazel-nuts, and sweeter than the kernels.
O, let me see thee walk. Thou dost not halt.

Katherine: Go, fool, and whom thou keep'st command.

Petruchio: Did ever Dian so become a grove
As Kate this chamber with her princely gait?
O, be thou Dian, and let her be Kate;
And then let Kate be chaste, and Dian sportful!

Katherine: Where did you study all this goodly speech?

Petruchio: It is extempore, from my mother wit.

Katherine: A witty mother! witless else her son.

Petruchio: Marry, so I mean, sweet Katherine.
And therefore, setting all this chat aside,

Performing Shakespeare

My Notes

Thus in plain terms: your father hath consented
That you shall be my wife your dowry greed on;
And will you, nill you, I will marry you.
Now, Kate, I am a husband for your turn;
For, by this light, whereby I see thy beauty,
Thy beauty that doth make me like thee well,
Thou must be married to no man but me;
For I am he am born to tame you, Kate,
And bring you from a wild Kate to a Kate
Conformable as other household Kates.
[Re-enter BAPTISTA, GREMIO, and TRANIO]
Here comes your father. Never make denial;
I must and will have Katherine to my wife.

Group 3

Act III, Scene II: Padua. Before BAPTISTA'S *house*

Baptista Minola: Is he come?

Biondello: Why, no, sir.

Baptista Minola: What then?

Biondello: He is coming.

Baptista Minola: When will he be here?

Biondello: When he stands where I am and sees you there.

Tranio: But say, what to thine old news?

Biondello: Why, Petruchio is coming in a new hat and an old
jerkin; a pair of old breeches thrice turn'd; a pair of boots
that have been candle-cases, one buckled, another lac'd; an old
rusty sword ta'en out of the town armoury, with a broken hilt,
and chapeless; with two broken points; his horse hipp'd, with an
old motley saddle and stirrups of no kindred . . .

Enter PETRUCHIO and GRUMIO

Petruchio: Come, where be these gallants? Who's at home?

Baptista Minola: You are welcome, sir.

Petruchio: And yet I come not well.

Baptista Minola: And yet you halt not.

Tranio: Not so well apparell'd
As I wish you were.

Petruchio: Were it better, I should rush in thus.
But where is Kate? Where is my lovely bride?
How does my father? Gentles, methinks you frown;
And wherefore gaze this goodly company
As if they saw some wondrous monument,
Some comet or unusual prodigy?

Baptista Minola: Why, sir, you know this is your wedding-day.
First were we sad, fearing you would not come;
Now sadder, that you come so unprovided.
Fie, doff this habit, shame to your estate,
An eye-sore to our solemn festival!

[after the wedding]

Enter PETRUCHIO, KATHERINE, BIANCA, BAPTISTA, HORTENSIO,
GRUMIO, and train

Petruchio: Gentlemen and friends, I thank you for your pains.
I know you think to dine with me to-day,
And have prepar'd great store of wedding cheer
But so it is—my haste doth call me hence,
And therefore here I mean to take my leave.

Baptista Minola: Is't possible you will away to-night?

Petruchio: I must away to-day before night come.
Make it no wonder; if you knew my business,
You would entreat me rather go than stay.
And, honest company, I thank you all
That have beheld me give away myself
To this most patient, sweet, and virtuous wife.
Dine with my father, drink a health to me.
For I must hence; and farewell to you all.

Group 4

Tranio: Let us entreat you stay till after dinner.

Petruchio: It may not be.

Gremio: Let me entreat you.

Petruchio: It cannot be.

Katherine: Let me entreat you.

Petruchio: I am content.

Katherine: Are you content to stay?

Petruchio: I am content you shall entreat me stay;
But yet not stay, entreat me how you can.

Katherine: Now, if you love me, stay.

Petruchio: Grumio, my horse.

Grumio: Ay, sir, they be ready; the oats have eaten the horses.

Katherine: Nay, then,
Do what thou canst, I will not go to-day;
No, nor to-morrow, not till I please myself.
The door is open, sir; there lies your way;
You may be jogging whiles your boots are green;
For me, I'll not be gone till I please myself.

My Notes

Performing Shakespeare

My Notes

'Tis like you'll prove a jolly surly groom
That take it on you at the first so roundly.

Petruchio: O Kate, content thee; prithee be not angry.

Katherine: I will be angry; what hast thou to do?
Father, be quiet; he shall stay my leisure.

Gremio: Ay, marry, sir, now it begins to work.

Katherine: Gentlemen, forward to the bridal dinner.
I see a woman may be made a fool
If she had not a spirit to resist.

Petruchio: They shall go forward, Kate, at thy command.
Obey the bride, you that attend on her;
Go to the feast, revel and domineer,
Carouse full measure;
Be mad and merry, or go hang yourselves.
But for my bonny Kate, she must with me.
Nay, look not big, nor stamp, nor stare, nor fret;
I will be master of what is mine own—
She is my goods, my chattels, she is my house,
My household stuff, my field, my barn,
My horse, my ox, my ass, my anything,
And here she stands; touch her whoever dare;
I'll bring mine action on the proudest he
That stops my way in Padua. Grumio,
Draw forth thy weapon; we are beset with thieves;
Rescue thy mistress, if thou be a man.
Fear not, sweet wench; they shall not touch thee, Kate;
I'll buckler thee against a million.

Exit PETRUCHIO, KATHERINE, and GRUMIO

Group 5

Baptista Minola: Nay, let them go, a couple of quiet ones.

Gremio: Went they not quickly, I should die with laughing.

Tranio: Of all mad matches, never was the like.

Lucentio: Mistress, what's your opinion of your sister?

Bianca: That, being mad herself, she's madly mated.

Gremio: I warrant him, Petruchio is Kated.

Act IV, Scene I: PETRUCHIO'S country house

Enter PETRUCHIO and KATHERINE

Petruchio: Where be these knaves? What, no man at door
To hold my stirrup nor to take my horse!
Where is Nathaniel, Gregory, Philip?

Servants: Here, here, sir; here, sir.

Petruchio: Here, sir! here, sir! here, sir! here, sir!
You logger-headed and unpolish'd grooms!
What, no attendance? no regard? no duty?
Where is the foolish knave I sent before?

Grumio: Here, sir; as foolish as I was before.

Petruchio: YOU peasant swain! You malt-horse drudge!
Go, rascals, go and fetch my supper in.
[Exit some of the SERVINGMEN]
[Sings] Where is the life that late I led?
Where are those—
Sit down, Kate, and welcome.

Katherine: Patience, I pray you; 'twas a fault unwilling.

Petruchio: A beetle-headed, flap-ear'd knave!
Come, Kate, sit down; I know you have a stomach.
Will you give thanks, sweet Kate, or else shall I?
What's this? Mutton?

First Servant: Ay.

Petruchio: Who brought it?

Peter: I.

Petruchio: 'Tis burnt; and so is all the meat.
What dogs are these? Where is the rascal cook?
How durst you villains bring it from the dresser
And serve it thus to me that love it not?
There, take it to you, trenchers, cups, and all;
[Throws the meat, etc., at them]
You heedless joltheads and unmanner'd slaves!
What, do you grumble? I'll be with you straight.
[Exit SERVANTS]

Katherine: I pray you, husband, be not so disquiet;
The meat was well, if you were so contented.

Petruchio: I tell thee, Kate, 'twas burnt and dried away,
And I expressly am forbid to touch it;
For it engenders choler, planteth anger;
And better 'twere that both of us did fast,
Since, of ourselves, ourselves are choleric,
Than feed it with such over-roasted flesh.
Be patient; to-morrow 't shall be mended.
And for this night we'll fast for company.
[Exit]

My Notes

My Notes

Group 6

Re-enter SERVANTS severally

Nathaniel: Peter, didst ever see the like?

Peter: He kills her in her own humour.
Re-enter PETRUCHIO

Petruchio: Thus have I politicly begun my reign,
And 'tis my hope to end successfully.
My falcon now is sharp and passing empty.
And till she stoop she must not be full-gorg'd,
She eat no meat to-day, nor none shall eat;
Last night she slept not, nor to-night she shall not;
As with the meat, some undeserved fault
I'll find about the making of the bed;
And here I'll fling the pillow, there the bolster,
This way the coverlet, another way the sheets;
Ay, and amid this hurly I intend
That all is done in reverend care of her—
And, in conclusion, she shall watch all night;
And if she chance to nod I'll rail and brawl
And with the clamour keep her still awake.
This is a way to kill a wife with kindness,
And thus I'll curb her mad and headstrong humour.
He that knows better how to tame a shrew,
Now let him speak; 'tis charity to show. *[Exit]*

Act IV, Scene III: PETRUCHIO'S house

Enter KATHERINE and GRUMIO

Katherine: The more my wrong, the more his spite appears.
What, did he marry me to famish me?
Beggars that come unto my father's door
Upon entreaty have a present alms;
If not, elsewhere they meet with charity;
But I, who never knew how to entreat,
Nor never needed that I should entreat,
Am starv'd for meat, giddy for lack of sleep;
With oaths kept waking, and with brawling fed;
And that which spites me more than all these wants—
He does it under name of perfect love;
As who should say, if I should sleep or eat,
'Twere deadly sickness or else present death.
I prithee go and get me some repast;
I care not what, so it be wholesome food.

Group 7

Enter PETRUCHIO, and HORTENSIO with meat

Petruchio: How fares my Kate? What, sweeting, all amort?

Hortensio: Mistress, what cheer?

Katherine: Faith, as cold as can be.

Petruchio: Pluck up thy spirits, look cheerfully upon me.
Here, love, thou seest how diligent I am,
To dress thy meat myself, and bring it thee.
I am sure, sweet Kate, this kindness merits thanks.
What, not a word? Nay, then thou lov'st it not,
And all my pains is sorted to no proof.
Here, take away this dish.

Katherine: I pray you, let it stand.

Petruchio: The poorest service is repaid with thanks;
And so shall mine, before you touch the meat.

Katherine: I thank you, sir.

Hortensio: Signior Petruchio, fie! you are to blame.
Come, Mistress Kate, I'll bear you company.

Petruchio: *[Aside]* Eat it up all, Hortensio, if thou lovest me.—
Much good do it unto thy gentle heart!
Kate, eat apace. And now, my honey love,
Will we return unto thy father's house
And revel it as bravely as the best,
With silken coats and caps, and golden rings,
With ruffs and cuffs and farthingales and things,
With scarfs and fans and double change of brav'ry.
With amber bracelets, beads, and all this knav'ry.
What, hast thou din'd? The tailor stays thy leisure,
To deck thy body with his ruffling treasure.
*[Petruchio tempts Kate with fancy clothing and accessories
and then takes it all away—claiming that it is not good enough.]*

Petruchio: Well, come, my Kate; we will unto your father's
Even in these honest mean habiliments;
Our purses shall be proud, our garments poor;
For 'tis the mind that makes the body rich;
And as the sun breaks through the darkest clouds,
So honour peereth in the meanest habit.
What, is the jay more precious than the lark
Because his feathers are more beautiful?
Or is the adder better than the eel
Because his painted skin contents the eye?
O no, good Kate; neither art thou the worse

My Notes

Performing Shakespeare

My Notes

For this poor furniture and mean array.
If thou account'st it shame, lay it on me;
And therefore frolic; we will hence forthwith
To feast and sport us at thy father's house...

Group 8

Act IV, Scene V: A public road

Enter PETRUCHIO, KATHERINE, HORTENSIO, and SERVANTS

Petruchio: Come on, a God's name; once more toward our father's.
Good Lord, how bright and goodly shines the moon!

Katherine: The moon? The sun! It is not moonlight now.

Petruchio: I say it is the moon that shines so bright.

Katherine: I know it is the sun that shines so bright.

Petruchio: Now by my mother's son, and that's myself,
It shall be moon, or star, or what I list,
Or ere I journey to your father's house.
Go on and fetch our horses back again.
Evermore cross'd and cross'd; nothing but cross'd!

Hortensio: Say as he says, or we shall never go.

Katherine: Forward, I pray, since we have come so far,
And be it moon, or sun, or what you please;
And if you please to call it a rush-candle,
Henceforth I vow it shall be so for me.

Petruchio: I say it is the moon.

Katherine: I know it is the moon.

Petruchio: Nay, then you lie; it is the blessed sun.

Katherine: Then, God be bless'd, it is the blessed sun;
But sun it is not, when you say it is not;
And the moon changes even as your mind.
What you will have it nam'd, even that it is,
And so it shall be so for Katherine.

Hortensio: Petruchio, go thy ways, the field is won.

Act V, Scene II: LUCENTIO'S house

Enter BAPTISTA, VINCENTIO, GREMIO, the PEDANT, LUCENTIO, BIANCA, PETRUCHIO, KATHERINE, HORTENSIO, and WIDOW. The SERVINGMEN with TRANIO, BIONDELLO, and GRUMIO, bringing in a banquet [after Bianca's wedding to Lucentio].

Baptista Minola: Now, in good sadness, son Petruchio,
I think thou hast the veriest shrew of all.

Petruchio: Well, I say no; and therefore, for assurance,
Let's each one send unto his wife,
And he whose wife is most obedient,
To come at first when he doth send for her,
Shall win the wager which we will propose.

Hortensio: Content. What's the wager?

Lucentio: Twenty crowns.

Petruchio: Twenty crowns?
I'll venture so much of my hawk or hound,
But twenty times so much upon my wife.

Lucentio: A hundred then.

Hortensio: Content.

Petruchio: A match! 'tis done.
[Petruchio wins the bet: Katherine proves to be the most obedient wife.]

Lucentio: Here is a wonder, if you talk of a wonder.

Hortensio: And so it is. I wonder what it bodes.

Petruchio: Marry, peace it bodes, and love, and quiet life,
An awful rule, and right supremacy;
And, to be short, what not that's sweet and happy.

Baptista Minola: Now fair befall thee, good Petruchio!
The wager thou hast won; and I will add
Unto their losses twenty thousand crowns;
Another dowry to another daughter,
For she is chang'd, as she had never been.

Performing Shakespeare

SCORING GUIDE

Scoring Criteria	Exemplary	Proficient	Emerging	Incomplete
Ideas	The performance • demonstrates a deep understanding of a scene and characters • uses a variety of physical and visual elements (facial expressions, movement, props or background sounds/images) effectively • shows evidence of extensive planning, rehearsal, and reflection.	The performance • demonstrates an adequate understanding of a scene and characters • uses some physical and visual elements (facial expressions, movement, props or background sounds/images) to convey meaning • shows evidence of sufficient planning, rehearsal, and reflection.	The performance • demonstrates a partial or flawed understanding of a scene and characters • uses distracting or basic physical and visual elements (facial expressions, movement, props or background sounds/images) • shows evidence of ineffective or insufficient planning, rehearsal, and reflection.	The performance • demonstrates little or no understanding of a scene and characters • lacks physical and/or visual elements • does not show evidence of planning, rehearsal, and reflection.
Structure	The performance • demonstrates strong evidence of collaboration • depicts a significant scene with a clear beginning, middle, and end • provides an engaging introduction and conclusion.	The performance • demonstrates adequate evidence of collaboration • depicts a scene with a beginning, middle, and end • provides an introduction and conclusion.	The performance • demonstrates uneven or ineffective collaboration • depicts a scene with an unclear beginning, middle, and/or end • provides a weak introduction and/or conclusion.	The performance • demonstrates a failure to collaborate • depicts a scene that is too short • lacks an introduction and/or conclusion.
Use of Language	The performer • demonstrates effective oral interpretation skills, including eye contact, volume, rate, inflection, tone, and rhythm • uses punctuation cues (periods, commas, semi-colons, dashes, exclamation points) accurately and consistently to inform vocal delivery.	The performer • demonstrates adequate oral interpretation skills, including eye contact, volume, rate, inflection, tone, and rhythm • uses some punctuation cues (periods, commas, semicolons, dashes, exclamation points) to inform vocal delivery.	The performer • demonstrates inadequate oral interpretation skills • uses punctuation cues (periods, commas, semi-colons, dashes, exclamation points) unevenly or inconsistently.	The performer • demonstrates flawed or ineffective oral interpretation skills • does not recognize punctuation cues, or uses them incorrectly.

Resources

Unit 1 Independent Reading List

Suggestions for Independent Reading

This list, divided into the categories of **Literature** and **Nonfiction/Informational Text**, comprises titles related to the themes and content of the unit. For your independent reading, you can select from this wide array of titles, which have been chosen based on complexity and interest. You can also do your own research and select titles that intrigue you.

Unit 1: Stories of Change		
Literature		
Author	**Title**	**Lexile**
Ada, Alma Flor	*My Name Is Maria Isabel*	860L
Alexie, Sherman	*The Absolutely True Diary of a Part-Time Indian*	600L
Avi	*The True Confessions of Charlotte Doyle*	740L
Black, Holly	*Geektastic: Stories from the Nerd Herd*	760L
Bradbury, Ray	*I Sing the Body Electric*	N/A
Bradbury, Ray	*R is for Rocket*	N/A
Bunting, Eve	*One Green Apple*	450L
Crutcher, Chris	*Athletic Shorts: Six Short Stories*	1010L
Flake, Sharon	*The Skin I'm In*	670L
Guthrie, Peter	*Little Worlds: A Collection of Short Stories for the Middle School*	N/A
Hidier, Tanuja Desai	*Born Confused*	890L
Jimenez, Francisco	*La Mariposa*	750L
Kadohata, Cynthia	*Kira-Kira*	740L
Keyes, Daniel	*Flowers for Algernon*	910L
Levithan, David	*Friends: Stories About New Friends, Old Friends, And Unexpectedly True Friends*	930L
Lin, Grace	*Dumpling Days*	710L
Park, Linda Sue	*Project Mulberry*	690L
Philbrick, Rodman	*Freak the Mighty*	1000L
Philbrick, Rodman	*The Mostly True Adventures of Homer P. Figg*	950L
Ryan, Pam Muñoz	*Esperanza Rising*	750L
Soto, Gary	*Baseball in April and Other Stories*	830L
Spinelli, Jerry	*Maniac Magee*	820L
Taylor, Mildred	*Roll of Thunder, Hear My Cry*	920L
Yang, Gene Luen	*American Born Chinese*	530L
Yep, Laurence	*Dragonwings*	870L

Nonfiction/Informational Text		
Author	Title	Lexile
Ahmedi, Farah and Tamin Ansary	The Story of My Life: An Afghan Girl on the Other Side of the Sky	850L
Jimenez, Francisco	The Circuit: Stories from the Life of a Migrant Child	880L
Myers, Walter Dean	Bad Boy: A Memoir	970L
Park, Linda Sue	*A Long Walk to Water: Based on a True Story*	720L
Paulsen, Gary	*Woodsong*	1090L
Pfetzer, Mark and Jack Galvin	*Within Reach: My Everest Story*	970L
Soto, Gary	*A Summer Life*	990L

Unit 2 Independent Reading List

Suggestions for Independent Reading

This list, divided into the categories of **Literature** and **Nonfiction/Informatinal Text**, comprises titles related to the themes and content of the unit. For your independent reading, you can select from this wide array of titles, which have been chosen based on complexity and interest. You can also do your own research and select titles that intrigue you.

Unit 2: The Power to Change		
Literature		
Author	**Title**	**Lexile**
Armstrong, William	Sounder	900L
Creech, Sharon	Hate That Cat	N/A
Creech, Sharon	Love That Dog	1010L
Creech, Sharon	Ruby Holler	660L
Creech, Sharon	The Wanderer	830L
DiCamillo, Kate	Because of Winn Dixie	610L
DiCamillo, Kate	The Tiger Rising	520L
Farley, Walter	The Black Stallion	680L
Funke, Cornelia	Dragon Rider	710L
George, Jean Craighead	Julie of the Wolves	860L
Gipson, Fred	Old Yeller	910L
Grogan, John	Marley: A Dog Like No Other	760L
Guest, Jacqueline	Hat Trick	710L
Hiaasen, Carl	Hoot	760L
Kadohata, Cynthia	Cracker! The Best Dog in Vietnam	730L
Korman, Gordon	No More Dead Dogs	610L
London, Jack	The Call of the Wild	1080L
London, Jack	White Fang	650L
Morey, Walt	Gentle Ben	740L
Mowat, Farley	Never Cry Wolf	1330L
Naylor, Phyllis Reynolds	Shiloh	890L
Paulsen, Gary	Guts	1230L
Paulsen, Gary	My Life in Dog Years	1150L
Peterson, Shelley	Sundancer	N/A
Rawls, Wilson	Where the Red Fern Grows	790L
Ryan, Pam Munoz	Paint the Wind	780L
Sewell, Anna	Black Beauty	650L
Sherlock, Patti	Letters from Wolfie	760L
Smith, Roland	Elephant Run	750L
Starr, Arigon	Super Indian (Series of 2)	N/A
Wedekind, Annie	A Horse of Her Own	1040L

Nonfiction/Informational Text		
Author	Title	Lexile
Chin-Lee, Cynthia	*Akira to Zoltan: 26 Men Who Changed the World*	N/A
Chin-Lee, Cynthia	*Amelia to Zora: 26 Women Who Changed the World*	N/A
Goodall, Jane	*My Life with the Chimpanzees*	910L
Grandin, Temple and Catherine Johnson	*Animals in Translation*	1130L
Guzman, Lila and Rick	*Cesar Chavez: Fighting for Fairness*	N/A
Hall, MH	*King Arthur and the Knights of the Round Table*	390L
Kehret, Peg	*Shelter Dogs: Amazing Stories of Adopted Strays*	940L
Lemke, Donald	*Investigating the Scientific Method with Max Axiom, Super Scientist*	760
Montgomery, Sy	*Temple Grandin: How the Girl Who Loved Cows Embraced Autism and Changed the World*	960L

Unit 3 Independent Reading List

Suggestions for Independent Reading

This list, divided into the categories of **Literature** and **Nonfiction/Informational Text**, comprises titles related to the themes and content of the unit. For your independent reading, you can select from this wide array of titles, which have been chosen based on complexity and interest. You can also do your own research and select titles that intrigue you.

Unit 3: Changing Perspectives

Literature

Author	Title	Lexile
Alvarez, Julia	*The Tia Lola Stories Series*	830L–850L
Applegate, Katherine	*Home of the Brave*	N/A
Ellis, Deborah	*Jakeman*	N/A
Fullerton, Alma	*Libertad*	N/A
Howe, James	*The Misfits*	960L
Kahn, Hena	*Night of the Moon*	780L
Khan, Rukhsana	*A New Life*	N/A
Krishnaswami, Uma	*The Grand Plan to Fix Everything*	770L
Na, An	*Wait for Me*	670L
Nye, Naomi Shihab	*19 Varieties of Gazelle: Poems of the Middle East*	970L
Smith, Greg Leitich	*Ninjas, Piranhas, and Galileo*	750L
Ursu, Anne	*Breadcrumbs*	720L

Nonfiction/Informational Text

Author	Title	Lexile
Anderson, Judith	*Know the Facts About Personal Safety*	N/A
Dipiazza, Frencesca Davis	*Friend Me: 600 Years of Social Networking in America*	1040L
Halls, Kelly Milner	*Saving the Baghdad Zoo: A True Story of Hope and Heroes*	N/A
Hoose, Phillip	*Claudette Colvin: Twice Toward Justice*	1000L
Lewis, Barbara	*The Kid's Guide to Service Projects: Over 500 Service Ideas for Young People Who Want to Make a Difference*	850L
Marrin, Albert	*Black Gold: The Story of Oil in Our Lives*	1070L
Norgren, Jill	*Belva Lockwood: Equal Rights Pioneer*	N/A
O'Brien, Anne Ibley and Perry Edmond O'Brien	*After Gandhi: One Hundred Years of Nonviolent Resistance*	1080L
Pollan, Michael	*The Omnivore's Dilemma: The Secrets Behind What You Eat* (Young Readers Edition)	930L
Rockliff, Mara	*Get real: what kind of world are you buying?*	890L
Schlosser, Eric	*Chew on This, Everything You Don't Want to Know About Fast Food*	1110L
Stearman, Kaye	*Taking Action Against Homelessness*	N/A
Warren, Andrea	*Orphan Train Rider: One Boy's True Story*	960L

Unit 4 Independent Reading List

Suggestions for Independent Reading

This list, divided into the categories of **Literature** and **Nonfiction/Informational Text**, comprises titles related to the themes and content of the unit. For your independent reading, you can select from this wide array of titles, which have been chosen based on complexity and interest. You can also do your own research and select titles that intrigue you.

Unit 4: The Final Act

Literature

Author	Title	Lexile
Allen, Laurie	Sixty Comedy Duet Scenes for Teens: Real-Life Situations for Laughter	N/A
Blackwood, Gary	Shakespeare's Scribe	870L
Detrick, Erin, editor	Actor's Choice: Monologues for Teens	N/A
Dickens, Charles	Oliver Twist	970L
Dumas, Alexandre	The Count of Monte Cristo	1080L
Kane, Bo	Acting Scenes and Monologues for Young Teens	N/A
Kipling, Rudyard	Captains Courageous	850L
Lamb, Mary and Charles	Tales from Shakespeare	1390L
Lewis, C.S	The Lion, the Witch, and the Wardrobe	940L
London, Jack	The Call of the Wild	1080L
Pegasus Illustrated Shakespeare Stories	The Comedy of Errors	910L
Pizzarello, Jason, editor	Actor's Choice: Scenes for Teens	N/A
Rafter, Dan (adapted by)	20,000 Leagues Under the Sea (Graphic Novel)	N/A
Shelley, Mary	Frankenstein	810L
Smith, Betty	A Tree Grows in Brooklyn	810L
Stevenson, Robert Louis	The Strange Case of Dr. Jekyll and Mr. Hyde	1010L
Twain, Mark	A Connecticut Yankee in King Arthur's Court	1080L
Verne, Jules	20,000 Leagues Under the Sea	1030L
Wagner, Lloyd (adapted by)	The Call of the Wild (Graphic Novel)	N/A

Nonfiction/Informational Text

Author	Title	Lexile
Ball, Jacqueline A.	Windsor Castle: England's Royal Fortress	680L
Barbara A. Somervill	Actor (Cool Arts Careers)	860L
Belli, Mary Lou and Lenney, Dinah	Acting for Young Actors: Ultimate Teen Guide	N/A
Carpenter, Angelica Shirley	Lewis Carroll: Through the Looking Glass	1080L
Prince, April Jones	Who Was Mark Twain?	910L
Stanley, Diane and Peter Vennema	Bard of Avon: The Story of William Shakespeare	1030L
Stanley, Diane and Peter Vennema	Good Queen Bess: The Story of Elizabeth I of England	1060L
Turnbull, Stephanie	Acting Skills	890L

Independent Reading Log

NAME _____ DATE _____

Directions: This log is a place to record your progress and thinking about your independent reading during each unit. Add your log pages to your Reader/Writer Notebook or keep them as a separate place to record your reading insights.

Unit _____

Independent Reading Title _____

Author(s) _____ Text Type _____

Pages read: from _____ to _____

_____

_____

_____

_____

_____

Independent Reading Title _____

Author(s) _____ Text Type _____

Pages read: from _____ to _____

_____

_____

_____

_____

_____

_____

Independent Reading Title _____

Author(s) _____ Text Type _____

Pages read: from _____ to _____

_____

_____

_____

_____

_____

_____

_____

Unit _____

Independent Reading Title _____

Author(s) _____ Text Type _____

Pages read: from _____ to _____

_____

_____

_____

_____

Independent Reading Title _____

Author(s) _____ Text Type _____

Pages read: from _____ to _____

_____

_____

_____

_____

Independent Reading Title _____

Author(s) _____ Text Type _____

Pages read: from _____ to _____

_____

_____

_____

_____

_____

Independent Reading Title _____

Author(s) _____ Text Type _____

Pages read: from _____ to _____

_____

_____

_____

_____

_____

SpringBoard Learning Strategies
READING STRATEGIES

STRATEGY	DEFINITION	PURPOSE
Chunking the Text	Breaking the text into smaller, manageable units of sense (e.g., words, sentences, paragraphs, whole text) by numbering, separating phrases, drawing boxes	To reduce the intimidation factor when encountering long words, sentences, or whole texts; to increase comprehension of difficult or challenging text
Close Reading	Accessing small chunks of text to read, reread, mark, and annotate key passages, word-for-word, sentence-by-sentence, and line-by-line	To develop comprehensive understanding by engaging in one or more focused readings of a text
Diffusing	Reading a passage, noting unfamiliar words, discovering meaning of unfamiliar words using context clues, dictionaries, and/or thesauruses, and replacing unfamiliar words with familiar ones	To facilitate a close reading of text, the use of resources, an understanding of synonyms, and increased comprehension of text
Double-Entry Journal	Creating a two-column journal (also called Dialectical Journal) with a student-selected passage in one column and the student's response in the second column (e.g., asking questions of the text, forming personal responses, interpreting the text, reflecting on the process of making meaning of the text)	To assist in note-taking and organizing key textual elements and responses noted during reading in order to generate textual support that can be incorporated into a piece of writing at a later time
Graphic Organizer	Using a visual representation for the organization of information from the text	To facilitate increased comprehension and discussion
KWHL Chart	Setting up discussion that allows students to activate prior knowledge by answering "What do I know?"; sets a purpose by answering "What do I want to know?"; helps preview a task by answering "How will I learn it?"; and reflects on new knowledge by answering "What have I learned?"	To organize thinking, access prior knowledge, and reflect on learning to increase comprehension and engagement
Marking the Text	Selecting text by highlighting, underlining, and/or annotating for specific components, such as main idea, imagery, literary devices, and so on	To focus reading for specific purposes, such as author's craft, and to organize information from selections; to facilitate reexamination of a text
Metacognitive Markers	Responding to text with a system of cueing marks where students use a ? for questions about the text; a ! for reactions related to the text; and an * for comments ,about the text and underline to signal key ideas	To track responses to texts and use those responses as a point of departure for talking or writing about texts
OPTIC	**O** (Overview): Write notes on what the visual appears to be about. **P** (Parts): Zoom in on the parts of the visual and describe any elements or details that seem important. **T** (Title): Highlight the words of the title of the visual (if one is available). **I** (Interrelationships): Use the title as the theory and the parts of the visual as clues to detect and specify how the elements of the graphic are related.	To analyze graphic and visual images as forms of text

STRATEGY	DEFINITION	PURPOSE
OPTIC (continued)	**C** (Conclusion); Draw a conclusion about the visual as a whole. What does the visual mean? Summarize the message of the visual in one or two sentences.	
Predicting	Making guesses about the text by using the title and pictures and/or thinking ahead about events which may occur based on evidence in the text	To help students become actively involved, interested, and mentally prepared to understand ideas
Previewing	Making guesses about the text by using the title and pictures and/or thinking ahead about events which may occur based on evidence in the text	To gain familiarity with the text, make connections to the text, and extend prior knowledge to set a purpose for reading
QHT	Expanding prior knowledge of vocabulary words by marking words with a Q, H, or T (Q signals words students do not know; H signals words students have heard and might be able to identify; T signals words students know well enough to teach to their peers)	To allow students to build on their prior knowledge of words, to provide a forum for peer teaching and learning of new words, and to serve as a prereading exercise to aid in comprehension
Questioning the Text* The AP Vertical Teams Guide for English (109–112)	Developing levels of questions about text; that is, literal, interpretive, and universal questions that prompt deeper thinking about a text	To engage more actively with texts, read with greater purpose and focus, and ultimately answer questions to gain greater insight into the text; helps students to comprehend and interpret
Paraphrasing	Restating in one's own words the essential information expressed in a text, whether it be narration, dialogue, or informational text	To encourage and facilitate comprehension of challenging text.
RAFT	Primarily used to generate new text, this strategy can also be used to analyze a text by examining the role of the speaker (R), the intended audience (A), the format of the text (F), and the topic of the text (T).	To initiate reader response; to facilitate an analysis of a text to gain focus prior to creating a new text
Rereading	Encountering the same text with more than one reading.	To identify additional details; to clarify meaning and/or reinforce comprehension of texts
SIFT* The AP Vertical Teams Guide for English (17–20)	Analyzing a fictional text by examining stylistic elements, especially symbol, imagery, and figures of speech in order to show how all work together to reveal tone and theme	To focus and facilitate an analysis of a fictional text by examining the title and text for symbolism, identifying images and sensory details, analyzing figurative language and identifying how all these elements reveal tone and theme
Skimming/Scanning	Skimming by rapid or superficial reading of a text to form an overall impression or to obtain a general understanding of the material; scanning focuses on key words, phrases, or specific details and provides speedy recognition of information	To quickly form an overall impression prior to an in-depth study of a text; to answer specific questions or quickly locate targeted information or detail in a text
SMELL* The AP Vertical Teams Guide for English	• Sender-receiver relationship—What is the sender-receiver relationship? Who are the images and language meant to attract? Describe the speaker of the text. • Message—What is the message? Summarize the statement made in the text.	To analyze a persuasive speech or essay by focusing on five essential questions

STRATEGY	DEFINITION	PURPOSE
SMELL* (continued)	• Emotional Strategies—What is the desired effect? • Logical Strategies—What logic is operating? How does it (or its absence) affect the message? Consider the logic of the images as well as the words. • Language—What does the language of the text describe? How does it affect the meaning and effectiveness of the writing? Consider the language of the images as well as the words.	
SOAPSTone*	Analyzing text by discussing and identifying Speaker, Occasion, Audience, Purpose, Subject, and Tone	To facilitate the analysis of specific elements of non-fiction literary and informational texts and show the relationship among the elements to an understanding of the whole
Summarizing	Giving a brief statement of the main points or essential information expressed in a text, whether it be narration, dialogue, or informational text	To facilitate comprehension and recall of a text
Think Aloud	Talking through a difficult passage or task by using a form of metacognition whereby the reader expresses how he/she has made sense of the text	To reflect on how readers make meaning of challenging texts and facilitate comprehension
TP-CASTT* The AP Vertical Teams Guide for English (94–99)	Analyzing a poetic text by identifying and discussing Title, Paraphrase, Connotation, Attitude, Shift, Theme, and Title again	To facilitate the analysis of specific elements of a literary text, especially poetry. To show how the elements work together to create meaning
Visualizing	Forming a picture (mentally and/or literally) while reading a text	To increase reading comprehension and promote active engagement with text
Word Maps	Using a clearly defined graphic organizer such as concept circles or word webs to identify and reinforce word meanings	To provide a visual tool for identifying and remembering multiple aspects of words and word meanings

*Delineates AP strategy

WRITING STRATEGIES

STRATEGY	DEFINITION	PURPOSE
Adding	Making conscious choices to enhance a text by adding additional words, phrases, sentences, or ideas	To refine and clarify the writer's thoughts during revision and/or drafting
Brainstorming	Using a flexible but deliberate process of listing multiple ideas in a short period of time without excluding any idea from the preliminary list	To generate ideas, concepts, or key words that provide a focus and/or establish organization as part of the prewriting or revision process
Deleting	Providing clarity and cohesiveness for a text by eliminating words, phrases, sentences, or ideas	To refine and clarify the writer's thoughts during revision and/or drafting
Drafting	Composing a text in its initial form	To incorporate brainstormed or initial ideas into a written format

STRATEGY	DEFINITION	PURPOSE
Free writing	Write freely without constraints in order to capture thinking and convey the writer's purpose	To refine and clarify the writer's thoughts, spark new ideas, and/or generate content during revision and/or drafting
Generating Questions	Clarifying and developing ideas by asking questions of the draft. May be part of self-editing or peer editing	To clarify and develop ideas in a draft; used during drafting and as part of writer response
Graphic Organizer	Organizing ideas and information visually (e.g., Venn diagrams, flowcharts, cluster maps)	To provide a visual system for organizing multiple ideas, details, and/or textual support to be included in a piece of writing
Looping	After free writing, one section of a text is circled to promote elaboration or the generation of new ideas for that section. This process is repeated to further develop ideas from the newly generated segments	To refine and clarify the writer's thoughts, spark new ideas, and/or generate new content during revision and/or drafting
Mapping	Creating a graphic organizer that serves as a visual representation of the organizational plan for a written text	To generate ideas, concepts, or key words that provide a focus and/or establish organization during the prewriting, drafting, or revision process
Marking the Draft	Interacting with the draft version of a piece of writing by highlighting, underlining, color-coding, and annotating to indicate revision ideas	To encourage focused, reflective thinking about revising drafts
Note-taking	Making notes about ideas in response to text or discussions; one form is the double-entry journal in which textual evidence is recorded on the left side and personal commentary about the meaning of the evidence on the other side.	To assist in organizing key textual elements and responses noted during reading in order to generate textual support that can be incorporated into a piece of writing at a later time. Note-taking is also a reading and listening strategy.
Outlining	Using a system of numerals and letters in order to identify topics and supporting details and ensure an appropriate balance of ideas.	To generate ideas, concepts, or key words that provide a focus and/or establish organization prior to writing an initial draft and/or during the revision process
Quickwrite	Writing for a short, specific amount of time in response to a prompt provided	To generate multiple ideas in a quick fashion that could be turned into longer pieces of writing at a later time (May be considered as part of the drafting process)
RAFT	Generating a new text and/or transforming a text by identifying and manipulating its component parts of Role, Audience, Format, and Topic	To generate a new text by identifying the main elements of a text during the prewriting and drafting stages of the writing process
Rearranging	Selecting components of a text and moving them to another place within the text and/or modifying the order in which the author's ideas are presented	To refine and clarify the writer's thoughts during revision and/or drafting
Self-Editing/Peer Editing	Working individually or with a partner to examine a text closely in order to identify areas that might need to be corrected for grammar, punctuation, spelling	To facilitate a collaborative approach to generating ideas for and revising writing.

STRATEGY	DEFINITION	PURPOSE
Sharing and Responding	Communicating with another person or a small group of peers who respond to a piece of writing as focused readers (not necessarily as evaluators)	To make suggestions for improvement to the work of others and/or to receive appropriate and relevant feedback on the writer's own work, used during the drafting and revision process
Sketching	Drawing or sketching ideas or ordering of ideas. Includes storyboarding, visualizing	To generate and/or clarify ideas by visualizing them. May be part of prewriting
Substituting / Replacing	Replacing original words or phrases in a text with new words or phrases that achieve the desired effect	To refine and clarify the writer's thoughts during revision and/or drafting
TWIST* The AP Vertical Teams Guide for English 167–174	Arriving at a thesis statement that incorporates the following literary elements: tone, word choice (diction), imagery, style and theme	To craft an interpretive thesis in response to a prompt about a text
Webbing	Developing a graphic organizer that consists of a series of circles connected with lines to indicate relationships among ideas	To generate ideas, concepts, or key words that provide a focus and/or establish organization prior to writing an initial draft and/or during the revision process
Writer's Checklist	Using a co-constructed checklist (that could be written on a bookmark and/or displayed on the wall) in order to look for specific features of a writing text and check for accuracy	To focus on key areas of the writing process so that the writer can effectively revise a draft and correct mistake
Writing Groups	A type of discussion group devoted to sharing and responding of student work	To facilitate a collaborative approach to generating ideas for and revising writing.

SPEAKING AND LISTENING STRATEGIES

STRATEGY	DEFINITION	PURPOSE
Choral Reading	Reading text lines aloud in student groups and/or individually to present an interpretation	To develop fluency; differentiate between the reading of statements and questions; practice phrasing, pacing, and reading dialogue; show how a character's emotions are captured through vocal stress and intonation
Note-taking	Creating a record of information while listening to a speaker or reading a text	To facilitate active listening or close reading ; to record and organize ideas that assist in processing information
Oral Reading	Reading aloud one's own text or the texts of others (e.g., echo reading, choral reading, paired readings)	To share one's own work or the work of others; build fluency and increase confidence in presenting to a group
Rehearsal	Encouraging multiple practices of a piece of text prior to a performance	To provide students with an opportunity to clarify the meaning of a text prior to a performance as they refine the use of dramatic conventions (e.g., gestures, vocal interpretations, facial expressions)
Role Playing	Assuming the role or persona of a character	To develop the voice, emotions, and mannerisms of a character to facilitate improved comprehension of a text

COLLABORATIVE STRATEGIES

STRATEGY	DEFINITION	PURPOSE
Discussion Groups	Engaging in an interactive, small group discussion, often with an assigned role; to consider a topic, text or question	To gain new understanding of or insight into a text from multiple perspectives
Think-Pair-Share	Pairing with a peer to share ideas; before sharing ideas and discussion with a larger group	To construct meaning about a topic or question; to test thinking in relation to the ideas of others; to prepare for a discussion with a larger group

Web Organizer

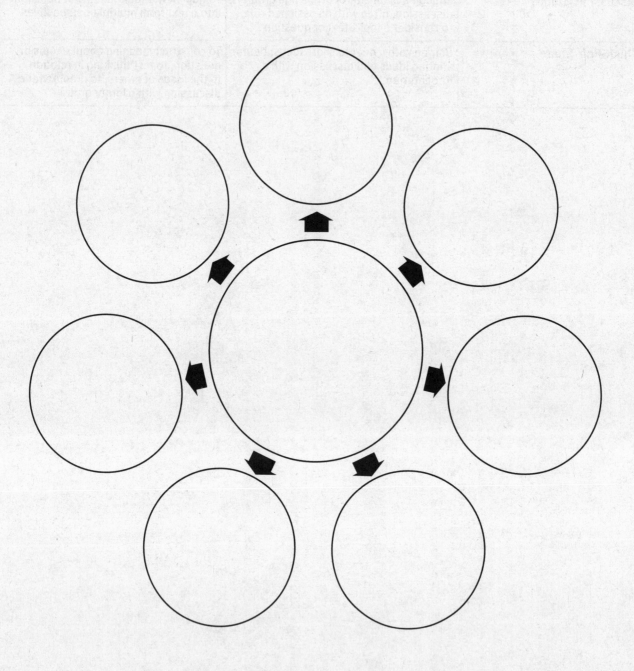

Word Map

Definition

Visual

Academic Vocabulary Word

Example

Example

Example

Verbal & Visual Word Association

Definition in Your Own Words	Important Elements

Academic Vocabulary Word

Visual Representation	Personal Association

Academic Vocabulary Tree

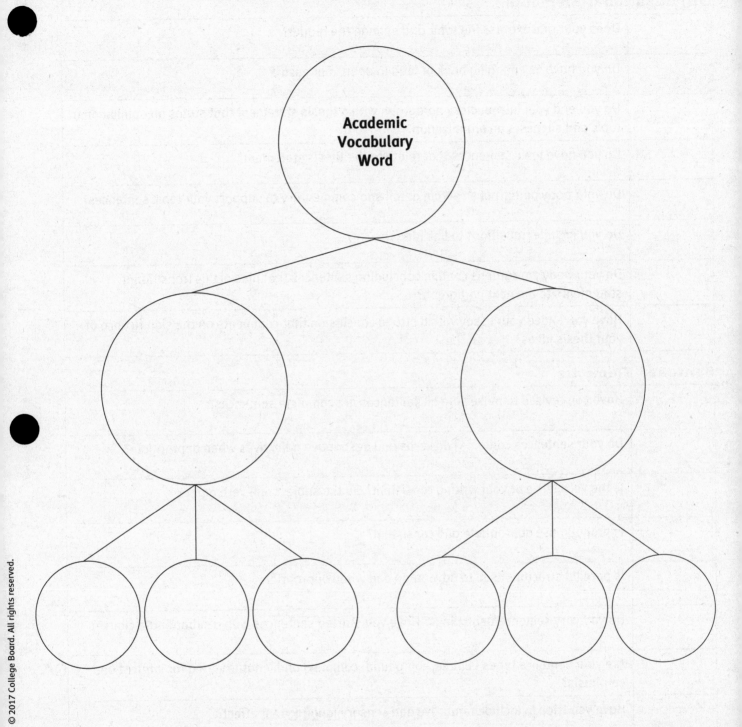

Editor's / Writer's Checklist

Organizational Elements

	Does your title express the topic and engage the reader?
	Do you have an engaging hook or lead to open your essay?
	Do you end your introductory paragraph with a thesis statement that states an opinion on a topic and suggests an organization?
	Do you have topic sentences that relate to the thesis statement?
	Do your body paragraphs contain detail and commentary to support your topic sentences?
	Do you include transitions to link ideas?
	Do your body paragraphs contain concluding sentences that also act as transitional statements to the next paragraph?
	Have you ended your essay with a strong conclusion that comments on the significance of your thesis ideas?

Sentence Elements

	Have you revised to make sure all sentences are complete sentences?
	Do your sentences contain vivid verbs and descriptive adjectives when appropriate?
	Is the verb tense of your writing consistent? Do the subject and verb agree?
	Is pronoun use appropriate and consistent?
	Is parallel structure used to advantage and when appropriate?
	Do you vary sentence beginnings? Have you started sentences with a subordinate clause?
	Are your sentence types (simple, compound, complex) and lengths varied for interest and emphasis?
	Have you tried to include figurative and sensory language for effect?
	Have you used appositives when appropriate?
	Have you checked punctuation use for correctness, especially for appositives, complex sentences and parallel structure?
	Have you incorporated and punctuated quoted material correctly?

Double-Entry Journal Graphic Organizer

Passage from Text	Page #	Personal Response/Commentary

Venn Diagram

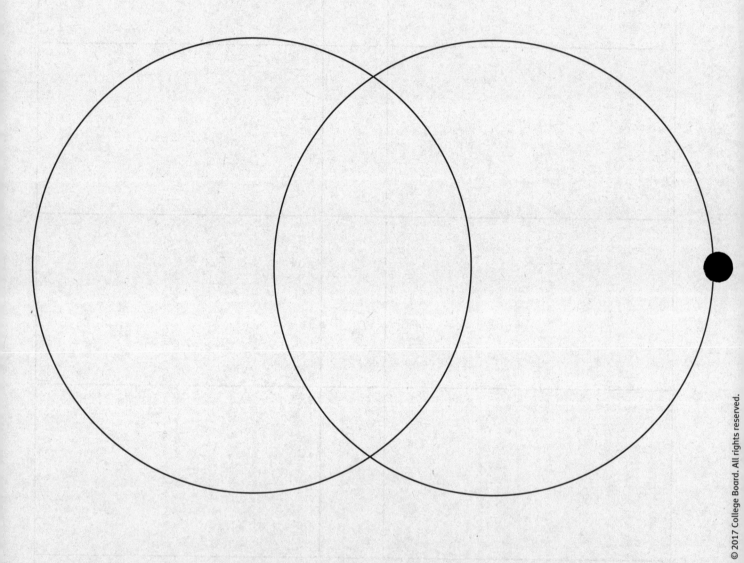

Evaluating Online Sources

The URL

What is its domain?

- .com = a for-profit organization
- .gov, .mil, .us (or other country code) = a government site
- .edu = an educational institution
- .org = a nonprofit organization

- Is this URL someone's personal page?
- Why might using information from a personal page be a problem?
- Do you recognize who is publishing this page?
- If not, you may need to investigate further to determine whether the publisher is an expert on the topic.

Sponsor:

- Does the web site easily give information about the organization or group that sponsors it?
- Does it have a link (often called "About Us") that leads you to that information?
- What do you learn?

Timeliness:

- When was the page last updated (usually this is posted at the top or bottom of the page)?
- How current a page is may indicate how accurate or useful the information in it will be.

Purpose:

- What is the purpose of the page?
- What is its target audience?
- Does it present information or opinion?
- Is it primarily objective or subjective?
- How do you know?

Author:

- What credentials does the author have?
- Is this person or group considered an authority on the topic?

Links

- Does the page provide links?
- Do they work?
- Are they helpful?
- Are they objective or subjective?

SOAPSTone:

SOAPSTone	Analysis	Textual Support
Speaker: What does the reader know about the writer?		
Occasion: What are the circumstances surrounding this text?		
Audience: Who is the target audience?		
Purpose: Why did the author write this text?		
Subject: What is the topic?		
Tone: What is the author's tone, or attitude?		

TP-CASTT Analysis

Poem Title:

Author:

Title: Make a Prediction. What do you think the title means before you read the poem?

Paraphrase: Translate the poem in your own words. What is the poem about? Rephrase difficult sections word for word.

Connotation: Look beyond the literal meaning of key words and images to their associations.

Attitude: What is the speaker's attitude? What is the author's attitude? How does the author feel about the speaker, about other characters, about the subject?

Shifts: Where do the shifts in tone, setting, voice, etc., occur? Look for time and place, keywords, punctuation, stanza divisions, changes in length or rhyme, and sentence structure. What is the purpose of each shift? How do they contribute to effect and meaning?

Title: Reexamine the title. What do you think it means now in the context of the poem?

Theme: Think of the literal and metaphorical layers of the poem. Then determine the overall theme. The theme must be written in a complete sentence.

TP-CASTT

Poem Title:

Author:

T		
P		
C		
A		
S		
T		
T		

Active Listening Feedback

Presenter's name: _____

Content

What is the presenter's purpose? _____

What is the presenter's main point? _____

Do you agree with the presenter? Why or why not? _____

_____

_____

Form

Did the presenter use a clear, loud voice? ☐ yes ☐ no

Did the presenter make eye contact? ☐ yes ☐ no

One thing I really liked about the presentation:

_____

_____

_____

One question I still have:

_____

_____

_____

Other comments or notes:

Active Listening Notes

Title: _____

Who?

What?

Where?

When?

Why?

How?

Cause and Effect

Title: _____

Cause: What happened?		Effect: An effect of this is

Cause: What happened?		Effect: An effect of this is

Cause: What happened?		Effect: An effect of this is

Cause: What happened?		Effect: An effect of this is

Character Map

Character name: _____

What does the character look like?

How does the character act?

What do other characters say or think about the character?

Collaborative Dialogue

Title: _____

```
┌─────────────────────────────────┐
│         "Wh-" Prompts           │
│                                 │
│      Who?   What?   Where?      │
│                                 │
│         When?   Why?            │
└─────────────────────────────────┘
```

Speaker 1

Speaker 2

Conclusion Builder

Evidence

Evidence

Evidence

Based on this evidence, I can conclude

NAME _____ DATE _____

Conflict Map

Title: _____

What is the main conflict in this story?

What causes this conflict?

How is the conflict resolved?

What are some other ways the conflict could have been resolved?

Conversation for Quickwrite

1. Turn to a partner and restate the Quickwrite in your own words.

2. Brainstorm key words to use in your Quickwrite response.

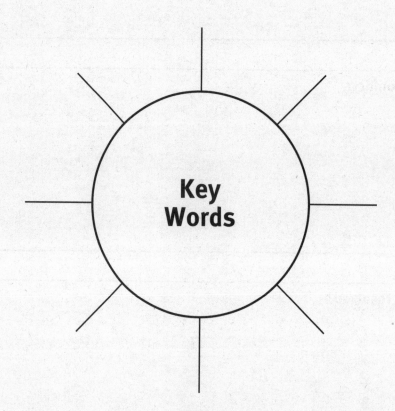

3. Take turns explaining your Quickwrite response to your partner. Try using some of the key words.

4. On your own, write a response to the Quickwrite.

Idea and Argument Evaluator

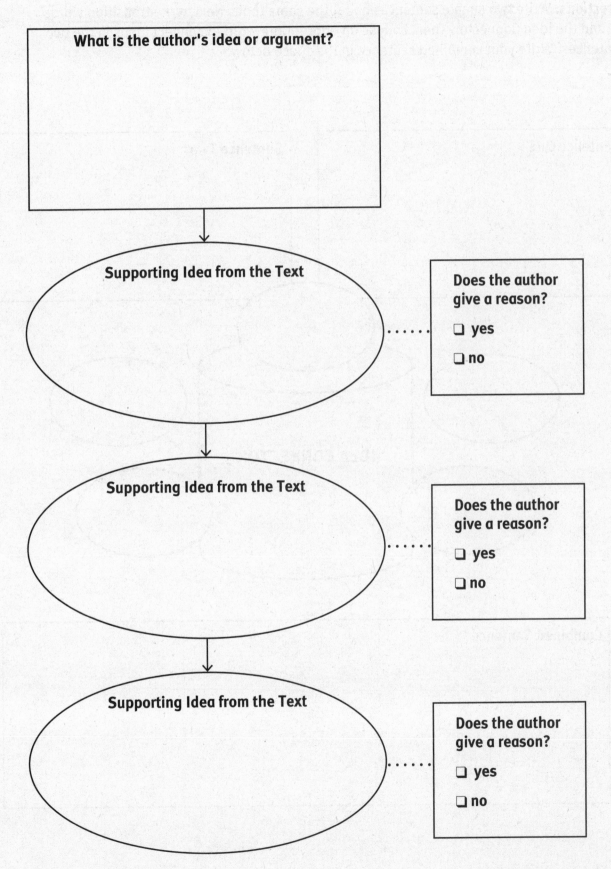

What is the author's idea or argument?

Supporting Idea from the Text

Does the author give a reason?

❑ yes

❑ no

Supporting Idea from the Text

Does the author give a reason?

❑ yes

❑ no

Supporting Idea from the Text

Does the author give a reason?

❑ yes

❑ no

Idea Connector

Directions: Write two simple sentences about the same topic. Next, write transition words around the Idea Connector. Then, choose an appropriate word to connect ideas in the two sentences. Write your combined sentence in the space below.

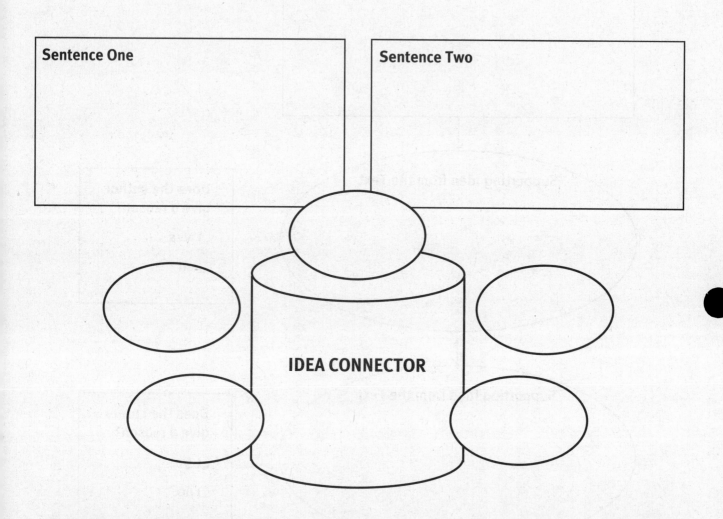

Sentence One

Sentence Two

IDEA CONNECTOR

Combined Sentence

Key Idea and Details Chart

Title/Topic _____

Key Idea _____

_____

_____

Supporting Detail 1 _____

_____

_____

Supporting Detail 2 _____

_____

_____

Supporting Detail 3 _____

_____

_____

Supporting Detail 4 _____

_____

_____

Restate topic sentence. _____

_____

Concluding sentence. _____

_____

_____

Narrative Analysis and Writing

Response

Response

Incident

Reflection

Reflection

NAME _____ DATE _____

Notes for Reading Independently

Title: _____

The main characters are	The setting is	The main conflict is

The climax happens when	The conflict is resolved when

My brief summary of _____

Opinion Builder

Reason

Reason

Based on these reasons, my opinion is

Reason

Reason

Paragraph Frame for Conclusions

Conclusion Words and Phrases

shows that

based on

suggests that

leads to

indicates that

influences

The _____ *(story, poem, play, passage, etc.)* shows that *(helps us to conclude that)* _____ _____ _____

There are several reasons why. First, _____ _____ _____ _____ _____

A second reason is _____ _____ _____ _____ _____

Finally, _____ _____ _____ _____

In conclusion, _____ _____ _____ _____ _____

Paragraph Frame for Sequencing

Sequence Words and Phrases

at the beginning

in the first place

as a result

later

eventually

in the end

lastly

In the _____ (story, poem, play, passage, etc.)

there are three important _____

(events, steps, directions, etc.)

First, _____

_____

_____

_____

_____

Second, _____

_____

_____

_____

_____

Third, _____

_____

_____

_____

_____

Finally, _____

_____

_____

_____

_____

Paraphrasing Map

What does _____ say?	How can I say it in my own words?	What questions or response do I have?

NAME _____ DATE _____

Peer Editing

Writer's name: _____

Did the writer answer the prompt? ☐ yes ☐ no

Did the writer provide evidence to support his or her reasons? ☐ yes ☐ no

Is the writing organized in a way that makes sense? ☐ yes ☐ no

Did the writer vary sentence structures to make the writing more interesting? ☐ yes ☐ no

Are there any spelling or punctuation mistakes? ☐ yes ☐ no

Are there any grammar errors? ☐ yes ☐ no

Two things I really liked about the writer's story:

1. _____
   _____
   _____

2. _____
   _____
   _____

One thing I think the writer could do to improve the writing:

1. _____
   _____
   _____
   _____

Other comments or notes:

Persuasive/Argument Writing Map

Thesis

Reason

Reason

Reason

Evidence

Evidence

Evidence

Evidence

Evidence

Evidence

Evidence

Evidence

Evidence

Conclusion

Roots and Affixes Brainstorm

Directions: Write the root or affix in the circle. Brainstorm or use a dictionary to find the meaning of the root or affix and add it to the circle. Then, find words that use that root or affix. Write one word in each box. Write a sentence for each word.

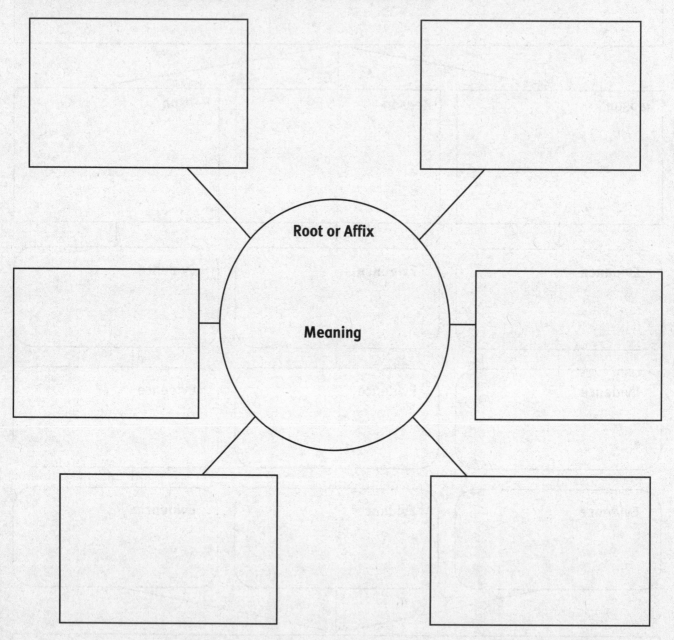

Root or Affix

Meaning

Round Table Discussion

Directions: Write the topic in the center box. One student begins by stating his or her ideas while the student to the left takes notes. Then the next student speaks while the student to his or her left takes notes, and so on.

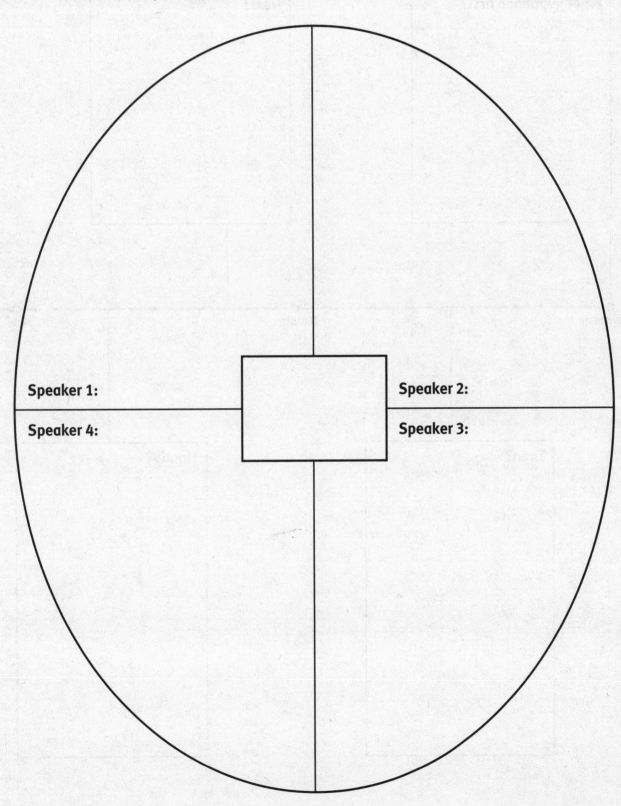

Speaker 1:

Speaker 2:

Speaker 4:

Speaker 3:

Sequence of Events Time Line

Title: _____

What happened first?

Next?

Beginning   Middle   End

Then?

Finally?

Text Structure Stairs

Finally, what happened last?

Next?

Then?

What happened first?

Unknown Word Solver

Unknown Word

Can you find any context clues? List them.

Do you recognize any word parts?

Prefix:

Root Word:

Suffix:

Do you know another meaning of this word that does not make sense in this context?

Does it look or sound like a word in another language?

What is the dictionary definition?

How can you define the word in your own words?

Venn Diagram for Writing a Comparison

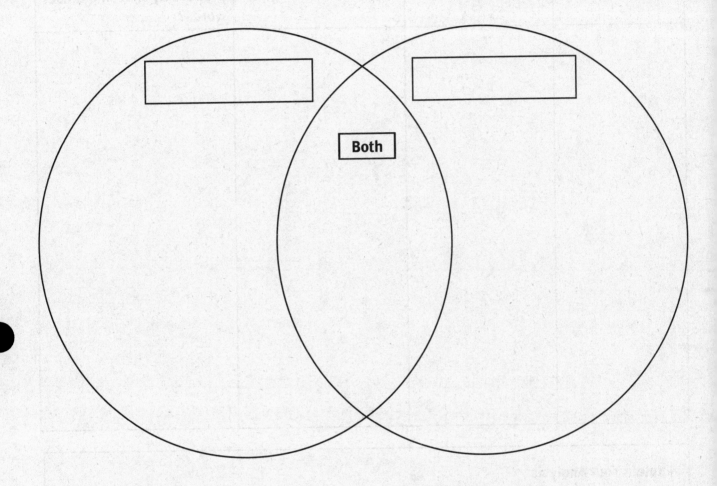

Both

They are similar in that _____
_____
_____
_____
_____
_____

They are different in that _____
_____
_____
_____
_____
_____

Word Choice Analyzer

Word or phrase from the text	What does the word or phrase mean?	What is another way to say the same thing?	What effect did the author produce by choosing these words?

Explain Your Analysis

The author uses the word or phrase _____ , which means

_____

Another way to say this is _____

_____

I think the author chose these words to _____

_____

_____

One way I can modify this sentence to add detail is to _____

_____

Glossary / Glosario

A

advertising: the use of print, graphics, or videos to persuade people to buy a product or use a service
publicidad: uso de impresos, gráfica o videos para persuadir a las personas a comprar un producto o usar un servicio

allegory: a story in which the characters, objects, or actions have a meaning beyond the surface of the story
alegoría: cuento en el que los personajes, objetos o acciones tienen un significado que va más allá de la superficie de la historia

alliteration: the repetition of consonant sounds at the beginnings of words that are close together
aliteración: repetición de sonidos consonánticos al comienzo de palabras que están cercanas

allusion: a reference to a well-known person, place, event, literary work, or work of art
alusión: referencia a una persona, lugar, obra literaria u obra de arte muy conocidos

analogy: a comparison of the similarity of two things; for example, comparing a *part to a whole* or the *whole to a part*
analogía: comparación de la semejanza de dos cosas; por ejemplo, comparar una *parte con un todo* o el *todo con una parte*

analyze (literary): study the details of a work to identify essential features or meaning
analizar (literario): estudiar los detalles de una obra para identificar características o significados esenciales

anecdote: a brief, entertaining account of an incident or event
anécdota: breve relato entretenido de un incidente o suceso

annotate: write notes to explain or present ideas that help you analyze and understand a text
anotar: tomar notas para explicar o presentar las ideas que te ayuden a analizar y a entender un texto

antonyms: words with opposite meanings
antónimos: palabras con significados opuestos

archetype: a character, symbol, story pattern, or other element that is common to human experience across cultures and that occurs frequently in literature, myth, and folklore
arquetipo: personaje, símbolo, patrón de un cuento u otro elemento que es común a la experiencia humana a través de diversas culturas y que aparece con frecuencia en literatura, mitos y folclor

argument: facts or reasoning offered to support a position as being true
argumento: hechos o razonamiento entregados para apoyar una posición como verdadera

artifact: an object made by a human being, typically an item that has cultural or historical significance
artefacto: objeto hecho por un ser humano, habitualmente un objeto que tiene significación cultural o histórica

atmosphere: the feeling created by a literary work or passage
atmósfera: sentimiento creado por una obra o pasaje literario

audience: the intended readers of specific types of texts or the viewers of a program or performance
público: lectores objetivo de tipos específicos de textos o espectadores de un programa o actuación

B

balanced sentence: a sentence that presents ideas of equal weight in similar grammatical form to emphasize the similarity or difference between the ideas
oración balanceada: oración que presenta ideas de igual peso en forma gramatical similar para enfatizar la semejanza o diferencia entre las ideas

bibliography: a list of source materials used to prepare a research paper or presentation
bibliografía: lista de las fuentes utilizadas para preparar una investigación o una presentación

body paragraph: a paragraph that contains a topic sentence, supporting details and commentary, and a concluding sentence and that is usually part of a longer text
párrafo representativo: párrafo que contiene una oración principal, detalles de apoyo y comentarios, y una oración concluyente que normalmente forma parte de un texto más extenso

C

caricature: a visual or verbal representation in which characteristics or traits are distorted for emphasis
caricatura: representación visual o verbal en la que las características o rasgos son distorsionados para dar énfasis

cause: an initial action; an event that makes something else happen
causa: acción inicial; suceso que hace que otra cosa ocurra

character: a person or animal that takes part in the action of a literary work
personaje: persona o animal que participa en la acción de una obra literaria

characterization: the methods a writer uses to develop characters; for example, through description, actions, and dialogue
caracterización: métodos que usa un escritor para desarrollar personajes; por ejemplo, a través de descripción, acciones y diálogo

citation: giving credit to the authors of source information
cita: dar crédito a los autores de información usada como fuente

claim: a writer's statement of a position or opinion about a topic
afirmación: declaración de un escritor acerca de una posición u opinión sobre un tema

cliché: an overused expression or idea
cliché: expresión o idea usada en exceso

climax: the turning point or the high point of a story
clímax: punto de inflexión o momento culminante de un cuento

coherence: the clear and orderly presentation of ideas in a paragraph or essay
coherencia: presentación clara y ordenada de las ideas en un párrafo o ensayo

collaborate: work together with other members of a group
colaborar: trabajar en conjunto con otros miembros de un grupo

comedy: an entertainment that is amusing or humorous
comedia: espectáculo que es divertido o cómico

commentary: explanation of the way the facts, details, and/or examples in a paragraph or essay support the topic sentence
comentario: explicación de la manera en que los hechos, detalles y ejemplos de un párrafo o ensayo apoyan la oración principal

commercialism: an emphasis on gaining profits through advertising or sponsorship
mercantilismo: énfasis en obtener utilidades por medio de la publicidad o el auspicio

communication: the process of giving or exchanging information. **Verbal communication** involves the written or spoken word. **Nonverbal communication** involves movement, gestures, or facial expressions.
comunicación: proceso de dar o intercambiar información. **La comunicación** verbal involucra palabras escritas o habladas. La **comunicación no verbal** involucra movimientos, gestos o expresiones faciales.

compare: to identify similarities in two or more items; *see also* contrast
comparar: identificar semejanzas entre dos o más elementos; *ver también*, contrastar

concluding sentence: a final sentence that pulls together the ideas in a paragraph by restating the main idea or by summarizing or commenting on the ideas in the paragraph
oración concluyente: oración final que reúne las ideas de un párrafo, reformulando la idea principal o resumiendo o comentando las ideas del párrafo

conclusion: the ending of a paragraph or essay, which brings it to a close and leaves an impression with the reader
conclusión: fin de un párrafo o ensayo, que lo lleva a su término y deja una impresión en el lector

conflict: a struggle between opposing forces. In an **external conflict**, a character struggles with an outside force, such as another character or something in nature. In an **internal conflict**, the character struggles with his or her own needs, desires, or emotions.
conflicto: lucha entre fuerzas opuestas. En un **conflicto externo**, un personaje lucha contra una fuerza externa, como por ejemplo otro personaje o algo de la naturaleza. En un **conflicto interno**, el personaje lucha contra sus propias necesidades, deseos o emociones.

connotation: the suggested or implied meaning or emotion associated with a word—beyond its literal definition
connotación: significado o emoción sugerida o implícita que se asocia con una palabra—más allá de su definición literal

consumer: a buyer; a person who acquires goods and services
consumidor: comprador, persona que adquiere bienes y servicios

consumerism: the buying and consuming of goods and products; the belief that it is good to buy and consume goods and services
consumismo: compra y consumo de bienes y productos; creencia de que es bueno comprar y consumir bienes y servicios

context clue: information in words and phrases surrounding an unfamiliar word that hint at the meaning of the unfamiliar word.
clave de contexto: información en las palabras y frases que rodean una palabra no conocida y que dan una pista acerca del significado de esa palabra.

contrast: to identify differences in two or more items; *see also* compare
contrastar: identificar diferencias entre dos o más elementos; *ver también*, comparar

controversy: a public debate or dispute concerning a matter of opinion
controversia: debate público o disputa sobre una cuestión sujeta a opinión

copy: the actual text in an advertisement
texto publicitario: información actual en un anuncio publicitario

counter-argument: reasoning or facts given in opposition to an argument
contraargumento: razonamiento o hechos dados en oposición a un argumento

credible: to be trusted or believed
creíble: ser confiable o creíble

criteria: the facts, rules, or standards on which judgments are based.
criterios: hechos, reglas o estándares sobre las cuales están basadas las opiniones.

D

debate: *n.* a discussion involving opposing points of view; *v.* to present the sides of an argument by discussing opposing points
debate: *s.* discusión que involucra puntos de vista opuestos; *v.* presentar los lados de un argumento discutiendo puntos opuestos

definition: the process of making clear the meaning or nature of something
definición: proceso de aclarar el significado o naturaleza de algo

denotation: the exact, literal meaning of a word
denotación: significado exacto y literal de una palabra

detail: in writing, evidence (facts, statistics, examples) that supports the topic sentence
detalle: en la escritura, evidencia (hechos, estadística, ejemplos) que apoya la oracón principal

dialogue: conversation between characters
diálogo: conversación entre personajes

diction: a writer's or speaker's choice of words
dicción: selección de palabras por parte del escritor u orador

dissolve: the slow fading away of one image in a film as another fades in to take its place
desvanecimiento: desaparición lenta de una imagen en una película a medida que otra aparece progresivamente para tomar su lugar

drama: a genre of literature that is intended to be performed before an audience; a play
drama: género literario destinado a ser representado ante un público; obra teatral

dystopia: an imagined place or state in which the condition of life is imperfect or bad
distopía: lugar o estado imaginario en el que las condiciones de vida son imperfectas o malas

E

editorial: a short essay in which a publication, or someone speaking for a publication, expresses an opinion or takes a stand on an issue
editorial: ensayo corto en el que una publicación, o alguien que representa una publicación, expresa una opinión o toma partido acerca de un tema

effect: the result of an event or action
efecto: resultado de un suceso o acción

epic: a long narrative poem about the deeds of heroes or gods
épica: poema narrativo largo acerca de las proezas de héroes o dioses

epilogue: a section at the end of a book or play that extends or comments on the ending

epílogo: sección al final de un libro u obra teatral, que extiende o comenta el final

essay: a short literary composition on a single subject
ensayo: composición literaria corta acerca de un único tema

ethos: a rhetorical appeal that focuses on the character or qualifications of the speaker
ethos: recurso retórico centrado en el carácter o las capacidades del orador

euphemism: an inoffensive expression that is used in place of one that is considered harsh or blunt
eufemismo: expresión inofensiva usada en lugar de una considerada cruel o ruda

evaluate: to examine and judge carefully to determine the value of something, such as an idea, a comment, or a source
evaluar: estudiar y juzgar cuidadosamente para determinar el valor de algo, tal como una idea, un comentario, o una fuente

evidence: the information that supports or proves an idea or claim; forms of evidence include facts, statistics (numerical facts), expert opinions, examples, and anecdotes; see also, anecdotal, empirical, and logical evidence
evidencia: información que apoya o prueba una idea o afirmación; algunas formas de evidencia incluyen hechos, estadísticas (datos numéricos), opiniones de expertos, ejemplos y anécdotas; ver también evidencia anecdótica, empírica y lógica

exposition: (*1*) a type of writing that explains, clarifies, defines, or gives information; (*2*) events that give a reader background information needed to understand a story
exposición: (*1*) tipo de escrito que explica, clarifica, define o entrega información; (*2*) sucesos que entregan al lector los antecedentes necesarios para comprender un cuento

expository essay: an essay that makes an assertion and explains it with details, reasons, textual evidence, and commentary
ensayo expositivo: ensayo que hace una afirmación y la explica con detalles, razones, evidencia textual y comentarios

expository paragraph: a paragraph that makes an assertion and supports it with details and commentary
párrafo expositivo: párrafo que hace una afirmación y la apoya con detalles y comentarios

F

fable: a brief story that teaches a lesson or moral, usually through animal characters that take on human qualities
fábula: cuento breve que enseña una lección o moraleja, normalmente por medio de personajes animales que asumen cualidades humanas

fact: a statement that can be proven
hecho: enunciado que puede demostrarse

[fairy tale]: a story that involves fantasy elements such as witches, [goblins], and elves. These stories often involve princes and princesses and today are generally told to entertain children.
cuento de hadas: cuento que involucra elementos fantásticos como brujas, duendes y elfos. A menudo, estos cuentos involucran a príncipes y princesas y hoy se cuentan generalmente para entretener a los niños.

falling action: events after the climax of a story but before the resolution
acción descendente: sucesos posteriores al clímax de un cuento, pero antes de la resolución

fantasy: a story based on things that could not happen in real life
fantasía: cuento basado en cosas que no podrían ocurrir en la vida real

fiction: writing that consists of imagined events
ficción: escritura que consiste en acontecimientos imaginados

figurative language: imaginative language that is not meant to be interpreted literally
lenguaje figurativo: lenguaje imaginativo que no pretende ser interpretado literalmente

flashback: a sudden and vivid memory of an event in the past; also, an interruption in the sequence of events in the plot of a story to relate events that occurred in the past
narración retrospectiva: recuerdo repentino y vívido de un suceso del pasado; además, interrupción en la secuencia de los sucesos del argumento de un cuento para relatar sucesos ocurridos en el pasado

fluency: the ability to use language clearly and easily
fluidez: capacidad de usar el lenguaje fácilmente y de manera clara

folk literature: the traditional literature of a culture, consisting of a variety of myths and folk tales
literatura folclórica: literatura tradicional de una cultura, consistente en una variedad de mitos y cuentos folclóricos

folk tale: an anonymous traditional story passed on orally from one generation to another
cuento folclórico: cuento tradicional anónimo pasada oralmente de generación en generación

folklore: the stories, traditions, sayings, and customs of a culture or a society
folclor: historias, tradiciones, dichos y costumbres de una cultura o sociedad

foreshadowing: clues or hints signaling events that will occur later in the plot
presagio: claves o pistas que señalan sucesos que ocurrirán mas adelante en el argumento

formal style: a style of writing or speaking that is appropriate for formal communication such as in academics or business
estilo formal: estilo de escribir o hablar adecuado para la comunicación formal como la académica o comercial

free verse: a kind of poetry that does not follow any regular pattern, rhythm, or rhyme
verso libre: tipo de poesía que no sigue ningún patrón, ritmo o rima regular

G

genre: a category or type of literature, such as short story, folk tale, poem, novel, play
género: categoría o tipo de literatura, como el cuento corto, cuento folclórico, poema, novela, obra teatral

global revision: the process of deeply revising a text to improve organization, development of ideas, focus, and voice
revisión global: proceso de revisar en profundidad un texto para mejorar su organización, desarrollo de ideas, enfoque y voz

graphic novel: a narrative told through visuals and captions
novela gráfica: narrativa que se cuenta por medio de efectos visuales y leyendas

H

headline: a short piece of text at the top of an article, usually in larger type, designed to be the first words the audience reads
titular: trozo corto de texto en la parte superior de un artículo, habitualmente en letra más grande, diseñado para ser las primeras palabras que el público lear

humor: the quality of being comical or amusing
humor: cualidad de ser cómico o divertido

hook: *n.* a compelling idea or statement designed to get readers' attention in an introduction
gancho: *n.* idea o afirmación atractiva diseñada para captar la atención del lector en una introducción

hyperbole: extreme exaggeration used for emphasis, often used for comic effect
hypérbole: exageración extrema usada para dar énfasis, habitualmente usada para dar efecto cómico

I

iamb: a metrical foot that consists of an unstressed syllable followed by a stressed syllable
yambo: pie métrico que consta de una sílaba átona seguida de una sílaba tónica

iambic pentameter: a rhythmic pattern of five feet (or units) of one unstressed syllable followed by a stressed syllable
pentámetro yámbico: patrón rítmico de cinco pies (o unidades) de una sílaba átona seguida de una sílaba tónica

idiom: a figure of speech that cannot be defined literally
expresión idiomatica: figura del discurso que no puede definirse literalmente

image: a picture, drawing, photograph, illustration, chart, or other graphic that is designed to affect the audience in some purposeful way
imagen: pintura, dibujo, fotografía, ilustración, cuadro u otra gráfica diseñada para producir algún efecto intencional sobre el público

imagery: descriptive or figurative language used to create word pictures; imagery is created by details that appeal to one or more of the five senses
imaginería: lenguaje descriptivo o figurativo utilizado para crear imágenes verbales; la imaginería es creada por detalles que apelan a uno o más de los cinco sentidos

improvise: to respond or perform on the spur of the moment
improvisar: reaccionar o representar impulsivamente

incident: a distinct piece of action as in an episode in a story or a play. More than one incident may make up an event.
incidente: trozo de acción distintivo como un episodio de un cuento o de una obra teatral. Más de un incidente puede conformar un suceso.

inference: a logical guess or conclusion based on observation, prior experience, or textual evidence
inferencia: conjetura o conclusión lógica basada en la observación, experiencias anteriores o evidencia textual

inflection: the emphasis a speaker places on words through change in pitch or volume
inflexión: énfasis que pone un orador en las palabras por medio del cambio de tono o volumen

interpretation: a writer's or artist's representation of the meaning of a story or idea
interpretación: representación que hace un escritor o artista del significado de un cuento o idea

interview: a meeting between two people in which one, usually a reporter, asks the other questions to get that person's views on a subject
entrevista: reunión entre dos personas, en la que una, normalmente un reportero, hace preguntas a la otra para conocer sus opiniones acerca de un tema

introduction: the opening paragraph of an essay, which must get the reader's attention and indicate the topic
introducción: párrafo inicial de un ensayo, que debe captar la atención del lector e indicar el tema

L

legend: a traditional story believed to be based on actual people and events. Legends, which typically celebrate heroic individuals or significant achievements, tend to express the values of a culture.
leyenda: cuento tradicional que se considera basado en personas y sucesos reales. Las leyendas, que típicamente celebran a individuos heroicos o logros importantes, tienden a expresar los valores de una cultura.

limerick: a light, humorous, nonsensical verse of few lines, usually with a rhyme scheme of a-a-b-b-a
quintilla: verso liviano, humorístico, disparatado y de pocas líneas, normalmente con un esquema a-a-b-b-a

listening: the process of receiving a message and making meaning of it from verbal and nonverbal cues
escuchar: proceso de recibir el mensaje y comprender su significado a partir de claves verbales y no verbales

literary analysis: the process of examining closely and commenting on the elements of a literary work
análisis literario: proceso de examinar atentamente y comentar los elementos de una obra literaria

local revision: revising a text on a word or sentence level
revisión local: revisar un texto a nivel de palabras o de oraciones

logo: a unique design symbol used to identify a company visually
logotipo: símbolo único de diseño, utilizado para identificar visualmente una empresa

logos: a rhetorical appeal to reason or logic through statistics, facts, and reasonable examples
logos: apelación retórica a la razón o la lógica por medio de estadísticas, hechos y ejemplos razonables

M

media: the various means of mass communication, such as radio, television, newspapers, and magazines
medios de comunicación: los diversos medios de comunicación masiva, como radio, televisión, periódicos y revistas

media channel: a type of media, such as television or newspaper
canal mediático: tipo de medios de comunicación, como televisión o periódicos

metaphor: a comparison between two unlike things in which one thing becomes another
metáfora: comparación entre dos cosas diferentes en la que una cosa se convierte en otra

monologue: a speech or written expression of thoughts by a character
monólogo: discurso o expresión escrita de pensamientos por parte de un personaje

mood: the overall emotional quality of a work, which is created by the author's language and tone and the subject matter
carácter: la calidad emocional general de una obra, que es creada por el lenguaje y tono del autor y por el tema

motif: a recurring element, image, or idea in a work of literature
motivo: elemento, imagen o idea recurrente en una obra literaria

media: the use of several media (for example, print, audio, and video) to communicate ideas
multimedia: uso de varios medios de comunicación (por ejemplo: impresos, cine, audio y video) para comunicar ideas

multiple intelligences: the variety of learning styles that everyone has in varying degrees. In each individual, different intelligences predominate.
inteligencias múltiples: diversidad de estilos de aprendizaje que todos tienen en diversos grados. En cada individuo predominan diferentes inteligencias.

myth: a traditional story that explains the actions of gods or heroes or the origins of the elements of nature
mito: cuento tradicional que explica las acciones de dioses o héroes o los orígenes de los elementos de la naturaleza

N

narrative: a type of writing that tells a story or describes a sequence of events in an incident
narrativa: tipo de escritura que cuenta un cuento o describe una secuencia de sucesos de un incidente

narrative poem: a story told in verse
poema narrativo: historia contada en verso

news article: an article in a news publication that objectively presents both sides of an issue
artículo noticioso: artículo de una publicación noticiosa que presenta objetivamente ambos lados de un asunto

nonfiction: writing that is based on facts and actual events
no ficción: escritura que se basa en hechos o acontecimientos reales

nonprint text: a text, such as film or graphics, that communicates ideas without print
texto no impreso: texto, como una película o gráfica, que comunica ideas sin imprimir

nonverbal communication: gestures, facial expressions, and inflection that form unspoken communication
comunicación no verbal: gestos, expresiones faciales e inflexión que forman la comunicación no hablada

novel: a type of literary genre that tells a fictional story
novela: tipo de género literario que cuenta una historia ficticia

O

objective: supported by facts and not influenced by personal opinion
objetivo: apoyado por hechos y no influenciado por la opinión personal

objective camera view: in film, when the camera takes a neutral point of view
visión objetiva de la cámara: en el cine, cuando la cámara toma un punto de vista neutro

omniscient: a third-person point of view in which the narrator is all-knowing
omnisciente: punto de vista de una tercera persona, en la que el narador lo sabe todo

onomatopoeia: the use of words that imitate the sounds of what they describe
onomatopeya: el uso de palabras que imitan los sonidos de lo que describen

one-liner: a short joke or witticism expressed in a single sentence
agudeza: chiste u comentario ingenioso que se expresa en una sola oración.

opinion: a perspective that can be debated
opinión: perspectiva que es debatible

oral interpretation: reading aloud a literary text with expression
interpretación oral: leer en voz alta un texto literario con expresión

oxymoron: a figure of speech in which the words seem to contradict each other; for example, "jumbo shrimp"
oxímoron: figura del discurso en la que las palabras parecen contradecirse mutuamente; por ejemplo, "audaz cobardía"

P

pantomime: a form of acting without words, in which motions, gestures, and expressions convey emotions or situations
pantomima: forma de actuación sin palabras, en la que los movimientos, gestos y expresiones transmiten emociones o situationes

paraphrase: to restate in one's own words
parafrasear: reformular en nuestras propias palabras

parody: a humorous imitation of a literary work
parodia: imitación humorística de una obra literaria

pathos: a rhetorical appeal to the reader's or listener's senses or emotions through connotative language and imagery
pathos: apelación retórica a los sentidos o emociones del lector u oyente por medio de un lenguaje connotativo y figurado

performance: presenting or staging a play
actuación: presentar o poner en escena una obra teatral

persona: the voice or character speaking or narrating a story
persona: voz o personaje que habla o narra una historia

personal letter: a written communication between friends, relatives, or acquaintances that shares news, thoughts, or feelings
carta personal: comunicación escrita entre amigos, parientes o conocidos, que comparte noticias, pensamientos o sentimientos

personal narrative: a piece of writing that describes an incident and includes a personal response to and reflection on the incident
narrativa personal: texto escrito que describe un incidente e incluye una reacción personal ante el incidente y una reflexión acerca de él

personification: a kind of metaphor that gives objects or abstract ideas human characteristics
personificación: tipo de metáfora que da características humanas a los objetos o ideas abstractas

perspective: the way a specific character views a situation or other characters
perspectiva: manera en que un personaje específico visualiza una situación o a otros personajes

persuasion: the act or skill of causing someone to do or believe something
persuasión: acto o destreza de hacer que alguien haga o crea algo

persuasive essay: an essay that attempts to convince the reader to take an action or believe an idea
ensayo persuasivo: ensayo que intenta convencer al lector de que realice una acción o crea una idea

phrasing: dividing a speech into smaller parts, adding pauses for emphasis
frasear: dividir un discurso en partes más pequeñas, añadiendo pausas para dar énfasis

pitch: the highness or lowness of a sound, particularly the voice in speaking
tono: altura de un sonido, especialmente de la voz al hablar

plagiarism: taking and using as your own the words and ideas of another
plagio: tomar y usar como propias las palabras e ideas de otro

plot: the sequence of related events that make up a story or novel
trama: secuencia de sucesos relacionados, que conforman un cuento o novela

point of view: the perspective from which a story is told. In **first-person** point of view, the teller is a character in the story telling what he or she sees or knows. In **third-person** point of view, the narrator is someone outside of the story.
punto de vista: perspectiva desde la cual se cuenta una historia. En el punto de vista de la **primera persona**, el relator es un personaje del cuento que narra lo que ve o sabe. En el punto de vista de la **tercera persona**, el narrador es alguien que está fuera del cuento.

prediction: a logical guess or assumption about something that has not yet happened
predicción: conjetura lógica o suposición acerca de algo que aún no ha ocurrido

presentation: delivery of a formal reading, talk, or performance
presentación: entrega de una lectura, charla o representación formal

prose: the ordinary form of written language, using sentences and paragraphs; writing that is not poetry, drama, or song
prosa: forma común del lenguaje escrito, usando oraciones y párrafos; escritura que no es poesía, drama ni canción

pun: the humorous use of a word or words to suggest another word with the same sound or a different meaning
retruécano: uso humorístico de una o varias palabras para sugerir otra palabra que tiene el mismo sonido o un significado diferente

purpose: the reason for writing; what the writer hopes to accomplish
propósito: razón para escribir; lo que el escritor espera lograr

Q

quatrain: a four-line stanza in poetry
cuarteta: en poesía, estrofa de cuatro versos

R

rate: the speed at which a speaker delivers words
rapidez: velocidad a la que el orador pronuncia las palabras

reasons: the points that explain why the author is making a certain claim
razones: los puntos que explican por qué un autor propone cierta afirmacón

reflection: a kind of thinking and writing that seriously explores the significance of an experience, idea, or observation
reflexión: tipo de pensamiento y escritura que explora seriamente la importancia de una experiencia, idea u observación

reflective essay: an essay in which the writer explores the significance of an experience or observation
ensayo reflexivo: ensayo en que el autor explora la importancia de una experiencia u observación

refrain: a regularly repeated word, phrase, line, or group of lines in a poem or song
estribillo: palabra, frase, verso o grupo de versos de un poema o canción que se repite con regularidad

relevant: closely connected to the matter at hand (for example, evidence supporting a claim)
relevante: relacionado estrechamente con el asunto en cuestión (por ejemplo, la evidencia que apoya una afirmación)

repetition: the use of the same words or structure over again
repetición: uso de las mismas palabras o estructura una y otra vez

research: (*v.*) to locate information from a variety of sources; (*n.*) the information found from investigating a variety of sources
investigar: (*v.*) proceso de buscar información en una variedad de fuentes; *también*, **investigación** (*n.*) información que se halla al investigar una variedad de fuentes

resolution: the outcome of the conflict of a story, when loose ends are wrapped up

resolución: resultado del conflicto de un cuento, cuando se atan los cabos sueltos

revision: a process of evaluating a written piece to improve coherence and use of language; *see also* local revision, global revision

revisión: proceso de evaluar un texto escrito para mejorar la coherencia y el uso del lenguaje; *ver también*, revisión local, revisión global

rhetorical appeals: the use of emotional, ethical, and logical arguments to persuade in writing or speaking

recursos retóricos: uso de argumentos emotivos, éticos y lógicos para persuadir al escribir o hablar

rhetorical question: a question asked to emphasize a point or create an effect; no answer is expected

pregunta retórica: pregunta que se hace para enfatizar un punto o crear un efecto; no se espera una respuesta

rhyme: the repetition of sounds at the ends of words

rima: repetición de sonidos al final de las palabras

rhyme scheme: a consistent pattern of end rhyme throughout a poem

esquema de la rima: patrón consistente de una rima final a lo largo de un poema

rhythm: the pattern of stressed and unstressed syllables in spoken or written language, especially in poetry

ritmo: patrón de sílabas acentuadas y no acentuadas en lenguaje hablado o escrito, especialmente en poesía

rising action: major events that develop the plot of a story and lead to the climax

acción ascendente: sucesos importantes que desarrollan la trama de un cuento y conducen al clímax

S

science fiction: a genre in which the imaginary elements of the story could be scientifically possible

ciencia ficción: género en que los elementos imaginarios del cuento podrían ser científicamente posibles

sensory language: words or information that appeal to the five senses

lenguaje sensorial: palabras o información que apelan a los cinco sentidos

sequence: the order in which events happen

secuencia: orden en que ocurren los sucesos

setting: the time and the place in which a narrative occurs

ambiente: tiempo y lugar en que ocurre un relato

short story: a work of fiction that presents a sequence of events, or plot, that deals with a conflict

cuento corto: obra de ficción que presenta una secuencia de sucesos, o trama, que tratan de un conflicto

simile: a comparison between two unlike things, using the words *like* or *as*

símil: comparación entre dos cosas diferentes usando las palabras como o *tan*

slogan: a catchphrase that evokes a particular feeling about a company and its product

eslogan: frase o consigna publicitaria que evoca un sentimiento en particular acerca de una empresa y su producto

source: a place from which information comes or is obtained

fuente: lugar de donde surge o se obtiene la información

speaker: the voice that communicates with the reader of a poem

hablante: la voz que se comunica con el lector de un poema

speaking: the process of sharing information, ideas, and emotions using verbal and nonverbal means communication

hablar: proceso de compartir información, ideas y emociones usando medios de comunicación verbales y no verbales

stanza: a group of lines, usually similar in length and pattern, that form a unit within a poem

estrofa: grupo de versos, normalmente similares en longitud y patrón, que forman una unidad dentro de un poema

stereotype: a fixed, oversimplified image of a person, group, or idea; something conforming to that image

estereotipo: imagen fija y demasiado simplificada de una persona, grupo o idea; algo que cumple esa imagen

subjective: influenced by personal opinions or ideas

subjectivo: influenciado por opiniones o ideas personales

subjective camera view: in film, when the camera seems to show the events through a character's eyes

visión subjetiva de la cámara: en el cine, cuando la cámara parece mostrar los sucesos a través de los ojos de un personaje

subplot: a secondary plot that occurs along with a main plot

trama secundaria: argumento secundario que ocurre conjuntamente con un argumento principal

sufficient: adequate for the purpose of supporting a claim or reason

suficiente: adecuado para cumplir con el propósito de apoyar una afirmación o razón

summarize: to briefly restate the main ideas of a piece of writing

resumir: reformular brevemente las ideas principales de un texto escrito

supporting details: in writing, evidence (facts, statistics, examples) that supports the topic sentence

detalles de apoyo: en la escritura, evidencia (hechos, estadísticas ejemplos) que apoya la oracon principal

symbol: an object, a person, or a place that stands for something else
símbolo: objeto, persona o lugar que representa otra cosa

symbolism: the use of symbols
simbolismo: el uso de símbolos

synonyms: words with similar meanings
sinónimos: palabras con significados semejantes

synthesize: to combine elements from different sources to create, express, or support a new idea
sintetizar: combinar elementos de diferentes fuentes para crear, expresar o apoyar una idea nueva

T

tableau: a purposeful arrangement of characters frozen as if in a painting or a photograph
cuadro: disposición intencional de personajes que permanecen inmóviles como en una pintura o foto

talking points: important points or concepts to be included in a presentation
puntos centrales: puntos o conceptos importantes a incluirse en una presentación

tall tale: a highly exaggerated and often humorous story about folk heroes in local settings
cuento increíble: cuento muy exagerado y normalmente humorístico acerca de héroes folclóricos en ambientes locales

target audience: the specific group of people that advertisers aim to persuade to buy
público objetivo: grupo específico de personas a quienes los publicistas desean persuadir de comprar

tempo: the speed or rate of speaking
ritmo: velocidad o rapidez al hablar

textual evidence: quotations, summaries, or paraphrases from text passages to support a position
evidencia textual: citas, resúmenes o paráfrasis de pasajes de texto para apoyar una position

theme: the central idea, message, or purpose of a literary work
tema: idea, mensaje o propósito central de una obra literaria

thesis statement: a sentence, in the introduction of an essay, that states the writer's position or opinion on the topic of the essay
enunciado de tesis: oración, en la introducción de un ensayo, que plantea el punto de vista u opinión del autor acerca del tema del ensayo

tone: a writer's or speaker's attitude toward a subject
tono: actitud de un escritor u orador hacia un tema

topic sentence: a sentence that states the main idea of a paragraph; in an essay, it also makes a point that supports the thesis statement
oración principal: oración que plantea la idea principal de un párrafo; en un ensayo, también plantea un punto que apoya el enunciado de tesis

transitions: words or phrases that connect ideas, details, or events in writing
transiciones: palabras o frases que conectan ideas, detalles o sucesos de un escrito

TV news story: a report on a news program about a specific event
documental de televisión: reportaje en un programa noticioso acerca de un suceso específico

U

utopia: an ideal or perfect place
utopía: lugar ideal o perfecto

V

verse: a unit of poetry, such as a line or a stanza
verso: unidad de la poesía, como un verso o una estrofa

voice: a writer's distinctive use of language
voz: uso distintivo del lenguaje por parte de un escritor

voice-over: the voice of an unseen character in film expressing his or her thoughts
voz en off: voz de un personaje de una película, que no se ve pero que expresa sus pensamientos

volume: the degree of loudness of a speaker's voice or other sound
volumen: grado de intensidad sonora de la voz de un orador o de otro sonido

W

wordplay: a witty or clever verbal exchange or a play on words
juego de palabras: intercambio verbal ingenioso u ocurrente o un juego con palabras

Literary Skills

Reading Skills

Writing Skills

Media Skills

Speaking and Listening Skills

Directions, 239
Drama games, 284, 288
Evidence, 184, 206, 214, 253
Expert group, 261, 269
Eye contact, 108, 253, 263, 272, 284, 285, 289, 299, 306, 307, 318
Facial expression, 107, 284, 285, 286, 289, 297, 299, 306, 307, 318
Feedback, 206, 215, 263, 285
Fishbowl strategy, 121
Formal style, 214, 215
Gestures, 107
Group discussions, 13, 17, 27, 49, 78, 79, 106, 114, 115, 206, 220, 307
    collaborative, 118, 123, 124, 183, 201, 206, 261, 263, 282, 299, 321
    communicating in, 107, 108, 109, 120, 124
    posing and responding to questions, 106, 107, 206, 215, 263
Images, 318
Inflection, 285, 287, 288, 289, 297, 299, 306, 307, 311, 312, 318
Jigsaw group, 263, 272
Literature Circles, 119, 123
    roles in, 119, 120, 123
Marking the text, 289, 297, 300, 304, 306, 307, 311
Movement, 107, 286, 318
Multimedia, 202, 259, 263
Multimedia presentation, 202, 259, 263, 273
Note-taking, 93, 114, 120, 123, 151, 263, 272, 282, 321
Oral interpretation, 287, 289, 306, 312, 319
Oral presentation, 171, 272, 273
Organization, 273
Pantomime, 284
Paraphrase, 163, 164, 206
Point of view, 184
Props, 286, 299, 306, 307, 318
Rate (of speaking), 287, 288, 289, 297, 299, 306, 307, 311, 312, 318
Reader's Theater, 276, 290, 297, 321
Reasons, 184, 185, 202, 254
Reflecting, 206, 216, 273, 299, 319, 321
Rehearsal, 273, 284, 286, 289, 290, 299, 306, 307, 312, 319, 321
    video recording of, 321
Research, 273
Rhythm, 312, 318
Role playing, 284, 311
Sentence starters, 215
Sound, 286, 318
Source citation, 214

Sources, 273
Summarizing, 56, 114, 202
Tableau, 284
Technology Tip, 273, 321
Tone (of voice), 214, 284, 285, 287, 289, 297, 299, 306, 307, 311, 312, 318
Verbal and nonverbal communication, 106
Viewing guide, 216
Visuals, 215, 216
Volume, 215, 253, 263, 272, 311

Language Skills

Adjectives, 235, 236, 282
    power adjective list, 234
    precise, 282
    predicate adjectives, 282
Adverbs, 282
    precise, 282
Appositives, 231, 232
    phrases, 232, 233
Clauses, 137
    dependent, 242
    independent, 105, 242
Compare and contrast, 100
Conjunctions
    coordinating, 63, 105
    subordinating, 256
Dependent markers, 242
Descriptive language, 28, 32, 286
    sensory language, 28, 32
    vivid verbs, 28, 42
Nouns, 193
    precise, 195
Parallel structure/parallelism, 137
Phrases, 15, 34, 65, 137
Power adjectives, 234, 235, 236
Power verbs, 235, 236
Prepositional phrase, 167
Prepositions, 167
Pronouns, 12, 26, 27, 41, 44, 100, 101, 105, 286
    agreement with nouns, 101, 114, 286
    indefinite, 64
    intensive, 19, 27, 101, 286
    number, 101
    objective, 26, 27, 101, 286
    person, 26, 101
    possessive, 26, 27, 71, 101, 286
    reflexive, 19
    subjective, 26, 27, 101, 286
    vague, 193, 286
Punctuation, 27, 41, 43, 124, 232, 288, 311
    commas, 15, 43, 105, 137, 288

dashes, 288
exclamation marks, 43, 288
periods, 43
question marks, 43
quotation marks, 20, 43, 231
semicolons, 105, 288
Repetition, 63, 241
Sentences, 260
    combining, 105, 137
    complex, 239, 242, 243, 260
    compound, 104, 105, 260
    fragments, 21
    repeated phrases in, 66
    simple, 21, 105, 260
Sentence variety, 63, 79, 86, 105, 118, 124, 242, 260, 262, 272
Series, 15, 137
Verbs, 32
    active, 193
    consistency of, 95
    irregular, 176
    power verb list, 235, 236
    regular, 176
    tenses, 95, 100, 105, 114
    vivid, 27, 28, 32, 42

Vocabulary Skills

Academic Vocabulary, 2, 4, 12, 17, 41, 48, 90, 100, 102, 107, 118, 127, 160, 162, 166, 172, 186, 187, 188, 189, 218, 229, 248, 255, 261, 264, 275
Acronyms, 38
Cognates, 7, 72, 172, 180, 198, 208, 251, 264, 265, 292
Connotation, 24, 27, 145, 163, 211, 266, 297
Content connections, 6, 194
Context, 5, 14, 50, 58, 64, 70, 80, 111, 143, 147, 166, 167, 200, 211, 253, 255, 257
Denotation, 24, 163
Diffusing, 138, 152, 269, 306
Etymology, 140, 144, 207, 259, 277
Multiple-meaning words, 55
QHT strategy, 4, 48, 92, 162, 218, 250, 275
Roots and affixes, 7, 55, 58, 106, 112, 131, 263, 284, 291
Synonyms, 195, 296
Thesaurus, 136, 138
Word relationships, 304
Word Wall, 136, 268, 282

ex of Authors and Titles

Unit 4

Image Credits